Maximilian Yorck von Wartenburg

Napoleon as a General

Maximilian Yorck von Wartenburg

Napoleon as a General

ISBN/EAN: 9783743438217

Printed in Europe, USA, Canada, Australia, Japan

Cover: Foto ©ninafisch / pixelio.de

More available books at **www.hansebooks.com**

NAPOLEON

AS A GENERAL

BY THE LATE
COUNT YORCK von WARTENBURG
COLONEL OF THE GENERAL STAFF OF THE PRUSSIAN ARMY

FORMING THE SEVENTH BOOK
OF
The Wolseley Series
EDITED BY
MAJOR WALTER H. JAMES

VOL. I.

Gibraltar, April 19th, 1897.

DEAR CAPTAIN JAMES,

I HAVE read with interest the list you have sent me of the military works to be published as "The Wolseley Series."

The subjects are wisely chosen, and the authors will be generally accepted as soldiers who are competent to express valuable opinions upon them.

I am much flattered by having my name associated with an undertaking that is designed to improve the professional knowledge of our officers, and I rejoice to feel that under your able editorship its success is assured. In some instances I see you are not only editor but also translator, for which duty, if you will allow me to say so, your intimate knowledge of the German idiom eminently qualifies you.

I hope the officers of her Majesty's army may never degenerate into bookworms. There is happily at present no tendency in that direction, for I am glad to say that this generation is as fond of danger, adventure, and all manly out-of-door sports as its forefathers were. At the same time, all now recognize that the officer who has not studied war as an applied science, and who is ignorant of modern military history, is of little use beyond the rank of Captain. The principle of selection, pure and simple, is gradually being applied to the promotion of all officers, especially in the higher grades. As years go on this system will be more and more rigidly enforced.

It is gratifying to know that a large proportion of our young officers are ambitious, and without doubt there is now many a subaltern who hopes to be a Field-Marshal or to be shot in the attempt. Experience enables me to warn all these determined men of how small their chance is of ever reaching any great position in the army unless they devote many of their spare hours every week to a close study of tactics and strategy as dealt with in the best books upon recent wars.

In this series of military works from the pens of first-class writers, the military student will find ample material to assist him in fitting himself for high command, and in the interest of the Empire and of the army I earnestly hope he will avail himself of it.

' I know how truly this work is undertaken as a labour of love by you as editor and by all who are helping you. But I also know that you and they will feel amply repaid if it assists the young officer to learn the science of his profession and, in doing this, to improve the fighting value of the service, to the true interests of which we are one and all sincerely devoted.

Believe me to be,
Very truly yours,
WOLSELEY.

THE WOLSELEY SERIES.

THE object of this series of books is to place before British officers and others translations of the best foreign military books in an English dress. It is also intended to add original works on portions of our military history which have, hitherto, been somewhat neglected. The great part played in national life by the armies of continental nations, has given rise to a much larger military literature than exists in England. The incessant struggle for supremacy has led to the production by master-minds of treatises on various parts of the art of war, which are of the highest importance, but many of which have hitherto only existed in their own language. It will be the aim of this series to make them available to English readers.

England has been engaged in no great war since the beginning of the century.[1] It follows, therefore, that both strategy and tactics have been more widely treated by foreign authors than by our own, not only for the reason set forth above, but also because having usually taken a personal part in them they are naturally more interested therein.

It is sometimes urged that lessons of continental conflicts are in no wise useful to ourselves; this is ridiculous. The guiding principles of the operations of war are the same, whether they are conducted against civilized or savage foes. If our army were prepared only to meet the latter it need scarcely be maintained in its present form, but no one can say with our widespread

[1] This was written in 1897.—ED.

Empire that we shall not be called upon to meet civilized opponents. If we are able to deal with them, we shall certainly have no difficulty in defeating savages, for it is by the training and discipline which render troops fit to meet those of their own state of civilization that they prove superior to the savage when they meet him in the field.

Strategy is the same, whether used against Arabs or Frenchmen. The tactics employed differ as the weapons of the enemy differ. But the soldiers trained to meet the highest class of opponents are, *ipso facto*, better qualified to deal with the inferior.

This series, therefore, will contain translations of well-known foreign writers, and it will also contain original English works dealing with the kind of warfare in which we are most frequently engaged, and with certain special phases of British military experience which have hitherto been somewhat inadequately dealt with. The history of British arms is replete with interest and is second to none in moving incidents of gallantry. Many of these have already been recorded, but the actual lessons to be learned from them have not always been systematically treated. It is hoped, as this series progresses, to do so, and to secure for future generations the practical deductions to be made from the deeds of British soldiers. A list of the volumes already arranged for will be found at the beginning of this book, and it will be the aim of the editor to add from time to time such works only as seem of the first importance in the theory and record of military achievement.

WALTER H. JAMES.

AUTHOR'S PREFACE

MILITARY historians commencing the study of the deeds of the great Corsican immediately after his fall, have rightly acknowledged that the moment had not arrived to collect together his strategical conceptions, to describe as a whole his characteristics as a general. Since that period numerous publications have thrown more and more light on his military attainments, and the publication of the *Correspondance de Napoleon* Ier completed in 1869, permits a complete judgment to be given on the great leader. But new events captivate the attention of the world and interest it more intimately, so that a proper estimate of Napoleonic literature from a scientific and literary point of view has been thrust somewhat into the background. These considerations account for the appearance of this book, and explain why it has not been attempted before by a more able pen.

As no complete relation exists of the campaigns of Napoleon of the nature of the publications issued by the Head-Quarters' Staff, I have been led to compile this account of the strategy of Napoleon, confining myself to those points which influence the main decisions of the General. I have in nowise attempted to write the history of his wars, or to trace in detail all the movements of each of the belligerents. Napoleon's own words as they are recorded in his correspondence and in the numerous works which have preserved them, have furnished the facts needed for a proper judgment. In default of any other merit, this work aims at contrasting the practice of Napoleon with his theories on war which serve as commentaries on the former, but which are somewhat widely dispersed.

In conclusion, I can only admit that I undertook the task because it has interested me so highly. Whether I have succeeded or not, I leave to the reader.

EDITOR'S PREFACE

Colonel Count Yorck von Wartenburg of the Prussian General Staff was well known in his own country as one of the most rising men in the German Army. His untimely death in China from suffocation due to a charcoal stove in an unventilated room has deprived the service of which he was so brilliant a member of one who was admittedly destined for a high career. The work of which this translation is offered to the British Army shows that he was a most capable military historian, an able and penetrating critic. For training in strategy no better field can be found than the study of the campaigns of the Great Emperor. Count Yorck von Wartenburg has produced a work which in a comparatively small space deals in a comprehensive way with them. No such book existed in English, and I have thought it well to include it in the Wolseley Series.

Walter H. James.

N.B.—The only maps published with the original work were those at the end of the second volume. I recommend the atlas published with Thiers' works on the French Republic and the Empire, as on the whole the best available.

CONTENTS

CHAPTER I.
YOUTH AND EARLY CAREER 1

CHAPTER II.
1796-97.
THE BEGINNING OF THE CAMPAIGN OF ITALY . . 24

CHAPTER III.
MANTUA. WÜRMSER'S ATTEMPT TO RELIEVE IT . . 50

CHAPTER IV.
MANTUA. ALVINTZY'S ATTEMPTS TO RELIEVE IT . 81

CHAPTER V.
THE CAMPAIGN OF 1797 102

CHAPTER VI.
1798-99.
EGYPT 123

CHAPTER VII.
SYRIA . . . 141

CHAPTER VIII.
1800.
MARENGO 164

CHAPTER IX.
1805.

ULM 198

CHAPTER X.

AUSTERLITZ 229

CHAPTER XI.
1806-1807.

JENA 267

CHAPTER XII.

EYLAU 303

CHAPTER XIII.

FRIEDLAND 343

NAPOLEON AS A GENERAL

CHAPTER I.

YOUTH AND EARLY CAREER.

EVERY one desirous of studying war must do so from the actual records; war must be studied by war itself. For "war, far from being an exact science, is a terrible and passionate drama."[1] It is therefore only by examining the history of former wars that we arrive at a just comprehension of what war really is.

Which part of this study is most valuable and improving to the soldier? The fact of knowing accurately the method in which some warlike operation was performed, or of knowing the date of some historical event, cannot be of much advantage to us, for no opportunity is likely to arise to reproduce facts, so to speak, in duplicate; what is of value to the student is to see how things have come to pass and thence to deduce the reasons for the results.

Now the actors in all these deeds were men, and the history of the birth of events lies in these men's mode of thinking. He who wishes to understand war must therefore learn to understand the men who waged it; the key to the history of war lies in the headquarters. The study of the history of war cannot therefore be separated from that of the generals, and this latter study must also

[1] Jomini, Formation des troupes pour le combat, 27.

embrace a knowledge of these generals as men, if it is to be truly instructive. To penetrate as it were the brain of a general for the purpose of finding out the origin of his resolution, will, moreover, exercise our minds in a similar way. For it will force us to follow, often laboriously, the development of great thoughts. The enthusiasm for individual personalities in the annals of war arising from this must inspire us to equally lofty aspirations, and enthusiasm is indeed the best result to be obtained from any study.

But where could we find a richer source of grand thoughts than in the mighty deeds of the man upon whose shoulders the whole of modern strategy rests? To study Napoleon as a *General* will be the most valuable and instructive work for a soldier, and it is our purpose to make the attempt.

If in commencing the history of the life of this man we wish, as our most natural starting-point, to begin with the date of his birth, we are confronted at the very threshold of our task by an insoluble difficulty; the fact is that the date of Napoleon's birth is by no means known with certainty. Lieutenant-Colonel Jung's interesting work gives all the documents referring to this matter, and these seem to justify the doubt whether Napoleon was not after all born at Corte on the 7th January, 1768; the author, however, rightly adds at once, that the decision of this matter is really unimportant, as we have to do with Napoleon as a historical personage, and as such he was and remains born at Ajaccio, on the 15th August, 1769.

About his childhood we have practically no authentic data; he spoke of himself as a restless, quarrelsome child. We may or may not regret the want of further evidence; in any case a history of his childhood is not of great value so far as a knowledge of the man is concerned. Napoleon himself was of the opinion that the proper development of our faculties begins in the time of sexual maturity, and that before this no definite judgment can be pronounced. As to any education or instruction, he enjoyed only a minimum of these as a child; his mother, the beautiful and energetic Letitia, had the greatest difficulty in keeping the household going, with insufficient means and an ever-increasing family. His father, of a yielding and sensitive temperament, was much away on his travels, and engaged above all in gaining the interest of influential patrons, in order to secure for himself wealth, and for his children a future. One of the results of these endeavours was the securing of a free scholarship at the military academy at Brienne.

On the 23rd April, 1779, the boy Napoleon entered this school. The small, thin Corsican boy with his foreign ways, who had hardly begun to master the French language, soon became the butt of his schoolfellows, and he felt all the more antipathy to them, as he had up till now, in his native isle, heard the name of France mentioned only as that of a recent enemy and present conqueror, and as yet he in no way felt himself a Frenchman. Thus he remained isolated, and his position was still more accentuated by his poverty, which formed a striking contrast with the more fortunate circumstances in which his schoolfellows, mostly sons of good and rich families, lived. The first document we possess written by himself, a letter to his father, dated the 5th April, 1781, expresses his annoyance at these circumstances, and shows in this boy of eleven a feeling of injured pride, rare at such an early age. Thus while he made satisfactory progress in his studies on the whole, there was developed in him at Brienne a pride which, being constantly excited by his surroundings, filled him with dissatisfaction with existing circumstances, and a leaning to solitude and taciturnity, as well as a wish to attain a position in which he could prove how much he was worth in comparison with his fellow pupils. Thus it does not seem as if M. de Keralio, who gave him the testimonial, "obedient, straightforward, and grateful," was an instructor gifted with great insight into the temperaments of his pupils.

But how under the pressure of such circumstances a precocious manliness may be developed in a powerfully endowed character, is shown by a second document in Napoleon's handwriting, the letter to his uncle Fesch, dated the 15th July, 1784. It is the letter of a youth of not quite fifteen, but who reasons in such an assured and firm manner on the subject in question, Joseph's future, as if the writer were not a younger brother, but the head of the family. The same impression is created by two other letters, which he wrote a year later to his mother and to his great-uncle Lucien, and in which he speaks of the recent death of his father (24th February, 1785) not without feeling indeed, but with the calmness of a man of experience.

At this time he was at the Military Academy of Paris, where he had been since the previous October, receiving his last preparation for a lieutenancy, in the artillery, as he had decided on this arm, having given up his first intention of entering the navy. His career there, however, forms no important chapter in his life, for he led a solitary existence; there also he met with the same circumstances in his fellow-students, and a pamphlet which he wrote there, and in which he rightly advocates a simpler education for future soldiers, betrays, in the fragment of it which has come down to us, the fact that he looked with secret envy upon the more favoured circumstances of others. Still the urgent wish to reform is evidence of a creative mind, which feels the capacity of constructing something new.

In the autumn of 1786 came the moment for his entry on life's career. In August of that year he had passed his examination, though without distinguishing himself in any special way; but the description of the young officer's character, contained in his testimonial from the Military Academy, and so well borne out by his future life, is of interest to us:—

"Retiring and diligent, he prefers study to amusements

of any kind, and delights in the reading of good authors; he is devoted to abstract sciences, with little leaning to others, is well versed in mathematics and geography; is taciturn, loves solitude, is obstinate, proud, and exceptionally inclined to egotism; speaks little, is energetic in his answers, ready and severe in his refutations; possesses much love of self, is ambitious and hardworking. This young man deserves to be pushed on."

His first garrison was Valence, and here the young officer found for the first time congenial society and showed himself sociable and communicative. Still he continued to occupy himself with science and with reading much in the most varied domains of thought, except in a military direction, which he seems to have somewhat neglected. But this peaceful state of mind did not last long; he had attacks of melancholy, partly attributable to physical causes, but to a greater extent due to his temperament, and these aggravated the feeling of hopeless monotony which garrison life produced in him; in this frame of mind he wrote: "Life is a burden to me, because the men, with whom I live and shall probably always have to live, have manners and customs as different from mine as moonlight is from sunlight. And since I cannot pursue the only mode of life which would render existence bearable to me, I feel a disgust for everything." A change of garrison, with two periods of leave spent in Corsica, a leave he got extended under various pretexts, fill up the time until 1789.

The political changes and cataclysms which had their beginning in this year opened to the capable and ambitious young officer, unrestrained by any narrow principles, a wide career. "Revolutions," said he at this time, "are a good time for soldiers possessed of intellect and courage."[1] He however felt at this time so little bound up with the fate of France, that he only took advantage of the new condition of things to obtain at once fresh leave to go to

[1] Victor, Mém., 149.

Corsica; this island as yet formed the limits of his ambition; to become its liberator from the French yoke, to be its lawgiver, to carry to an end the part played by Paoli, whether alone or as his fellow-worker, but with more good fortune and success, these were more or less the ideals of his youthful imagination. Arrived in Corsica, he threw himself eagerly into the political arena, and his address to Matteo Buttafuoco is a characteristic evidence of this activity. In it great keenness of logical reasoning is united with much pathos, and the passionate expression of an excitable temperament endowed with a full insight into human nature and its weaknesses.

But whilst his pen in this document, written while he was violently excited by the political circumstances, struck a note, if exaggerated, still on the whole appropriate, another of his pamphlets, which appeared soon afterwards, showed how little he was affected by the feelings which move the mass of mankind. The Academy of Lyons had offered a public prize for the best answer to the question: "What truths and what feelings is it most important to inspire men with for their happiness?" The little pamphlet which Napoleon sent in to this is an astonishingly feeble production; its style is bad; the development of the most commonplace thoughts confused; in short, only the name of its author would induce anyone to read it. It not only failed to gain the prize, but met with very adverse criticism. We may mention here a secondary circumstance which illustrates Napoleon's views about mankind. The phrase with which he started was: "Food, a dwelling, clothing, and a wife are of absolute necessity for happiness." It is worthy of note that he here classes a wife as a chattel, and looks upon her as created merely for the happiness and requirements of man. This reminds us of Mme. de Rémusat's words: "The emperor despises women . . . their weaknesses appear to him an irrefutable proof of their inferiority."[1]

[1] Mme. de Rémusat, Mém., I. 112.

In the midst of this occupation as an author his active zeal in the political affairs of his native country did not remain idle. A *coup d'état* which he had planned failed, it is true, in its very birth, but without any ill consequences to him. And if we marvel, how in a European state an officer of the army could cause civil troubles so recklessly, and play so strange a political part, we must remember the *rôle* we have seen General Skobelev play of late, and reflect how very much the conditions of France at this time resembled those of the republic of Rome in the century before our era. There was the same general feeling that the existing conditions were not destined to be the eventual form of the state, there was the same uncertainty as to who was eventually to rule, and therefore also to punish; and there were men who, like Napoleon, had little to lose and everything to gain. It is true, in Rome Catiline failed before Cæsar succeeded, while in Corsica Napoleon was fortunate enough to escape Catiline's fate and finally himself became Cæsar.

For the moment indeed he considered it advisable to leave his home and to return to his regiment in France, where he resumed his varied studies. He often afterwards, and not without pleasure apparently, recalled this time, during which, in spite of his straitened circumstances, he had his brother Louis living with him, who was nine years younger than he, and for whom and for whose education he made many sacrifices: " I lived like a bear, always alone in my room with my books, then my only friends; " and he reproached the King of Holland, when the latter laid down his crown, with the fact that he did not recall that time with a similar feeling.

Whoever thinks the man Napoleon may be described with the one word, "egotist," does not, though his judgment may not be wrong, give due weight to the complications of the human mind; Napoleon was ruled by egotism, it is true, but no man is in everything and at all times an egotist; no human life is quite so logically built up on one principle alone.

During the year 1791, the flood of revolution rose from day to day. Napoleon took with heart and soul the side of the new political ideas, and felt a restless, burning desire to take an active part in them. He wrote to his great-uncle Lucien: "Send me three hundred francs; this sum will be sufficient to take me to Paris. There a man can at least be up and doing and conquer obstacles. Everything tells me I shall succeed." But since there was as yet no place for him in the principal theatre of action, he soon returned to his native island, preferring a participation in the development of events there to garrison-service. "What man," he exclaimed at this time, "would not wish to be assassinated, on condition of having been Cæsar! One ray from his crown of glory would indemnify one richly for an early death."

And here we must put to ourselves the question, What was the mainspring of Napoleon's actions, the thirst for fame or the longing for power? The judgments of history vary on this point. "We cannot say he really loved fame, for he did not hesitate to prefer success to it."[1] "No conquest was in his opinion complete as long as the monument was absent which would hand down its remembrance to posterity. Glory, and nothing but glory, he desired for France and for himself."[2]

"Bonaparte is consumed by two devouring passions, the desire of fame and war. . . . In all his actions the present time was subordinate to the future ages."[3] Both these judgments have had their day. Bourrienne lived in close contact with the general and the consul; Mme. de Rémusat only knew him in the last days of the consulate and during the empire.

Was not Napoleon compelled, the longer he ruled over

---

[1] Mme. de Rémusat, Mém., I. 106.
[2] Bourrienne, Mém., IV. 53.   [3] The same, III. 212, 215.

men, to become the more eager for an increase of his power; did not his own great deeds necessarily make it more and more difficult for him to gain still greater glory, and was not the very magnitude of the renown he had gained calculated to render him indifferent to its augmentation? He himself said on his return from Tilsit: "Military glory is soon used up in modern times. Fifty battles scarcely produce more effect now than five or six used to do. I am and ever shall be for the French the man of Marengo much more than that of Jena and Friedland."[1] How interesting to compare with this what he said immediately after Marengo: "Well, well! A few more great deeds like this campaign and I may be spoken of by posterity."[2] The same Marengo which appeared a mere beginning to the young man, consumed by a thirst for glory, which might at the most be worthy of half a page in the annals of the world, this same Marengo the emperor, grown colder after numberless successes, looked upon as the apogee of his glory, never to be excelled in the eyes of posterity, and the exercise of ever increasing power seemed to him then the only thing worth striving for and attaining.

Thus we must think of him as eager for glory and action when he landed again in Corsica in September, 1791. Not long after his arrival his great-uncle died, and henceforth he looked upon himself as the head of the family. "We could not argue with him," says Lucien, "he was annoyed at the least opposition and angered by the least resistance."[3] Thus he remained in Corsica for a time, heedless of the fact that he was breaking his leave, that his regiment was being mobilized, and that the Legislative Assembly ordered a return of the entire army, and decreed that all absentees should be looked upon as deserters. Napoleon was determined to

---

[1] Mme. de Rémusat, Mém., III. 65.
[2] Bourrienne, Mém., IV. 170. [3] Lucien. Mém., 49.

secure his election to a superior post in the volunteer battalions with elective officers, which were at that time formed in Corsica, and the violence, boldness, and lawlessness with which he went to work is worthy of note. The election was conducted at Ajaccio by three Government commissaries, whose influence would necessarily be decisive. Two of these were favourable to Napoleon's claims; as to the third, Murati, he had him brought to his house on the eve of the election by a few armed men, and received him there with the words: " I could wish that you were free, entirely free. You were not so in Peraldi's house," and—prevented him appearing at the election the next day. The result was his election as second lieutenant-colonel of the second battalion. Scarcely was he in possession of this post than he endeavoured to use it for his further projects.

Again he planned to capture the citadel of Ajaccio from the French garrison, in order to promote a national rising, which might open a field of action for his ambition. But again the enterprise failed, and he considered it wise to leave Corsica once more and to return to France.

There he had, it is true, been not only struck off the list of his regiment on account of his absence, but also denounced to the secretary of war on account of the troubles he had excited. Still he succeeded in obtaining from the authorities of his native land testimonials of good behaviour, and thus he set out (in May, 1792) to meet an uncertain future with the unconcern which alone can lead to great successes. Youth acts recklessly, and thus often finds ways and means where a man who takes things more seriously only sees difficulties.

He went to Paris, where he occupied himself at first in vain efforts to procure his reinstatement in the army, made the most varied plans, and had to live on very slender means. The rising of the 20th June took place at this time, and he was present as a spectator in the crowd congregated around the Tuileries. However revolutionary his own behaviour had been in Corsica, his innate leaning to order and authority was disgusted at the action of the dregs of the people, and he exclaimed indignantly: "Che coglione (what fools). How could they admit this rabble? Four or five hundred of them should have been blown away by cannon, and the rest would have run for their lives."[1] The 10th of August brought with the fall of Royalty a favourable change in his own fate; officers were wanted, and, forgetting the past, he was reappointed to his old rank.

He immediately returned to Corsica under the pretext of having to escort his sister home from the College of St. Cyr, and resumed his appointment in the 2nd battalion of volunteers. Along with it he was told off for an expedition to occupy Sardinia, which, however, came to nothing on account of the small military qualifications of both sailors and soldiers.

Meanwhile the "Convéntion" had seized the helm of the State in France, and between its severe and rude government and the actual ruler of Corsica, Paoli, disputes soon arose. Napoleon took sides with the former, represented in Corsica by Saliceti. The latter appointed him inspector-general of the artillery on the island, and in this capacity he again endeavoured to seize the citadel of Ajaccio, but again unsuccessfully; the population, partisans of Paoli, expelled the Bonaparte family and destroyed their dwelling-house. Thereupon Napoleon quitted Corsica with all his relations in June, 1793.

At last he joined his regiment at Nice. In Southern France there broke out at this time a counter-revolutionist and royalist movement, which found support principally at Lyons, Marseilles, and Toulon. To prevent the junction of the reactionary parties, Colonel (afterwards General) Carteaux was sent to Avignon. In front of this town Captain Napoleon Bonaparte met him; he had been sent thither from Nice to fetch some guns from Avignon. This town having been evacuated by the enemy, he

[1] Bourrienne, Mém.

remained in it, to organize a park of artillery, and during this interval of leisure he wrote "The Supper of Beaucaire," a pamphlet in every way differing from his former ones. In this he took definitely the side of the "Mountain," which was at that time in full power; he explained in a lucid and sober style the political and military situation in the south, and predicted the certain success of the arms of the republic. The pamphlet was favourably received, and justly so, by the deputies Saliceti, Gasparin, and the younger Robespierre, who had just arrived at Avignon, and they ordered it to be printed at the expense of the State. In this manner he became known to the men then in power, and this fact was soon to procure him quick promotion.

The most serious question of the moment was Toulon. It was too late to prevent the occupation of this most important seaport by the English; it had to be retaken, and in this enterprise Napoleon's star for the first time shone in the sky.

On the 28th August the English fleet had entered the harbour; on the 29th the republican vanguard under Mouret arrived in the defile of Ollioules, but was immediately driven out again. The recapture of this point was decided upon and undertaken on the 7th September. Here a wound received by Dommartins led to Napoleon succeeding him as commander of the artillery, a post he filled with the greatest energy. But at first, Carteaux's corps could not, on account of insufficient means, undertake anything against Toulon; only when the division Lapoype, ordered up from the army of Italy, began gradually to arrive, was a regular siege begun. Carteaux was soon recognized as incapable, and was replaced by Doppet, the latter, on his own confession of being unsuited to the work, giving place immediately to Dugommier, a zealous and active officer and a straightforward and open soldierly character. He held, on the 25th November, a council of war, at which Napoleon was present, he having on the 14th of the month already forwarded to the minister of war a plan for the capture of Toulon, which had been favourably received. There is evidence that he laid down his views in this with as much firmness and assurance as if he had been one of the best known and most experienced of generals. In this council of war the general plan of the siege, agreeing in its main points with Napoleon's proposals, was determined upon and put into execution without delay.

Dugommier had divided the army into two divisions: the left under Lapoype and the right under Mouret; the younger Duteil commanded the whole artillery, Napoleon that of one brigade of the division Mouret. He certainly distinguished himself remarkably during the siege by his activity and military insight, and his advice was repeatedly listened to and followed; his superior officer Duteil allowed his young subordinate, whose capacities he appreciated, a free hand with respect to the artillery; but the latter did not in any way occupy the position at this time, or have the influence upon the conduct of the siege as a whole, which he ascribed to himself at St. Helena. It is possible, however, that twenty years of the most tremendous successes and absolute command may have obscured the emperor's recollection of the small importance of a battalion commander. But whatever his real share in the capture of Toulon may have been, one thing is certain, the young officer made a considerable and extraordinary impression; the originality of his ideas, the power and vigour with which he expressed them, astonished and interested; he already knew how to captivate men, and possessed an eagle eye to detect capacity; Junot's, Marmont's, and Victor's careers date from this period.

After the capture of Toulon (the 19th December, 1793) he was, on the recommendation of the deputies Saliceti and Robespierre the younger, whose confidence he had fully gained, rewarded with the rank of brigadier-general.

His first appearance had, it is true, not given Napoleon an opportunity for a full display of his abilities; but if we examine it more closely, we shall find even here the indications of the true general. In fixing upon the plan to be followed, he did not enter into local considerations, but picked out at once the point of most importance; he determined this upon grounds of a military and moral nature, such as the situation as a whole furnished, his reasoning being as follows:—The main point is, to command the roadstead; the moment the hostile fleet can no longer hold this, the town will be abandoned, for without a fleet the garrison has no means of retreat; now the English will abandon the town and destroy the defences of the harbour rather than employ for its protection a garrison, the surrender of which must be only a question of time. But if the garrison prefers to hold out, then and only then the siege may be begun advantageously. Thus having settled the main question, he proceeded to determine the points, the possession of which must lead to the attainment of the main object, viz. the command of the roadstead; he therefore decided on the occupation of the point l'Eguillette as the operation upon which all efforts must, to begin with, be centred. This once admitted, he pointed out how to carry it into execution.

It is one of the surest marks of a true general, that he knows in every situation how to set aside details and matters of secondary importance, and to combine and direct all the moral and physical forces at his disposal to the principal aim; once the latter fixed upon, the necessary details follow almost as a matter of course, at any rate any capable officer on the staff of the general can determine them. Marmont says very justly: "I never met with a single man of distinction, and capable of the conduct of great affairs, who was not in the habit of putting on one side all details and contenting himself with regarding the work he had entrusted to

YOUTH AND EARLY CAREER

others." No general of modern times exhibited this freedom of judgment never unobscured by any concern for details, in such a high degree, as Napoleon; in this alone lies the explanation of his splendid successes. "The greater, the more active, the wider an intelligence, the less it can linger over commonplace and trivial details."[2]

At the close of the siege of Toulon Napoleon was appointed to the army of Italy and proceeded accordingly to Nice. This army made soon after this (April, 1794) a forward movement and seized the entrances to the passes of the Alps. Under these circumstances a meeting of the leaders took place on the 20th May, at which the future plan of campaign was decided upon. Its framework was due to Napoleon, and we may therefore assume, broadly, that it represented his views; it is therefore the first document capable of throwing a light upon Napoleon's views with regard to the conduct of an army in a campaign, and shows us his ideas on this point. But before we proceed farther, we must mention one important consideration.

(1)

Napoleon, an upstart, was not in a position to carry out fully his ideas as to the conduct of war at the head of an army; this reward of the soldier's career became his only in the after course of events. We may divide into three periods his career as a general. In the first he acted as adviser and collaborator in plans of operations, checked by considerations of things and persons; in the second he stood, it is true, at the head of an army, independent on his own theatre of war and free to develop his capabilities, but still only a link in the war as a whole, provided with definite forces for definite purposes; and only in the third period did he dispose absolutely of the whole army and State, and was thus in a condition to exercise the highest art of the general, viz., to determine where and with what forces

[1] Marmont Mém.   [2] Mém. de Ste Hel., II. 193.

the final issue of war is to be decided. Now, of these three periods, the first, in which he merely planned campaigns, comprises the time between the siege of Toulon and his assumption of the command-in-chief in Italy; the second, in which he conducted campaigns, the period from this to the 18th Brumaire; and lastly, the third, in which he conducted wars, includes the rest of his career up to the moment when he stepped on board the *Bellerophon*.

Not to be able to get beyond the first of these stages was, among the generals of Napoleon's stamp, the fate of Gneisenau, and bitterly did he feel it, as such a nature must: "It is a hard fate never to be considered worthy of an independent command, always to have to work for another!"[1] the second stage, which is the goal of the ambition of every true soldier, but for which few only are chosen by fate, was reached, among modern generals, by Robert Lee; lastly, as to the third stage, Cæsar and Napoleon alone reached it of those not born on a throne. It was Hannibal's ruin that he could not get beyond the second stage.

We are as yet only at the beginning of the first chapter in our considerations, we must therefore not expect to find in the plans of campaigns of which we are now speaking, all that rendered the later strategy of the emperor so magnificent. The above-mentioned plan[2] began as follows: "We can only invade the plain of Piedmont with forces superior in numbers to those of the enemy; in order to attain this superiority, the Army of Italy must be united with that of the Alps." This exordium showed already the man, who nineteen years later wrote: "You must know that it is my principle to advance in masses."[3] Having settled upon a junction of forces, he determined the point at which this must take

---

[1] To Hardenberg. Gonesse, 30th June, 1815.
[2] C. N. Colmars, 2nd Prairial, an. II.
[3] C. N. To Eugéne. Erfurt, 28th April, 1813.

place, and with regard to this he said: "The junction of the two armies can only take place in the valley of the Stura, if we are to profit by the positions and lines of advance seized by the army of Italy."[1] Then he pointed to the fact that the line of contact of the two armies ran to the spot where the Stura valley debouched into the plain of Lombardy, and that therefore their most natural point of junction lay there. Then he proceeded to lay down the details of execution. The army of the Alps was to furnish two columns of observation (each of 4000 men) and three columns of attack (4000, 5000, and 8000 men respectively). The former were to watch the valleys of the Varaita and the Maira, and to advance as the enemy fell back. The latter were to push forward towards the valley of the Stura, in order to take the enemy's positions there at Argentera, Berezio, and Sambuco, in flank; after this reinforcements were to be sent forward to the Varaita, which, in conjunction with the columns of observation there (altogether 11,000 men), were to capture the position of Castel Delfino. In the Stura valley Demonte was to be invested.

The army of Italy was to watch the passes from the valley of the Tinea into that of the Stura, as well as the country towards Mondovi on its right, and was to form four columns of attack of 16,000, 6000, 4000, and 2000 men respectively. Of these the first two would push forward towards Borgo San Dalmazzo, the other two were to assist in the attack of the army of the Alps in the Stura valley. The forward movement to Borgo was principally intended to entice the enemy's forces thither, and thus to facilitate the opening of the passes on the upper Stura.

If we examine the details of this plan, we shall, it is true, be compelled to acknowledge the appropriateness of the measures and the accuracy of all the calculations it contains, but we shall feel somewhat surprised to catch Napoleon in the act of conceiving so artificial a plan,

[1] C. N. Colmars, 2nd Prairial, an. II.

calculated upon the correct working together of such a large number of different columns. For he was the very man who, in his later strategy, never made plans depending for their success upon the fitting-in of everything exactly as calculated, so that accidents beyond the control of the general might spoil the whole. Of course among mountains the temptation to split up a force into many columns, as also the excuse for it, is greater than in a plain, yet they must all finally emerge at one point only, and thus the defensive position of the enemy is easily rendered altogether untenable; still we shall have to look for other reasons in explanation of the case before us. It will assuredly not be approved of as a general rule, that each column should be told minutely what it is to do every day in such or such a case; this, however, must be put down to the complete inexperience of the subordinate officers of that time, and was therefore possibly a matter of necessity. Above all, however, we must again remember that Napoleon had not a free hand in the drawing up of this plan, that he could not arrange everything according to his own judgment, and thus we may explain the matter in the most natural way by seeing in it a compromise between divergent views, and in this case we must admire the skill with which after all an acceptable plan of attack was worked out.

This plan, however, did not remain quite unaltered. On the 2nd Messidor, at Nice, Napoleon put another draft on paper, which showed a few alterations of detail, though it was the same in its main outlines. By it the Army of the Alps was only to lend 16,000 men for the common object, who were to push forward in two columns against Castel Delfino (7000 men) and along the Stura valley (9000 men). Should the former meet with resistance, it was to be supported by the latter. We notice here that Napoleon had given up the idea that the occupation of the Stura valley was the main object, upon the attaining of which the enemy would abandon Castel

Delfino of his own accord. This was no improvement; but in view of all he did later, we may assume with certainty that we have to do here not with a modification of his own views of the situation, but with a yielding to the wishes of the Army of the Alps.

The Army of Italy was to form only three columns, of which the one destined to directly support the attack of the Army of the Alps in the Stura valley was reduced to 3000 men, whilst those which were to push on to Borgo, close the pass, and ensure the success of the whole operation, now appeared as by far the larger portions, viz. 20,000 and 7000 men. Moreover, he says expressly: "This is really the corps which will afford support to the whole army and the whole line from Castel Delfino to the Tanaro." As to the details of this plan, the individual inferior officers were allowed greater liberty of action, and the whole had been simplified; in this respect the alteration was a happy one.

However, this plan too was not put into execution. The political changes of the 9th Thermidor, which took place not long after this in Paris, of course greatly influenced the state of affairs in the armies as well, and Robespierre's fall more particularly affected Napoleon's position most seriously. The confidential relations between him and the younger Robespierre, and the favours he had received from the latter, had excited envy against him, and his enemies seized the opportunity to injure him. A secret mission with a view to reconnoitring, on which he had been sent to Genoa, served as a pretext to arrest him on his return; but, as no serious facts could be proved against him, he was soon set at liberty again, and before long appointed to the Army of the West. He went for the present to Paris, and remained there, dissatisfied with his employment on the scene of civil war, yet eager to be on the spot should fresh political changes occur in the capital. Being thus for the moment without any military duties to speak of, he again took up his pen and wrote among other things a memorandum on the Army of Italy, which he presented to the Committee of Public Safety.[1]

In this memorandum we already discover the germ of the whole of that ever memorable campaign of 1796. The idea of advancing along the depression between the Alps and the Apennines, the anticipation that the divergent interests of the Austrians and Piedmontese would immediately make themselves felt, and that consequently the former would take up a position for the protection of Lombardy and the latter for that of Piedmont, as well as driving the Austrians back to Alessandria, the quick flank movement against the Piedmontese for the purpose of compelling them, by the threat of a march to Turin, to make peace—all this was already set down in detail. The subsequent course of events also was already outlined. With that sure confidence in the infallibility of his own conceptions, with which only true genius or hopeless incapacity is endowed, he took success for granted, and depicted in a few bold strokes the results to which it might lead. He showed here by the extent of his mental vision that his assurance was that of genius, for incapacity is ever timid; true military genius alone is gifted with that vivacity of imagination which immediately foresees the remotest results that may ensue from a given state of affairs. He proceeds to show how, after having forced a peace on Piedmont, Lombardy would be conquered, the Tyrol invaded, a junction effected with the army of the Rhine, and how, by an irruption into the very heart of the Austrian states, France would be in a position to dictate peace.

But in another respect also this memorandum challenges our attention. The soldier who studies the campaign of 1796 without being acquainted with the history of Napoleon's life, is too much given to look upon this general, 27 years old, as a dazzling meteor, improvis-

[1] C. N. Mémoire sur l'armée d'Italie ; and Mémoire militaire sur l'armée d'Italie.—Paris premiers jours de thermidor, III.

ing, so to speak, unconsciously from his own natural gifts one of the most brilliant of campaigns. But wherever we examine historical events more narrowly, we shall find in the end that the course of things in the world is after all not quite spontaneous. We see, for example, by this memoir, that these great successes were preceded by a long and close study of the theatre of war and a weighing of all the factors, and that when Napoleon assumed the command-in-chief of the army in Italy, he only found himself in a situation with which he had long been most intimately acquainted; indeed, we venture to say that great results are only born of great labours. We may remind the reader of what Bourrienne says of Napoleon: "Whatever great deeds he did as emperor were only the results of plans which he had conceived long before, and at a time when his future rise was only a dream, or rather a natural outcome of his powers of imagination."[1] Only the man who is constantly occupied with great thoughts will be able to form a great resolve when the decisive moment appears.

Whether as a result of this memorandum or of the recommendations of Barras and other patrons, the young general, who was still putting off the moment of his departure for his post as commander of an infantry brigade with the Army of the West, was appointed by the Committee of Public Safety to the section of the staff for drawing up plans of campaign. In this position he quickly gained the approval of the members of the committee who superintended this branch, and soon orders were sent to the army of Italy and the Alps, conveying Napolean's ideas without modifications. It is true the reception these met with shows that the plans of genius can only be put into execution by leaders of genius. Kellermann replied their author was fit for a madhouse, and Scherer, unconsciously hitting the right nail on the head, that whoever made these plans should carry them out himself.

[1] Bourrienne, Mem., IV. 279.

In this post Napoleon remained, however, only for a brief time; shortly afterwards he was not only removed from it, but struck off the active list of generals altogether, because he had not considered it necessary to enter upon his post in the Army of the West, at this time engaged in quelling the royalist risings. Thus he remained for the moment without any employment whatever, though he no longer suffered from straitened means. At one time he had entertained the idea of going to Turkey, in order to reorganize the army there; he now took up this plan again, but the events of the 13th Vendemiaire were already visibly brewing, and when they came near, Napoleon, who had hitherto always shown himself zealous for republican ideas, and whose military capacity was acknowledged, and who, being without employment, was ready to take advantage of any turn of fortune's wheel, was the man whom Barras chose to conduct he fight in the streets of Paris. The result of this is too well known for us further to allude to it in detail.

Overjoyed at the result, he wrote to Joseph on the 14th, "Fortune has declared for me," and Marmont, who immediately after this became his aide-de-camp, says that he noticed in him an extraordinary confidence and quite a new air of greatness and importance. He sought in every way to exploit the position thus gained, and one of its consequences was his marriage.

It is perhaps difficult, as regards all human resolutions, to fix upon any one motive as the decisive one, indeed the causes of the origin of any resolution are generally very complicated; this was very likely the case here; violent, southern passion was undoubtedly to a great extent present, and undoubtedly also the prospect of the chief command in Italy, held out to him by Barras, had its share in it; at any rate we cannot and will not attempt to determine to what his resolution was finally due.

But one thing we may mention: the interesting sidelights cast by Josephine upon her suitor show us how Napoleon appeared to men at the moment when his career as a general was about to begin. "I admire the general's courage, and the extent of his knowledge of all sorts of subjects, upon which he converses equally well, and the vivacity of his mind, which makes him understand the thoughts of others, almost before they are expressed in words; but, I confess, I am frightened by the power which he seems to wish to exert over all that surround him. His searching glance has something strange and inexplicable in it, which impresses even our Directors." He himself says to Josephine: "Do they think I need their favour in order to rise? Some day they will all be only too happy if I extend mine to them. My sword is at my side, and with it I shall go far." And Josephine refers to this as follows: "I do not know how it is, but sometimes this ridiculous confidence captivates me so much, that I believe everything possible which this odd fellow puts into my head; indeed, who can calculate what he may not be capable of accomplishing with his powers of imagination?"

CHAPTER II.

1796-97.

THE BEGINNING OF THE CAMPAIGN OF ITALY.

(1) On the 2nd March Napoleon was appointed commander-in-chief of the army of Italy, on the 9th he married Josephine, on the 11th he left for the army, and on the 27th he took command of it, issuing this celebrated proclamation:—

"Headquarters, Nice, 7th Germinal IV.
"Soldiers!—You are naked and ill fed; the Government owes you much but can give you nothing. Your patience, your valour among these rocks have been admirable, but they bring you no glory; not a ray falls upon you. I will lead you into the most fertile plains on earth. You will conquer rich provinces and large towns, there you will find honour and glory and wealth. Soldiers of Italy, will you be wanting in courage or endurance?"

From this moment dates the historical importance of Napoleon. Hitherto we have hurried with hasty steps over events, endeavouring only to give a general picture of the circumstances which had most influence upon the development of the man; now the study of him as a general only begins to claim our attention exclusively, and with it comes the necessity for a more detailed treatment. Here we cannot refrain from expressing the regret, which the military student must feel on entering upon the history of Napoleon's wars, that the story of none of these ever memorable campaigns should have appeared in a comprehensive form, based upon documentary evidence. It ought indeed to be the business of the French staff, who alone have at their disposal the most important documents on the subject, to publish a really authentic delineation of this most glorious chapter in French military annals; may they soon realize this obligation![1]

Now, how are we to picture to ourselves this young general, whose youth we have described, in order to explain both his early successes and his later empire? Born in revolutionary times, he began his career without recognizing any other authority than power and success, with a character untamed by experience, hard and self-willed, of a nervous temperament, easily roused, passionate, but withal endowed with a mind that was never troubled by trivial matters, ever looking forward to great things, and possessing a power of will which nothing could daunt. But exactly because this iron will found means to overcome every obstacle, it changed into unyielding obstinacy, and because his mind, led by such a will, acknowledged no limits to his greatness, it changed gradually into a delight in the gigantic. It was his nature to be unable to bear any constraint either in small or great things; while dressing he tore and threw away whatever in the least annoyed him, and in politics he never listened to the wise counsels of Talleyrand, but always gave way to his mood of the moment. Everything had always and immediately to yield to his will; his nature was that of a tyrant, if not always that of a ruler. Neither men, nor facts, nor his environment influenced him; his irresistible impulses led him to subdue men and things and to bend circumstances to his own will; but as he never would conquer nor

[1] Since the author wrote these lines an admirable account of the Campaign of Prussia (1806-7) has appeared by Lettow Vorbeck, giving the Prussian views, while Foucart in his Campagne de Prusse, the publication of which commenced about the time Count Yorck began his, gives an excellent detail history from the French point of view.—ED.

restrain himself, all his successes ended eventually in unsuccess.

His personal appearance had at this time nothing of dignity about it; owing to his thinness, his features were almost ugly in their sharpness; his walk was unsteady, his clothes neglected, his appearance produced on the whole an unfavourable impression, and was in no way imposing; but in spite of his apparent bodily weakness he was tough and sinewy, and from under his high forehead there flashed, despite his sallow face, the eyes of genius, deep-seated, large, and of a greyish-blue colour, and before their glance and the words of authority that issued from his thin pale lips, all bowed down.

The army to command which he was called, Napoleon found in the following position. Of the main body there stood on the left wing the division Garnier, with its centre at the Colle di Finestre and its left extended as far as Isola. Next came the division Macquart along the road Sospel-Tenda, as far as the Col di Tenda; these two divisions served to keep up communication with the Army of the Alps and were not to take any immediate part in the offensive operations for the present. Next came the division Serurier on the road Pieve-Ormea-Garessio, and on the right behind this the division Augereau with its right wing resting upon the seashore at Laigueglia. The divisions of Laharpe and Meynier in the van under the orders of Massena covered the coast from Voltri up to the division of Augereau. The cantonments of the troops covered a good deal of ground. As to cavalry, in any case of little use in such country, Napoleon had 2500 men, which he placed under the command of General Steingel, forming them into two divisions and stationing them along the coast road in reserve behind the infantry; the first in advance towards Loano, the second in its rear.

On the other hand the Piedmontese army under Colli stood in the valley of the Tanaro and the Upper Bormida;

The Beginning of the Campaign of Italy

the Austrians under Beaulieu, an old man of seventy-one years, nominally also commander-in-chief of the Piedmontese, had their outposts advanced into the Northern Apennines, whilst their main body was on the point of concentrating in the plain near Alessandria.

Napoleon determined at once to take the offensive; as early as the 28th of March he wrote:[1] "Citizen directors! Your intentions shall be carried out; I shall march shortly." Before this could be done, however, some questions of administration and organization had to be attended to, so that the advance of the army might not be arrested by such considerations as retarded MacMahon's march to Mezières so much in 1870, when the only chance of its success lay in the rapidity of its execution. Here also rapidity of execution had to justify the boldness of the operations, and thus the general employed the first few days in organizing his commissariat and the communications in the rear of his army. It is altogether wrong to picture Napoleon as always pushing forward without any thought of his commissariat; he always kept his eye on it, only it never obscured the clearness of his military insight, nor did he permit it to interfere with the course and directions of his operations, and with respect to it as a rule, he always adhered to the phrase: "In the conduct of our armies we must be guided by the principle that war must support war."[2]

He had employed the few days following his arrival to such good purpose, that he could, immediately after taking up the chief command, write to Carnot:[3] "Our commissariat is secured for one month; our communications are assured," and he could now proceed to that concentration of the army on the right wing, which was to be the second step before the commencement of operations, and about which he said himself:[4] "The change from a defen-

[1] C. N. Headquarters, Nice.
[2] C. N. Mém. sur l'armée d'Italie, premiers jours de Therm.
[3] C. N. Nice, 28th March.
[4] C. N. Mém. Campagnes d'Italie, I. 101.

sive to an offensive attitude is one of the most delicate of operations." His plan was on the whole the same as that which he had laid down in his report made in 1795: An advance against the centre of the allies, whose divergent interests would induce them, once separated, to fall back in different directions; then a peace rapidly forced on the Piedmontese, followed by a struggle with the Austrians, who would then stand alone. As the most suitable point for this advance against the centre, he had selected the depression between the extremity of the Alps and the Apennines, where the mountains were lowest; this spot was marked by the road Savona-Cadibona-Altare-Carcare.

At the head of his staff was General Berthier, forty-three years old, the man who was to retain this post thenceforward during all Napoleon's campaigns, only to forsake his general, whose deeds covered him too with immortal glory, and who heaped upon him more honours and riches than upon any one else, in a shameful manner, at the moment when his star was setting. Indeed Napoleon at St. Helena called him contemptuously "one of the ganders, whom he had made half eagles," and all that is handed down to us about him by his comrades-in-arms confirms, what his short conduct of the army in 1809 proved to the world, namely, that he possessed an inexhaustible capacity for work, that he was untiring both at the work-desk and in the field, and an experienced master of all the details of military affairs, but that he was entirely lacking in the gift of understanding the great thoughts he had to convey to the army. Even as the steam hammer, moved by the power of steam, can crush everything and force it into the shape desired by the master, but is an inert mass without him, so was Berthier in Napoleon's hands, and moulded by his spirit. Separated from him he sank back into nothingness.

Whilst the divisions of the army were thus engaged in concentrating, and garrison troops were coming up from the rear according to the commander-in-chief's orders, in order to secure the line of retreat of the army by their occupation of Nice, Albenga, and Savona, Napoleon's headquarters left Nice on the 2nd April and advanced along the coast by short stages. But the enemy also did not remain idle. The vanguard of the French troops at Voltri had aroused in Beaulieu apprehensions for Genoa, and thus some forward movements of the Austrians in that direction, beginning on the 31st March, proved to Napoleon that his intention to surprise them in their winter quarters had failed. Meanwhile, Colli had been concentrating his forces in close cantonments around Mondovi and Ceva. At this moment[1] Napoleon overestimated the Piedmontese; he put them at 45,000 men, the Austrians correctly at 37,000, whilst he himself had 45,000. At the actual commencement of operations we may fairly compute the active strength of the armies in the field as follows: Colli 25,000, Beaulieu 35,000, Napoleon 37,000; the allies, however, had a very considerable superiority in artillery, the French being very weak in this arm.

On the 9th April Beaulieu opened the campaign by advancing in person on the left with 7000 men towards Voltri, whilst Argenteau, disposing altogether of 9000 men, which, however, were not all at hand, pushed forward in the centre towards Sassello; Colli remaining at Ceva. Napoleon, who had been on the point of joining the division Serurier, now hurried in person, surprised by these movements, to Savona, in order to be on the scene of action. The next day, the 10th, Beaulieu advanced against the brigade of Cervoni, stationed at Voltri, and by nightfall the latter had to fall back upon its division Laharpe, which it rejoined on the 11th near Madonna di Savona. On this same day Argenteau forced the French posts back through Montenotte, but behind this village, at some earthworks thrown up on Monte Legino, and

---

[1] C. N. Headquarters, Albenga, 6th April.

defended by the brave Colonel Rampon, met with a resistance which he could not overcome.

The arrival of these reports rendered it clear to Napoleon that the enemy were advancing on the west, though he was not of course acquainted with the actual distribution of their forces. At the same time he recognized two things : first, that the columns advancing upon Voltri and Savona could not support each other directly ; and secondly, that he was at least equal to one of these columns if he massed the greater portion of his army against it; he therefore resolved upon an immediate attack on the Austrians advancing *viâ* Montenotte; these once beaten, he would stand on the inner line between Beaulieu and Colli, who would then be separated from each other, at Voltri and Ceva, by thirty-eight miles of impassable mountainous country. Thus the French general would be free to throw himself upon either of them, before the other could come up.

Therefore he issued on the afternoon of the 11th April the following orders : [1]—" Augereau will march with 6000 men to Mallare; on the morning of the 12th at five o'clock he will start thence for Cairo, where he will wait for further orders. He will overthrow all opposition. Massena will push forward along the road *viâ* Altare with 9000 men, as soon as he has collected these troops. Laharpe will march at daybreak on the 12th with 7000 men to the Monte Legino to reinforce the corps stationed there. Serurier will be informed of the intended attack and demonstrate against Colli." This was, in fact, tactically a combined attack in full force on the right wing of the Austrian column advancing *viâ* Montenotte, and strategically, a piercing of the enemy's centre.

Napoleon himself left Albenga at one o'clock in the morning and accompanied Massena's column. The result (2a) answered his expectations. Argenteau, who had collected only 3000 men for his offensive movement, was turned by

[1] C. N. **Headquarters, Albenga.**

The Beginning of the Campaign of Italy

Massena near Montenotte-inferiore and completely driven back with very heavy losses. Augereau had no chance of joining in the fight, being forced by some movements of Colli in the direction of the Bormida valley to keep his eye upon the Piedmontese, in order to protect the left flank of the French advance against any danger threatening it from them; he therefore went back from Cairo to Montefreddo.

Immediately after this success Napoleon turned his attention to the Piedmontese, and as he found them within reach, he decided to attack them. Augereau and the larger portion of Massena's division, altogether 10,000 men, were to advance *viâ* Millesimo and Castelnuovo upon Montezzemolo, whilst Serurier penetrated into Ceva, and sought to turn the right wing of the enemy with his left, his own right wing assisting in the attack upon Montezzemolo. Massena himself, with the remainder of his division and Laharpe, advanced against the Austrians in the direction of Dego, in order thereby to cover the attack upon the Piedmontese on this side. (2b)

In executing these orders Augereau met the left wing of the Piedmontese on the morning of the 13th at Millesimo. General Provera, commanding here, threw himself, in face of superior numbers, into the ruined castle of Cosseria, and all efforts to wrest from him this position were unsuccessful during that day. But the next morning Provera was forced by want of water and ammunition to surrender the castle to Augereau. Being now secure on this side, Napoleon determined to take Dego, to which an Austrian division had advanced, so as to secure his right flank during his further operations against the Piedmontese. Massena and Laharpe, who had the evening before arrived in front of this position, attacked from the right, turning the enemy, whilst Napoleon ordered a half-brigade of the troops planted before Cosseria to assist. At one o'clock in the afternoon the attack on the position, only occupied by 4000 men, commenced.

Beaulieu, who had at the first news of Napoleon's advance against Argenteau, hastened back to Acqui, was as a matter of fact still busy with concentrating his army at this place, and had planted the above-named post in Dego to cover this operation. The latter was now entirely destroyed by Napoleon's combined attack with superior forces, and all the guns (eighteen) and almost all the men fell into the French hands.

Thus on the evening of the 14th of April the separation of Beaulieu's and Colli's forces was a *fait accompli*, and Napoleon, having returned to Carcare, resolved now to direct his attacks against the latter, and thus to force the Piedmontese to conclude peace. Accordingly he issued at 10 p.m. the following orders:—Massena to collect his forces at Dego and remain there; all the rest to start at 8 a.m. and march upon Montezzemolo. The cavalry, hitherto left behind in their old positions, were now moved up to Carcare.

(2c) But on the 15th with the break of day an Austrian column of 3000 men pushed forward to Dego, and by eleven o'clock in the forenoon captured this village from the French, who undoubtedly had neglected to take ordinary measures for safety. This column consisted of five battalions coming from Sassello, who ought really to have come up in time for the fighting on the 14th. The French, taken by surprise, were driven back in disorder; soon, however, Napoleon himself hastened thither on Massena's request for assistance. Indeed, before the beginning of the attack information had already reached him that Beaulieu himself intended to advance upon Dego, and he had in consequence countermanded the advance of Laharpe's division and halted it at Rochetta. About two o'clock in the afternoon the French took the offensive again and threw back the Austrians in disorder with heavy losses upon Spigno. Meanwhile on the left wing Serurier had advanced the same day in the Tanaro valley against Ceva, whilst Augereau, forcing the opposing troops of Colli back on his side, had reached the position of Montezzemolo, and had thus come in touch with Serurier.

Thus Napoleon had once more definitely repulsed the Austrians on his right wing and was doubly secure, whilst his left was within striking distance of the enemy, prepared to detain them until he could turn their flank from Dego. The sum total of successes against the Austrians was, a loss of 10,000 men, and such a strong moral effect, that Beaulieu, convinced of the French superiority of numbers, now thought only of concentrating his troops at Acqui and protecting Lombardy.

On the 15th success seemed still more within Napoleon's reach than on the evening of the 14th. It was of no use whatever to advance against the Austrians. He was not in touch with them; they might evade him, in which case he would have missed his stroke, whilst in the meantime Colli could fall back upon Turin and place both his army and the capital in safety. Then all chance of forcing a peace upon one of his opponents, thus getting rid of him, and having the advantage in regard to numbers on his own side, would be lost. Now the whole plan was based upon compelling the Piedmontese, after separation from the Austrians, to make peace, and thus gaining a safe base for future operations against the other isolated opponent. There are many examples in the annals of war of a general being carried away by success in battle and neglecting his general plan of operations, in order to reap the direct advantage of his success. But Napoleon, who was now at the turning-point of his movements, kept his main object well in view, and accordingly moved against the Piedmontese.

To begin with, it is true he took steps towards moving the division of Laharpe to Sassello, and even told off Massena to support it; nor can we clearly understand the aim of this movement. And here we may mention that the "Correspondance de Napoleon I." is but an incomplete guide for the early part of the campaign of 1796; probably much was settled by word of mouth, for Napoleon constantly endeavoured as far as possible to see to everything personally.¹ "You cannot imagine my life here," he wrote to the Directory, "I arrive tired, but have to keep awake all night to settle questions of administration, and be all over the place to restore order."

On the 16th April Augereau had proceeded to attack the entrenched position of the Piedmontese at Ceva and had driven them from it; they fell back on the road to Mondovi as far as Lesegno. On the 17th we find Laharpe recalled to Dego, and Massena and Serurier sent forward to Ceva; the latter occupied this place the same evening. The next day the whole cavalry was placed under Serurier's orders and Napoleon himself moved his head-
(2d) quarters to Saliceto. On the 19th the attack upon Colli began. Serurier advanced upon San Michele by a flank movement on the left, in order to cut off his road to Mondovi, Augereau marched upon Castellino in order to outflank him on the right, while Massena pushed on straight to Ceva. Colli, wishing to retreat by Mondovi, met Serurier and engaged him successfully, it is true, but without any really decisive result. As to Napoleon, he had proceeded to Ceva; he fixed his headquarters for the night at Lesegno, still further in advance, and from here he ordered at one o'clock in the night a general attack upon Colli. All further arrangements were to be made in the course of the next day, for only then probably would he become acquainted with the actual position of the enemy. Accordingly Massena was to advance upon Lesegno, and a part of Augereau's force was put under his command. The rest of the latter took up positions, partly at Castellino, in order to threaten the enemy's left flank, and partly at Mombarcaro, in order to observe the Bormida valley, along which the Austrians might approach. For security against the latter, Laharpe also was to

¹ C. N. Carrú, 24th April.

march to Mombarcaro, and to occupy the fortified position of Ceva, leaving only one brigade as rearguard in Cairo.

At two o'clock in the morning of the 21st, Massena crossed the Tanaro and advanced upon Lesegno; on the same morning Serurier received orders to push forward over the bridge of Torre and to attack the right wing of the enemy posted behind the Cursaglia. The enemy, however, did not wait for this attack, but retreated *viâ* Mondovi. Serurier encountered a division left behind at Vico to cover this retreat, and defeated it completely. In the evening Napoleon was at Mondovi, but returned again to Lesegno. On the 22nd his army took up a position along the line Mondovi-Niella-Castellino, that is, generally speaking, remained in its place; probably because the quality of the republican troops was such, that an interval of comparative rest was absolutely necessary for the restoration of tactical order; besides Napoleon was not altogether sure whether Colli might not advance again; when no such advance occurred, he ordered Serurier, on the 23rd, to move forward on the road to Fossano, Massena on that to Cherasco, both as far as the other side of the Pesio; Augereau went to Dogliani, and Laharpe was to follow on the 24th as far as Niella. From Lesegno a General Order was issued on the 23rd, to stop the numerous excesses of his subordinate officers, more particularly all looting.

It is true, Napoleon, like all great leaders, laid an enemy's country under contribution for the benefit of his army to the utmost extent, yet he always looked upon looting as a cancer that must be rooted out, inasmuch as it destroyed all discipline. He himself said: "I have thought much on this subject; I have often been tempted to reward my soldiers by permitting it, and I should have done so had I considered it of advantage. But nothing is more calculated to disorganize an army and to ruin it entirely;"[1] and it was this conviction which made him

[1] Mém. de Ste. Hél.

write angrily to the Directoire : " I shall restore discipline or cease to command these robbers ! "[1] Altogether plundering was distasteful to his nature. " Great men are never cruel without necessity,"[2] he justly said himself, and though indeed he was inexorable when he met with resistance, or when his policy demanded it, he was never personally cruel. He ordered the plundering of Pavia to cease after three hours, because he took pity on its inhabitants ; if, during his passage to Egypt, a man fell overboard, he did not rest until he was saved, and all who were intimately associated with him testify unanimously that he was not without a certain kindness for individuals, as long as his interests were not at stake, nor his anger roused. General Foy, assuredly a trustworthy witness, says : " Do not let us mistake a despot, whose anger never overstepped the limits of what he considered his interests, for a tyrant, passionate, blind and bloodthirsty. Napoleon was not wicked by nature ; he always showed himself full of leniency for his people ; even his enemies he could not hate long or vehemently."[3]

Whilst his columns were crossing the Pesio, Napoleon received that same day, the 23rd, a letter from Colli requesting an armistice. Napoleon declared himself ready to grant it, on condition that two of the three fortresses, Cuneo, Alessandria, and Tortona, were surrendered, and that definite negotiations for peace were begun immediately. These conditions were accepted, and the truce was signed on the 28th ; Cuneo and Tortona were surrendered to the French.

Therewith the first chapter of Napoleon's first campaign came to a successful end, and an examination of it gives us the first (and that a valuable) insight into Napoleon's methods. In the first place we are struck with the confidence with which the youthful leader accepted his task

---

[1] C. N. Carrú, 24th April.   [2] Mme. de Rémusat, Mém.
[3] Hist. de la guerre de la péninsule.

and carried it through; no half-success, no failure forced him into an irksome apprenticeship; from the first he showed himself as a master of his art, as did Alexander, Hannibal, and Charles XII. Doubtless physical and mental qualities have to be combined to render such a result possible, but still it is certain that there are, on the other hand, things in the art of war which can be learned, and must be learned, in order to achieve success. The greatest elasticity of mind cannot dispense with the mechanical side of the art of war. "Achilles was the son of a goddess and a mortal; this is a symbol of the spirit of the art of war,"[1] says Napoleon. We have seen how fully prepared he himself was in entering on his career, how Italy as the scene of a probable war had been made by him the object of especial and mature study, and as those qualities which fortune alone can grant were present in him in a rich measure, his success was both deserved and inevitable. Gambetta on the other hand furnishes us, in our own time, with a proof that even the highest energy, coupled with undoubted genius, does not suffice to ensure victory, if a knowledge of the mechanical part be lacking.

And if we examine Napoleon's work in detail, we shall appreciate his plan and its execution at their full value only after clearly understanding the danger of the strategical conditions under which he assumed command of the army. Widely scattered as it was over the narrow belt of land between the Ligurian Alps and the sea, its only line of communication in the rear, with Marseilles, was extremely exposed, both on the side of the mountains, where an enemy advancing over the Col di Tenda might cut the French off completely, and also on the side of the sea, on which the English fleet held undisputed sway. Nor did this single line of communication lie in the exact rear of the army and covered by it, but along the prolongation of its left flank, one of the most unfavourable strategical positions imaginable, as Napoleon proved most

[1] Précis des guerres du maréchal de Turenne.

strikingly to the Prussian army in 1806. And what did he accomplish in this unfavourable position? In three weeks the French army was concentrated, one enemy beaten and thrown back upon his communications, the other's capital threatened, and the French army had its line of communication in its rear and covering all the space from Saluzzo to the sea.

In this opening of the campaign we immediately recognize the characteristic stamp of Napoleon's whole generalship: a clear perception of what masses can effect. Jomini, whose admirable system is based on the deeds of the greatest master of the practice of war, says in the chapter on the fundamental principle of war,[1] that it consists of the following:—

1. To lead the bulk of the army by strategical combinations successively to the decisive points of the theatre of action, and as much as possible upon the enemy's lines of communication without endangering one's own;

2. To manœuvre in such a manner that the bulk of one's forces act only against detached portions of the hostile army.

Napoleon was from the first fully alive to these principles. As early as 1794 he says: "The same rules obtain in the conduct of campaigns as in the siege of fortresses; the fire must be concentrated upon one point. The breach once made, the equilibrium is disturbed, all the rest becomes useless and the fortress is taken. . . . The attacks should be concentrated, not scattered."[2] When in 1799 he met Moreau for the first time and the two men discussed strategy, the latter said: "It is always the greater numbers that win!" "You are right," broke in Napoleon eagerly, "it is always the greater number that beats the lesser,"[2] adding by way of explanation: "When with inferior forces

---

[1] Précis de l'art de la guerre.
[2] C. N. Rapport sur la position polit. et mil. des armées de Piémont et d'Espagne.
[3] Gohier, Mém.

I had a large army before me, I concentrated mine rapidly and fell like lightning upon one of the enemy's wings and routed it. Then I took advantage of the confusion which this manœuvre never failed to produce in the opposing army, to attack it on another point, but always with my whole force. Thus I beat it in detail, and the victory which was the result, was always, as you see, the triumph of the larger number over the lesser."

The carrying out of this principle was the secret of Napoleon's strategy; but it is necessary in addition to be able always to distinguish readily the point at which the concentrated attack should be delivered and to possess the strength of mind to disregard all secondary matters, however important they may seem to be, in order to bring your whole force to bear at the decisive point. It is above all this clearness and logical pursuit of strategical plans that we admire in Napoleon, and which make the study of him as a general profitable. When, after the conclusion of the whole campaign now under consideration, he had marched victoriously through Italy into the heart of Austria, he himself said with reference to his strategy: "There are in Europe many good generals, but they see too many things at once; as for me, I see only one thing, namely the enemy's main body. I try to crush it, confident that secondary matters will then settle themselves."[1] Thus we see here how he calmly left the road to Genoa open to Beaulieu, when the latter began the campaign, and how he only watched Colli for the time being and threw himself with superior forces upon Argenteau's force, the centre of the allies; between the 11th and the 15th he defeated all the Austrian divisions opposed to him. This is an example of the employment of superior numbers at the decisive point, for since his opponents were not united, and moreover were drawn from several nations, the most effective course was to separate them by pushing between them. If after the first few blows the principal enemy, the Austrians, fell

[1] Berthezène, Souvenirs milit.

back, Napoleon might reckon that the secondary force, the Piedmontese, would only think of the immediate protection of their own country, and would not consider that they could best protect their country by joining Beaulieu, in order to fight a pitched battle with their united forces. This calculation, based upon a correct appreciation of human motives, was justified by events. Indeed the same thing may be found often in the history of war, when allies are engaged; that the Prussians acted differently and in accordance with the rules of war, in marching on the 17th June, of 1815, to Wavre, and on the 18th to Belle-Alliance, sacrificing all their communications, is a glorious testimony to Gneisenau's judgment and Blücher's decision.

Beaulieu being beaten and having fallen back, Colli's army became the proper objective, and immediately the French general turned with superior forces on him, merely guarding against attack on the side of the Austrians. From the 16th he operated solely against Colli, and after seven days the latter asked for a truce. It is worthy of notice also, that Napoleon ordered up troops who had stopped behind in order to observe the Austrians, as soon as he saw that the latter remained inactive, and that the further he advanced, the further he left them behind him. It was ever his aim to keep his forces together as much as circumstances permitted, while any fighting was anticipated, for, "We must separate to live, but unite to fight!"[1]

He thus showed the clearest perception of what is essential in war and the most resolute adherence to what he recognized as essential.

To this must be added his careful regulation of the commissariat, his care in securing his base, his indefatigable personal energy, and his stern maintenance of discipline; and thus Napoleon, taken altogether, presents to us an example, such as no other modern military leader has

---

[1] C. N. Rapport sur la position, etc.; see p. 38 and footnote.

shown in full perfection at the commencement of his career.¹

Scarcely had Napoleon attained his first object, viz. the removal of one of his opponents from the field, than he directed his attention to the next point. It is significant that it was just at the moment when he found himself in front of numbers in a favourable position compared with his opponent, that he began to ask the Directory for reinforcements and for the assistance of the Army of the Alps; for he was well aware of the great expenditure of forces which an advance on a large scale, such as he had in view, would entail. His first success had only increased his appetite for further successes, and he wanted to set in motion proportionately larger forces. This dissatisfaction with the success achieved, this desire to place the goal aimed at further and ever further ahead, is the stamp of the true general.

After Colli's offer of a truce on the 23rd April, Napoleon had at first continued his advance upon Turin, in order to thoroughly impress the Piedmontese with the necessity of yielding. The latter fell back without resistance, and on the 27th Napoleon crossed the Stura. As to the doings of the Austrians he had no accurate (3) information, but as his advance into Lombardy would in any case bring him in contact with them, he did not trouble about this, and no sooner was the truce concluded than he wrote: "To-morrow I shall march against Beaulieu; I shall force him to retreat behind the Po; I shall cross this river in his immediate rear, seize the whole of Lombardy, and before a month is passed, I hope to be among the mountains of the Tyrol, to meet the army of

¹ Thus Wellington's Talavera campaign cannot be for one moment compared with that of Vitoria, which was as brilliant as Napoleon's Marengo campaign. On the other hand, Marlborough's first great campaign, 1704, was assuredly his greatest master-piece. The strategy of this was entirely due to the English commander, although German authors, probably through ignorance, habitually ignore this fact.—ED.

the Rhine, and in conjunction with it carry the war into Bavaria.¹ On the same day, the 28th April, he issued orders regulating the garrisons of the places taken or handed over, thus securing his base, and also for his army to set itself in motion towards the East in the general direction of Tortona. He ordered the divisions Macquart and Garnier up from the Alps *viâ* Cuneo as reinforcements, and had now, after deducting garrisons, 35,000 men at his disposal for his operations. Beaulieu's force he correctly estimated at 26,000.

This latter general, having made a vain attempt to capture Tortona and Alessandria and thus to secure some points of support on the theatre of war on the right of the Po, retreated before the approaching French, on the 1st May by Valenza behind the Po, on the 2nd behind the Agogna. On this day Napoleon's headquarters were at Bosco, Augereau had reached Frugarolo, Laharpe Rivalta, and Massena Castellazzo; Serurier had followed at an interval of one day's march and was at Alba.

The French general had, as we have seen, determined at the very moment of the conclusion of the truce with the Piedmontese, to proceed immediately to the conquest of the whole of Lombardy, and thus he had, in order to mislead his enemy, inserted a clause in that convention, permitting the French army to cross the Po at Valenza. Now when Beaulieu fell into this trap and took up his position behind the Agogna on the road to Pavia, Napoleon was at once ready to take advantage of this mistake, brought about by his action, and to effect a crossing lower down, and thus not only become immediately master of a larger extent of territory, but also place himself on the flank and rear of the Austrians and turn their posts of defence on the Agogna, the Terdoppio, the Ticino, and the Lambro by a single movement; besides, the crossing would be a surprise, and therefore more likely to succeed.

¹ C. N. To the Directory. Cherasco, 28th April.

The Beginning of the Campaign of Italy

On the 3rd May, accordingly, Napoleon ordered from his headquarters at Tortona the formation of four battalions of Grenadiers and two battalions of Carbineers to be ready for the march on the 5th. This picked body was to surprise the point selected for crossing. Meanwhile he continued to hoodwink the Austrians. On the 4th he advanced *viâ* Castelnuovo, Sale, and Bassignana towards the Po; on the preceding day he had written to the governor of Alessandria,[1] that a division would without delay appear before Valenza, to cross the Po there. All communication with the left bank was interrupted and an embargo laid on all boats, etc. But at the same time, on the 4th, the newly formed picked body was assembled at Casteggio and placed under the command of General Dallemagne. To this same place, 1500 cavalry and six guns were dispatched on the 5th, whilst the army executed a movement to the right along the Po.

All these arrangements show how conscious Napoleon was of his superiority in judgment and power of will over his opponent; he dictated to him his course of action, was quite sure that he would keep to it and commit the mistakes on which he reckoned and which he had led him on to do. This consciousness of mental superiority, one of the strongest guarantees of victory, was always felt by Napoleon. We shall see how at Austerlitz too he led his enemy into errors through his own dispositions, and how he predicted with certainty these errors and the manner in which he himself would take advantage of them. But we may well ask ourselves, whether this feeling of superiority, naturally increased by success, must not in the end lead to a complete contempt for any opponent, and thus to fatal errors, which, though they are to those of men like Beaulieu, Brunswick, Mack, and Massenbach as dissipation is to impotence, yet lead to the same end; for as Napoleon himself said on his retreat from Moscow: "To be too much accustomed to great successes often

[1] C. N. To Chevalier Solar-Bosco.

leads to great reverses."[1] Was it not indeed this same contempt of the enemy arising from a consciousness of superiority which induced Frederick the Great to attempt a decisive battle at Kolin with 34,000 men against 53,000; was it not this insolence of success which led Charles XII. to the field of Pultawa, which probably affected Alexander, which detained Napoleon so long in Moscow, and which made him exclaim even on the 12th October, 1813, with reference to the battle-field of Leipzig: "I shall only fight if I like. They will never dare to attack me there,"[2] and which finally caused him, on the 18th June, to reject obstinately the thought of any possibility of the Prussians appearing on the field?

But Frederick learned from experience. Immediately after Kolin he abandoned the whole of Bohemia, and renounced during all the subsequent years of the war the thought of dictating a peace under the walls of Vienna; a king should act thus, because, as Napoleon says, A *king* must not aim merely at victory, but at its consequences.[3] But just because a *general* should aim merely at victory, Napoleon will be for us soldiers the greater example. The "Halt," which Napoleon should have cried as regards himself when he became a sovereign, will be imposed upon *us* by the State; for *us* the one guiding principle of warfare must ever remain, a complete overthrow of the enemy, and nothing more; and therefore we should continue to study the example of this man, who, a soldier himself, was ever dominated by this principle, so much so indeed, that even in 1814, forced back almost under the walls of his capital by superior numbers, he exclaimed after the successful engagement at Champaubert: "If we gain such a success to-morrow over Sacken as we gained to-day over Olssufiev, the enemy will recross the Rhine more quickly than he crossed it, and I shall find myself once more on the

---

[1] Ségur, Hist. de Nap. et de la grande armée. At Orscha.
[2] Marmont, Mém.   [3] Mém. de Ste. Hél.

The Beginning of the Campaign of Italy

Vistula."[1] Such self-confidence, such powers of imagination, grasping the remotest bearings of every success, well befits a general.

On the 6th May Napoleon commenced his march upon Piacenza. Dallemagne reached Castello San Giovanni, Augereau Broni, Laharpe and the cavalry under Kilmaine Stradella; Serurier remained in front of Valenza, and Massena at Sale. Being so placed, Napoleon said to himself: "Should my advance on Piacenza induce Beaulieu to evacuate the Lomellina, I shall cross quietly at Valenza. Should Beaulieu remain in ignorance of our march to Piacenza for twenty-four hours, I shall cross during the night if I can obtain boats and materials for rafts in this town."[2] In any case this latter resolution was the more likely for him to adopt, for, "I may be accused of rashness, but never of slowness."

In order to receive as early as possible all intelligence coming in from both wings, Napoleon had not yet removed his headquarters from Tortona, though another circumstance also may have influenced him in this. Since a crossing at Piacenza was more probable, and since this crossing could only be successful as a surprise, he rightly considered it advisable to allow his headquarters to remain as long as possible in the vicinity of Valenza, so as to confirm the Austrians all the more in their mistakes. This was one of those precautions which he never lost sight of when it was a question of concealing from the enemy any movement begun. Of this we shall see a fine example in 1805, when he remained quietly in Paris at first and then betook himself to a forward position at Strasburg, facing the passes in the Black Forest, whilst his army made its preliminary movements for the magnificent stroke of turning the flank of the Austrians posted on the Iller.

The whole of the 6th May was spent in deciding what

[1] Marmont, Mém.
[2] C. N. To the Directory, Tortona, 6th May.

was to be done; therefore when his choice fell upon Piacenza, the crossing could no longer be effected during the night, but had to be postponed until the morning of the 7th. In the evening of the 6th Napoleon at Tortona issued the following orders: " Massena will on the 7th proceed to Voghera, Laharpe will start at five o'clock and march to Calendasco, Augereau at six o'clock to Castello San Giovanni, Dallemagne at four o'clock to Borgo San Antonio." Napoleon himself went to Castello San Giovanni, and ordered on the same evening the banks of the Po to be reconnoitred and a few boats to be collected. On the 7th,

(4) at four o'clock in the morning, Dallemagne started, and his division, accompanied by the commander-in-chief, arrived at Piacenza at nine o'clock. On the other bank of the Po only some 150 Austrian cavalry were to be seen. At this sight, Napoleon, now certain of being able to effect his passage here, at once sent orders to all his subordinate officers to push forward by forced marches. Dallemagne immediately began to cross, and by two o'clock in the afternoon his division stood on the left bank. The enterprise had succeeded, and Napoleon could say with a sneer: " Beaulieu has lost his head; he calculates very badly; he falls continually into the traps prepared for him."[1] Laharpe crossed next, his being the first entire division to do so.

On the same day the French came in contact with Beaulieu's outposts. The latter had on the 4th dispatched General Liptay with 5000 men down the Po to protect its banks, he himself following on the 6th *viâ* Gropello. General Liptay arrived at Guardamiglia on the 7th and forced the French to fall back as far as the Po. But at one o'clock in the afternoon of the 8th, Napoleon, who had now sufficient troops on the further side, pushed forward in his turn, and the hostile division, which had taken up a position at Fombia, was driven back to Pizzighettone, a portion of it being utterly routed. In the evening Laharpe was at

[1] C. N. To Carnot, Piacenza, 9th May.

The Beginning of the Campaign of Italy 47

Codogno, Dallemagne pushed forward as far as the neighbourhood of Pizzighettone. About ten o'clock at night, a fresh Austrian division, advancing along the road from Casalpusterlengo, met with Laharpe's outposts and repulsed them, but was subsequently driven back in its turn; it had hurriedly been sent out at noon from Belgiojoso by Beaulieu when he learnt that the French had crossed the Po. During this encounter Laharpe fell, and was succeeded in command by Menard. Napoleon being informed of these events, was not alarmed at this advance of detached bodies of troops, and merely remarked: "Perhaps Beaulieu means to fight a battle; the man has the audacity of madness, though not that of genius."[1]

Beaulieu did in fact intend to deliver a general attack, and ordered it in the evening of the 8th; but after receiving further news as to events, he recognized that his forces were not sufficiently concentrated for a battle, and he therefore countermanded his orders soon after midnight and began his retreat across the Adda. He now took up a position near Lodi. Napoleon employed the 9th in allowing the divisions of Massena and Augereau, the latter at Veratto, to complete the passage and pushing them forward towards Lodi. Augereau reached Borghetto, (5) Massena Casalpusterlengo, Dallemange, under the latter's command, advanced to Zorlesco, and Menard took his place at Maleo in front of Pizzighettone. Napoleon himself left Piacenza during the night and arrived at three o'clock in the morning at Casalpusterlengo. He immediately sent Dallemagne forward against Lodi, and when the latter found this town occupied, he himself advanced with the divisions of Massena and Augereau.

Beaulieu had immediately continued his retreat towards Cremona, and Lodi was only covered by a division of 7000 men, who were to follow and form the rearguard. At 11.30 a.m. Napoleon arrived before the town, drove out the Austrians, and in the afternoon, after six o'clock, formed

[1] C. N. To Carnot, Piacenza, 9th May.

a close column, which, when its advance had been to some extent prepared by artillery fire, made about seven o'clock the famous assault on the bridge with astonishing rapidity and irresistible impetus. This performance, which he himself described as the boldest of the campaign, inspired him with unwavering confidence in his lucky star. Even at St. Helena he said: "Vendemiaire, and even Montenotte, had not yet led me to consider myself a being apart. Not till after Lodi did I feel that I was destined in any case to play a foremost part on our political stage: that first kindled the spark of boundless ambition in me?"[1]

We can understand why this feat should have inspired him with such confidence, when we consider that he expected to find the whole Austrian army defending the passage at Lodi, and indeed may have imagined even on the evening after the engagement that he had really beaten its main body. Though we know now that this was not the case, Lodi still teaches us the lesson, that in war a bold resolve is often unexpectedly favoured by fortune. Mere reasoning could scarcely have led him to expect success there, still the enterprise was undertaken with determination. Yet at Lodi the main body of the Austrians was not present, nor was any firm determination shown by them to bar the passage at all costs. Napoleon was by no means inclined to avoid the obstacle, as he might have done; he dreaded the loss of time, for he thought with Gneisenau that "Strategy is the art of making use of time and space. I am less chary of the latter than the former. Space we can recover, lost time never."[2]

On the 11th May, Napoleon remained with the bulk of his forces near Lodi, sending forward some detachments to Crema and towards Milan; his immediate intention was, "to pursue Beaulieu and to take advantage of his being stunned, to strike him another blow."[3]

---

[1] Mém. de Ste. Hélène.
[2] C. N. To Stein, Dammartin le St. Père, 7th January, 1814.
[3] C. N. To Carnot, Lodi, 11th May.

The Beginning of the Campaign of Italy

Since the Austrians, as he had learnt, had fallen back upon Pizzighettone, he started in the early morning of the 12th in that direction; Massena and Dallemagne pushed forward along the left bank of the Adda; Menard advanced on the right, Serurier, still at Piacenza, was, if necessary, to support Menard. Augereau received, in the course of the 12th, orders to follow *viâ* Crema towards Pizzighettone. However, Beaulieu was no longer there; he had drawn together his troops at Cremona, and then crossed the Oglio. Pizzighettone surrendered on the 13th after a short bombardment.

Being now convinced that, on the one hand, Beaulieu, retreating towards Mantua, was no longer to be overtaken, and on the other, that nothing further was to be feared from him for the present, Napoleon determined to complete the conquest of the country occupied by him, and sent Massena to Milan, Augereau to Pavia, whilst Serurier remained at Piacenza, and Menard at Codogno and Pizzighettone. Napoleon himself entered Milan in triumph on the 15th May; and thus the second chapter of the campaign, the conquest of Lombardy, came to an end seventeen days after the beginning of operations against Beaulieu.

CHAPTER III.

MANTUA. WÜRMSER'S ATTEMPT TO RELIEVE IT.

(6) ON the 14th May, at the moment when all the plans of Napoleon had been crowned with such complete success, he received at Lodi from his Government the information that he would in future, after the arrival of the army of the Alps, have to share the chief command with Kellermann. The latter would conduct the campaign on the left bank of the Po, and he, Napoleon, would have to march in the first instance to Rome and Naples.

He immediately replied that, under these circumstances, he would give up the command of the army altogether. All he said on this point is most pertinent: "I have conducted the campaign without asking anybody's advice; I should have done no good if I had had to take anybody else's views into consideration. Everyone has his own way of carrying on war. General Kellermann has had more experience, and will no doubt carry it on better than I; but together we should do very badly."[1]

"I may add that I am of opinion that it would be better to have one bad general than two good ones. War is like government, it is a question of tact;"[2] and he was convinced that the decision the Directory would now come to with respect to the chief command, was more important than the 15,000 men by whom Beaulieu would probably be reinforced.

Every general will feel it his duty to act as Napoleon acted here. Whoever is conscious of being fit to fill the

---

[1] C. N. To the Directory, Lodi, 14th May.
[2] C. N. To Carnot, Lodi, 14th May.

office of commander-in-chief, must claim to be treated with full confidence; still, the history of war is not wanting in examples of leaders who did not possess sufficient self-control to refuse a great command, though coupled with limitations; but in such cases we may say with justice, that any reverses suffered tarnish the réputation of the man, who, tempted by the glory of a high command, accepted it, although deprived of full liberty of action. Bazaine, on the 12th August, 1870, is an example of this; Blücher, on the 11th August, 1813, a glorious instance to the contrary. Napoleon himself considered this matter worthy to be discussed at some length in his Memoirs, where he declared most emphatically, that a general at the head of an army should only carry out such plans as he himself approves of. He said distinctly: "Every commander-in-chief who takes upon himself to execute a plan which he considers bad or ruinous is culpable; he ought to remonstrate, to insist upon alterations, and, if necessary, rather resign, than become the means of the defeat of the force entrusted to him." [1]

With what firmness in the midst of the most difficult circumstances he had wielded this chief command, which was now to be divided! The army which he took over was destitute in every way, and the means by which it afterwards sought, as we have seen, to remedy this destitution, viz. plunder, was more dangerous than the original disease. And yet it had won such victories, accomplished such marches! This proves that a leader of genius knows how to gain victories, whatever the condition of his troops may be; it proves also that Jomini is right when he says: "I believe Napoleon would not have done more even with the best equipped troops, nor Frederick less, had the conditions been reversed." [2]

More important still than the efficiency of the men is that of the subordinate officers. "It is the officers who gain

---

[1] Mém. de Ste. Hel., Observations sur les campagnes de 1796 et 1797.
[2] Traité des grandes opérations mil., I. p. 430, 4th edit.

victories, or enable them to be gained."[1] In this respect Napoleon was fortunately placed; his subordinate commanders were young, ambitious, enterprising, and yet already experienced in war. Still, he had to put up with one evil. When Napoleon joined the army of Italy, he found in its ranks men, who were to be his subordinates, who thought they were in no way inferior to himself in courage, talent, and capacity for the chief command; his appointment had excited astonishment and to some extent envy as well. Massena, dissolute, rapacious, but ambitious and unsurpassed as a leader; Augereau, frivolous, boastful, but brave and clever: Serurier, a tall, stern figure, and of great experience; Laharpe, simple and capable; Steingel, indefatigable, the model of a leader of advance-guards ;—all these were men already possessed of a wide experience of war, though still in the prime of life; for at that time people thought what Napoleon soon expressed in words: "The great art of government is not to let men grow old."[2]

And now there came among all these men, as their commander-in-chief, this Bonaparte—small, of delicate appearance, and not yet twenty-seven years old, younger than any, and barely known to a few among them as a capable general of artillery.

But this youthful leader brought with him a strong opinion as to the necessity of absolute command on the one side and unconditional obedience on the other. It was his conviction that "unless the limits of every man's authority are well defined, the whole becomes confusion."[3] However much the party of opposition, Serurier, Kilmaine, Vignolle, etc., grumbled, success was on his side, and he contented himself with saying contemptuously: "The position of a general after a battle is more awkward than before it, for in the first instance he could take one resolu-

[1] C. N. Rapport du Gén. Clarke au Directoire. Milan, 7 déc., 1796.
[2] C. N. To Carnot. Verona, 9th August, 1796.
[3] C. N. To Pille, Nice, 16th June, 1794.

tion only, in the latter he may be criticized by all those who would have taken another."[1] Still, if any objections had reached him, he would have rejected them coldly, for "it does not do for those who are not behind the scenes to pass judgment on the way the strings are pulled."[2] Marmont, who was at this time, together with Junot and Murat, with him as aide-de-camp, says: "Bonaparte's bearing was, from the moment of his arrival, that of a man born to rule. Even the dullest saw clearly that he would know how to enforce obedience," and Duroc told De Pradt, a relative of his, that Napoleon even then kept as much aloof from his generals and everyone else as he did later on in the midst of his guards at the Louvre. He indeed knew how to compel obedience to such a degree, that during the whole course of this campaign not one instance is reported by anyone of resistance to his authority or departure from his orders: a sure sign of a true general.

But if we compare his stern and assured manner as commander, and the unconditional obedience which he knew how to enforce, with his own rather insubordinate behaviour as a lieutenant, we shall be compelled to say, that the men most suited to command are often least inclined to obey; and in this respect Napoleon says himself:

"I do not believe in the proverb that in order to be able to command one must know how to obey.[3] This experience must assuredly render still more difficult the task of those who are called upon to regulate the promotion of officers in time of peace; because obedience must be exacted, and yet insubordination may be only the evidence of a strong mind."

In consequence of Napoleon's representations the Directory relinquished, as early as the 21st May, their mistaken idea of a division of the chief command. Meanwhile the French general, allowing his troops only a few

[1] C. N. To Letourneur 6th May, 1796.
[2] C. N. To Berlier, 2nd July, 1794.
[3] C. N. To Joseph, Finkenstein, 5th May, 1807.

days of urgently needed rest, was busy settling the administration of the conquered districts, in order to secure his rear with a view to a further advance. But on the 19th he issued orders for a fresh forward movement towards the Adda; and on the 23rd for another, towards the Oglio. The vanguard, under Kilmaine (five battalions of grenadiers, three of carbineers and 1600 horse), was to start at four o'clock in the morning of the 24th, proceed as far as Soncino, and occupy the passage of the Oglio; the other divisions were to start at five o'clock in the morning and march as follows: Augereau from Cassano to Fontanella, Massena from Lodi to Offanengo, Menard from Codogno to Soresina, and Serurier from Cremona to Casalbuttano. The headquarters were moved to Crema.

Scarcely had Napoleon arrived at that place the next day, the 24th, than he received news of a rising of the country people of Lombardy, which had spread to Milan and Pavia. Immediately he wrote a note in pencil to Berthier, ordering him to send three battalions, two regiments of cavalry and four guns to Milan; he himself hurried thither in advance, arriving there that same evening; meted out punishment on the 25th, and marched immediately to Pavia. Into this town about 8000 armed peasants had forced their way and compelled the small French garrison to surrender. On the 26th, Napoleon appeared before the gates and, as some resistance was offered, forced an entry; he ordered a number of the rebels to be cut down, the commander of the garrison, which had surrendered, to be shot, and the town to be set on fire and plundered for a few hours. This rapidity in arriving at and carrying out, and his determination and want of scruple as to the means employed, are among the reasons of his successes. That done, he hastened after his army, which meanwhile had, according to his orders, advanced further towards Brescia.

By the 25th it had crossed the Oglio, and Kilmaine had arrived at Brescia, Massena at Casaglio, Augereau at Baitella; Serurier at Quinzanello. In these positions the army halted for the day. On the 27th, Napoleon, arriving at Soncino, rejoined it, and advanced early in the morning of the 28th to the Chiese, his vanguard moving beyond it as far as Lonato; this latter and a demi-brigade sent to Salo were to lead the enemy to suppose that Napoleon was turning northwards round Lake Guarda towards the Tyrol; and for this purpose also the right wing, under Serurier, was left that day at Ghedi. Not till the 29th did Serurier reach the Chiese at Mezanno; Augereau crossed this river and arrived at Desenzano; Massena was at Montechiaro; Kilmaine marched to Castiglione. On the 30th the entire force started at two o'clock in the morning to force the passage of the Mincio at Borghetto. Kilmaine was sent thither direct, the other corps were stationed five to eight miles from it in readiness. Napoleon himself accompanied the vanguard.

Beaulieu had determined to defend the line of the Mincio. But though he had so repeatedly experienced the effects of Napoleon's strategy, this had not sufficed to teach him the secret of the phrase: "Separate to live, unite to fight."

Having at first been alarmed for the Tyrol on account of Napoleon's movements to the left, he had divided his forces in such a manner that 9000 men were posted at Peschiera, 6500 at Valeggio, 3500 at Goito, whilst in and near Mantua there were 11,000 men. Afterwards, with the intention of barring the passage of the Mincio, he distributed his 19,000 men, so far as they were not required at Mantua, pretty equally along the nineteeen miles of the course of the Mincio from this latter fortress as far as Peschiera. Napoleon's effective force amounted to 28,000 men.

It was natural, considering the concentration of Napoleon's forces and the distribution of Beaulieu's, that the former should break the latter's line merely by marching on Valeggio. He thus furnished a good illustration of the principle, that the art of strategy consists in assembling the largest possible force at the most important points of any line of operations."[1] In accordance with his dispositions Kilmaine arrived with the vanguard at seven o'clock in the morning in front of Borghetto, and drove the enemy's outposts back, and at nine o'clock his grenadiers crossed the river by a ford. At noon he drove the defenders of the left bank, who were inferior to him in numbers, back upon Valeggio, and then still farther, upon Castelnuovo. Napoleon now determined to turn against the right wing of the Austrians, which was nearest to him and was concentrating at Castelnuovo, so as to head it off from the Tyrol; besides, he probably expected here to meet Beaulieu's entire main body.

Accordingly Kilmaine stood fast for the present at Valeggio to cover Massena's passage, whilst Augereau, having crossed in the meantime, advanced along the Mincio towards Peschiera. At five o'clock he arrived before this town; the Austrians fell back, and he occupied it, but did not succeed in blocking the enemy's road to the Tyrol. Kilmaine likewise had been ordered to advance on the road to Castelnuovo, after Massena had completed his crossing and had his whole force at Valeggio. Serurier was in the rear at Guidizzolo on the right bank. The headquarters were at Valeggio.

The next morning Augereau and Kilmaine pushed forward towards Castelnuovo, in the hope of finding the Austrians still there and being able to attack them; Massena was sent to Villafranca with orders to attack whatever forces he might find there; Serurier was ordered across the Mincio to Valeggio. But Beaulieu had retired during the night over the Adige by the shortest route; the troops composing his left wing had also arrived there in time, and thus the Austrians entered the Tyrol along that river, and Napoleon was able, eight days after his start from the banks of the Adda, to announce triumphantly:

[1] Jomini, Traité des grandes opérations mil., III. 337, 4th edit.

"The Austrians are completely driven out of Italy. Our outposts hold the line of the mountains of Germany."[1]

Napoleon's march to the Chiese *via* Brescia was in the first place intended to create the impression that it was his purpose to march to the left into the Tyrol, just as his leaving Massena and Serurier before Valenza had been intended to create the impression that it was not his purpose to march to the right, to Piacenza. As he had done on the Po, he turned rapidly to the point chosen for his passage and crossed, before the scattered Austrians had time to oppose him in sufficient force. The rapidity with which he here again came to a decision, is characteristic of the General, who said that in war he only knew three things: "to march daily thirty miles, give battle, and then bivouac in peace." It is true, one must also know the most effective direction in which to march the thirty miles a day, as Napoleon knew it; for "the secret of war never lies in the legs, it lies altogether in the head, which sets those legs in motion; an army may make forced marches during a whole campaign and yet be lost if these marches are in the wrong direction."[2] Here on the Mincio, for example, the turning movement effected on the Po could not be repeated, for the Austrians were protected against any flank movement by the formidable obstacle of Lake Guarda, and Napoleon could not therefore, as on the Po, choose his crossing-point elsewhere than in front. Once across the Mincio, however, he immediately attempted the most effective of all operations, viz. forcing the enemy from his line of retreat; he ordered Augereau to Peschiera, whilst he himself endeavoured to hold the enemy by his attacks upon Villafranca and Castelnuovo. The latter only escaped by a complete retreat, which settled the issue of the campaign.

The Austrians being for the present driven from the

[1] C. N. To the Directory, Peschiera, 1st June
[2] Jomini, Traité. etc., I. 429, 4th edit.

whole of Upper Italy, Napoleon proceeded with his further operations for securing his conquest. He had to keep his eye upon three things: first, a continued observation of the lines of approach of the Austrians, in order to oppose at the right moment their return; secondly, the capture of Mantua, in order to obtain full and assured possession of Upper Italy, and of the whole line of the Mincio as his future base; and thirdly, the wresting of as advantageous a peace as possible from the States of Southern Italy, especially Rome and Naples. This last point had indeed been less one of the objects which Napoleon had in view, than a wish of the Directory. As we have seen above, the latter had even intended to make of this an operation of equal importance with the campaign in Upper Italy. However, Napoleon succeeded both in retaining the sole chief command and also in reducing this operation to its proper place as a secondary affair. The Directory was in this matter on a par with those " many good generals in Europe"; it saw " too many things at once ;" but Napoleon saw only one thing, the enemy, that is the Austrians; these once beaten, secondary matters such as Rome and Naples would come right as a matter of course.

But, the Austrians being beaten, Napoleon considered it feasible to satisfy his Government with regard to these secondary matters, and proceeded therefore to a new distribution of his army, now swelled by some reinforcements from the army of the Alps. Massena received 18,000 men (including 5000 men of the division Sauret placed under his command) with instructions to cover the movement from the Austrians; he was to post three demi-brigades at Salo and three at Monte Baldo, to the west and east of Lake Guarda, and as a reserve one at Peschiera, one at Verona, and one in a camp between the Adige and Lake Guarda. Serurier received 5000 men, with orders to advance upon Mantua, and if possible to begin the investment of that place. The divisions of Augereau, Vaubois (drawn from the army of the Alps) and Dallemagne's advance-guard (three grenadier battalions), in all 12,500 men, remained at the commander-in-chief's own disposal. Finally, 9000 men were in garrison in various places in Lombardy.

Napoleon gave orders in the first place for the fortifications of Peschiera to be rapidly repaired; this place was to be put in a state of defence as speedily as possible. Then he joined Massena at Verona, and established his headquarters at Roverbella, whence he conducted the investment of Mantua. The first steps to be taken were as follows: Augereau was to block the two high roads leading to the right bank of the lake, Serurier the two leading to its left bank; Dallemagne remained at Roverbella in reserve, but he soon relieved Augereau, and the latter was sent to Bologna in order to co-operate with Napoleon in his further operations against Tuscany and Rome. These operations were soon brought to a close by negotiations more or less advantageous, from a pecuniary point of view, with the individual princes concerned; in a military sense they were of no interest.

On the 5th July Napoleon was back in his headquarters at Roverbella, and proceeded with the siege of Mantua in earnest. Meanwhile, however, news had been constantly arriving about the reinforcements which were reaching the Austrians in the Tyrol, and at this time Napoleon estimated the forces assembled there under Würmser at 59,000 men; it is true he probably overestimated them purposely, in order to induce his Government to accelerate the despatch of reinforcements to himself. His own army consisted of 42,000 men. The garrison in Mantua he estimated wrongly at 8000 men, it being in reality 13,000. His plan at this moment was to capture Mantua as quickly as possible; as to Würmser, he would only move against him should he approach too near the line of the Adige, now occupied by Massena with 15,000 men and Augereau with 6000. On the west of Lake Guarda stood the division of Sauret, 5000 men, under

(7)

Massena's chief command, as a corps of observation; the division of Despinoy, 5000 men, was on its march from Milan to the Adige, and Serurier with 8000 was investing Mantua. An attempt to seize this place by a *coup de main* failed owing to ill-luck, for, as Napoleon himself predicted, "All enterprises of this kind are entirely dependent on luck; a dog or a goose may wreck them."[1] 3000 cavalry under Kilmaine were at Valese; and Napoleon, sharply watching from Verona all the movements of the enemy in the Tyrol, felt that the decisive moment was at hand, and exclaimed, "Woe to him who is wrong in his calculations!"[1]

In the night of the 18th to the 19th July the first parallel before Mantua was begun and the following night completed. The siege now proceeded rapidly. Napoleon himself, who was present at the cutting of the trench, soon departed again to join the troops in position facing the Tyrol, in order to be at hand there during Würmser's attack, which, as he had been informed, was to take place without delay. It was delivered on the 29th. Würmser had divided his army into two columns; the one under Quosdanovich, 18,000 men, marched along the west shore of Lake Guarda against Salo, drove back Sauret, penetrated as far as Gavardo, and occupied Brescia with one corps, Sauret retiring upon Desenzano; the other column under Würmser himself, 24,000 strong, attacked at three o'clock in the morning the positions of Massena's vanguard at La Corona and turned it, forcing it back with heavy losses; and one corps on the flank, 5000 men, advanced along the valley of the Brenta with the intention of misleading the French. On hearing this, Napoleon, who was just then at Montechiaro, ordered a junction of Massena, Despinoy, and Kilmaine that day, the 29th, at Castelnuovo, whilst Augereau was to concentrate at Zerpa and advance *via* Villanuova upon Montebello, in order to attack the enemy there the next day; Napoleon seems

[1] C. N. To the Directory, Verona, 12th July.

therefore really to have taken the corps in the Brenta valley for a main column. However, on further information arriving, he was undeceived as to the strength of the column advancing through the valley of the Adige, and learned also, though without any further particulars, that the division of Sauret had been attacked and had fallen back.

And here we are confronted by an entirely new development in Napoleon. Although he had long looked forward to this attack, yet now it had come he seemed for the moment extremely uneasy and inclined to be alarmed at his situation. It is true he did not yet order the siege of Mantua to be suspended, but all the baggage, all the vehicles and State property in the rear of the army were sent back to Milan, and the citadel of this town was ordered to be placed in a state of defence. To Serurier he wrote: "Perhaps we shall recover ourselves; still, affairs force me to take serious measures to secure a retreat."[1] Neither this "perhaps" nor any mention of a probable retreat shall we ever again find mentioned by Napoleon. The orders to Augereau were immediately countermanded, and he was ordered to retreat to Roverbella and Villafranca. The next day Napoleon wrote to him: "The following is the unfortunate position of our army. The enemy have broken through our line in three places, they are masters of La Corona and Rivoli, two important points. Massena and Joubert[2] have been compelled to yield to superior forces, Sauret has evacuated Salo and begun his retreat to Desenzano, and the enemy has captured Brescia and the bridge of San Marco. You see that our communications with Milan and Verona are cut off."[3]

In such situations it may happen that subordinate officers, upon whom no such weighty responsibility rests, remain more calm and judge more correctly; still, we must

---

[1] C. N. Montechiaro, 29th July.
[2] Brig.-Gen. under Massena. He was at Rivoli.
[3] (No place), 30th July.

be careful not to put them on that account in the same category with the commander-in-chief, whose mind, being more active and more occupied, realizes the awkwardness of a situation in all its bearings to the fullest extent. Thus Massena wrote at this time: "I expect indeed to find that the strength of the force which appeared yesterday in Vicenza has been over-estimated. You will see, citizen-general, it is after all merely a reconnaissance;"[1] and Sahuguet writes: "Up to now, in spite of the usual exaggerations, nothing justifies the idea that the hostile corps which has moved upon Brescia is of any great strength."[2] The opinion of these two men was in this case a more calm and correct view of the situation than Napoleon's at the first moment; still, each of these inferior officers knew that their young, excitable and fiery commander-in-chief alone could at the moment of action lead the army to victory. However capable each felt in his own domain as a corps leader, still it was fully felt that the conduct in chief of the operations required a wider view. This had been shown during those few days at the end of May when Napoleon was absent in Milan and Pavia for the purpose of quelling the revolt there; a feeling of insecurity had at that time seized the lower officers, the nearer they approached the enemy without him, and Berthier wrote to him: "The army . . . is impatiently longing for you."[3] So great is the ascendency of a really great mind.

The fact is, as Jomini says, "War is not a science, but a passionate drama," and the tremendous and sudden vicissitudes of this drama tax all the powers of a man, and not only his intellect. This explains why we may sometimes find hours of doubt, nay, moments of despair, coming upon even the greatest generals; but it also justifies the glory which accrues to those exceptional minds who with-

---

[1] C. N. To Napoleon, Pieverono, 29th July.
[2] C. N. To Napoleon, Milan, 31st July.
[3] C. N. Crema, 25th May.

stand the storm of alternating emotions successfully and thereby get the better of their enemy. Only phlegmatic natures would remain untouched by some hesitation when great decisions have to be formed, and such never achieve any great deeds.

Napoleon was, like all great men, nervous, easily excited and highly emotional; a nervous twitching of the corner of his mouth and his right shoulder betrayed this outwardly; he suffered from a constant restlessness, which became most noticeable when the decisive moments in his campaigns were at hand. He was easily roused to anger or moved to tears. It is not rare to see him moved to such a degree that he shed a few tears; they seem to be due to some kind of nervous excitement, and mark its crisis. "I have very rebellious nerves," he says, "and they would expose me to the danger of going mad, if my pulse did not continue to beat slowly through it all." That remarkable scene of his parting from Josephine and Talleyrand at Mayence in 1806, when the Emperor was on the point of beginning his campaign against Prussia, is well known; it shows how tremendously excited great men are at decisive moments, even those whom history has called specially cold and firm in their resolution; and it forms an interesting pendant to that other scene which took place sixty years later at the council of war in Nikolsburg, when the Prussian staff desired to carry the war forward into Hungary, and which the principal actor in it has himself described in the following words: "But they remained unmoved, and I spoke in vain once more against this plan. Then I left the apartment and went into my own room, separated from the other only by a wooden partition. I threw myself on my bed and wept from nervous excitement. And after a while silence fell upon them in the other apartment, and the plan was not carried out."[2]

[1] Mme. de Rémusat, Mém., I. 124.
[2] Die Grenzboten, 1879, III. 493.

But if Napoleon for a moment considered his situation unfavourable, and wavered in his resolutions, yet the final result was, that he judged clearly and acted vigorously, and this it is that makes the great general. Although at first he had said that the enemy's columns had broken through his line, yet he now recognized the advantage which was his if he acted quickly from his central position between the disunited advancing forces of the Austrians, and he "feels that he must form a great plan."[1] In the first place he went to Desenzano, and resolved to attack the column which was advancing on the west of Lake Guarda, threatening his communications; he therefore ordered Sauret and Despinoy, of whom the latter had been moved up to Desenzano on this very day, the 30th July, to advance upon Salo on the morning of the 31st and to attack the enemy there. He himself started for Castelnuovo and ordered Massena, who had been forced back as far as this, to take up a position near Peschiera behind the Mincio, and to occupy the bridge of Valeggio with a detachment.

(8) Augereau's and Kilmaine's forces were at this moment at Castellaro and Roverbella, to cover Mantua against Würmser's advance, but the siege could no longer be continued, and Serurier was ordered to suspend it, to withdraw the siege artillery as far as possible, and then to reinforce Augereau. The same night Napoleon arrived on this part of the theatre of war at Roverbella, and despatched Augereau, Kilmaine and a part of Serurier's force in all haste forward to Montechiaro *viâ* Goito. Serurier himself, with the investing corps from the right bank of the Mincio, was to fall back to the Oglio and take up a position near the bridge of Marcaria, in order to secure the threatened line of retreat, Cremona—Pizzighettone—Pavia. Massena was to advance further upon Lonato. Thus the whole army was withdrawn behind the Mincio, and thereby secured from Würmser's immediate attack;

[1] C. N. To the Directory, 6th August.

while it fell with united forces upon Quosdanovich alone.

The latter had meanwhile, after occupying Brescia, advanced to Montechiaro on the 30th; on the 31st he met Napoleon's forces. Napoleon himself had already hastened thither; his restless activity during these decisive days is indeed worthy of admiration, and contributed materially to the energetic execution of his plan; indeed, only leaders in the strength of their youth are able to be so untiring and, so to speak, omnipresent; in these days the commander-in-chief rode five horses to death.

On the side of the French, Sauret now pushed forward on the 31st to Salo, quite on the left flank of the Austrians, seized this town, and released a French detachment there, which had remained behind on the 29th; then he fell back again upon Desenzano. Meanwhile Despinoy and Massena's advance guard had also repulsed an Austrian corps at Lonato; and Quosdanovich, recognizing their superiority in numbers, and alarmed for his communications after the capture of Salo, commenced at ten o'clock in the evening his retreat to Gavardo. On the 1st August Augereau arrived at Brescia after a night march; this advance reopened Napoleon's line of communication with Milan and restored his magazines and other depôts in Brescia to him; he was now no longer reduced to his one line of retreat to Pavia. On the same day Sauret was again sent forward to Salo, and Despinoy advanced from Lonato; Augereau was ordered to support this movement, whilst Massena led his force in all haste to Lonato. In the meantime Serurier had, during the night of 31st July—1st August, suspended the siege of Mantua, but being unable to remove the siege train, he destroyed it as far as possible.

Würmser, who on the 31st had reached Valeggio, now resolved, knowing that Mantua was relieved, to cross the Mincio and to attack the French, who were advancing against Quosdanovich, in the rear; however, during the 1st August he contented himself with sending an

advance-guard to Goito and ordering one corps to cross at
(9) Borghetto. On the 2nd he commenced his advance across
the Mincio at Goito. On the same day Napoleon, who
during the preceding evening had himself arrived in Brescia,
recalled Augereau thence to Montechiaro; the divisions
of Sauret (now under the command of Guieu, Sauret
having been wounded) and Despinoy advanced upon Salo
and Gavardo, in order to drive Quosdanovich still further
back. Massena collected his troops as a general reserve
at Lonato and San Marco bridge; one of his corps had
been observing the Mincio and had then fallen back before
Würmser as far as Castiglione, which latter position it
now received orders to hold. But after a slight resistance
it allowed itself to be driven from it by the vanguard of
Würmser's forces, whereupon Napoleon immediately
cashiered its commander before his whole corps.

On the 3rd August the forces met. Napoleon himself advanced with Massena *viâ* Lonato, and encountered one of Quosdanovich's corps, which was likewise advancing towards this town. But when this corps deployed in order to outflank the French, he at once recognized this movement as "a sure pledge of victory," and pierced its centre in column, routed it, forced it back upon Desenzano, and, cutting off its retreat, compelled almost the whole of it to surrender. A second division approaching was thrown back with heavy losses. On the other hand, an attack by Guieu upon Quosdanovich's divisions stationed at Gavardo was repulsed, and the former was forced to retreat to Salo. Despinoy's advance also failed, and in the evening he was back at Brescia.

On the opposite front, that is against Würmser, Augereau had been set in motion at two o'clock in the morning towards Castiglione; he drove Würmser's vanguard out of this town and forced it back as far as Solferino, where Würmser himself had taken up his position; Augereau's attacks upon this latter were continued until the evening, but without success. In the evening, Napoleon himself joined Augereau, examined his position, and then returned to his headquarters at Castelnedolo, to prepare for further operations. On the morning of the 4th, Despinoy and (10) Guieu received orders to advance again from Brescia and Salo towards Gavardo. But Quosdanovich was already in full retreat; he had resolved on the preceding day to attempt a junction with Würmser from the north, by Lake Guarda. But a detached corps found this line already barred by the French columns, which had pushed forward, and in attempting to break through to Würmser *viâ* Lonato, it naturally met with Massena's troops, and was forced to lay down its arms at Napoleon's summons, who had arrived in person in Lonato during the afternoon.

These events made it clear to Napoleon, that he had nothing further to fear at present from Quosdanovich, and he determined to throw himself upon Würmser on the next day with all the troops at his disposal.

This latter general had made a few slight alterations in his position on the 4th, but had done nothing to secure a preponderance in numbers or a certain co-operation on the part of Quosdanovich during the attack, which was now inevitable. Napoleon on the other hand ordered, at 8 o'clock in the morning, the division Serurier (for the moment commanded by General Fiorella, on account of Serurier's illness) to march upon Guidizzolo; Despinoy also was to come up as speedily as possible; Massena took up a position to the left of Augereau; and thus Napoleon brilliantly acted up to his own principle: "If you wish to fight a battle, collect all your corps, do not neglect one of them; one battalion sometimes may decide the day."[1] And not only did he concentrate all his forces, but he so determined the line of advance of his reinforcements, that the enemy might not only be beaten but annihilated. This trait is especially characteristic of Napoleon's strategy. Fiorella's march on Guidizzolo shows us "that a battle should not merely be fought, so

[1] Précis des guerres de Fréderic II.

as to gain a victory, but so as to complete the annihilation of the organized corps of the enemy."[1]

In order to occupy the enemy until the arrival of Fiorella, who was following closely behind Napoleon, the latter attacked on the morning of the 5th August. Würmser moved to his right, in order to turn the French left wing, and if possible to come in touch with Quosdancvich. This movement filled Napoleon with joy, for it favoured his own better-laid plan of turning the Austrian left wing. He allowed Würmser to proceed, and moved also to the right; but as soon as he observed Fiorella's arrival he began the general attack. Würmser could not of course withstand this combined attack with superior forces; still, he succeeded in effecting his retreat to Borghetto, where he crossed the Mincio. The French pursued him up to this river, and Napoleon, fully satisfied, said: "Thus in five days another campaign has been brought to a close."[2]

At first Würmser attempted to make a stand behind the Mincio. Napoleon ordered Augereau to cross the river at Valeggio, whilst Massena was to cross at Peschiera and turn the Austrian right wing. These movements commenced on the 6th. Early in the morning Massena arrived at Peschiera at 8.30, whilst Augereau occupied the enemy at Valeggio by a cannonade. The former threw the Austrians before him back, and upon this Napoleon sent Fiorella and Augereau after him, *viâ* Peschiera. But in the evening Würmser ordered a general retreat into the Tyrol, and escaped thereby all further pursuit. Massena in the main took up his former positions again, as did Sauret (who had resumed his command) to the west of Lake Guarda, forcing the Austrians back; in this Augereau supported Massena and then took up a position near Verona; Fiorella led his troops back again to Mantua and resumed the investment of this fortress.

[1] Jomini, Hist. crit. des camp. de F. II. 468, 4th Edit.
[2] To the Directory, Castiglione, 6th August.

The result of this nine days' compaign from the beginning of Würmser's advance to his retreat behind the Mincio was therefore that Napoleon drove him back again and inflicted a loss of 16,000 men on the Austrians. But this result had been purchased by the interruption of the siege of Mantua and the sacrifice of the whole siege train, so that now the town could only be taken by blockade, necessarily a slow proceeding. Here we have a new phase of Napoleon's strategy. Up till now he had advanced without a check, turning or breaking through one line after another of the Austrian defence, acting always on the offensive. Thus he reached the Adige and therewith the limit of every rapid advance far into an enemy's country, namely the point where the natural or artificial advantages attendant on fighting on one's own ground counterbalance the strength of the invader, weakened as he is by his own advance. The natural obstacle which here caused him to pause was the Alps, which could only be crossed after a further reinforcement of the French troops; the artificial obstacle was the fortress of Mantua, which must be captured before any further advance could take place. Napoleon himself had, before the beginning of the war, pointed to the Adige as the best line of defence against the Austrians, which must of necessity be occupied, and thus he was from the 1st June reduced to the defensive, though there was, for the time, no opponent in the field.

And how did he interpret this defensive? He formed a siege corps to invest before Mantua and a corps of observation facing the Tyrol; herein his guiding principle was exemplified, for as soon as the Austrians left the mountains with adequate forces, he would go to meet them and make Mantua's fate dependent on a pitched battle. He has been reproached with the fact that this solution of the question could lead to his immediate aim, the capture of Mantua, only by a round-about way, and therefore incur loss of time. This is quite true; but considering the proportion

of strength of the two opponents, there was no other way.
If we consider the other alternative which has been put
forward as the better one, we can hardly believe that it
would have led to success in the end. This other alternative
was that Napoleon should have drawn lines of investment
round Mantua, and held them with his whole army until
the fall of the fortress, which might certainly be expected
very soon. But what would have happened then? The
advance in two bodies of the Austrians would have been
of no disadvantage to them, or, rather, they would have
derived from it all the advantages they expected, for their
opponent would then have done exactly what they counted
on his doing. Quosdanovich would have cut Napoleon's
communications with Lombardy with impunity, and then
the united Austrian army would have assembled before
the French lines. 42,000 French would in that case have
been placed between 13,000 Austrians in the fortress and
47,000 outside it, and the disparity of strength would have
made itself fully felt. Even if we suppose that the French
could with the help of their intrenchments have resisted
the united efforts of the two Austrian armies—although
Napoleon was entirely convinced that "it is an axiom in
strategy that he who remains behind his intrenchments
is beaten; experience and theory are at one on this point"[1]
—even if we take for granted that the fortress soon surrendered, still, what then? Napoleon would in that case
only have become the besieged instead of the besieger,
and would have been invested with his 42,000 men, plus
13,000 prisoners, in a town which had already had some
difficulty in provisioning its own garrison. He would in
that case himself have stood in need of being relieved. Or
was he to leave a sufficient garrison in the place and break
through with some 32,000 men? Even if he had succeeded
in this, he would again have been compelled to fight
in the open, and with only 32,000 men, against the united
47,000 Austrians—he who at the commencement of the

[1] Souper de Beaucaire.

operations, after relinquishing the siege, could march with 42,000 men against the enemy, who were as yet separated. But would a sortie have been successful? The history of war shows us, since Marcellus broke out of Nola in 216 B.C., not a single example of an army invested in a fortress delivering itself by its own strength; while, on the other hand, it shows us many examples of such armies which had to surrender along with the fortress. It is acknowledged to be a difficult operation to emerge from a defile in the face of an opponent; and he who wishes to break out from a fortress is always in that position, at whatever point he may attempt it.

Since Napoleon was not strong enough to continue the siege and at the same time face the relieving army, to abandon the siege and put all his forces in the field was not merely the best, it was the only judicious plan. His immediate aim, it is true, was the capture of Mantua, but his principal aim was, after all, to succeed in holding the line of the Mincio and with it the whole of Lombardy; if he had shut himself up in Mantua, he would have abandoned this dominating idea. In this very instance we ought to admire the masterly way in which Napoleon held fast to his main object and set aside secondary objects. It was in this way alone that the division of his opponent's forces could be utilized, thus only could he make up for his inferiority in numbers by the rapidity of his movements, and give a signal proof that the effective strength of an army may, like "momentum" in mechanics, be taken as mass multiplied by velocity.[1]

How just was his decision becomes still more evident if we compare this situation with that of another beleaguered Austrian fortress, and with the final result in that case—a comparison suggested by Napoleon himself. When in 1757 Frederick the Great stood before Prague, and Daun was marching to its relief, the former could not make up his mind to suspend the siege for the moment,

[1] Mém. de Ste. Hel. Observations, etc., I. 392.

to leave only a weak corps of observation in front of the fortress and to fall upon Daun with all his strength. He "saw too many things at once;" he did not bring the masses to bear upon the decisive point, and was beaten, when with 34,000 men he attacked 53,000. And as a result he had not only after all to give up the siege, but lost the whole campaign as well.

To sum up: the characteristic feature of this first example of Napoleon's defensive tactics is, that he succeeded in avoiding the most common failing of such tactics, viz. a want of initiative. It is contrary to the nature of a true general to have his course of action imposed upon him by the enemy, and it was Napoleon's instinctive determination to force his opponent to do as he wished, more than any other consideration, that dictated to him his line of action here, and this fact justifies him more than any other argument. In this point Lee resembles him most of more recent leaders, Lee, who being as a rule forced to act on the defensive on account of his inferiority of numbers and political circumstances, yet always managed to keep the initiative to himself.

Würmser having been thus forced back into the mountains, Napoleon found it first of all necessary to restore the discipline and see to the commissariat and the equipment of his army, all of which had considerably suffered. Besides, he wished, before assuming the offensive in the Tyrol, to wait until his promised reinforcements had arrived, and until the French army in Germany had made some further progress, so that he might not be likely to meet with too superior forces there. For those who think they recognize in Napoleon's successes merely audacity favoured by good luck, this pause of the youthful and ever-victorious general in face of the Alps, this recognition of the fact that his present inferiority of numbers did not allow of any immediate pursuit of his successes, are facts worth pondering over. The value of numbers was fully appreciated, and by none more than himself. This was a distinctly new departure from the method of conducting war in the eighteenth century.

After a few changes in the commanders, the position of the French army at the end of August was the following: the division of Sahuguet, 8000 men, was investing Mantua, which had received some reinforcements and now contained 17,000 men (of whom, however, 4000 were sick); Augereau with 9000 men was at Verona; Massena with 13,000 at Rivoli; Vaubois with 11,000 at Storo, to the west of Lake Guarda. On the 31st August Napoleon wrote from Brescia to Moreau, the commander-in-chief of the army of Germany, that they were now in a position to act in concert; he was going to start for Trent with his army on the 2nd September. (11)

In this latter town Würmser had at this time his headquarters. He was at the head of 41000 men in the Tyrol, and decided to divide them into an army of defence and an army of attack. The former, under Davidovich, was to hold the valley of the Adige, whilst he himself was to advance with the other along the Brenta valley towards Bassano, and from thence wheel round to the Adige at Legnago. Accordingly he entrusted 20,000 men to Davidovich, of which 8000 were stationed at Roveredo, 5000 behind these as a reserve at Trent, and the remainder in the Grisons and the Vorarlberg; 21,000 men he despatched to Bassano, and of these 11,000 arrived there on the 31st August, 4000 being then at Pergine, and 6000 still at Trent. On the 7th September the whole force was to be assembled at Bassano.

While Würmser had thus begun his advance to Bassano, Napoleon also had given orders for the same purpose. On the 1st September, at 10.30 in the evening, he issued these orders from Verona: "Massena will move forward on the 2nd along the Adige valley as far as Ala; Augereau will follow in his right rear as far as Lugo-Rovere; both will start at noon. Kilmaine will remain behind with 2000 men for the protection of Verona." Vaubois had the day before already received orders to march round the northern extremity of Lake Guarda on the 2nd September to Torbole. Sahuguet, who was before Mantua, was informed that the army was about to enter the Tyrol. Napoleon was aware of the presence of some hostile troops at Bassano, but he supposed the main body to be at Trent ; as to any advance on the part of the latter *via* Bassano to Verona, in order to relieve Mantua, he considered it unlikely; "should the enemy, however, commit this folly,"[1] Kilmaine was to avoid them by retiring behind the Mincio, and Sahuguet to at once give up the investment of Mantua and retire behind the Oglio. Peschiera was to be held under any circumstances. The preliminary movements thus ordered were not completed until the 3rd, some weak Austrian outposts were driven in at Ala and Serravalle, and the combined advance of all the three divisions upon Roveredo was ordered for the 4th.

This opening of the operations was again characteristic of Napoleon's strategy. According to his opinion, "it is an axiom, that the junction of the different corps of an army should never take place near the enemy."[2] Already at the beginning of April he had given an example of this in the Riviera by desiring to concentrate the army from its extended positions to begin with on the right wing, before crossing the mountains and commencing operations. In other words he rejected all concentric operations which had for their object the junction of separated offensive columns on the battle-field itself, in presence of the enemy; and thus we see here that he took care to effect a junction of his columns in the neighbourhood of Serravalle-Mori, before approaching the enemy's position at Roveredo. But even this operation was not sufficiently secure in Napoleon's eyes, and he afterwards criticized it thus : "It cannot be said that this march was absolutely without

[1] C.N. To Berthier, Verond, 2nd September, in the morning.
[2] Précis des guerres de Fréd. II., IV. 218.

danger, but it did not present much danger."[1] So convinced was he of the excellence of the great principle of an "advance in one body."

And rightly so. There is, indeed, something alluring about concentric operations; they render the march of the columns easier on account of their being separated; and they hold out a hope of surrounding the enemy entirely, if they succeed; only one too often forgets that, as General Willisen says, this can only happen "if the enemy are stupid enough to allow it."[2] Napoleon also alludes expressly to this: "I see that you are wrong in a military sense; I see that you imagine two columns surrounding one and a half must have an advantage; but this is not so in war, for the two columns will not act in concert, and the enemy will beat them, one after the other. Certainly we should surround the enemy, but first we must be united ourselves."[3] And he himself, the great master, proved often what chances an enterprising leader has against separated hostile columns, even though their total forces outnumber him considerably. An army thus divided not only exposes itself to accidents, which may hinder or delay the march of any one of its columns, but also, instead of there being one commander with a united force capable of conducting great operations, there must be two, one for each of the independent columns, because otherwise their appointed meeting might be prevented by divergent views of the situation.[4]

On the 4th September Davidovich's vanguard, which on the preceding day had been forced to fall back, was attacked at Marco and Mori by superior numbers, all three French divisions advancing simultaneously, and driven back to Roveredo with heavy loss. Indeed, the French entered this town at the same time with it and forced it

---

[1] Observations, etc., I. 401.   [2] Der Feldzug von, 1866, 250.
[3] C.N. To Jerôme, Finkenstein, 18th May, 1807.
[4] This is as given in the German Text. The author would appear to postulate that the two commanders had received like instructions; but yet their different views of the situation might lead to non-junction of their columns.—ED.

to retreat to Davidovich's main position at Caliano. Napoleon drew his troops together near Roveredo, and, having quickly restored tactical order, pushed forward again. The narrow defile of La Pietra, very easy to defend, was found to be occupied by one regiment only; one determined attack was sufficient to force it, and then Davidovich's troops on the other side near Caliano, who were encamped there in fancied security, were surprised and entirely scattered.

Meanwhile Würmser's corps had continued its march through the Brenta valley according to the plan agreed upon; the rearguard was on that day at Borgo, and Würmser, who was still at Trent, even after he had at 5.30 in the evening been informed of what had happened at Caliano, did not in any way alter his plan. On the contrary, he set himself in motion on the road to Bassano, leaving orders behind for Davidovich to hold Trent. This, however, the latter could no longer do, but was forced to fall back as far as Lavis.

Consequently Massena entered Trent unopposed at eight o'clock in the morning of the 5th, and Vaubois followed at noon, but Augereau was still on the road. Here for the first time Napoleon learnt that he had not hitherto had Würmser's main body before him, and that the latter had marched along the valley of the Brenta; but he did not consider this movement to be an advance for the relief of Mantua, but an attempt at withdrawal brought about by his own method of attack. He determined to follow him in order to cut him off and so attack him, but first he wished to settle with the opponent whom he had immediately before him, so as not to have anything to fear in his own (12) rear. Therefore Vaubois advanced in the afternoon, and by the evening Davidovich was driven from his position at Lavis and retired further up the Adige. In the meantime Massena was sent to Pergine, and Augereau likewise from the Adige valley *viâ* Val Sorda to Levico in the valley of the Brenta, in pursuit of Würmser.

On the 6th September Napoleon continued his movements. Vaubois remained at Lavis to protect the rear, and only lent a detachment from the grenadiers of his force as a reinforcement to the columns of attack. Massena marched to Levico; Augereau with the headquarters to Borgo, their outposts being pushed forward as far as Ospedaletto; they had driven a small Austrian force from Levico in the morning. On the 7th Cismone was reached, after another Austrian corps had been driven back from Primolano. At two o'clock on the morning of the 8th, Napoleon started, ordered Massena to cross to the right bank of the Brenta at Carpane, and then advanced again towards Bassano. At seven o'clock he came in sight of the Austrians. Würmser had, it is true, still adhered to his plan of a further march forward to Verona *via* Vicenza, and therefore one half of his army was already at Montebello, whilst he himself with the other was still at Bassano; but now the resolute advance of the French in his rear seemed to make him lose his head altogether, and thus he accepted battle here, although this was in no way in accordance with his real plan of operations, and although he could not have done worse than fight with only half his force at hand. The result of course was a defeat and a retreat to Vicenza which resembled a flight; many stragglers scattered in different directions and lost sight of the main body altogether. After a junction with the other half of his army at Montebello the retreat was hurriedly continued to Legnago, which place was reached on the morning of the 10th. But Würmser had now only 12,000 men under his command. (13)

Already on the 8th Napoleon had sent his divisions in pursuit, Augereau to Padua, in order to cut off the Austrians' retreat to Friaul; whilst he himself with Massena advanced to Vicenza, and reached this town during the afternoon of the 9th. He now received some more reliable but still indefinite reports as to Würmser's movements, which led him to see through the latter's intention to escape to Mantua *viâ* Legnago, and while he therefore, with Massena, continued the pursuit *viâ* Montebello, Augereau received orders to march to Legnago. At 10 p.m. Massena began to cross the Adige at Ronco, and Augereau marched upon Montagnana; Würmser's forces, as a whole, remaining stationary at Legnago. Napoleon, faithful to his principles, while sacrificing all matters of secondary importance, hastened to draw all his troops together for a decisive blow against Würmser. Kilmaine, with the garrison of Verona, was to march to Isola della Scala; Sahuguet was to assemble his forces at Goito. On the 11th the two met at Castellaro, Augereau's vanguard arrived before Legnago in the evening, and Massena reached Roverchiara. On this same day Würmser continued his march to Mantua and arrived late at night at Nogara, after having had to fight his way through at Cerea, where he fell in with the head of Massena's column. After a short halt, he continued his march on the 12th very early in the morning; hearing of Sahuguet's presence at Castellaro, he left the main road, and, striking to the left, reached Mantua unmolested at noon, by a detour *viâ* Villempenta. Hereupon Napoleon hurried up with all the men he could collect, and proceeded to force Würmser to throw himself with his whole force into Mantua; and resumed the investment of this town. It was entrusted to Kilmaine with 9000 men; Vaubois with 10,000 was still at Trent; Massena with 9000 was sent to Bassano and Treviso; while Augereau with 9000 men took up a position near Verona. The division of Macquart, 3000 men, was ordered up from the rear as a general reserve, and stationed at Villafranca. Napoleon himself went for the present to Milan. By the beginning of October the above positions were finally taken up, and the effectives of the various bodies reached the figures above mentioned, the ranks being filled by drafts from the rear. To oppose them, Würmser was in Mantua with 28,000 men (5000 being sick), Davidovich in the Tyrol with 14,000, and scattered about the Vorarlberg there were 3000 more, and on the Isonzo and among the passes into Carinthia 4000 men.

What more especially strikes us in Napoleon's strategy during this time is the rapidity of his movements; that rapidity which Jomini has more than once compared to lightning, and which led the French soldiers to remark in 1805: "The Emperor has invented a new method of waging war; he makes use of our legs instead of our bayonets."[1] In the afternoon of the 5th September Napoleon's columns began to enter the valley of the Brenta, and by 7 a.m. on the 8th he came in contact with the Austrians in position at Bassano; that is in about 60 hours he had marched about 57 miles and had moreover engaged the enemy at Levico and Primolano. Having beaten Würmser at Bassano, he sent his divisions without delay in pursuit, and Massena reached Vicenza in the afternoon of the 9th, that is, in 36 hours he had fought a battle and marched 21½ miles; and during the next 24 hours he again moved 21½ miles and, besides, crossed the Adige. Augereau, who after the battle of Bassano had been sent to Padua, but subsequently ordered up to Legnago, arrived in front of this place on the evening of the 11th, and had thus, counting from the morning of the 8th, marched over 60 miles and fought a battle within 84 hours. Altogether Napoleon's troops had, between the 5th and the 11th September, that is within 6 days, fought two engagements and one battle and covered the following distances: Massena, 100 miles, including the passage of one river by a ferry; Augereau, 114 miles. It is only genius who can compel ordinary human beings to perform such feats.

Theoretically, nothing appears easier than to pursue a fugitive enemy vigorously after a victory, and yet nothing is rarer in the history of war than a really effective pursuit; and many a general has been able to gain a victory on the field of battle by his great endurance and by great efforts, and yet not known how to reap all the

[1] 6⁰ bull. de la grande armée. Elchingen, 18th Oct., 1805.

advantages possible to be gained from it. The great results which a vigorous pursuit secures by no means follow as a matter of course. This is owing to the constitution of human nature; for after a victory the soldiers are exhausted, and long for that rest which they think they have earned, and this exhaustion has to be overcome. Besides—and this is still more important—the commander-in-chief will have to conquer the same feelings within himself, though he is less to be a prey to them. The tremendous tension of all the moral and physical forces which is necessary to gain a victory, relaxes as soon as the end to which it was to lead, and for which these forces were exerted, is attained. The human mind is but little inclined to rouse itself immediately to fresh efforts, and so to speak to pile up new difficulties, and as after the victory there is no longer an enemy present to render such efforts imperative, any mind that does not stand out far above the common level, yields easily to the temptation of indulging in what Müffling appositely calls "the necessary digestion of one's joy over a victory."[1] Whoever in such a situation overcomes not only the exhaustion and the passive resistance of his men and subordinate officers, but also rouses himself to immediate fresh efforts, whoever, like Gneisanau after Belle-Alliance and like Napoleon almost invariably, engages in vigorous pursuit after a victory, has by such an exhibition of mental power justified his title to a place among the greatest generals.

[1] Aus meinem Leben, 76.

CHAPTER IV.

MANTUA. ALVINTZY'S ATTEMPTS TO RELIEVE IT.

ON the 24th September the command of a fresh army (14) of relief was entrusted to Alvintzy, and vigorous measures were taken to enable it to take the field. One month later it was considered ready to do so, and Alvintzy issued orders that the troops collected at Friaul, 29,000 men, were to start on the 22nd October, concentrate at Pordenone, cross the Piave, and take Bassano on the 3rd November. On the same day the troops in the Tyrol under Davidovich were to take Trent. Immediately afterwards the two columns were to advance and unite on the Adige. In pursuance of this plan, the column from Friaul under Alvintzy himself arrived on the 30th October on the Piave, a little beyond Conegliano.

By the 25th Napoleon was informed of the enemy's advance in the direction of the Brenta. It was his intention to let Vaubois attack the troops in the Tyrol, and drive them beyond Neumarkt, and then to withdraw 3000 men from Vaubois' force, in order to reinforce his own main body. Meanwhile Massena was to fall back on Vicenza, in case the enemy advanced in force on Bassano. Later on, after the arrival of Vaubois' reinforcements, Napoleon intended to throw himself with his whole strength upon the enemy, thoroughly exhausted by a long march in continuous rain and by bad roads.

On the 29th Massena pushed forward to the Piave with a small force to reconnoitre, and had ascertained the presence of the enemy on the other bank. He accordingly collected his division at Bassano and continued to watch the Piave. On the 2nd November Alvintzy crossed this river; a fact which Massena immediately reported to Napoleon, then at Verona. On the 3rd Alvintzy reached Barcon, Massena still standing fast at Bassano. Napoleon still watched calmly from Verona the approach of the enemy; he had sent Berthier to Vaubois, in order to have someone there who would carry out his wishes implicitly. On the morning of the 4th, Alvintzy advanced against Bassano and occupied this town without resistance, as Massena had evacuated it at 5 a.m. and fallen back on the road to Vicenza. On the same day Augereau, whom Napoleon now sent forward, reached Montebello, followed in person by his leader. On the 5th Massena and Augereau joined forces at Vicenza, whilst Alvintzy remained at Bassano.

In the meantime Vaubois had advanced along the valley of the Adige against Davidovich in accordance with his orders. On the 2nd November he moved off at three o'clock in the morning and attacked the Austrians' advanced positions at San Michele and Segonzano; he did not, however, succeed in capturing them, and fell back to Lavis in the evening. On the 3rd Davidovich in his turn advanced and assembled his troops at Sevignano, facing the French right wing. Vaubois, fearing to be cut off, withdrew his left wing to Trent. On the 4th Davidovich began the attack, and drove Vaubois back so effectually, that the latter evacuated Trent during the night and took up his position in the defile of La Pietra with his whole force. Against this position Davidovich advanced on the 5th, with the view of attacking, at the same time sending a column to the right to Nomi and Torbole, in order to turn the French.

On the 6th an encounter took place on the Brenta. Napoleon had started in the early morning and pushed forward; Augereau towards Bassano, and Massena towards Cittadella; but at both places all his attacks, incessantly repeated from 7.30 in the morning until nightfall, failed to force the passage of the Brenta, defended by the Austrians. On the same day Davidovich had assailed the position of La Pietra, though without success, in front; but the turning-column had taken the villages of Nomi and Torbole and threatened Vaubois' retreat. Thus Napoleon's plan of driving back Alvintzy behind the Brenta and then marching along the valley of this river to place himself in Davidovich's rear, had failed, and when in addition he received news from Vaubois during the night, confirming the latter's retreat to Caliano and anticipating further retrograde movements, he saw the necessity of abandoning the offensive for the present and of preventing Davidovich's threatened appearance in his rear at Verona, near where the Adige emerges into the plain. Accordingly he ordered the same night Augereau and Massena to begin their retreat to Vicenza; he himself betook himself to that town on the 7th, and, after giving his troops a short rest, continued his retreat at nightfall to Verona, which he reached in the forenoon of the 8th.

Meanwhile Vaubois had on the 7th again been attacked at Caliano, but this time his position was captured soon after four o'clock in the afternoon, and by the evening he saw himself forced back as far as the line La Corona-Rivoli. Alvintzy also had on the 7th approached within five miles of Vicenza with his outposts, and on the 8th his main body reached this town, whilst Davidovich on the same day arrived at Rivalta.

This period is one of especial interest to the student of Napoleon's genius as a strategist. We see that he was by no means uniformly lucky in what he undertook, but was now and then thrown into dangerous and disadvantageous situations, when running great risks; and if victory ended by returning to his standard, it was not owing to Fortune's favour, but his own perseverance and skill. On the whole we shall find, when we study historical events more closely, that luck is generally fairly evenly divided between two combatants; even the one who is vanquished in the end has had moments, hours and days when fortune smiled on him, and when he could have gained the victory had he resolutely taken advantage of the favouring circumstances; but letting the chance slip, and then subsequently acting too late or unskilfully and meeting with ill success, he puts it down to circumstances beyond his own control. Napoleon, on the other hand, was always true to the principle: "Take advantage of all your opportunities. Fortune is a woman; if you let her slip one day, you must not expect to find her again the next."[1] And thus we readily forget, seeing his eventual success, that errors and even failures were not absent from his strategy, and that a change of fortune was brought about only by his energy and skill.

In the case before us, used to victory as he was, he had conceived a plan, which certainly was not without danger. Although on the whole the weaker, he wished to take the offensive against both the advancing Austrian columns; so that, having forced back Alvintzy behind the Brenta, he might, by marching along the valley of that river against Davidovich from the south, repeat the manœuvre that had been so successful in the beginning of September against Würmser from the north. But when Vaubois was seriously defeated and he himself could not force the passage of the Brenta, he saw that only the most rapid change of plan could free him from his awkward position. And it is the readiness with which he abandoned his first plan and formed a fresh one that here excites our admiration. Luck had not attended his first somewhat risky projects, and he was immediately prepared to make the best of the circumstances, such as they were, though so unlike what he hoped for. "A great general must say several times a day to himself, 'What should I do if the enemy appeared in my front, on my right or on my left flank?' If he finds it difficult to

[1] Dix-huit notes sur l'ouvrage intit. Consid. sur l'art de la guerre, Mem. Ste. Hel.

answer such questions, he is not in a good position, or all is not as it should be, and he must alter it."[1] As he said, so he acted, and therefore every vicissitude found him ready to turn the changed conditions to his advantage.

One of the hardest yet most important things for a general is to possess the firmness to keep his aim steadfastly in mind, and at the same time the versatility to choose the means necessary for his end, so as to suit varying circumstances. "He who does not hold life fast like a wrestler, alive to its lightest movement, as if he had a thousand limbs, to every turn of the fray, and on the watch for every forward or backward sway, will not have his way even in conversation, much less in battle."[2]

But must not this quality be inborn? Assuredly, and especially must it be possessed by a great general to a very high degree, for the colour-blind cannot become painter. Still, this gift of nature must, like any other, be cultivated; and here I think the study of military history will be of the greatest use. Whoever endeavours to understand the varying fortunes of bygone campaigns and the generals that took part in them, and constantly practises himself in considering what resolutions led in the one case to victory, in the other to defeat, what happened and what might have happened, will thereby strengthen the capacity of his own mind for rapidly taking in and judging of new conditions. At any rate, no less a man than Napoleon himself recommends the study of the campaigns of all great masters, and goes so far as to say: "This is the only way to become a great general, and to grasp the secrets of the art;"[3] while Jomini says: "The military history rightly interpreted is the true school of war."[4]

In their estimate of the advantages to be derived directly

---

[1] Mém., Observations, etc., I. 405.
[2] H. v. Kleist, Von der Ueberlegung.
[3] Observations, etc., III. 497.
[4] Précis, etc.

from the study of military history, some great leaders have placed them very high indeed. General Skobelev, for example, as bold and energetic a soldier as ever was, liked during battles to quote from his extensive reading similar instances and to demonstrate to what in those former instances success or failure had been due; nay, Napoleon himself wrote to Marmont on the 14th October, 1813, when he arrived at Breitenfeld, and there was every likelihood of a battle being fought there: "I send you an account of Gustavus Adolphus's battle, treating of the positions you are occupying."[1] Still, it would be erroneous to suppose that a knowledge of the history of war consists in a mere collection of examples, to which one has only to refer in order to find a model which may be imitated without modification, although there is no doubt but that practice in such studies must facilitate the forming of a correct opinion, and that what originally was an incomplete natural talent, will thereby be changed into a firmly-seated and self-reliant quality. Of Napoleon it is said: "As long as passion urged him on, he saw only his aim, but once this was reached, he examined the obstacles which he might have met with;" and so *we* also may learn by study how obstacles are to be overcome, so as to go straight to the point when we are called upon to act, and to do it with confidence, convinced that the result will depend, not on good luck, but on our own capacity. *We* also can then say: "There are no great and memorable events which are merely the work of chance and luck; they are always due to forethought and genius. Great men are rarely seen to fail, even in their most hazardous undertakings. Look at Alexander, Cæsar, Hannibal, the great Gustavus, and others; they always succeeded. Did they become great only by good luck? No; but because they were great, they knew how to bend Fortune to their will. If we study the causes of

---

[1] C.N. Headquarters, Reudnitz.

their successes, we are astounded to see all they did in order to gain them." [1]

To resume, on the 8th November, Napoleon himself stood with 21,000 men at Verona, Vaubois with 8000 at La Corona. Opposed to them in the neighbourhood of Rivalta was Davidovich with 16,000 men, and Alvintzy with 27,000 near Vicenza. On the 9th the latter advanced to Montebello, whilst Davidovich, influenced by the rumours of reinforcements, which were said to have reached Vaubois under Massena, remained idle. On the 10th nothing was done, except that Alvintzy pushed his vanguard of 8000 men forward beyond Caldiero. The next day he himself followed to Villanuova. During these days Napoleon had not stirred. His first thought had naturally been, that Davidovich, taking advantage of these propitious circumstances, would push forward resolutely, in which case he himself would have been between two fires, and he therefore resolved to keep Davidovich at any cost at a distance, in order not to lose his line of retreat behind the Mincio, should he require it. Therefore Massena was to join Vaubois. But when Massena, who had been sent on in advance to La Corona, returned on the evening of the 8th with somewhat reassuring news as to Vaubois' position, and when a second report the next day proved to Napoleon that Davidovich had for the present no intention of taking the offensive, Massena's division was kept where it was, and Napoleon, allowing his troops a few days of rest, awaited, during the 9th and 10th, the further development of the enemy's plans. It was not until about three o'clock in the afternoon of the 11th, that the approach of hostile forces to Verona, on the road from Vicenza, was reported to him.

He immediately resolved upon a counter offensive. He repulsed the foremost bodies, a part of the Austrian vanguard, with ease, and they, continuing their retreat during the night, reached the position of Caldiero, where the

[1] Mém. de Ste. Hélène, VII. 236.

vanguard determined to make a stand on the 12th. In the early morning of this day, Napoleon advanced against it, and soon after eight o'clock the attack commenced. At first he gained some partial successes, Augereau advancing along the road against the front of Caldiero, while Massena turned the right wing at Colognolo; but by four o'clock in the afternoon the troops of Alvintzy's main body began to come up. Now the French were repulsed along the whole line, and retired during the night upon Verona. Alvintzy followed on the 13th as far as Vago, his cavalry even approaching the gates of Verona. During this time Davidovich had again done nothing; still, Napoleon's situation had now become exceedingly precarious. It is true he could still fall back either upon the force that was besieging Mantua, or behind the Mincio, but in either case he would be immediately followed by the Austrian superior forces after their junction on the Adige, and he would no longer have had any chance of investing Mantua or holding the plain of Lombardy. But whilst almost any other general would have saved his army from its dangerous position by retreating, regardless of the loss of ground, Napoleon's keen glance still saw a way of striking at the enemy, while yet separated. Alvintzy alone, it is true, was superior in numbers to him, and he must avoid any too direct attack, but he determined to go completely round him, capture his transport and reserve artillery, and then attack him in the rear.

(16) But even his great and bold spirit required time to mature such a resolution under the pressure of constantly changing and often conflicting news, and to complete the material preparations for it, and thus it was not till the evening of the 14th that Napoleon set his troops in motion for this turning movement, by which he intended to entirely alter the situation. In Verona he left Kilmaine with 3000 men, whom he had for this purpose recalled from the investing corps before Mantua. Napoleon himself marched upon

Ronco, where, having thrown a bridge across, he passed the Adige on the morning of the 15th. Here he found himself on the marshy ground which formed the angle between the Adige and the Alpone, and could only be traversed by the dykes which led on the left to Belfiore di Porcile, on the right to Albaredo, and in the centre to Arcola. Thus Massena advanced on the morning of the 15th along the dam to Belfiore, Augereau along that to Arcola.

The Austrians intended on this day to push forward on the one side direct to Verona, and on the other side to cross the Adige at Zevio with the same purpose, so as to surround the enemy supposed to be near Verona; but it was with this concentric movement as it often is in such cases: the enemy "was not stupid enough to allow it to be carried out;" he had not stood still, and his advance now took the Austrians altogether by surprise. It was only about noon that Alvintzy set his troops in motion towards the points threatened. But now the nature of the ground was in favour of the Austrians, forced to act on the defensive. Massena was stopped even before reaching Belfiore; Augereau's repeated furious attacks on the bridge of Arcola over the Alpone failed; even Napoleon's personal example could not command success, nay, in the confusion of falling back the commander-in-chief was himself forced from the dam into the marsh, and was for a few moments in the most imminent danger of being made prisoner by the pursuing Austrians. And although about seven o'clock in the evening a small column, which had been sent out *viâ* Albaredo under Guieu to turn the position, impregnable in the front, arrived before Arcola and forced the Austrians to evacuate it during the night, still Napoleon's plan of advancing quickly to surprise Villanuova in the rear of the enemy, had failed. Alvintzy's troops now lay partly to the east of the Alpone, partly near Caldiero and facing Massena, whilst Napoleon, thus threatened on both sides by forces conjointly superior to his in numbers, considered it wiser to retreat behind the Adige during the night, all the more as he could not be sure whether Vaubois also was not repulsed.

In the course of that night he learnt with certainty that Vaubois had not yet been attacked, and thereupon he resolved to resume his attacks against Alvintzy on the 16th (17a) Augereau therefore again moved forward to Arcola on the morning of that day, and Massena to Belfiore; in both directions the Austrians were forced to fall back, but the bridge of Arcola remained in their possession, and again Napoleon considered it advisable in the evening not to pass the night in this region of dams and marshes, but to put the Adige between himself and the enemy, and thus at the same time ensure the possibility of a march to (17b) join Vaubois. He now resolved to give up his proposed front attack upon Arcola on the 17th and to cross the Alpone lower down, and therefore gave orders the same night, to begin throwing a bridge across. In the morning of the 17th, having been informed that Vaubois had on the 16th still not been attacked, he attempted for the third time to advance across the Adige with the division of Massena, ordering Augereau to pass the Alpone on the new bridge. Massena's attack upon Arcola failed, but when the Austrians pushed forward on the dam behind the retreating French, as far as Ronco, this isolated column was surrounded on all sides and entirely routed. Augereau, at first engaged in this encounter, now immediately began to cross the bridge over the Alpone just completed and to attack Arcola on the left bank; but this attack also the defenders once more repulsed.

However, the strength of the Austrians was almost exhausted. Already in the morning Alvintzy had written to Davidovich that he could, it is true, resist one more attack, but was unable to assume the offensive. Both leader and men had come to the turning-point, where the balance between success and failure being even, the least push would suffice to incline it to the one side or the other, and thus prove the truth of Napoleon's dictum: "The fate of a battle is a question of a single moment, a single thought; ... the decisive moment arrives, the moral spark is kindled and the smallest reserve force settles the matter;"[1] and in another place also he expresses the same conviction, saying: "There is a moment in engagements when the least manœuvre is decisive and gives the victory; it is the one drop of water which makes the vessel run over."[2] Alvintzy, who was of opinion that he could resist one more attack, but not gain a complete victory, could not command that spark, but in Napoleon it flashed out and gave him the victory. Thus the apparently insignificant decisive factor must not be put down to good luck in such a case. One energetic push forward—nay, the mere semblance of such—is at such times sufficient to throw the necessary weight into the scale. Here also it was the mere semblance of an attack which turned the scale. Some fifty horsemen, sent by Napoleon to the rear of the Austrians, with orders to lead them to expect a great cavalry charge by sounding numerous trumpets and riding boldly forward, actually caused the enemy to waver and led them to leave the approach to Arcola open. This happened at three o'clock in the afternoon. At the same time Massena and Augereau charged again, and a division called up from the garrison of Legnano advanced by Albaredo. A general attack upon Arcola now began on both banks of the Alpone, and at five o'clock the position was in the hands of the French. The Austrians fell back to Villanuova and San Bonifacio; indeed, the troops retreating from Caldiero had to fight their way through the French who were pursuing from Arcola. On the 18th Alvintzy continued his retreat *viâ* Montebello as far as Olmo. Thus Napoleon's greater (14) persistency had secured victory, and he was well aware of

[1] Mém. de Ste. Hélène, II. 15.
[2] Précis des guerres de J. César, XXXII. 104.

this when he said :. "Never yet has a battle-field been so hotly disputed as that of Arcola."[1]

Meanwhile Davidovich too had begun to move. On the 17th November he commenced his turning attack upon Vaubois' position at Rivoli, at seven o'clock in the morning. The result could not be long in doubt, considering his superior numbers, and by two o'clock in the afternoon Vaubois, compelled to abandon his position, was in full retreat upon Verona. After a short halt in Bussolengo, he continued his retreat to Castelnuovo during the night, and on the morning of the 18th withdrew behind the Mincio at Peschiera. Davidovich remained on the battle-field on the evening of the 17th; on the 18th he advanced as far as Pastrengo.

When Napoleon was informed of Vaubois' defeat, and saw at the same time on the morning of the 18th that Alvintzy had no longer any intention of making a standing at Villanuova, he only sent his cavalry in pursuit of the latter, and ordered Massena to march forward along the right bank of the Adige to Villafranca, and Augereau by the left bank to Verona. On the 19th Davidovich received news of Alvintzy's retreat and Napoleon's advance against himself, and he therefore began his own movement to the rear on the 20th. In the meantime, however, Alvintzy, perceiving that he was not pursued, had decided to turn back and to advance again upon Verona, in order to relieve Davidovich, and, while the latter retreated, Alvintzy advanced on the 20th as far as Villanuova. Meanwhile Napoleon had effected a junction between the corps of Massena and Vaubois, and ordered their joint advance against Davidovich; at the same time Augereau pushed forward across the mountains from Verona to Dolce in the valley of the Adige, in order to cut off the enemy's retreat.

On the 21st Alvintzy reached the position of Caldiero, after having driven out some weak French divisions left

[1] To Carnot, Verona, 19th November.

behind there, his vanguard being in the vicinity of Verona. On the same day, in the morning, Davidovich was just evacuating his position at Rivoli on the approach of Vaubois and Massena, when he received news of Alvintzy's fresh advance. He immediately wished to reoccupy the position just evacuated, and gave orders to this effect, but finally changed his mind and determined to continue his retreat. This vacillation was of course bound to cause mistakes and disorder. Therefore, when the French attacked, the fight immediately took an unfavourable turn for the Austrians; they were repulsed with heavy loss, and when in addition news of Augereau's advance *via* Lugo to Peri, threatening their rear, arrived, a general retreat as far as Ala was ordered. But Augereau had already reached Peri, and thus the way had to be cleared there by further fighting. In this unfavourable position Davidovich's troops were utterly routed, and only escaped by flight, incurring heavy losses.

During the next few days no movements of importance took place. On the 23rd Alvintzy received information of Davidovich's defeat, and saw himself forced to retreat behind the Brenta, which he did during the night before the 24th. A sortie on the part of Würmser from Mantua on the 23rd was repulsed, for Napoleon had now had time to send the troops, drawn from the investment corps, back to it. Thus on the 24th this campaign too was finished; again Napoleon had victoriously solved the problem of acting on the defensive, he had maintained his position.

The French army now occupied the following positions, (18) and by the end of December reached the figures given below:—Serurier (who had taken the place of Kilmaine, who was sick) was investing Mantua with 8000 men; Massena lay at Verona with 9000; Joubert (who had succeeded Vaubois in his command) lay at Rivoli with 10,000 men; Augereau at Legnago with 9000; and as reserves there were the division of Rey, 4000 men, near and in front of Brescia, for the observation of the valley of the Chiese, and Victor's brigade, 2000 men, at Castelnuovo and Goito. There came now a pause in the active operations, for Napoleon had of course no reason for reassuming the offensive before the capture of Mantua, and the Austrians were compelled to reform and reinforce their army first. This was completed by the beginning of 1797; and Alvintzy now projected a second attempt to relieve Mantua. He had at present 9000 men under Provera near Padua; these were to start from there on the 7th January, and to seize Legnago on the 9th. Bajalich had 6000 men at Bassano; these were also to start on the 7th and take Verona on the 12th. The main army, under Alvintzy himself, 28,000 men, was to advance against the position of Rivoli and attack and capture it on the 13th January. Accordingly, Bajalich and Provera started on the 7th; the former reached Villanuova on the 9th, and the latter Montagnana after an encounter with Augereau's advanced guard on the preceding day. Augereau reported this to Napoleon on the same day, though he did not as yet credit the enemy with any serious intentions against Legnago, and he therefore assembled only a portion of his troops there, keeping the rest at Ronco under Guieu.

Napoleon received the news at Bologna on the 10th. He immediately sent the 2000 men stationed there to Rovigo under Lannes, to support Augereau, whilst he himself, for the present, joined Serurier. On this day Bajalich advanced but a little way; his vanguard reached Caldiero; Provera remained stationary; Alvintzy's main body was still engaged in concentrating. But on the 11th January, Bajalich arrived before Verona; Provera again remained stationary at Montagnana, and Alvintzy's columns were beginning to reach the Monte Baldo. Meanwhile nothing was altered, generally speaking, in the French positions, although, both on the Adige and at Rivoli, all were standing to their arms because the advance of the enemy along the whole line rendered the direction of their main attack still a matter of doubt.

On the 12th Bajalich attacked Verona unsuccessfully, for he had sent the larger part of his troops to Alvintzy along the Val Pantena[1]; and in the afternoon he retreated to Caldiero. The first troops of Alvintzy arrived before Joubert's outposts at La Corona; their attack, however, was wanting in unanimity, and the position remained in the hands of the French. Provera again remained inactive. On the same day Napoleon arrived in Verona. His first impression, after Augereau's message, was that the enemy intended to reach Mantua by the lower Adige, and he had therefore sent orders from Roverbella to Massena to hold himself ready for a march to Legnago. But when he came to Verona and noted Bajalich's attack there, he kept Massena back, although as yet without any clear conception of the situation. However, Joubert's report of the advance against La Corona now arrived, and Napoleon began to doubt whether the enemy's main force was after all facing Augereau. He said to himself on the morning of the 13th: "Here at Verona I have about 6000 men before me, whom I shall attack to-day. Joubert must be able to report to-day also, whether the force before him exceeds 9000 men; if this is the case, there cannot be more than 10,000 men at the most facing Augereau. The enemy is therefore nowhere in full strength, and I can, on whatever wing he wishes to cross the Adige, throw myself upon him with superior numbers." However, in any case Napoleon must find out with certainty on which wing the larger portion of the Austrians were, if he did not wish to make a thrust at random; once aware of this, the quickest movement of the army in that direction would be necessary, and every moment would be precious. Therefore his carriage had been standing ready, with the horses put to, since the evening before, so as to take him immediately to the threatened point; meanwhile he was awaiting the solution

---

[1] The Val Pantena is one of the minor valleys between the Brenta and Adige valleys.

of the state of affairs with the greatest anxiety. It came that very day.

Joubert had already recognized that the enemy had resolved to force him from his strong position, and had therefore his main forces there; he consequently evacuated his outlying positions at La Corona in the early morning of the 13th and collected his troops on the plateau of Rivoli. The Austrian columns, now advancing undisturbed, threatened however to turn this position during the afternoon. In the meantime Napoleon had recognized Alvintzy's plan from Joubert's reports, and resolved at once to act, as he had always done hitherto, in the way which, in imitation of his example, the theory ot strategy now lays down as an invariable principle; namely, to throw himself in full strength upon the enemy's main column, without for the time troubling about the advance of any minor columns. He therefore issued the following orders at three o'clock in the afternoon: "Victor will at once march to Villafranca," and at five o'clock: "Rey will advance to Castelnuovo, where he will wait for further orders as to his march to the battle-field; Massena will leave Verona with a small garrison and march immediately, so as to take up a position to the left of Joubert." He himself hastened thither in advance. Joubert received orders to hold the position of Rivoli.

(19) This latter general, at ten o'clock in the evening, before the threatened turning movement of the Austrians, had already begun to evacuate the position of Rivoli, when Napoleon's above-mentioned orders arrived just in time to keep him in this position. The Austrians, pushing forward in six columns, reached the line from Caprino to the chapel of San Marco with four of these in the evening, the fifth being at Rivalta, the sixth on the other side of the

(18) Adige at Dolce. Provera had collected his troops at Minerbe with the intention of crossing the Adige by night at Anghiari; Bajalich, having been attacked in the morning by Massena's vanguard, retired at nightfall to Villanuova.

Mantua

At two o'clock in the morning Napoleon joined Joubert. (19) In the bright moonlight he distinctly saw the Austrians in position in a semicircle around him, and resolved to break through their turning attack by making an offensive move against their extended line. Before daybreak he therefore ordered Joubert to force back the enemy's outlying troops, and to advance as far as the position near the chapel of San Marco; the left wing of the French stood at Trombalora, whilst their right blocked the hollow way leading to the plateau near the inn Della Dogana. At daybreak the Austrian columns commenced the attack. That on their extreme right, the first, was to turn the position of Rivoli completely and then attack it in the rear from the heights of Mt. Pipolo. The sixth, near Ceradino, was to occupy the defile of Chiusa on the left bank of the Adige and cannonade Rivoli. In the front, the columns second, third and fourth were to attack the position of Rivoli, whilst the fifth was to await at Incanale the result of this attack, and then to storm the hollow way near the inn. Napoleon, on his side, decided to leave only a very small force on his flanks, thrown back towards Trombalora and the inn, because he expected Massena and Rey to come up in a very short time. (The latter had received orders at Castelnuovo to continue his march at once.) With Joubert's main body he intended to take the offensive against the attack of the three central Austrian columns; these, forming the main body, once beaten, he would be able to cut off the isolated columns and the two wings and capture or destroy them.

To begin with, however, the Austrians were advancing, and the second column, pushing forward over Caprino, even threatened for a moment to force Joubert altogether away from Rivoli, by turning his left wing, and to throw him back upon the Adige. But this danger was averted, for already the head of Massena's column was coming up on Joubert's left at Trombalora. Nevertheless, the Austrians continued their main advance. The position of the chapel of San Marco was captured, that near the inn was being attacked in the rear by their fourth column, whilst the fifth was forcing its way in front up the hollow way, and the defenders of this important ascent were giving way, towards the plain of Rivoli. It was noon.

(20) But however threatening matters looked for the moment, Napoleon did not yet feel any apprehension, for he was too conscious of his superiority over his opponents, not only of his actual superiority in numbers—for after the arrival of Massena and Rey he could bring a larger number of troops to the battle-field—but still more of his personal superiority in generalship. He remained perfectly calm, and with that marvellously clear insight which was one of his greatest attributes, recognizing the point at which the decisive attack would be delivered, he now sent all the forces he had at his disposal against the fifth column, just then ascending the plateau from the inn. This column, met by his attack, before it was in a position to deploy, was thrown back down the hollow road in utter (21) disorder. At the same time the three other Austrian columns in the centre fell back before the French, who now advanced along the whole line, and their retreat soon degenerated into a rout. Thus the first Austrian column, which, as we mentioned, had marched to the rear of the position of Rivoli, was now completely cut off from its fellows, and when in addition Rey appeared in its rear during the afternoon, it was so hard pressed and surrounded, that all order was lost, and by noon of the next day all the troops of this column had fallen into the enemy's hands.

Napoleon was on the point of advancing past the inn, although night was already falling, in order to annihilate the (22) fifth column also, when he received the news that Provera had during the preceding night crossed the Adige at Anghiari. He resolved immediately to hasten to cover Mantua, and therefore ordered Joubert, with Rey under him, to resume his pursuit vigorously the next morning early. He kept Massena back at Rivoli and ordered him to leave on the 15th at break of day for Villafranca. As soon as Joubert no longer needed Rey, he was to despatch him also to that place.

As we have seen, Provera had got his troops in readiness during the evening of the 13th January at Minerbe to cross the Adige during the night. This he did successfully, although Guieu hurried up with that part of Augereau's forces which stood at Ronco and attacked the head of Provera's column. The latter then continued his march towards Mantua, and reached Nogara. But Guieu and Augereau (whom Lannes had joined the evening before) marched immediately from two sides against Provera's column, and though they did not succeed in blocking its way, yet they delayed its advance and even cut off its rearguard entirely at Cerea.

On the 15th one more encounter took place before (21) Rivoli, for both Joubert and Alvintzy were advancing, the latter in order thereby to relieve his isolated first column and also to free Provera. But he was soon forced to fall back, and Joubert, noticing this, ordered his wings to be turned, while keeping the centre engaged. The Austrian soldiers, having for some days past suffered from want of provisions and ammunition, and being disheartened by their defeat the day before, fell back in disorder, and left a large number of prisoners in Joubert's hands. Altogether these two days at Rivoli, the 14th and 15th, gave to the French 13,000 prisoners of war.

Provera had meanwhile continued his march to Mantua, (22) and arrived at noon before the suburb San Giorgio, which had been occupied and fortified by the French. After having succeeded in informing Würmser of his arrival, the two resolved upon a combined attack on La Favorita and San Antonio on the morning of the 16th. Napoleon reached Roverbella on the evening of the 15th with the troops of Massena and Victor, whom he had taken with him from Villafranca. At Roverbella he learnt that Provera had arrived at noon before San Giorgio, but that this suburb was still in the hands of the French. He now ordered Augereau to press vigorously from the rear, and Serurier to take up a position at La Favorita, in order to oppose any sortie from the fortress; he himself decided to approach from the north with Massena and Victor, and thus to complete the circle around Provera. It is true, Augereau had not immediately followed the Austrians on the 15th, but had occupied himself with blocking their retreat to the Adige; he received his orders for an advance to La Favorita, however, in time to assist there actively the next day.

On the 16th, in the morning, Provera began his attack upon La Favorita. Soon, however, he saw himself surrounded on all sides through Napoleon's dispositions, described above, and about noon he resigned himself to having to lay down his arms. Thus this attempt failed, even more disastrously than all the previous operations of the Austrians for the relief of Mantua, nine days after its commencement; it was destined to be the last. Of the 43,000 men with whom Alvintzy had opened the campaign, he scarcely brought 25,000 men back. Mantua's fate was now sealed, and on the 3rd February the fortress surrendered to the French, and its garrison became prisoners of war.

For eight months the place had been a bone of contention, and four relieving armies had been defeated and partly annihilated by Napoleon. And herein also he proved of what different material he was made, compared to ordinary generals. The latter are liable to lose their energy for new enterprises by long protracted operations, even though they be successful; to them the glory already gained seems not only well earned, but an entirely satisfactory consummation of their lives; they have no desire to increase it, they only wish to preserve it, forgetful of the great saying, "He who fears to lose his fame, is sure to do so."[1] Only a

[1] Napoleon to the Directory, Leobon, 16th April, 1797.

genius of the first rank will aim so high, that every success appears only a step to higher successes, and therefore inspires him with energy to pursue new aims. This is the same mental operation as the one we spoke of above, when treating of the question of pursuit. Therefore we are forced to admire the freshness with which Napoleon prepared to face each of these four successive armies as well as the boldness with which he dealt with them ; his great deeds had not exhausted, but rather fortified his energy.

CHAPTER V.

THE CAMPAIGN OF 1797.

(22) THE last attempt to relieve Mantua having failed, and the town having surrendered, the Austrians had retreated into the mountains of the Tyrol and of Friaul. They immediately went to work again, however, to collect large reinforcements, in order to have a fresh army ready, capable of carrying on the war; but it was no longer possible for them to re-enter Italy or to assume the offensive; their reconstructed army was only intended for the defence of their own borders. Indeed, for the present there were only 7000 men in the Tyrol and 24,000 on the Brenta to withstand a first attack.

With the fall of Mantua, Napoleon of course at once resumed the idea of taking the offensive, but he too was waiting for reinforcements, without which, indeed, no vigorous advance, no crossing of the Alps or invasion of the heart of Austria would be possible. He therefore only ordered Massena and Augereau for the present to move forward to Bassano and Cittadella, and in consequence of this movement the Austrians quitted the Brenta and retired behind the Piave. They likewise fell back behind the Avicio before Joubert, who was also advancing. But after this the French remained stationary, and Napoleon proceeded with one corps of 8000 men to Rome, for both his Government and he himself had resolved to come to an immediate definite settlement with this State, which had shown animosity during the struggle with the Austrians and while the fate of Italy was still undecided. As the Austrians

The Campaign of 1797

were too weak for a resumption of the contest at present, there was a pause in hostilities. Napoleon's march against the few and indifferent Roman troops is without any strategical interest for us, and on the 19th February the conditions of peace, dictated by Napoleon, were signed at Tolentino on behalf of the Papal Government.

Meanwhile the French general had been receiving continuous reports about the massing of ever-increasing numbers of Austrian troops, and on the 17th he wrote: "In a few days I shall return to the army, where, as I notice, my presence is becoming necessary;"[1] and among the reasons which he quoted to the Directory as influencing his conclusion of peace with Rome, he mentioned: "(4) Because my presence with the army is indispensable."[2]

In the meantime the Archduke Charles had been appointed commander-in-chief in the place of Alvintzy. He joined the army in the beginning of March, and on the 10th it was stationed as follows: In the van 10,000 men on the Piave; behind the Tagliamento from Gemona down stream 17,000 men; in the Tyrol, at Salurn and in the valleys of the Avicio and the Nos, 14,000 men, besides 10,000 Tyrolese volunteer riflemen. (23)

Napoleon also had returned to his army, and was at this date (10th March) at Bassano; his army consisted, after the arrival of reinforcements, of the following forces: Bernadotte, with 10,000 men, at Padua; Serurier, 9000, at Asolo; Massena, 12,000, at Bassano; Guieu, 10,000 (Augereau's late division), at Castelfranco. Joubert stood in the Tyrol on the Adige with his own division of 10,000 men, Baraguey d' Hilliers had 6000, and Delmas 5000. In Verona and Mantua there were respectively 2000 and 1500 men as garrisons.

The disposition of the Austrians in two bodies was well known to Napoleon, and his plan consisted of throwing himself with the larger portion of his army, 41,000 men,

[1] To Joubert, Tolentino.   [2] Tolentino 19th February.

upon the enemy's main body, probably not more than 30,000 men, under the personal command of the commander-in-chief and in position on the direct road to Vienna. He moreover intended to advance in such a manner as to place the French army between the two Austrian forces, thus separating them, as he had done Beaulieu and Colli in the previous April; then to attack the main body when it had no hope of any assistance from the corps in the Tyrol. Accordingly he ordered Massena to turn the archduke's right wing by advancing *viâ* Feltre and Belluno, and cut his communications with the Tyrolese corps. Napoleon himself intended to attack the Austrian front with Serurier, Guieu and Bernadotte, with Massena on his left, meaning to push forward with his whole strength against the pass of Tarvis. Baraguey would be sent to Primiero, to cover Massena's turning movement against the Tyrol, and to render the separation of the Friaul corps from that of the Tyrol more effectual. Should Joubert be attacked by superior forces, a thing scarcely to be expected, he was to retreat slowly along the Adige towards Castelnuovo, continually facing about, and occupy the excellent positions that the valley afforded. But should Joubert, as was likely, considering his large force, also advance and reach Botzen, Napoleon would order him up through the Puster valley, during his own advance against Villach. Then he would be with his united forces on the shortest road to Vienna.

On the 10th March Napoleon opened the campaign by ordering Massena to Feltre. The Austrian vanguard on the Piave immediately fell back and assembled behind the Livenza, only observing the Piave.

On the 11th Guieu and Serurier advanced nearer to the much swollen stream, and Massena pushed forward a little beyond Feltre. On the 12th, at daybreak, Napoleon ordered the passage of the Piave to be begun, and therefore Guieu crossed at Nervesa to the south of the wood of Montello, and Serurier to the north of this wood at Ciano, the cavalry reserve preceding him. Guieu reached Conegliano on the same day, with Serurier a little in his rear, Bernadotte followed in support to Castelfranco, and Massena arrived at Belluno. Baraguey occupied Primiero on this day; the weak Austrian advanced troops falling back along the whole line as far as the Livenza.

On the 13th the Austrians, about 10,000 strong, who had retreated from the Piave, assembled near Pordenone on the high road to Udine; their rear guard, however, was compelled on the evening of this day by Guieu to evacuate Sacile. Serurier reached Conegliano and Bernadotte Treviso. Massena remained with his main body at Belluno, but seized the pass of La Fossa, further up the Piave. Napoleon, now at Conegliano, was, from what had happened hitherto, convinced that he would succeed in arresting the enemy on the Tagliamento and force him to accept battle. But he intended to fight only after having been joined by Massena, and therefore sent orders to the latter to hasten up *viâ* Aviano, and if this was not possible, to march to Sacile. Therefore Massena set his troops in motion on the 14th towards Serravalle, Serurier arrived at Porto Buffole, Bernadotte at Conegliano, Guieu collected his forces at Sacile, and to this latter town the headquarters also were moved. We see distinctly from these dispositions how Napoleon was endeavouring to mass his forces, so as to have all his troops in hand, before advancing across the Tagliamento to attack the enemy's position. The Austrians drew all their outlying corps on this day to the Tagliamento; their main body was posted behind this river, with its centre at Codroipo and its wings extending to San Daniele and Latisana. The archduke himself was at Udine.

On the 15th Napoleon did not advance far. He himself with Guieu reached Pordenone; Bernadotte, Sacile; Serurier crossed the Livenza and arrived at Belvedere. As to Massena, Napoleon expected he would reach Serravalle on this day, and sent him orders at nine o'clock to march *viâ* Sacile and Pordenone to Cordenons, where he was to arrive, if possible, by the 16th. The Austrians now withdrew their outposts behind the Tagliamento, but otherwise scarcely changed their positions. On this same day Napoleon wrote a very remarkable letter to Joubert on the situation.[1] First he informed him of his intention to effect the junction of his two army corps in the valley of the Drave, to turn to the north after crossing the Tagliamento, and to take the pass of Pontafel; Joubert was to drive the enemy beyond Brixen. Having thus pointed out his main object, Napoleon proceeded to a consideration of the following eventualities:—

1. If Joubert should be beaten and driven back as far as Mantua;

2. If hostile bodies of troops advanced *viâ* Feltre to Primolano into the valley of the Brenta, in order to cut off Joubert from Napoleon;

3. If a hostile column turned one of Napoleon's wings and made its appearance on the Piave or the Brenta, before he could change front.

Now in this there were two things characteristic of Napoleon. First, the perfect calm with which he viewed the possibility of his first assumption coming to pass. Let the enemy advance in his direct rear and drive back Joubert to the Po, this general would be able to hold out with his base in Mantua, and using the Po as his line of supply until the decisive blow had been struck on the Tagliamento; then Napoleon, returning, would on his side cut off and annihilate the hostile corps, which had advanced so boldly and interrupted his communications with his base for a moment. Secondly, we must notice that he, although taking three different possibilities of the enemy's movements into consideration, still did not continue enumerating in detail all he expected his subordinate general to do in each case, but, after having given him general advice as to the most probable eventuality, the

[1] From Sacile.

first, he dismissed the second as unlikely, and did not consider the third at all. It is indeed generally conceded to be a mistake to attempt to give a distant corps minute instructions for all and every eventuality, and thus this letter of Napoleon's is a fresh proof of the natural gifts as a strategist with which he was born. Of course an energetic, enterprising and youthful subordinate officer like Joubert, a contemporary of Napoleon, was necessary before the commander-in-chief could view with calmness such movements between himself and his base, which are always liable to make a great impression on both the leader and the troops.

On the morning of the 16th, Napoleon set his divisions in motion against Valvasone, in order to cross the Tagliamento that day. Guieu arrived first, and was ordered against the right wing of the Austrian lines which extended from Codroipo as far as Torrida; while Bernadotte, who arrived about noon, was sent against their left wing. Serurier followed later in the right rear to Codroipo as a reserve. About three o'clock in the afternoon the French columns began crossing, whilst the Austrians kept up a desultory fight until the evening, in order to cover their retreat towards Palma, which had already begun. In the course of the night the Austrian troops assembled at Palma, leaving a rearguard on the Cormor. Massena had not been able, as we have seen, to assist actively in this day's preparations for the crossing of the Tagliamento, though it had been Napoleon's intention that he should do so, the mountain roads by which he had to march having delayed his advance too much. But now Napoleon ordered him to start at eleven o'clock in the evening, and to march as quickly as possible to Spilimbergo.

The Archduke Charles wanted to wait for his expected reinforcements to come up before engaging in a decisive battle; he therefore continued his retrograde movement on the 17th to Gradisca. The French advanced but a short distance on this day; Napoleon seemed to consider it necessary to be thoroughly clear as to whether the enemy had really evaded him to the southward, or was still on the road to Tarvis with his main force. The successes which the archduke, a young man of twenty-five years, had gained during the preceding year in Germany, had secured him a sufficient reputation for his opponent, himself only twenty-seven years old, to be on his guard, for Napoleon never omitted to take the personal qualities of the leaders opposed to him into consideration in his strategical plans.

However, every day Napoleon's apprehensions as to the archduke's powers as a general vanished more and more, and by the 25th of March he was in a position to say: "Up to this hour Prince Charles has manœuvred worse than Beaulieu and Würmser; step by step he has committed blunders, and very gross ones too; he has had to pay dearly for them, and he would have had to pay far more dearly for them if his reputation had not deceived me up to a certain point and prevented me from being sure about certain mistakes which I perceived indeed, but considered to have been caused by intentions, which afterwards proved to have had no existence." [1]

This shows us moreover what a great effect the reputation of a general, when once gained, has on his subsequent deeds. The most striking instance of this is Napoleon himself; for when, in the year 1814, with scarcely a handful of raw levies he had to face the allies, who outnumbered him three to one, the weight of his name alone had such a tremendous effect upon them, that no superiority of numbers seemed sufficient to render them sure of a victory wherever Napoleon appeared in person. And if from the before-mentioned example we see that even a Napoleon was, for a time, influenced in the same way, we shall, on the one hand, understand how those who were infinitely his inferiors succumbed to it altogether; but

[1] C.N. To the Directory, Goritz.

The Campaign of 1797

on the other we shall be moved to a just admiration for the steadfastness of Blücher, whom no such considerations ever affected.

For the rest we must say, in considering this first occasion on which Napoleon and the Archduke Charles measured swords, that the annals of war could probably not furnish the names of two leaders who, both as generals and as men, differed so widely from each other. Napoleon, violent, intractable, full of an unbridled desire of glory and power; the archduke, cold, calculating and ever awake to the call of duty in all his actions. Napoleon, the son of an insignificant Corsican lawyer, only lately ennobled, breaking through all the legal restrictions of his adopted country in arbitrary fashion for his own aggrandizement; the archduke, the first prince of the blood, acquiescing in all the commands of his Government, without any idea of opposition. Napoleon, as in his own life, ever grasping at the highest, so in his strategy ever resolutely choosing the boldest course and pursuing it unflinchingly; the archduke, as in his own life, always retiring, so in his mode of waging war, never seeking for personal glory, though often dilatory when the greatest haste was necessary, shrinking from the risk of staking the whole weal of his army and country on one cast of the dice. So, too, Napoleon ever growing in greatness, though but in one direction, the highest ideal of every soldier, yet the terror of every sovereign who looked to the future; while the archduke, no great conqueror of nations or destroyer of States, was a pattern to every subject, placed in the highest and most responsible position, not thinking for himself. The archduke acknowledged his opponent's military superiority unreservedly and ungrudgingly, and openly expressed his admiration for him; whilst Napoleon, who had not, and could not have any conception of such a noble nature, which was ncapable of being tempted by any bait from the path of duty, exclaimed angrily and characteristically,

"He is a blockhead!"[1] when in the year 1805 he for the first time became personally acquainted with the archduke. These two instances suffice to show the wide gulf which separated the two men.

On the 18th March, the archduke withdrew his army wholly behind the Isonzo, and took up his position to the east of Görz. Napoleon had, at seven o'clock on the evening before, issued the following orders from Valvasone:—" Bernadotte will start at 3.30 in the morning and proceed to Palma; Serurier will follow him, and be followed in his turn by Guieu. Massena will push forward by San Daniele and Gemona and seize the Chiusa at the entrance to the Pontafel pass (Chiusa veneta)." Joubert also received orders to advance to Brixen. Palma was found evacuated and was occupied, after which Napoleon formed his army on the right bank of the Torre. In the early morning of the 19th, Napoleon's army was ready to cross the Torre. Bernadotte crossed first and marched to Medea, Napoleon accompanying this column. The Austrians offered no resistance whatever. Serurier then marched across the river and pushed forward to Villesse, and both divisions proceeded to Gradisca. This town was invested, and its garrison surrendered at nine o'clock in the evening.

The archduke determined to continue his retreat, and did so during the same night. He intended to effect a junction at Villach with the reinforcements that were on the way to him. For this purpose he divided his army into two columns; the larger of these he sent in the direction of Laibach, so as to move it up afterwards *viâ* Krainburg to Tarvis; the other he ordered to march to the same point by ascending the Isonzo valley. He himself hastened in advance to Villach. Massena, having by forced marches recovered the lead he had lost, and having entered the pass of Pontafel, stormed the bridge of Casasola that day, the 19th, which had been occupied by

[1] Mme. de Rémusat, Mém., II. 235.

THE CAMPAIGN OF 1797

a weak detachment, and formed one of the defences of the pass. The Austrians retreated to Pontafel.

On the 20th Napoleon pushed forward up the Isonzo, as far as Görz, with Bernadotte on the right bank and Serurier on the left; Guieu marched in the direction of Cormons. But during the course of the day Napoleon was informed that a somewhat considerable portion of the enemy's forces had retreated to Laibach, and although he had no intention of following them there with his main body, still he sent Bernadotte on the 21st to Czernitza, to keep watch on that road; indeed, the latter came in touch with the enemy's rearguard. Guieu marched that day to Cividale, and Serurier pushed farther up the Isonzo valley. Massena had meanwhile continued his forward movement through Pontafel on the 20th, and reached Tarvis with a portion of his troops; a small Austrian detachment stationed here for the protection of the pass fell back before him to Wurzen. Thus on the 21st Massena was already at Tarvis with part of his force when the Austrians, retreating by the Isonzo valley, started for the same place from Caporetto; they reached Predil on that day. They had been informed of the presence of the enemy at Tarvis, and determined to force their way through them. To facilitate this movement, the force which had retreated before Massena to Wurzen was ordered to advance from there in the direction of Tarvis.

On the 22nd the Austrians actually succeeded in capturing Tarvis again; Massena's troops, which had arrived there, fell back upon their division at Malborghetto, and the Austrians occupied the position at Tarvis, collecting all their forces; they sent one corps forward to Saifnitz against Massena and left a rearguard in the Predil pass to hold the hermitage of Flitschl. On the same day Guieu had pushed forward from Cividale to Caporetto, driving an Austrian detachment out of Stupizza. The Serurier's division (under the command of Chabot, Serurier being ill since the evening before) remained stationary, as a general reserve. On the 23rd, in the morning, Guieu took the Flitschl hermitage by storm, whilst on the other side Massena advanced and captured the position of Saifnitz and then Tarvis also; thus all that remained of the Austrians in the Predil pass, some 2000 men, were cut off and surrendered to the French. Meanwhile Bernadotte had advanced on that day on the road to Laibach as far as Präwald; Chabot was likewise ordered thither, and reached Czernitza.

It was the archduke's intention to assemble his whole force for the present near Klagenfurt; a part of his expected reinforcements had already arrived in Villach, about 5000 men, and these were ordered to await the troops retreating from Tarvis. Napoleon, on his side, ordered Massena and Guieu to advance upon Villach; Chabot, who, as we have seen, had been sent along to the road to Laibach, received counter orders, and marched up the Isonzo valley. Bernadotte remained for the present at Präwald. Villach was evacuated before the approach of the French, and in this situation Napoleon awaited news of the events in the Tyrol.

There operations had meanwhile begun. At first Joubert had, of course, waited until he received information about Napoleon's advance. Then he immediately opened the campaign by crossing the Avicio on the 20th March. Everywhere the Austrians were surprised and thrown back upon Neumarkt with the loss of numerous prisoners. Joubert reached Salurn. During the next few days the Austrians continued their retreat. Joubert followed, and on the 22nd reached Botzen. Here the main body of the enemy, some 8000 men, had taken the road into the Eisack valley, but their right wing, finding this road already blocked, had retreated to Meran. Joubert, on his side, left Delmas behind at Botzen to cover his rear, and with the remainder of his troops followed in the track of the Austrians into the Eisack valley. The latter had stationed their rearguard in the defile near Klausen, and their main body in a position near Brixen.

On the 23rd Joubert reached Teutschen. On the 24th he advanced against Klausen, stormed the pass, and then pushed on to Brixen; the Austrians, however, made no stand there, but fell back to Mühlbach, so that Joubert in the evening reached Brixen. The next day the Austrians continued their retreat to Sterzing, leaving only a rearguard of 1500 men behind at Mühlbach to protect the pass entrance into the Puster valley; but this detachment was attacked by Joubert on the 26th and driven out. But having no fresh news of Napoleon, the latter stood fast at Brixen.

In the meantime, on the 28th, the Austrians had effected their junction near Klagenfurt, and numbered 13,000 men, only one corps of 5000 remaining in the neighbourhood of Laibach on the left bank of the Save. The archduke had been informed of the events in the Tyrol. Napoleon, as we have seen, united Massena's and Guieu's corps in the first place at Villach, whilst Chabot was still on the march from the rear. On the 29th he started, forced the Austrian vanguard back, and occupied Klagenfurt, the archduke having retreated to St. Veit on this day. But again Napoleon had to wait, partly in order to bring up Chabot, before advancing further, and partly in order to obtain definite information as to Joubert's situation and as to the enemy's forces facing Bernadotte.

On the 31st March Napoleon advanced from Klagenfurt to St. Veit, whilst Bernadotte marched upon Laibach. The Austrians retreated again, and took up a position behind the Gurk. But when, on the 1st April, the French appeared before this position, the archduke, still resolved to wait for further reinforcements before accepting battle, determined to retreat still farther. But Napoleon followed him closely in this retreat, which began early in the morning of the 2nd April, came up with the rearguard, and defeated it with heavy loss. His troops reached

Neumarkt that day, and Bernadotte received orders at once to come up by forced marches *viâ* Klagenfurt. The enemy's capital was now the objective, and the only thing worthy of consideration for the moment was the enemy's force which blocked the road to that capital. This was now the decisive point, and therefore it was here that Napoleon collected all his forces, not caring whether the road *viâ* Laibach to Trieste and Udine remained open or not. Thus he again obeyed "the principles of concentration, which are the true principles of strategy."[1] With respect to Joubert he said : "At this moment we have not assumed the offensive in a sufficiently marked manner, and Vienna is not yet so directly threatened that the enemy can have really given up all thought of resuming the offensive in the Tyrol, but within forty-eight hours everything will be changed."[2] And therefore he wrote to Joubert : it was certainly possible that he might order him up, but for the present he should only endeavour to keep the road open to him in the Drave valley towards Lienz.

The Austrians continued their retreat in the night from the 2nd to the 3rd April; and the detachment left behind before Laibach also received orders to fall back with all speed to Bruck *viâ* Graz. Here we may see again how effective is the plan of massing your troops on the decisive point. It is true, Napoleon left the road to Laibach open by ordering Bernadotte up; but the enemy, threatened by the French full strength at his most vulnerable point, was unable to take advantage of it, being himself compelled to order the detached force to fall back as quickly as possible. In the early morning of the 3rd, Napoleon pushed on after the archduke, and again overtook his rearguard at Unzmarkt. This headlong and untiring advance of Napoleon was not only due to his natural desire to keep his retreating opponent in sight, it was partly also due to his hope of capturing one of the

[1] Mém., Observations, etc., I. 414.
[2] To Joubert, Friesach, 3rd April.

latter's columns, which, as he was informed, had been separated from the Tyrolese army corps and was endeavouring to join the archduke by the valley of the Mur. This news was inaccurate, but its result was the eager pursuit of the archduke; and this furnishes a proof that with a generally correct appreciation of what is really important in warfare, even mistakes, which must frequently occur, may do no great harm.

During the next few days the Austrians continued their retreat, and reached Bruck on the 6th, their rearguard being at Leoben. That day plenipotentiaries from the emperor arrived in Napoleon's headquarters at Judenburg, and the negotiations, which began now, put an end to the campaign. By the 7th a truce was concluded. But Massena, foremost in the pursuit of the Austrians, arrived in the evening of this day before Leoben and demanded and obtained the evacuation of this town. Joubert, having in Brixen received news and orders from Napoleon, had on the 4th ordered Delmas to leave Botzen and join him, and had then begun his march to the Puster valley, and had arrived in Lienz.

Thus the head of Napoleon's columns was at Leoben, only ninety-five miles from Vienna, twenty-eight days after they were set in motion against the archduke, and one year, to the very day, from the beginning of the operations from the Genoese littoral against Beaulieu.

This last campaign assuredly furnishes food for much reflection, and to us who desire to investigate Napoleon's idea as a strategist, it teaches one lesson in particular. We have already pointed out that it was his great fundamental axiom to mass his troops before coming in touch with the enemy. Does not this campaign, however, exhibit a violation of that principle, and can we, in view of this violation, still consider the above as his guiding axiom? On this very question he himself wrote at St. Helena, and argued with much show of reason that there was in this campaign no instance of columns joining only in the presence of the enemy, nor of concentric operations. But his argument is immaterial for our purpose. Even if no one were convinced by it, the very circumstance that Napoleon considered it necessary to defend himself against the imputation that he had employed any concentric operations, would be sufficient. The fact remains that he did look upon such strategy as radically wrong, and considered the principle of an advance by a single line the only correct one; and it is this conviction of the great strategist which is of importance for us, and not whether he did or did not, in any given case, adhere strictly to his own principle. "To operate in divergent directions without any lines of communications is a mistake, and it generally entails another. The detached column has orders only for the first day; its operations on the second depend on what the main column has done; the former therefore loses time in waiting for orders, or it must depend on good luck."[1]

And here we must again emphatically point out that Napoleon did recognize the existence and necessity for certain rules and principles in the art of war, for the tendency of our days is to say that no such exist, that every case in war is something new, which must and can be considered only by itself, and that practical experience and not theory is the key of the art. To such men Napoleon, who certainly cannot be accused of following in the beaten track of theory, answers: "The art of war is an art with principles, which should never be violated,"[2] and again, "All the great generals of antiquity, as well as those who have since worthily followed in their footsteps, accomplished their great deeds only by obeying the rules and principles of the art, i.e. by the correctness of their combinations and a careful balancing of means and results, efforts and obstacles. They have been successful only by adapting

---

[1] Mém., Observations, etc., I. 396.
[2] Memorandum for the King of Spain, Chalons-sur-Marne, 22nd Sept., 1808.

themselves to these rules, whatever in other ways the boldness of their undertakings and the extent of their operations may have been. They never ceased to make of war a real science. To this extent are they our great examples, and only by imitating them in this manner can we hope to emulate them;"[1] and the same general replied angrily, when the word "a methodical campaign" annoyed him: "Every well-conducted war is a methodical war. . . . The principles of the whole art of war are those which guided the great generals whose grand exploits history has handed down to us."[2] Of what value, indeed, would it be for us to study the deeds of those men if no universal truths were to be deduced from them? The work of selecting what was common to all the deeds of great generals and welding it into a science was done in the camp of this great strategical genius, whose deeds form its best illustration. It was under the influence of Napoleon's successes that Jomini recognized the fundamental axiom of strategy "to direct the bulk of the forces at the disposal of the commander upon the decisive point, whether of the theatre of war or of a battle-field;"[3] it was during Napoleon's wars that Jomini wrote his most important works, and to the experience gained in them his "Précis of the Art of War" owes its origin; it is their ripest fruit and the clearest exposition of how the art should be practically taught.

And now, if we turn to the consideration of the Italian campaign as a whole, the first thing assuredly that strikes every eye is the inborn genius for war of this youthful leader. There was now, indeed, but one opinion about him: "Here there is no one but looks upon him as a man of genius. He has great power over the men who form the Republican army. . . . His judgment is sure; his resolutions are carried out with all his powers. His calmness amid the most exciting scenes is as remarkable

[1] Mém. de Ste. Hélène, VII. 238.
[2] Mém., Dix-huit notes, etc., III 415.
[3] Introduction to the Study of great Combinations in Strategy and Tactics, 8.

as his extraordinary rapidity in changing his plans, if forced to do so by unexpected circumstances." [1] It is true people noticed, also, that he never spared his men, that he was hard, impatient, masterful; but his bearing, his look, his manner of speaking were those of a man born to command; everyone felt this and submitted. And yet his companions in arms at that time speak with praise of his easy and vivacious ways, his sparkling, brilliant conversation, his jokes and good humour, where duty was not in question: in one word, of that singular charm which surrounded this genius in the freshness of his youth.

And how striking, how original, his first appearance had been! It is true, the revolution, with its gigantic levies, had already led up to the abandonment of the eighteenth-century strategy, which we may call that of Frederick, after its greatest exponent; but as yet the new departure was incomplete, as yet the leaders, men of talent, but not of the first rank, had not freed themselves wholly from old traditional methods, nor realized all the logical conclusions to be deduced from the new state of affairs; they did not possess creative genius. It was Napoleon who threw aside completely and without distinction all and every tradition, and became, by his victorious march from Nice to Leoben, at once the creator and greatest representative of modern strategy, personifying in himself all its ideas. This is the real significance of the campaign of 1796. The leaders of the revolution also had begun to cast aside the hindering chains of the magazine system of Frederick's school; they had, however, looked on this emancipation not as a means of giving their powers free play, but rather as an element which often led to confusion. It is true, Napoleon found the old methods already broken down, but it was the great work of his genius that he put new ones in their place, and " assuredly the greatest creative effort of the human mind is that which

[1] Rapport du Gén. Clarke au Directoire. Milan, 7 déc., 1796.

makes real what was not so before."[1] The fact is, he had original thoughts; and this is rarer than people think, for original thought creates new things, and "wherever there is the creation of new things, there must be genius."[2]

Originality, then, is the most salient feature of this campaign. But even if we admit this, there is still wide room for admiration of the manner in which the original conception was carried out. In the first place. it is the planning of the individual movements which strikes us by its simple grandeur. One guiding principle is always present: "Strategy consists in always having, in spite of an army of inferior strength, a larger force than the enemy at the point attacked, or at the point which the opponent attacks."[3] Keeping this always in view, and having once made his plans, it seemed henceforth as if Napoleon saw through the enemy's intentions, as if he were guiding their movements himself; accidents occurred without interfering with the course of the campaign—nay, without being much noticed by the spectator, so clear and all-embracing was Napoleon's glance.

"Military science," he said, "consists in carefully weighing all possible eventualities, and then, almost mathematically, eliminating chance. It is here that no error must be made, for a decimal more or less may change everything. But this discrimination between skill and chance can only be exercised by a real genius."[3]

This enlistment of chance, which "must ever remain a mystery for mediocre minds, and which becomes of importance to men of mark,"[4] goes hand in hand with a full command of all one's mental powers, such as Napoleon possessed at all times and in every situation. This is what has been called "two-o'clock-in-the-morning courage, i.e. spontaneous courage, which, in spite of the most unexpected occurrences, leaves us always the same

[1] Mme. de Rémusat, Mém., I. 333.   [2] The same.
[3] Bourienne, Mém. Napoleon's dictation, I. 185.
[4] Mme. de Rémusat, Mém., I. 333.

freedom of mind and judgment and decision;"[1] and with respect to this, Napoleon added, he had found that he himself possessed this kind of courage in an eminent degree, and that he had seen but few individuals who were not much inferior to himself in this point. His contemporaries were indeed struck by the extraordinary rapidity with which Napoleon was able to judge correctly of any question. "The habit," says a writer in addressing him, "which I recognized in you of seeing correctly, yet very rapidly."[2]

And one other phase of moral courage must be alluded to here, namely, the urgent desire to bring about a decision by battle. This desire also is characteristic of great generals; it was this that raised Frederick the Great so high above the other commanders of his time; for it is always a sign of self-confident mental power. Napoleon, looking back upon more victorious battles than any general in the annals of war, says: "People have a mistaken idea of the strength of mind necessary to engage, with full consideration of its consequences, in one of those great pitched battles on which may depend the fate of an army or a country and the possession of a throne,"[3] and he adds, that but few generals were eager to fight battles.

The fact is, he possessed in the highest degree what he himself considered as most desirable, namely, the quality of "being four-square, that is, of being as broad as one is long,"[3] as he called it. He meant by this, a complete balance of perception and character or courage. "If courage," he continued in his observations on this point, "preponderates too much, a general will undertake things above his grasp and commit errors, and on the other hand, if his character or courage is much inferior to his perception, he will not dare to execute what he has conceived."[3]

[1] Mém. de Ste. Hélène, II. 17.
[2] Comeyras to Napoleon, Milan, 15th July, 1796.
[3] Mém. de Ste. Hélène, II. 18.

Suppose Napoleon had fallen in the midst of his undertakings, would not any one of his subordinates, whichever of them we may imagine at the head of the army, have shown a want of one or the other? Would Bernadotte or Serurier in his place have had moral courage enough to carry out what Napoleon's foresight had planned; would Massena or Augereau have been able to carry those bold enterprises with equal skill to a successful issue? Indeed, in Napoleon the clearest perception of what was best was combined with the utmost daring in carrying it out, however rash it might be.

And finally, all these qualities were inspired and set in motion by an extraordinary ambition. Only this constant keen desire to excel all others can call forth an indefatigable activity, and thereby enable a soldier to bring all the talents given him by nature into play, and to gain ultimate success. Ambition is the fire, without which no machine, however well put together and provided with material, can begin its work; without ambition a soldier resembles that horse of Roland's which was possessed of every perfection, only, alas! he was dead. How was it that Napoleon was at Leoben whilst Moreau and Hoche had barely crossed the Rhine? It had been his personal ambition, ever urging him forward, ever thirsty for glory and conquest, which had carried him on; and just for this reason Napoleon's name is rightly placed far above those of his contemporaries. Had Moreau and Hoche been inspired by an equal ambition, they would never have awaited on the Rhine the good pleasure of the Directory. In his wrath, Napoleon wrote at that time: "The armies of the Rhine can have no blood in their veins. . . . If you mean to enter on a campaign, nothing ought to stop you!"[1]

But such an ambition must not be mean; it must not seek to rise by humiliating others; it must be an ambition like that which made young Cæsar weep before

[1] To the Directoire, Leoben, 16th April.

the statue of Alexander, because the latter at his age had already conquered the world; an ambition like that, which caused Napoleon to say: "I hold the immortality of the soul to be the remembrance which we leave behind in the minds of men. This thought is an inspiring one; it were better not to have lived at all than to leave no trace of one's existence behind." [1]

Indeed, if we consider collectively the many-sidedness and the great qualities necessary for a great general, and recognize in what a happy manner they were combined in this one youthful soldier, we shall agree with what Desaix said, when Marmont spoke to him of Napoleon's genius, at that time as yet unknown to the world: "The chief-command of an army is the most difficult thing on earth; it is the one work of all others which requires the display of the greatest number of qualities in a given time." [2]

---

[1] Bourienne, Mém., IV. 280.   [2] Marmont, Mém., I. 80.

CHAPTER VI.

EGYPT.

1798-99.

NAPOLEON'S many victories, Leoben, the 18th Fructidor, and Campo Formio had raised him above the rank of a mere general; he was henceforth for his own and foreign Governments a power which had to be reckoned with. After having played the sovereign in Italy, to return to Paris and become a simple citizen again was impossible; he felt this himself, and the Directory understood it; hence the expedition to Egypt.

To begin with, it is true he engaged in some political intrigues, in order to gain a position worthy of his ambition and capacities; but on the one hand his passionate soldier nature was not yet experienced enough in those mazes, and on the other the whole political situation was not yet suitable, the pear, as he said himself, was not yet ripe. Thus he was between two dangers, that of ruining himself by precipitation, or of disappearing in the crowd. He feared the latter himself: "In Paris all is soon forgotten. If I remain here long without doing something or other, I am lost."[1] Thus, to help himself out of the difficulty, he chose what of old had led Cæsar to Gaul, a foreign expedition at the head of an army.

At first the command of an army to invade England was entrusted to him, but a personal examination of the position of affairs soon caused him to reject this project

[1] Bourrienne, Mém., II. 32.

entirely, and his unquenchable desire for action sought another outlet. " My glory is already at an end; there is not enough of it in this little Europe. I must go to the East; all great glory comes from there." Indeed, to the East his looks had long been directed; to that land which inflamed his imagination with its wonders. Already during the negotiations with Austria at Passeriano he had said: "Europe is a mole-heap; only in the East have there ever been great empires and great cataclysms; in the East there are six hundred millions of human beings."[1] The Directory, which had long since begun to mistrust and fear him, and yet could not make up its mind to remove him, was glad to get rid of him, even at the cost of a good army, which France might very soon want again. " He gets all he asks for. It seems as if the Directory wanted to get rid of such a dangerous warrior at any cost."[2]

People have admired Napoleon very much at this juncture for having, as they say, forecast the future so truly, and having realized that he must give the Directory time to work out its fate, while he himself kept at a distance and acquired new glory, in order to be hailed hereafter the saviour by all parties. True, so it turned out, and some such calculation probably was in part at the bottom of his Egyptian plan; still, if we assume for example that a revolution had taken place and another man had seized the political power in France during his absence, a thing which might any day have happened as things then were, in that case would not the judgment of history condemn a man like Napoleon, who considered himself called upon to some day be the head of the State, for leaving France for the sake of an expedition to Egypt at a moment when everything at home was still in an unsettled state? The English ministry undoubtedly read his scheming mind correctly, when it mentioned in the preface to the " Intercepted Correspondence of the French Army in Egypt," that Napoleon certainly reckoned only

[1] Bourrienne, Mém., II. 34, 44.   [2] Gohier, Mém., I. 29.

upon a short stay there, as far as he himself was concerned, and meant to return, accompanied by a few faithful followers and covered with glory, so as to be fêted as the conqueror of Egypt. Aboukir ruined that well-devised plan.

Still we shall have to confess, that in the uncertainty of human life no definite plans can be based upon such far-reaching calculations. One thing we may be sure of, that Napoleon was even then aiming at becoming the master of France; but the means to that end were not yet quite clear to him. He could not remain quietly at home. Egypt lay ready to satisfy his impetuous desire for action; he seized the opportunity, and, as is so often the case, Fortune favoured the brave. He expected much of Fortune, and it gave him even more than he asked. It was his very absence that paved the way for the realization of his highest ambition. A shrewd observer of things human said: "I am certainly of opinion, that it is better to be too impetuous than too cautious, for Fortune is a woman, and whoever wishes to render her subservient to himself, must beat and buffet her; indeed, we see that she lets herself be mastered by such men, rather than by those who take her coolly. And for this reason Fortune, like a woman, always favours youth, because it is more inconsiderate and passionate and orders her about with more freedom."[1]

On the 19th May, 1798, Napoleon set sail from Toulon on board the *Orient*, and on the 1st July he arrived before Alexandria. Here he was informed that Nelson, who was eagerly searching the Mediterranean for him, had likewise been off this town on the 28th June, but having, contrary to his expectations, not found the French there, had departed immediately for Syria. Astonished at his good luck, Napoleon determined to commence the landing of his troops at once, in spite of the high sea and the distance they lay from the shore. Bruey's advice to

[1] Machiavelli: The Prince, 55.

the contrary he set aside with the words: "Admiral, we have no time to lose. Fortune gives me only three days; if I do not make the most of them, we are lost."[1] The landing commenced in the evening and continued during the whole night without any particular mishap, and by the morning about 4000 men of the divisions of Menou, Kleber and Bon were on shore in the Bay of Marabout. With these troops Napoleon himself set off immediately, at three o'clock in the morning, Reynier having orders to see to the landing of the rest of the troops.

The army at this time was thus constituted :—
Chief of the staff: Berthier.
Kleber's Division: 2nd Light Infantry, 25th, 75th demi-brigades of the line.
Desaix's Division: 21st Light Infantry, 61st, 88th demi-brigades of the line.
Bon's Division: 4th Light Infantry, 18th, 32nd demi-brigades of the line.
Menou's Division: 22nd Light Infantry, 13th, 69th demi-brigades of the line.
Reynier's Division: 9th, 85th demi-brigades of the line.

Each division numbered about 4500 men; the cavalry under Dumas 4000 men; the artillery reserve 3000 men.

Besides the above-mentioned commanders, there were also with him in various capacities many officers whose ability Napoleon had recognized, and thus we find here under his orders a large number of the men who afterwards acquired the highest military glory under the Empire: Murat, Lannes, Rampon, Junot, Marmont, Davont, Friant, Belliard, Lanusse, Vial, Caffarelli, Duroc, Bessières, Rapp: all men worthy to accompany such a commander-in-chief with such great deeds before him.

By nightfall on the 3rd July the landing of the French troops was virtually completed. In the meantime Napoleon had reached Alexandria on the 2nd. The Arabs tried at

[1] Bourrienne, Mém, II. 86.

first to resist, but when the French, attacking and turning them, forced the Rosetta Gate, envoys were soon sent to the camp announcing the surrender of the town. The transports were now brought into the roads of Alexandria and the fleet anchored in the bay of Aboukir. Napoleon collected his army in Alexandria, but Desaix was sent straight from the landing-place to Al Beda on the road to Damanhur, and ordered to advance upon that town. Napoleon's first move would be to seize Cairo. But the army remained for the next few days in Alexandria to wait till all the baggage and transport were landed. Napoleon formulated the following rule to guide his strategy under these new conditions: "My task will here consist in keeping all my extraordinary resources hidden, and using them only when I have to engage great masses; they will then be all the more telling."[1]

On the 5th the divisions of the army were set in motion. In the assault upon Alexandria, Kleber and Menou had been wounded; the former therefore was made commandant of that place, and the latter was destined for the same post at Rosetta. Consequently Kleber's division was led by Dugua, and Menou's by Vial. Reynier reached Al Beda on the 5th, whilst Desaix was already on the march from that place to Damanhur; Vial followed in Reynier's rear, and behind Vial came Bon, night marches being of course common in this climate. Dugua was sent to Rosetta on the evening of the 5th. On the afternoon of the 7th Napoleon himself followed the army on the road to Damanhur, which town Desaix had reached on the 6th.

This first march had given the French soldiers a sufficient foretaste of those exertions, privations and sufferings which this enterprise was to entail on them in such rich measure, that soon there was no one, with the exception of the commander-in-chief, but longed with all his soul to quit the country, and cursed the campaign. He alone remained unmoved by all the terrors of the climate, being only

[1] To Desaix, Alexandria, 3rd July.

concerned about the glory he would gain; and at a time when men had begun to commit suicide to escape from their present misery, he tapped the chief of his staff contentedly on the shoulder and said: "Well, Berthier, here we are at last."[1] And how tremendously his powers of imagination were excited by the grandeur of scenes around him! "In Egypt I saw myself freed from the fetters and constraints of civilization; I dreamt all sorts of things, and saw the means of carrying out what I had dreamt. I established a new religion; I pictured myself on the road to Asia on an elephant, a turban on my head, and holding in my hand a new Koran, which I had written myself from my own inspiration. I should have combined in my enterprises the traditions of the two worlds, putting under contribution for my own advantage the whole domain of history; I should have attacked the British Empire in India, and restored my connection with old Europe by that conquest. The time spent in Egypt was indeed the happiest of my life, for it was the most ideal."[2]

At Damanhur Napoleon assembled his army and continued on the 9th his march to the Nile towards Ramanieh, to which place Dugua also received orders to march from Rosetta. On the 10th the army reached Ramanieh. During this march the enemy was encountered for the first time. Egypt stood at that time nominally under the suzerainty of Turkey, but it was actually ruled by the warlike caste of Mamalukes, whose capital was Cairo. In this town Murad, universally acknowledged as the most powerful of their beys, collected, upon the news of the landing of the French, an army consisting, according to the custom of the country, mostly of cavalry. Some flying columns, sent out by him to reconnoitre, met Desaix's division on the 10th.; but the superiority of European arms and tactics immediately became evident, and the Mamalukes were soon repulsed by Desaix's fire.

---

[1] Miot, Mém, 33.   [2] Mme. de Rémusat, Mém., I. 274.

On the 12th, after Dugua had also come up, the French left Ramanieh once more, and, advancing along the Nile, reached Minieh Salameh. Murad, who had started from Cairo on the 6th, had meanwhile taken up a position near Schebreket and entrenched himself there. On the 13th the encounter took place. An armed flotilla on the Nile accompanied the march of the French army. This flotilla, being in advance of the army, met in the neighbourhood of Schebreket a similar armament of the Mamalukes, and had at first a hard tussle; but finally, thanks to the superiority of the French arms, victory rested with them. On land meanwhile the army also came up, forming divisional squares. The Mamalukes, about 5000 men, having several times tried to find a point where their cavalry might penetrate, but in vain, retreated to Cairo, with but little loss. Napoleon, who had been satisfied with a passive resistance, as he wished on this day only to familiarize himself with his enemy's mode of fighting, christened this insignificant skirmish "the battle of Schebreïss."

On the 21st he continued his march up the Nile, and in sight of Cairo met the main force of the Mamalukes, near Embabeh, with its left wing resting on the Pyramids, in position for the defence of the capital. The French army formed in the same order of battle as at Schebreket, the divisions being posted chequer-wise in large squares, supporting each other. But Napoleon, being now acquainted with the effectiveness of this formation, and also with the enemy's mode of attack, did not intend merely to await their attack, but to advance as well. In advancing he brought his right wing more and more forward, so as to force the enemy from his line of retreat and to hem him in with his back to the Nile. A great cavalry charge of the Mamalukes' left wing against the turning divisions of Desaix and Reynier having failed on account of the heavy fire of the latter, their right wing in the entrenched camp of Embabeh was now attacked by Bon and Vial. This camp was taken by storm, and the greater portion of its defenders perished in the waters of the Nile. The remainder of the Mamalukes took flight, partly under Murad into Upper Egypt, and partly under Ibrahim to Belbeïss and Salahieh on the road to Syria. The French army halted in the evening at Embabeh and round Gizeh.

On the 22nd the citadel of Cairo was occupied by Bon : on the 23rd Desaix marched by Gizeh up the Nile and took up a position commanding the road to Upper Egypt ; on the 24th Napoleon moved his headquarters to Cairo, and his divisions encamped in and around this town. From here various arrangements were made to secure the country conquered. Vial occupied Damietta with a small detachment, Lannes taking his place at the head of Menou's division. War contributions were levied, arms confiscated, punishments decreed and mercilessly enforced, for "the Turks can only be ruled by the greatest severity ; every day five or six heads are cut off in the streets of Cairo by my orders. Up till now we have been forced to be lenient with them, in order to wipe out the reputation of terror which preceded us ; but now, on the contrary, we must make these tribes obey, and they only obey where they fear."[1]

It was now Napoleon's intention to hunt Ibrahim altogether out of Egypt into Syria, in order to secure what he had conquered ; with Murad he attempted at first to enter into negotiations. As a commencement of his operations against Ibrahim he sent a vanguard on the 2nd of August to Kanka, where it arrived on the 3rd. But on the 5th it was driven out of this town by Ibrahim and retired along the road to Cairo, where it met with Reynier, whom Napoleon had likewise sent thither ; and on the morning of the 6th the French returned to the position of Kanka. Napoleon had on the evening of the 5th already learnt what had happened, and now considered the moment propitious to execute his plan of defeating Ibrahim and driving him from Egypt. Therefore he started himself on the 7th

[1] To Menou, Cairo, 31st July.

with Lannes for Kanka, after having entrusted to Desaix the chief command at Cairo and its safety against attacks from Upper Egypt.

With the commencement of this new enterprise the general dissatisfaction, the enormous disillusion and dejection, which had come over leaders and men from the moment of landing at Alexandria, for the first time broke out and showed itself in grumbling and mutinous words. But it did not go any further; for, before any actual disobedience occurred, without any punishments or violent measures, Napoleon managed to reconcile the men to their duty by the mere force of his words and his personality, and, as Savary says: " So great was the confidence General Bonaparte had in himself, that he left Cairo in spite of what had happened."[1]

On the 7th he arrived at Kanka, followed on the same day as far as Matarieh by Dugua, who was also to take part in the expedition against Ibrahim. On the 9th Napoleon reached Belbeïss, Ibrahim retreating before him to Salahieh. On the 10th the headquarters were at Koreïn, and on the 11th, Napoleon, hurrying forward in front of his infantry, with his cavalry, only some 300 strong, came up with Ibrahim at Salahieh. But the latter had already begun his retreat into Syria, and all the French attacks on his rearguard failed to induce him to make a stand. The cavalry of the Mamalukes outnumbered the French, and when the infantry came up, the enemy had already disappeared into the desert. Napoleon now determined to make Salahieh a dépôt, and ordered it therefore to be fortified as an earnest of his intended campaign in Syria. Reynier was left behind there, and Dugua sent to Manssurah on the 13th. The commander-in-chief himself hastened back immediately to Cairo with the rest of the troops.

Scarcely had he left Salahieh, when an aide-de-camp arrived with a despatch from Kleber; it contained the

[1] Mém., I., 89.

news of the destruction of the French fleet by Nelson at Aboukir. Whatever may have passed at this moment through Napoleon's mind, his companions read no sign of it in his face. Of course he understood what a terrible impression this stroke must make upon his army, already so disheartened; but he only felt the increased necessity of meeting the frowns of Fate and the dejection of his men with firmness, and the classical phrase, "Si fractus illabatur orbis, impavidum ferient ruinæ," might well have been applied to his conduct at this juncture. Both leaders and men felt now more than ever that the future safety of the army depended solely on this man of genius, who set Fate at defiance.

This Egyptian enterprise is indeed less suited to serve as a distinct military lesson than his other campaigns, for the climate as well as the enemy were too much unlike those to be met with in Europe. Still, the great principles of warfare, true under all circumstances, were here, too, acted on, and may here also be studied. For instance, we see how Napoleon, after having once planned the move against Ibrahim, collected all the forces at his disposal, although he would have been sure of victory even with inferior numbers; but he adhered to the maxim that all available troops should be collected whenever it is intended to give battle.

And when afterwards, as we shall see presently, Desaix was sent to Upper Egypt against Murad Bey, and issued orders for concentric advance movements, in order not only to defeat but also surround the enemy, Napoleon immediately gave fresh evidence of the dislike he had already shown in Italy for such complicated manœuvres, dependent for their success upon the punctual arrival of several columns; and he hastened to write to his subordinate officer: "You know that, as a rule, I dislike laboriously-planned attacks. Seek to meet Murad, wherever you can, but do so with your collected forces. If he then, on the battle-field, makes a stand, you will take measures to inflict as severe a defeat upon him as possible."[1] And on this occasion he also thought it advisable to impress the same lesson upon the chief of his staff; indeed, he wished to see his whole army as convinced as he was himself of the efficiency of an advance in full strength, so that even in his absence this great principle might be followed; and he therefore wrote to Berthier: "You will order General Desaix to attack Murad Bey whenever and wherever he may find him, but always to keep his troops together; it is not my wish that he should divide his forces in order to turn him."[2] This simple lesson, always to keep one's forces massed, reminds us of Jomini's words, which he calls an indisputable truth, namely, that "the simpler an important manœuvre, the more certain its success."[3] We may therefore, even in Egypt, learn some lessons in warfare; still, this campaign outside of Europe is more important on the whole as bearing on the character of Napoleon than on his strategy.

The news of Aboukir brought about an immediate change of feeling in Egypt; the whole population, besides the Mamaluke beys Murad and Ibrahim, were inspired with new hopes of being able to get rid of the French; and the Porte also determined to declare against France. Still, for the present, a time of comparative rest began for the French, of which they took advantage to establish a civil administration and secure their conquest. Desaix only was sent to Upper Egypt. His troops were embarked on Nile boats on the 25th August, and reached Siut on the 14th September; but here he was informed that Murad, having eluded him by marching through the Great Desert to the right, was advancing upon Cairo. Desaix therefore immediately descended the river again on the 19th; he met Murad on the 7th October at Sediman, and defeated him. After this, he remained in the neighbourhood of Benissuoff, and busied himself with the subjugation of the country.

[1] Cairo, 4th September. [2] Cairo, 4th September. [3] Précis, etc., 228.

We may say that this period proves Napoleon's unflinching firmness of mind in carrying out any enterprise once entered on, even more than his imperturbability after Aboukir, and this I consider the most significant characteristic of him as a general. A weak man may indeed withstand the shock of a great misfortune; it is the continued daily renewed struggle against misfortune, never allowing any relaxation, which ends by exhausting the energy of strong men. And what desperate difficulties of various kinds Napoleon had to encounter day by day, let us gather from eye-witnesses, and most of all himself.

The whole population around him was hostile; the people of the country, though defeated, were not subjugated, nor would they be so for a long time.[1] The smallest transport, every messenger had to be escorted by troops; resistance was always cropping up in all quarters; Frenchmen were murdered. "Faith, it is a war, worse than that of La Vendée."[2] Such orders as the following were constantly being issued by Napoleon:— "Citizen-general, you must utilize the days during which the division of General Dugua can remain in Damietta, to disarm the town, to imprison the suspects, and to send them to Cairo, to disarm the villages, and take hostages."[3] "I am annoyed, citizen-general, to learn that the five villages, which have behaved so badly, have not yet been disarmed."[4] "You will order General Lannes to march to-morrow at daybreak with 400 men to the village of El Katah, on the Rosetta arm, in order to punish its inhabitants for having stopped two dschermes (Nile boats) loaded with artillery, this morning."[5] Again and again such punitive measures had to be taken, and we

---

[1] Correspondence de l'armée française. Girey to Ramcy. Rosetta, 28th July, 1798.
[2] The same. Damas to Kleber. Bulak, 27th July.
[3] To Vial, Cairo, 26th September.
[4] To Dugua, Cairo, 6th October.
[5] To Berthier, Cairo, 1st November.

may judge from the strength of the above-mentioned detachment how unsafe the country was.

And yet with what severity resistance was punished! "You will have the kindness, citizen-general, to give orders to the commandant of the place to cut off the heads of all who are caught red-handed. Let them be led this night to the banks of the Nile, between Bulak and Old Cairo, let their headless trunks be thrown into the river.[1] Every night we cut off some thirty heads, especially of the ringleaders; this will, I think, be a lesson to them.[2] The stage-coach of Damietta has been attacked, citizen-general, and the officials have been murdered, as, I fancy, by the villagers of Ramleh, etc. Try to capture the ringleaders, and have their heads cut off."[3]

Above all, the French did not forget, in the meantime, to levy indemnities, and to confiscate private property. The orders to this effect were very numerous, for the army was in urgent need of funds, so much so, indeed, that as Bourrienne, one of those immediately about Napoléon's person, admits, it was customary at this time to resort to shooting men in order to get their money; and the following order of Napoleon confirms this disclosure:—"Enclosed, citizen-general, you will find an order, which you will communicate to Koraïm; according to the usual course of these matters in this country, I give him this day to redeem his life by handing over 30,000 talars to the military chest."[4] By such stringent measures, order and security were gradually restored to some extent.

But another enemy had to be dealt with day by day, namely, the state of the army itself. Want of discipline and habits of plunder on the part of the soldiers, as well as embezzlements on the part of the officials, had, even in

---

[1] To Berthier, Cairo, 23rd October.
[2] To Reynier, Cairo, 27th October.
[3] To Lanusse, Cairo, 27th October.
[4] To Dupuy, Cairo, 5th September

Italy, been the order of the day. All these evils were repeated here: "We loot the villages, ruin the natives and violate their women."[1]

But a new element was here added to those evils. In Italy officers and privates were enthusiastic in doing their duty, they hailed the continuance of the war with delight; here the very opposite of this was the case. Egypt had been painted to them as a promised land, but the first step on its soil brought bitter disappointment.. "This is a land of misery. The inhabitants are savages, who have in every way incurred the curse of nature; they have not one thing in their favour. In every village of Lower Egypt one is, so to speak, in the midst of a band of murderers."[2] No sooner did the troops enter the first town, than they came to the following conclusion: "There is nothing on earth so wretched, so miserable, so unhealthy as Alexandria; the houses are mud hovels, with holes instead of windows ... in a word, imagine the ugliest and worst-built pigeon-cotes, and you will have a correct idea of Alexandria."[3] Nor did Cairo please them any better. "This town is horrible; the streets breathe the plague on account of the filth, the people are disgusting and brutalized."[4] "This abominable hole of a Cairo is inhabited by lazy vagabonds, squatting all day long before their disreputable hovels."[5]

Every march, every movement of the army, entailed the greatest sufferings. "Since we have been in Egypt, the army has not ceased to suffer. The tremendous exertions we have had to make in the desert; the great heat, which seemed to make the soil red-hot; the necessity of being constantly on the march, though entirely without provisions: all this has led to many volunteers dying, falling suddenly

---

[1] Correspondence de l'armée française, 2e partie, IV., Cairo, 26th July.
[2] The same.
[3] The same, 1e partie, Rosetta, 27th July.
[4] Dupuis to Carlo, Cairo, 29th July.
[5] Damas to Kleber, Bulak, 27th July.

down from sheer exhaustion."[1] On all sides an intense longing showed itself to get away from this country. "I assure you, that if I ever have the happiness to set foot on my native soil once more, it will be never to leave it again. There are not four Frenchmen among the forty thousand here but think the same."[2] "It is almost impossible for me to convey any idea to you of what we have suffered; sufferings upon sufferings, privations, misery, fatigues, we have gone through them all to the utmost."[3] "We are living in a country of which everyone is sick to death. If the army had known it before leaving France, not one of us would have embarked; we should all have preferred death a million times to exposing ourselves to the wretchedness in which we are here."[4]

Not a few indeed confirmed the truth of these last words by their suicide. "Several soldiers have blown out their brains, others have cast themselves into the Nile; some dreadful things have happened."[5] "We have had men here, who committed suicide in the very presence of the commander-in-chief, saying to him, 'This is your work!'"[6] Thus the army was not far from mutinying. "Some soldiers have been overheard to remark, on seeing their generals pass, 'There they are, the butchers of the French,' and a thousand other expressions of the same kind."[7]

But whenever the dissatisfaction with the Egyptian campaign went so far as to induce officers to send in their resignation, Napoleon resorted to severe censure. "The commander-in-chief acknowledges the letter of resignation sent in by citizen Beauvais, adjutant-general. An officer who quits the service in good health in the middle of a

---

[1] Dezirard to Adeline, Cairo, 17th August.
[2] Tallieu to his wife, Rosetta, 4th August.
[3] Colbert to Collasse, Tersi, 25th July.
[4] Rozis to Grivet, Alexandria, 9th September.
[5] Gay to his parents, Cairo, 14th October.
[6] Rozis to Grivet, Alexandria, 9th September.
[7] Boyer to his parents, Cairo, 28th July.

campaign cannot have entered on it with the intention of gaining glory and assisting in the establishment of universal peace; he must have been induced to join by some other motive, and is therefore not worthy of the men whom I command."[1] And when this public disgrace was not sufficient to overcome in officers their disgust for Egypt, Napoleon wrote in answer to a request for leave to return to France on the part of another officer: "The commander-in-chief's reply to this request is, that it is his desire that you should employ this officer constantly in outpost duties, since he gained his rank as major-general in Paris and without seeing a shot fired."[2]

And to crown all, sickness appeared, as might have been expected considering the climate and the efforts made. "The greater part of the army suffer from diarrhœa, and although victorious, will perish miserably after all."[3] "About 200 blind are starting this day, citizen-general, for Rosetta; it is my desire that they should be sent home to France."[4] At the beginning of 1799 the plague, that scourge of the East, broke out.

But is it not, considering all these circumstances, a most convincing proof of the greatness of this general, only twenty-nine years old, that in spite of all this, the restraints of discipline still held good, and that the army, in spite of all, remained manageable? The fact is, there was, in all these men, outweighing even their sense of suffering, the consciousness that Napoleon alone was able to cope with the situation; indeed, the very circumstances which would have destroyed the influence of an ordinary nature, gave to his genius its incontestable dominion over his men. "When the officers and men saw Alexandria and the deserts surrounding it, they were stupefied with amazement. Bonaparte put new life into them."[5] "Our confidence in

[1] Ordre du jour, Cairo, 14th October.
[2] To Dommartin, Cairo, 10th December.
[3] Pistre to Pistre, Cairo, 16th August.
[4] To Berthier, Cairo, 28th January, 1799.
[5] Jaubert to Bruix, anchorage of Aboukir, 9th July.

Bonaparte is unlimited."[1] "You may easily imagine how difficult our situation in this country has become through this event (Aboukir), which would rob the army of all hope were we not aware of the commander-in-chief's genius. Therefore we confidently lay upon him the burden of extricating us from the difficulties in which we find ourselves."[2]

In studying such a campaign the question forces itself upon us whether, under similar circumstances, we should have done more than those men or borne everything with greater fortitude than they did ; and there may be moments when we might hesitate to answer in the affirmative. At such moments we admire Napoleon, as he deserves. He never forgot that Menou, half-deranged as he was, was at this time one of the few who did not give up hope of an ultimate happy issue to the enterprise. And his later career was a proof that Napoleon so remembered it. It would be a mistake to suppose that the egotism, which was apparently such a marked characteristic of his, was of a narrow kind ; on the contrary, he ever held services rendered in faithful memory, most of all those rendered to him at the time when his career had not as yet reached its climax ; and he knew how to reward them lavishly. "Bonaparte," as Marmont testifies, "never forgot any proofs of attachment he received."[3]

The positions of the French army in the autumn and winter of 1798 were as follows :—

Headquarters : Cairo.
Dugua at Manssurah, afterwards at Damietta.
Reynier at Salahieh.
Desaix near Benissuof.
Lannes and Bon at Cairo.

This latter town was, according to Napoleon's order of the 9th October, put in a state of defence and forts erected

---

[1] Le Père to Beytz, Alexandria, 5th August.
[2] Miot to Miot, Cairo, 15th August.
[3] Mém., I. 412.

round it. A rising of the populace, which broke out on the 22nd October, was quickly and sternly quelled the very day after its outbreak.

The 69th demi-brigade of the line, forming part of Lannes' division, was sent to Alexandria, where Kleber commanded, whilst the 4th Light Infantry, of Bon's division, was sent to Rosetta, where Menou was in command.

CHAPTER VII.

SYRIA.

ALTHOUGH no regular news had been received since Aboukir and the blockade of Alexandria by the English immediately after that battle, Napoleon managed in various ways to get some general information as to the plans of his enemies.. England and Turkey were to make common cause against him, and the attack was to be made by their combined forces. One Turkish army was collecting in Syria, under the chief command of Achmed Pasha, surnamed Djezzar (butcher) on account of his cruelty; another Turkish army was assembling at Rhodes, to land in Lower Egypt; and the operations were to be supported by an English fleet.

But Napoleon resolved, as he had already done so often in Italy, not to give time to his opponents to carry this combined plan into effect, but to throw himself quickly upon one of them. This could of course only be done against Djezzar. No landing had as yet been effected in Lower Egypt, therefore there was as yet no enemy there to fight against; but the army in Syria was already fully formed, it had occupied Gaza, and pushed its vanguard forward as far as El Arish. Here then there was an opponent, and a march to Syria was therefore determined on. On the 2nd December, Bon was sent to Suez with a small detachment, to establish a depôt there. On the 26th, Napoleon arrived there in person and stayed three days, in order to examine the locality and make various arrangements. On the 2nd January, 1799,

Reynier advanced as far as Katieh, and on the last day of this month Napoleon gave orders for the general advance.

The army of operations in Syria consisted of the divisions of Kleber, Reynier, Bon and Lannes; each of these, however, being obliged to leave detachments behind to garrison Egypt, only numbered 2500 men; of cavalry, artillery and engineers there were about 3000 men with them. In Alexandria, Marmont held the chief command in the place of Kleber; that of Cairo was entrusted to Dugua. The whole army moved in the first place on El Arish: Napoleon himself left Cairo on the 10th February at 10 p.m. Lannes was at Belbeïs on the same day, and Bon at Salahieh.

Meanwhile, Reynier had arrived in front of El Arish the day before, had taken this village by storm, though it was obstinately defended by about 2000 men, and had thrown its defenders, still numbering 1500 men after their losses in the fight, back into the fort. And now the French were forced to open trenches against the latter, though it possessed no guns, and to place field artillery in position so as to effect a breach, for they could not with their small numbers afford the losses which an assault would entail. On the 12th, Kleber also arrived in front of El Arish. But, meanwhile, hostile troops were approaching from Gaza as well, and their numbers increasing daily, until they reached several thousands, they encamped on the 13th behind a dried-up watercourse in the face of the French. During the night of the 14th-15th, they were, however, surprised by Reynier, who had turned their position, and utterly routed. On the 17th, Napoleon himself arrived here, and on the 18th he could say: "The four divisions of infantry and the cavalry are assembled before El Arish, citizen-general, after having crossed the desert with ease, thanks to the measures which had been taken."[1] In the afternoon of the 20th,

[1] To Dugua, before El Arish.

El Arish surrendered, after a breach had been effected; but the resoluteness of the defenders in resisting to the utmost procured them very favourable conditions.

On the 21st February, Kleber was sent on in advance along the road to Gaza, and on the next day Bon and Lannes followed, Reynier remaining near El Arish until the 25th. Napoleon himself started on the 23rd, but when he arrived in Chan Junes, he ascertained that his divisions had lost their way, and did not succeed till the next day in concentrating them near this place. There was some hostile cavalry in front of him, but it fell back upon Gaza, and the French army, continuing its march, arrived before this town on the 25th. Here a corps of several thousand men was in position under Abdallah; but when Napoleon ordered his army to deploy and advance, they fell back without any serious resistance.

The army remained only two days in the neighbourhood of Gaza. Both the fort there and that of El Arish were placed in a proper state of defence, a precaution Napoleon never neglected for the security of his communications, for this bold and victorious general always took the possibility of a reverse into account in his plans of operation. Herein his art of war differed from his methods in politics. " You will understand that events may happen which would make El Arish the most advanced post of our line of operations, and, as this fort can hold out for a fortnight or even a month, it may be of incalculable value to us." [1]

On the 28th, the army, with Reynier's division as rearguard, started once more from Gaza, and on the 3rd March it arrived before Jaffa, Reynier following two days later. The capture of this town would give Napoleon access to the sea, and he was expecting supplies, as well as portions of a siege train from Alexandria by sea. Here again trenches were opened, the field guns placed in position, and Bon and Lannes began regular siege operations;

[1] To Caffarelli, Jaffa, 10th March.

Kleber being ordered forward on the road to Acre, to cover the siege. The garrison offered a determined resistance, and even ventured upon two sorties, which, however, were easily repulsed. On the 7th March, in the afternoon, the place was taken by storm, after a breach had been made, and the garrison, having refused to surrender, " were put to the sword, the town was given over to plunder, and suffered all the horrors of a place taken by assault." [1]

Indeed, it was not merely the fury of the soldiers, infuriated by resistance, that proved fatal to the defenders of Jaffa, but also the deliberate calculation of the commander-in-chief. About 2000 Turks had been taken prisoners. It was impossible for the French to carry them with them, for already the difficulties of the commissariat were exceedingly great; to liberate them on parole would have been a measure which, even among civilized nations, has often proved ineffective with respect to private soldiers, and, indeed, instances of officers of high rank could be quoted who broke their parole; to send them to Egypt would have required an escort which Napoleon could not spare, as well as provisions and stores which could not be procured or conveyed. For two days Napoleon thought about the matter, then issued this order: " You will order the adjutant-general on service to convey all the gunners and other Turks who were captured in Jaffa with arms in their hands to the sea-shore, and have them shot, taking care that none escape." [2]

In the eyes of mere didactic historical writers, this deed may appear horrible and revolting, but practical military history must not consider it as such. The safety of one's own army, on which the possibility depends of ultimately gaining the victory, must outweigh all other considerations. If such an act is necessary for the safety of one's army, it is not only justified, but its repetition in

[1] Napoleon, Mém., Camp. d'Egypte et de Syrie, II. 32.
[2] To Berthier, Jaffa, 9th March.

any future war would be advisable, and no convention could alter this fact. In the exceptional circumstances of warfare, no other motto is permissible but this, "Salus publica summa lex!" and any conclusion of conventions can, and is meant to be, binding only as far as the above principle allows. Cases will indeed occur in every war where the combatants are forced to violate the literal text of conventional laws for their own safety, and in such cases recriminations may indeed be defensible for political purposes, but are, for all that, untenable. Napoleon himself considered his action at Jaffa as quite natural, and spoke of it as such to his subordinate officers; it did not enter his head to discuss the necessity for his resolution. He wrote to Marmont: "The capture of Jaffa has been a brilliant affair; 4000 of the best troops of Djezzar and the best gunners of Constantinople had to be put to the sword;"[1] and to Kleber: "The garrison of Jaffa consisted of nearly 4000 men; 2000 were killed in the town, and nearly 2000 were shot between yesterday and to-day."[2] We mentioned some time ago that Napoleon could not really be said to have been cruel, but he did possess the strength of mind to be hard and to look on men at certain times as mere counters; and this strength of mind a general must possess.

Jaffa was now again placed in a state of defence, and three frigates received orders to set sail from Alexandria to that place; Reynier was left behind there for the present, whilst on the 14th March the army started upon its march to Acre. On the next morning Napoleon met a hostile corps at Korssum; it was forced to fall back, it is true, but owing to the broken ground, where the agility and local knowledge of the natives were of special advantage against the tactics of the French, it inflicted some losses upon Lannes' division which was pressing it too close; a fact which brought upon this general a

[1] Jaffa, 9th March. [2] Ibid.

reprimand from Napoleon: "We are not in a position to indulge in such feats of daring."[1] On the 17th the army entered the plain of Acre.

Napoleon took up his position on the reverse slope of a ridge, which stretched towards the north as far as the sea, and the occupation of which cut off Acre from the land, as this town lies on a sort of peninsula. Kleber was on the right wing, Lannes and Bon in the centre, Reynier, who had followed at an interval of two days' march, on the left wing. On the 19th the town fortifications were reconnoitred, and their appearance gave hopes that this town would fall no less speedily than Jaffa; a slight wound, however, which the reconnoitring engineer-officer sustained in his hand, induced him to give up any further attempt to gain a nearer view, and on his return he reported that the place had no counterscarp. The attack was begun on the 20th by opening trenches; it was directed against the eastern front. This front was formed by two sides meeting at a right angle; at the apex of this projecting angle there was a strong tower, commanding the other works of defence, and enfilading the two sides of the angle, and it was against this projecting tower that the attack was more especially directed.

To cover the siege from any attack from the outside, Napoleon watched the line of the Jordan, and stationed for this purpose four corps of observation at Haifa, Nazareth, Safed, and before Tyre. Having done this, he impressed upon their commanders the necessity of seeing that nothing crossed this line without their knowledge. "We shall feel secure, convinced that you will allow no enemy to cross this line between the mills of Daud and Sherdahm, without letting us know at once."[2]

On the 28th March the works had advanced so far that the breaching batteries could open fire against the tower, and in the afternoon, at three o'clock, the breach

---

[1] Bourrienne, Mém., II. 229.
[2] To Murat, before Acre, 10th April.

was considered practicable and orders were given for an assault. This, however, was foiled by the counterscarp of the ditch, an obstacle the existence of which was only now perceived. It is true, under the assumption that some counterscarp was probably in existence, a mine had been sunk, but it had not taken effect. Meanwhile, the town had received, about the beginning of March, a most valuable reinforcement in the shape of an English squadron under Sidney Smith; no complete investment was thus possible, and the road remained open for the arrival of war materials and provisions, besides which the fleet captured the vessels which were bringing up the heavy siege guns to Napoleon, and thus the latter was reduced to a great extent to mining for the further continuation of the siege; and we know what that means for the besiegers. Djezzar, aided by a late French officer of artillery and former comrade of Napoleon at the Paris Academy, Picard de Phélippeaux (he had left it number forty-first on the list, Napoleon being forty-second, next), as well as by some English officers and gunners, offered a resistance, of which the annals of Turkish warfare furnish so many examples in the defence of places open to assault or having practicable breaches in their walls; still, the various vigorous sorties he made were repulsed.

Meanwhile a relieving army was beginning to assemble in the neighbourhood of Damascus, and in the first week of April Napoleon received news that hostile bodies of troops were crossing the Jordan, both to the north and the south of Lake Tiberias, and also that depôts were being formed at Tiberias. A strong reconnaissance, conducted by Junot, met with superior forces no further off than Lubi, halfway between Nazareth and Tiberias, and fell back fighting to Nazareth.

To guard against these movements Napoleon sent Kleber to Nazareth, and on the 11th April the latter effected a junction with Junot. Advancing thence to Lubi, he met on the further side of Kana about 4000 men, mostly cavalry, and threw them back upon the Jordan; then, however, he retired to Nazareth, for he was justly afraid of being compelled, if he advanced immediately, to engage the whole relieving army.

The latter now crossed the Jordan in full strength by the Medschamia bridge to the south of Lake Tiberias; a detached corps crossing the bridge of Jakub on the north of the lake, invested Safed. Napoleon, in order to block the retreat of the latter, sent Murat early in the morning of the 14th, to the bridge of Jakub, ordering Kleber at the same time to continue to watch the relieving army and to prevent it moving on Acre. However, it was not at present advancing directly on Acre, but moved on the 14th to the left to the plain of Esdrelon, where it received reinforcements from Samaria and Nablus; its total strength possibly amounted at this time to 15,000 men.

Kleber noticed this movement and remembered Napoleon's injunction: "If, in the varied movements which may occur, you can find means to put yourself between the enemy and the Jordan, do so, without being deterred by the thought, that this might cause them to march against us,"[1] he therefore resolved now to carry out this manœuvre, and reported that he would start on the 14th. Thereupon Napoleon conceived the plan of acting according to the principle which he followed before Mantua, namely, first to deal with the relieving army and to employ as many troops as possible from the besieging army for this purpose; of course the great tactical superiority of his army permitted him in this case to keep up the siege at the same time.

Consequently he started on the 15th with Bon's division *via* Nazareth, in order to come in touch with Kleber. The latter had meanwhile gained the line of retreat of the Turkish army to the Jordan, and resolved to attack it during the night of the 15th-16th, again acting on Napo-

[1] Before Acre, 13th April.

leon's directions: "Should the enemy dare to pitch his camp close to yours, the commander-in-chief is sure you will make a night attack on him, which will have the same result as that of El Arish."[1] However, this plan failed. The morning of the 16th came before Kleber reached the enemy, and in the plain, bounded on the north-east by Mount Tabor, he saw himself soon surrounded on all sides and attacked by superior forces. He formed his troops into two squares, and in this formation he was successful in repulsing all attacks, until Napoleon appeared, who in the meantime had quite turned the enemy and shut him in between himself and Kleber. The Turks succumbed entirely to the combined attack and fled with great losses, partly beyond the Jordan and partly into the mountains. Then Napoleon returned with Bon to the army before Acre; Kleber resumed his position near Nazareth, after having first pursued the fugitive enemy on the 17th as far as the Jordan.

Meanwhile, at Acre a mine had been constructed, in order to open a breach in the large tower, and Napoleon reckoned with full confidence upon success; in a letter to Dugua he already anticipated the surrender of the town on 25th April. Besides, nine heavy guns had been landed safely at Tantura by three frigates coming from Alexandria, and these were now on the road to the besieging force.

On the 24th Napoleon ordered the great mine to be fired, but the result was insufficient, part of its effect being lost in a subterranean chamber, and the breach was not sufficiently practicable to begin the assault. Consequently the bombardment continued for a few days in order to complete the breach, and on the 30th April the first heavy guns were placed in position.

In addition to the breach in the great tower, Napoleon now gave orders to direct the guns, so as to open a breach in the curtain to the east of it, and pushed forward mines in

[1] Before Acre, 14th April.

order to destroy the counterscarp opposite the proposed second breach. In the meantime, however, the enemy began a counter attack, and ran counter approaches along the front of attack from two places d'armes; an attempt to eject them from these works had only a temporary success; whilst they on their side succeeded in reaching and destroying the mine in front of the curtain opposite the counterscarp. Now Napoleon's efforts were again directed against the big tower and the enemy's outworks. After a fruitless attempt on the 6th, he succeeded in the evening of the 7th May in taking the enemy's places d'armes and the works on the glacis, and also in occupying the large tower. On the 9th, the batteries resumed their fire, after want of powder had silenced them for a few days; the main fire was now directed against the curtain, for, being masters of the ditch, the French were now able to make use of the breach there; but there was as yet no access to the town from the tower, and the besieged had thrown up new defences inside the inner wall.

Early in the morning of the 10th, the French army prepared for the assault; Kleber also had been ordered up for it; the breach in the curtain appeared practicable; the principal storming column indeed reached it, but the defenders were successful in recovering their places d'armes, and from them, advancing along the ditch, they attacked this column in the rear, whilst the breach itself was meanwhile so effectually enfiladed from the traverses and a tower on the wall, that the storming party could not stand their ground in it. The men fell back, and the assault had failed.

This was the first real check Napoleon met with, for the repulse of this assault meant the loss of the campaign; the number of days which he could still stop before Acre were very few. He could not repeat the assault; in his army the plague was raging; from Egypt news was continually arriving of fresh troubles having broken out, and the landing of a Turkish army in Lower

Egypt was now impending. And what hopes had he not built upon the fall of Acre, whilst lying before the place with 10,000 men and 3000 sick and wounded! He had intended to call up the nations of the Orient, take possession of Constantinople, overthrow the Turkish empire, found a new empire under his own rule, and return victorious through Vienna to Paris. And this whole tremendous edifice of his imagination had now crumbled at a blow.

Here already we may see in his mind some premonitory symptoms of his ultimate fate, which indeed, it would almost seem, are inseparable from the nature of the greatest soldiers, namely, a want of control of the imagination. He who restrains himself will do deeds that will live, and in this respect the poet's address to the Great Elector is profoundly true :[1]

> "The dullard's aim, not thine it is,
> To try to win Fate's brightest crown."

'Tis true, the highest success, though we can grasp it in imagination, will always be beyond our realization, for our means, finite, like all human things, militate against the infinity of our aims. But the general who at all times cultivates self-restraint, risks stopping short also of what is possible, and lessens his chances of success, and therefore he will satisfy our highest expectations only by never being satisfied himself, and aiming, after each success, at something still higher. "A general has only one aim, a general who is also a sovereign must have two. His actions as a soldier will always be subordinate to politics."[2] But only he who devotes himself fully and wholly to one thing is able to attain perfection, and therefore the ideal sovereign will never be an ideal general ; politics lay restraints upon a sovereign in his career as a general, and if he be a great sovereign he submits to these restraints, but just because

---
[1] Kleist, Prinz von Homburg, II. 293.
[2] Müffling, Die Feldzüge der Schlesischen Armée, 52.

he restrains himself and does not seek for the highest success, he cannot be considered the highest ideal of a general. A shrewd student of biography said of Charlemagne: "He was a military leader greater than most, but he was not ambitious of glory gained in battle, still less did he envy his generals such glory, and in this also he differed from the most eminent heroes of ancient and modern times. For actual war was ever, with him, only a means to an end. He himself gained several decisive victories as leader of his army; but he conducted many campaigns by proxy, for he felt that his task was a higher one, and this, the highest virtue of a king, he showed not only in his more advanced age, but even in his youth."[1] Had Napoleon acted thus, he would have died on his throne as one of the most admired founders of a state and dynasty; but he would never have marched in triumph into Vienna, Berlin, Madrid, or Moscow, and military history would have lost its highest exemplar.

On the 17th May, Napoleon issued a proclamation to his army, in which he announced its approaching return to Egypt, and veiled as much as possible of his defeat. All preparations were made for the start, all stores were destroyed, the guns, which could not be transported, were blown up or sunk in the sea, and on the 18th and 19th all the wounded, sick, and non-combatants were sent on in advance, whilst all the time the fire against Acre was kept up vigorously. At last, on the 20th May, at nine o'clock in the evening, the army itself began its retreat. Lannes was at the head, followed by Bon and then Reynier, Kleber for the present remaining in position to cover the departure, and then acting as rear-guard with his division. In this order the army retreated, suffering the most severe hardships, in forced marches, moving by Tantura and Cæsarea, yet overtaken by the enemy, whose effective pursuit was rendered difficult by a complete devastation of the country. On the 24th Jaffa was reached, where the exhausted

[1] Freytag, Aus dem Mittelalter, 321.

army was granted a few days of rest; these days were employed in blowing up the fortifications of this town and destroying its means of defence. On the 28th, the army continued its march to Egypt; at El-Arish, Napoleon left a small garrison, and from Katieh, which also received a garrison, he sent Kleber to Damietta, he himself marching towards Cairo with the other three divisions. He entered this town in state on the 14th June, that is, on the twenty-sixth day after his start from Acre. The distance traversed during this time by his army amounted to over 300 miles, without reckoning détours, a performance which if executed on a European theatre of war would be mentioned with respect, but which is really nothing less than marvellous under the circumstances, after a severe siege, in such a climate, without proper roads, and considering the continual struggle with want of water and stores, with sickness and with the desert.

Once more at Cairo, Napoleon again occupied himself with the administration of the country and the organization of his army; he more particularly endeavoured to devise means to raise the numerical strength of the latter. His losses up to that time he computed at 5344 men, and this number, although not very high, considering the circumstances, may probably be taken as accurate, for he reported it to the Directory in a despatch in which he asks for reinforcements, in which, therefore, he had no reason for underrating his losses; though, on the other hand, he was desirous, for obvious reasons, of making the best of his position. Meanwhile he wrote to Desaix: " I should like, citizen-general, to purchase 2000 or 3000 negroes, above sixteen years, and put about 100 of them into each battalion."[1] This indeed points to ominous gaps, and therefore we may assume, that to the above-mentioned number of losses must be added a considerable number of sick and wounded, on whose recovery Napoleon reckoned, and whom he therefore did not include in his

[1] Cairo, 22nd June

losses. In the course of the coming year, Napoleon anticipated a further loss of 6000 men, and estimated the eventual active strength of his army at 15,000 men; thus he was at that moment at the head of about 21,000. But this computation was probably intentionally low, as he based upon it his demand for reinforcements. If we deduct from the original number of 30,000 men a loss of 5000, he ought still to have had 25,000 at his disposal, that is, 4000 more than above reckoned; and, assuming that about one half of these 4000 were unfit for active service, from wounds or sickness, there would remain in June, 1799, an effective force of 23,000 men; a very favourable result, indeed, and one which was of course owing to the fact that his losses in battle against such opponents were infinitesimal.

Napoleon's plan of incorporating 3000 negroes in his army shows, moreover, very distinctly how little he cared about the quality of his instruments in the consciousness of his innate genius; he counts by heads; it is the value of numbers in warfare, which becomes evident here; indeed Napoleon's strategy introduced this value as the decisive factor in the modern art of war; the strategy of Frederick's day did not recognize it. This new element in strategy and its importance was at first, as is always the case with anything new, scarcely acknowledged and in no way utilized; and thus it came to pass that Napoleon in 1805, and again in 1807, appeared in the field against two great military powers with an overwhelming superiority of numbers. Of the few voices which at that time already advocated the principle of masses, one of the most notable was that of Bülow, a man of the highest abilities: "The superiority of the larger number of combatants over the lesser is very evident in modern strategy, if only on account of the necessity of preventing turning movements, and the advantage which turning movements afford. If you have more men than the enemy and know how to use them properly, the greater ability and bravery of the soldiers of your opponent is of no account."[1]

Napoleon found Egypt on the whole in a peaceful state. Dugua had managed to maintain order and to nip a few attempts at revolt in the bud. Desaix had meanwhile traversed Upper Egypt, and had arrived at Assuan on the cataracts of the Nile on the 1st February, 1799, forcing Murad Bey back into Æthiopia (the Soudan). This latter chief now retired into the desert, and numerous incursions of the Arabs into the Nile valley from the desert on both sides of the stream compelled Desaix's troops to make incessant marches and counter-marches. Murad even attempted in the beginning of July to reach Cairo by advancing through the province of Fayoum; but Napoleon, informed of this plan by Desaix, sent Murat to meet him, and Murad immediately fell back into the desert, but pushed forward at once again towards Gizeh. Murat followed him, and Napoleon sent a small detachment towards the Pyramids on July 14th to reconnoitre. He was intending to join this detachment himself, when he received news from Marmont that a Turkish fleet, apparently with land forces on board, had appeared in the roadstead of Aboukir.

He now determined to evacuate the whole of Upper Egypt and to bring up Desaix to Cairo, whilst he himself would go to meet the invading army, as soon as he was convinced that the object of the fleet was to land troops to any serious extent. For the present he sent orders to Desaix to move towards Benissuof. Napoleon himself proceeded on the morning of the 15th to the Pyramids of Gizeh, but Murad had already begun his retreat, and only a few shots were exchanged with his skirmishers. But now fresh news arrived from Marmont, announcing a reinforcement of the hostile fleet by some twenty ships, and reporting a landing of troops as imminent. With characteristic rapidity of resolve, Napoleon now formed the

[1] Spirit of Modern Strategy, 209.

plan of throwing himself on the invading army, and carried this project into execution without delay. He handed over the chief command in Cairo to Dugua, sent orders to Kleber to march to Rosetta, ordered Desaix up to Cairo, whilst Lannes and Rampon (the latter of whom had taken the place of Bon, who had died of the wound received in Syria) at once began their march towards Ramanieh on the 16th at one o'clock in the morning; Murat was to precede them with his advance-guard, accompanied also by the detachment collected at Gizeh against Murad. Napoleon started for Lower Egypt with 6000 men in all.

Here, meanwhile, the Turkish army, 12,000 men, had effected their landing at Aboukir and seized this fortified place on the 15th; it entrenched itself immediately on the peninsula. Marmont, who had at first marched with the garrison at Alexandria, 1200 men, on the morning of the 15th, in order to resist the landing, wheeled about upon hearing that this had already been effected, and resolved to hold out in Alexandria until Napoleon's arrival. The latter had arrived in Ramanieh on the 19th July, and remained there until the 22nd, in order to collect his army.

The following was now his view of the situation, as he explained it in a letter to Kleber: "It seems as if the enemy had really landed at Aboukir and was at this moment in possession of the works there."[1]

"My line of operations is Alexandria, Birket, Rosetta. I shall remain at Birket with the main body of the army." (In a letter to Menou, he said: "Birket is the centre of all my operations.")[2] "General Marmont is at Alexandria, you are at Rosetta, with about equal forces; you, therefore, form the right wing, General Marmont the left, and I the centre. If the enemy is in strength, I shall give battle on favourable ground, by joining either my right or my left wing, and I will try to arrange that

[1] El Ramanieh, 20th July.   [2] El Ramanieh, 21st July.

whichever of you cannot be present with me may be able to come up in support so as to form a reserve."

The whole plan of operations in Lower Egypt thus again illustrated the two great principles which we have recognized so clearly in his strategy hitherto:—

1. Not to advance against the enemy in separate columns, but to form mass first.

2. To collect all possible forces to the last man for the delivery of a battle.

The former was shown first by the fact that Napoleon collected the troops, which he intended to lead against the Turks, from their different quarters in the country, at Ramanieh, that is, at a point which he was sure of reaching before the enemy. But here one might have expected him to operate by separate columns, for the purpose of turning the enemy: Marmont from Alexandria, Kleber from Rosetta, Napoleon from Birket, all marching simultaneously to Aboukir; they stood, so to speak, ready for some such movement. But no, the conviction, that his forces must be united before coming in contact with the enemy, was too deeply rooted in Napoleon, and he therefore determined, first to effect a junction with one of his wings, since it was no longer possible to call in both, and then to give battle. The other wing, moreover, he did not send to Aboukir, in which movement it might perhaps, if the Turks advanced, have met, unsupported, their superior forces, but he ordered it up to join him as a reserve.

Kleber accordingly received orders to keep himself in readiness for a start at a moment's notice, either for Birket or for Etko; meanwhile he was to remain in continual touch with Napoleon; Dugua was ordered to send up whatever troops he could possibly spare, for "the commander-in-chief requires all his forces in order to attack the enemy."[1] Murat was sent forward on the 20th to Besseïntuan and Birket, to reconnoitre and open

[1] El Ramanieh, 20th July, 8 o'clock in the evening.

communications with Marmont. The latter was advised to keep a good look-out; should the enemy offer him a capitulation, he was to hint that, if he really saw himself shut in, he would not be disinclined to consider it, "for I should look upon it as a great stroke of luck, if the ease with which they have taken Aboukir induced them to invest you, for in that case they would be lost."[1]

But on the 22nd Napoleon was forced to realize that the enemy had no intention of undertaking anything against Alexandria, but had intrenched themselves at Aboukir; he therefore resolved to march against them to see whether it would be possible to attack them; and ordered, on this day, Lannes to Birket, and Lanusse (who had replaced Bon) to Besseïntuan. On the 23rd the army was accordingly at Birket, during the night it advanced further towards Alexandria and encamped ten miles from that town. Napoleon himself, hastening on in front of the army, arrived, in the evening of the 23rd, at Alexandria to join Marmont; he inspected his works, which he found in good condition, and learned that the enemy numbered about 15,000, and were still engaged in intrenching themselves at Aboukir; he now selected a small detachment from the garrison and occupied with it a position important on account of its wells, about half-way between Alexandria and the enemy. He immediately sent orders to his army to join him, and in the night between the 24th and 25th, about midnight, it was assembled there; Kleber had sent news that he was at Fuah on the Nile.

Napoleon now issued the following orders: "Murat with the whole vanguard (together with the detachment brought from Alexandria to be added also) will start at two o'clock and make straight for the enemy; the army will follow Lannes on the right, Lanusse on the left. Kleber will follow as quickly as possible to Aboukir as a

[1] El Ramanieh, 21st July.

reserve. Menou will make a sortie from Rosetta with a few hundred men, so as to harass the enemy and engage his attention in that quarter."

Thus in the early morning the army marched upon Aboukir. There the Turkish army had placed itself in battle array in front of the fortress in two imperfectly intrenched lines, with its wings resting on the sea. The infantry of Napoleon's van-guard began the attack on the right wing of the enemy's first line, whilst Lannes faced the left wing; Murat with all his cavalry formed the centre; Lanusse was in the second line behind the left wing. The enemy's right wing immediately relinquished its position and fell back upon their second line; their left wing, now quite isolated, was entirely turned by Lannes' attack, and cut down or forced into the sea to the last man. Some bodies of troops from the second Turkish line advancing to its support, were thrown back upon their comrades, part being driven into the sea. And now the French army reformed, before proceeding to the attack of the second line.

This line, situated in front of the fort of Aboukir, consisted of a strong earthwork in the centre, from which to the right and left there ran trenches. Napoleon now ordered the infantry of the van-guard to attack the earthwork in front, whilst the whole cavalry was to keep the enemy's left wing in check; Lanusse, who had by this time marched in position on the left wing, was ordered to turn the enemy's right wing completely, by engaging it in front with the 32nd demi-brigade[1] and interposing with the 18th between it and the sea. This attack, however, undertaken under the enfilading fire from the earthwork, failed; Lanusse did not succeed in either driving the Turks from their trenches or turning their right flank, and had to fall back. But now Lannes delivered with two battalions an assault upon the earthwork itself, whilst at

[1] As is well known, this is equivalent to "regiment," a term abandoned on political grounds.—TR.

the same time Murat overthrew the cavalry on the enemy's left wing, and Lanusse led the 18th demi-brigade once more to the attack of the enemy's right wing. The assault on the earthwork was successful; Lannes entered it by the gorge and from the right, and as one of Murat's squadrons, breaking through the enemy's lines, got behind the work, its defenders lost all chance of retreat and were partly cut down, partly taken prisoners. From the earthwork the whole right wing of the enemy was rolled up and driven into the sea, the Turkish army was entirely shattered, some weak remnants only taking refuge in the fortress.

It was a regular Napoleonic battle, a battle which annihilated the enemy, and he wrote triumphantly to Dugua : " The general staff will have informed you of the result of the battle of Aboukir; it was one of the finest I ever saw, not a man escaped of the army landed." [1]

On the next day Napoleon summoned the fortress of Aboukir to surrender; this was however refused. The bombardment which began immediately was resisted as well as was possible under the circumstances ; but on the 2nd August the garrison had at last to surrender.

Having waited for the fall of this fortress, Napoleon left Alexandria on the 5th and arrived on the 10th again in Cairo. But his resolution to leave Egypt without delay was already taken. It is probably impossible to determine definitely when it became matured ; very likely it had always been secretly entertained by him. He could scarcely have conceived it for the first time after an envoy, sent to the English fleet in consequence of Aboukir, returned with the latest news from Europe. He probably was not so completely cut off from all news as he and his suite afterwards pretended ; too many people in France, more especially his brothers, were anxious to keep him posted in current affairs, nor had he himself ever lost sight of that country in all his plans.

[1] In front of Aboukir, 27th July.

Be this however as it may, being now fully informed of the unfortunate position of affairs in France, and of the successes of the allies against that country, he considered the time had come to throw his sword there into the scale and to take a decisive position in the Government. "What is the use of those incapable men at the head of affairs? With them there is nothing but ignorance, stupidity, and venality. I, I alone, have borne the burden and have given stability to this Government by my uninterrupted successes, for without me it could never have come into existence nor have lasted."[1] In spite of the exaggeration contained in these utterances, Napoleon was more or less justified in speaking thus, for the great majority of Frenchmen looked upon matters in exactly the same way as he did, and saw in him the only possible saviour. And now his new laurels of Aboukir allowed him to appear in France with all the ascendency of a victor; after Acre he could not have left Egypt; this victory rendered it possible, and it was for this that he had this enigmatical utterance to Murat on the night before the battle: "This battle will decide the fate of the world."[2]

For the present he occupied himself with administrative duties, ever desirous of discrediting by his actions all rumours of his departure, which kept arising in spite of all his attempts to secure secrecy; for he was well aware that his army, seeing in him their sole salvation, would never let him leave them without opposition.

It is true the great principle of the effect of masses is the most important factor in strategy, but it is the work of the master mind to set these masses in motion and to employ them at the decisive point, and therefore victory is due to the master mind, that is, to the general himself; the thousands who are drowned in the sea, shot down or surrender helplessly as prisoners of war, succumb to the physical power of the enemy who outnumber them in that one place, but it was the brain of the general that brought

[1] Marmont, Mém. II. 32.   [2] Miot, Mém. 258.

those superior numbers there. The greater the mass the larger its resistance from inertia or obstinacy, and consequently the more comprehensive and energetic the mind of him who sets it in motion must be. Therefore, in his very fondness for employing masses, lies the proof of Napoleon's genius as a strategist. In this sense his march to Russia, which condemned him as a statesman, was his greatest achievement as a strategist.

In the middle of August Marmont, whom Napoleon had entrusted with this mission, sent news that the moment seemed favourable. Sydney Smith, who had been watching the coast of Alexandria, had just sailed for Cyprus in order to replenish his water supplies. Immediately, on the 18th of the month, Napoleon left Cairo, went to Alexandria, sent from there orders to Kleber to assume chief command of the army, and set sail on the 23rd, at five o'clock in the morning, on board the frigate "Muiron," accompanied by Berthier, Murat, Lannes, and Marmont. In the morning of the 9th October he landed at Fréjus, and was received by the populace with joyful acclamations.

The marvellous good luck which allowed him during the forty-seven days of this passage to escape again and again from the most imminent danger, made no less an impression upon his companions than his victories. "We felt that we owed it to the intervention of Providence. If ever a human being had reason to believe in the protection of a divine hand, in a guiding power watching over him and preparing all things necessary for the success of his enterprises, it was Bonaparte."[1] Indeed, the occurrences of life prove so often the insufficiency of human foresight, that surely almost every man has had reason to exclaim : "I entered upon this enterprise, though it seemed to me sufficiently foolhardy; in this as in a thousand other circumstances the want of prudence will assuredly be compensated for by boldness

[1] Marmont, Mém. II. 41.

of execution, and Fortune will probably once more crown with success endeavours which cool reason would never have dreamed of."[1] Indeed it is exactly courage in conceiving assurance of success, and resolution in execution, which ensure the happy issue of a project. Those very persons who looked upon Napoleon's good luck with an astonishment akin to superstition, used to say: "It is true, he knew *when* to run risks, and this quality is the most necessary of all in the accomplishment of great deeds. He risked much, but he risked at the right moment, and if circumstances never left him in the lurch, it was because he was always equal to the occasion."[2]

[1] Kleber to the Countess of . . . Toulon, 8th May, 1798.
[2] Marmont, Mém. II. 41.

CHAPTER VIII.

MARENGO.

1800.

THE 18th Brumaire had, in fact, invested Napoleon with the full powers of an autocratic sovereign. The first appearance of the modern representative system of government on the continent had furnished ample evidence of the vacillating and constantly changing nature of such governments, and shown at the same time that such a system must, in the exposed position of a continental state, lead quite logically to constant disaster. Therefore the whole nation greeted Napoleon with acclamation when he seized the sceptre in accordance with the principle : "If a man feels within himself the strength and capacity for government, he should, if possible, seize the rudder of the state, if it is in incapable hands."[1]

We shall not dwell here on how he wielded his power as a statesman. We will only say one thing, and that briefly. We have spoken of his strategy as the most perfect of modern times, and in this point even Frederick must yield him the palm. But his acts as a sovereign are a different matter. Frederick's conquests were acquisitions, which, being soon absorbed by his own people, augmented the strength of the latter, and made it capable of greater extension and development. Napoleon's conquests remained alien incorporations, which did not open up any new sources of strength, but rather required ever

[1] Bülow, Campaign of 1805, II. 138.

fresh exertions of strength for their retention. The form of Frederick's despotism soon came to nothing, but the training it had afforded his nation continued to influence, and is still influencing it; the forms created by Napoleon's despotism are still in power in France, but whatever this country may possess of lasting political ideas and real strength, it owes to another despot, a greater statesman, Richelieu. In comparing the statecraft of a Richelieu, a Frederick, a Bismarck, with that of Napoleon, we recognize in the former a positive, limited fixed goal, something attainable, as distinguished by something indefinite in the latter.

Napoleon inaugurated his reign by negotiations for peace. But the whole situation of Europe was at that time too unsettled to allow of the possibility of a lasting peace. On both sides the negotiations were carried on with a want of sincerity, and could not therefore lead to any decisive issue. They were therefore soon broken off, and it was decided to resume hostilities.

In the beginning of 1800, the military situation on the frontiers of France was the following :— (25)

In Italy, Massena was posted with 30,000 men on the line Genoa—Savona—Col di Tenda; some 10,000 more occupied the passes of the Alps. Opposed to these was Melas, with 80,000 men in Piedmont, whilst some 20,000 of his troops were distributed as garrisons throughout Upper Italy, Tuscany, and the Romagna.

In Germany, Moreau had 120,000 men facing Alsace and Switzerland; in front of him was Kray, on the other side of the Rhine, with 120,000 men at Donaueschingen, with his right wing on the Kinzig and his left at Schaffhausen. If the French Republic wished to retrieve the situation created by its unfortunate campaigns in 1799, and deal its adversaries some great blow, it would have to put very large forces in the field. Napoleon, of course, was of this mind, and therefore he gave orders to Berthier, who was at that time secretary, to organize a reserve army, the chief command of which he reserved for himself. It was to consist of a right wing, with its depôt at Lyons, a centre, with Dijon as depôt, and a left wing with its depôt at Chalons-sur-Marne, each of these corps of a strength of 18,000 to 20,000 men. His orders concluded with these words: "You will keep the formation of this army in every way secret, even from your assistants, from whom you will ask for only the most indispensable information."[1]

Here, then, we see Napoleon for the first time acting independently in the initiation of a war as a whole. The question he had to decide was what to do with the new army, to use it in Italy or in Germany, against Melas or Kray. The map will show us that Germany was the decisive point. Kray once beaten, the French would be able to march without resistance to Vienna, or take Melas in rear with superior numbers in Italy. Napoleon himself explained this with perfect clearness: "In this campaign, the frontier of Germany is the decisive point, the littoral of Genoa a secondary one. Indeed, any events which might occur in Italy would not have any direct or immediate effect upon the state of affairs on the Rhine, whilst all the events which would happen in Germany would have a necessary and immediate effect upon Italy."[2] "As a matter of fact, should the army of the Republic be defeated on the Rhine, though it were victorious in Italy, the Austrian army could penetrate Alsace, Franche-Comté, or Belgium, and complete their success without the French army being in a position to create any diversion, or arrest its course. But if the French army at the decisive point were successful, even though that of Italy were beaten, all that would have to be feared would be the capture of Genoa, an invasion of Provence, or perhaps the siege of Toulon, but in that case, a portion of the army of Germany would, by descending

---

[1] C. N. Paris, 25th January.
[2] Mém. de Ste. Hél. Ulm—Moreau, II. 485.

from Switzerland into the valley of the Po, immediately arrest the victorious enemy in Italy or Provence."¹

Therefore, Napoleon turned first to Germany, to strike the decisive blow of the war, and it was his intention to unite the reserve army with that of Moreau, in order, thus, to have a decided superiority of numbers as against Kray. His plan was to concentrate his whole army, covered by the Rhine, in the neighbourhood of Schaffhausen and Stein, then to cross the Rhine at Schaffhausen, and appear at the very commencement of the campaign with superior forces on Kray's left flank and rear, to cut him off from all his communications, and to force him towards the Rhine, then his army would be destroyed, and the road to Vienna would be perfectly open.

It is this method of opening campaigns which shows the Napoleonic strategy in all its inspired simplicity, in all its directness, aiming at a complete annihilation of the enemy. He planned his operations against Kray's left wing, just as he did those against Melas' right wing, and he carried out the same methods in 1805 against the Austrian right, and in 1806 against the Prussian left wing; the same plan was also formed for his advance over the Saale in April, 1813. The principles, few but great, which he thereby formulated and obeyed, are the following:—

First, the principle of having only one line of operations. Napoleon always kept the mass of his army massed in one direction; any other method, such, for example, as that of Frederick in 1757, when he advanced into Bohemia along four lines of operation, at a considerable distance from each other, he rejected as false, since it gave the enemy the chance of attacking one column with his whole strength.

Secondly, the principle of making the main body of the enemy's army the objective.

¹ Mém. de Ste. Hél. Notes sur le précis des événements mil., &c. (M. Dumas), II. 592.

Thirdly, the principle of choosing the line of operation in such a manner as to place oneself on one flank, or, if possible, on the rear of the enemy, and thus cut his communications.

Fourthly, the principle, which follows logically upon the third, of turning, what Willisen calls the enemy's strategical wing, that is, the one, the turning of which will most effectually drive him off his lines of communication. Had Napoleon, for instance, in the case before us, planned to turn Kray's right wing, the most he could have hoped to do was to drive him into the Tyrol, and one line of communications would still have remained open to him.

Fifthly, the principle of keeping one's own communications open.

But personal considerations forced Napoleon to alter his magnificent plan to some extent. He had of course intended to take into his own hands the supreme command of the reserve army united with Moreau's; but it now became evident that Moreau refused to serve under him, and Napoleon's position was not yet sufficiently assured, either to remove this general without further ado, or to entrust Moreau with the chief command of both armies; the latter might easily have gained too much political influence thereby. Moreover, as soon became evident, the plan of a genius, simple though it be, requires the genius of its originator to carry it out properly. For when Napoleon proposed to Moreau the execution of this very plan, for which indeed the latter's army was strong enough by itself, Moreau was unable to agree with Napoleon's ideas. Strange to say, he considered such a concentrated advance dangerous, and would rather have seen the crossing of the Rhine effected at various points along the line from Strasburg to Schaffhausen; a glance at the map will show that he would thus meet Kray frontally, and thereby the kernel of the whole plan, namely, placing the enemy at the very commencement of the campaign in the most unfavourable position, and striking at his weakest point, would be lost. When Napoleon, therefore, commanded him on the 1st March to concentrate between Bâle and Constance, and to send his chief of the staff immediately to Paris, where the general plan of operations would be communicated to him, this officer brought such entirely divergent views about the method of opening the campaign with him, that Napoleon soon saw he could never have his ideas carried out by Moreau.

And he was all the more ready to leave it to Moreau to cross the Rhine and open the campaign in whatever manner he thought fit, as this theatre of war and the operations upon it would no longer play the decisive part from the moment when he relinquished the idea of using the reserve army in Germany. The army of Germany was, therefore, directed on the 22nd March to cross the Rhine between the 10th and 20th April, to push forward to Stockach, and to throw the enemy behind the Lech; one division under Lecourbe was to remain in Switzerland as a reserve. As soon as the above was done, this division and the three first divisions of the reserve army were to cross the St. Gothard into Italy, whilst the three remaining divisions, consisting of troops of inferior quality, were to follow as a reserve to Zurich at the end of April. It was therefore in Italy that the decisive blow was now to be struck, and it was left for Moreau to cover the rear and left flank of this army while invading Italy, by an advance to the south of the Danube.

Let us now glance at Italy. As early as the 5th March Napoleon had communicated his views to Massena, as to the latter's situation. It was his advice to concentrate four-fifths of all his forces at Genoa, and to push on from that place, always with his force well in hand against one point only of the Austrian line of advance; this plan would undoubtedly bring about some secondary results, for the Austrians were sure to indulge again in concentric operations of separated columns: "the enemy is sure to make three attacks in the Austrian manner, along the Levante, *viâ* Novi and *viâ* Montenotte; you will avoid two of these attacks and meet the third with your full strength." The eternal principle: "A division of forces against several objects at the same time results in the inability to act with proper effect against any one of them. One weakens oneself thereby, and affords the enemy an opportunity of annihilating his opponent in detail. One can only expect to be successful, where one can bring larger numbers to bear than the enemy. It is the masses which decide. Union is strength, division weakness."[1] Bülow preached this doctrine, Jomini and Willisen concur in it, Napoleon's actions demonstrate it, and his words confirm it.

On the 8th March official orders were issued, that a reserve army of 60,000 men was to be formed and was to assemble at Dijon; the First Consul himself would assume the chief command. But one of the articles of the constitution forbade the First Consul to take the command of any army in person, and therefore Berthier was appointed to the chief command of the reserve army on the 2nd April. Marmont observes with justice, "this was the same thing as keeping him under another name as chief of the staff." Napoleon was used to him and his methods of doing business: we have indeed evidence that he was not, generally speaking, fond of changing his men, he "was a creature of habit, and disliked nothing more than change, and, as he himself said, new faces."[2]

The Reserve Army was, according to the official notice, to concentrate at Dijon, but in reality the various troops forming it were all immediately set in motion for Switzerland; the public notification of Dijon as the point of

[1] Bülow, Geist des neueren Kriegssystems, 57.
[2] Bourrienne, Mem. III. 119.

concentration was intended to mislead the enemy, and the news which the Austrians obtained as to the importance of the forces at Dijon, soon had the effect of destroying their belief in the existence of any real reserve army.

On the 18th March Napoleon, presuming it to have arrived at Zurich, drew up the line of march to be followed from thence to Bergamo *viâ* the Splügen. We shall see presently how, in accordance with events, the point of crossing was gradually shifted westward. On the 9th April he wrote to Massena and communicated to him the plan agreed upon for the operations of the Army of the Rhine; he enjoined him to keep strictly on the defensive until the army, falling from Switzerland upon the enemy's rear, either by the Gothard or the Simplon, had appeared in Italy, when he was immediately to attempt a junction with its right wing *viâ* Turin. In the meantime, however, Melas had, on the 6th April, already assumed the offensive against Massena with 60,000 men, and exactly as Napoleon's keen military insight had anticipated, namely by advancing concentrically from three directions, Massena opposed a resistance to these superior numbers, which showed his military capacity in the most brilliant light. Taking the utmost advantage of the mountainous nature of the country, and being always prepared to reassume the offensive, he exhibited a splendid example of the way to conduct a retreat, yielding step by step, and a magnificent illustration of Napoleon's words: " To act otherwise would no longer be called waging war; for the art of war consists only in gaining time, if one's forces are inferior."[1] By the 19th April, Massena was forced back upon Genoa and surrounded in his position there.

Napoleon had only very uncertain news about these events; the turning movement of Melas and his superior forces had soon cut off all Massena's communications with France, and therefore Napoleon knew even on the 24th April, nothing more than that " the Army of Italy is

[1] C. N. To Joubert. 17th February, 1797.

engaging the Austrians;"[1] for the rest, he continued: "but whether it win or lose, it is absolutely necessary that the Reserve Army should not waste an hour." Berthier therefore received orders to lead the army to Geneva, and thence to invade Italy either by the Great St. Bernard or the Simplon; his army Napoleon estimated at this time at 40,000 men. Now Moreau had, with his usual caution, in spite of all his promises, not yet opened the campaign; therefore Napoleon wrote: "Do repeat to Moreau the command to attack the enemy. Try to make him understand that his constant delay endangers the safety of the Republic materially." The fact was, Moreau's advance was to render possible the march across the Alps, for otherwise the army so employed would have exposed its left wing, nay, possibly even its rear, to Kray's attack.

Here for the first time we find the St. Bernard mentioned; that is to say, the point of crossing the Alps has been changed from the Splügen to the St. Bernard, some 140 miles off, and the point of entrance into Italy from Bergamo to Ivrea, or some 90 miles further west. When, through Moreau's inaction, the speedy and final decision with Kray appeared less and less likely, the more extensive operation over the Splügen was given up, and the Gothard or Simplon taken into consideration. Then, when Melas took the offensive, it became necessary to act speedily and effectually; so the point of crossing had to be fixed on still nearer home, so as to expedite the operation.

Indeed, it will usually happen, if the enemy's army itself is the objective, that the originally chosen line of operations is gradually altered, for the enemy rarely remains on the same spot; it is like aiming at a moving target. The movement against Ulm in 1805 was of the same nature. Thus the Napoleonic principle, to assemble the mass of troops on one line of operations only, becomes of all the greater importance; for if a general

[1] C. N. To Carnot. Paris.

has been deceived, as often happens, with respect to the enemy's position or movements, he will then be at least able to bring his whole force to bear, in accordance with the changed conditions. But in Frederick's march with four separate columns into Bohemia, a march we mentioned as an example of the opposite principle, it was no longer possible for him, if the Austrians did not happen to be at the expected point, or if their army made any unexpected movements, to change the direction of all the four columns at a given moment, or adapt their four several movements to altered circumstances.

On the 24th April Napoleon had, as we have seen, left the choice between the Simplon and the Great St. Bernard to Berthier, and the latter wrote at that time: "According to circumstances, I shall start from Geneva on the 13th or 14th May, in order to cross into Italy either over the St. Bernard or the Simplon or the Gothard. I shall only decide at the last moment. The Simplon is impassable for sledges. The St. Bernard and St. Gothard are the most suitable points to cross at." [1] But the news which arrived of the state of affairs near Genoa necessitated a very prompt decision, and thus Napoleon wrote on the 27th: "I am no longer disposed to cross by the St. Gothard; I consider this operation would be possible and prudent only if General Moreau had gained a great success over the enemy.

"For the rest, it is possible that we shall no longer be able to go to Milan, but shall have to march in all haste to Tortona, in order to relieve Massena, who, if he be defeated, will have shut himself up in Genoa, where he has provisions for thirty days. I desire therefore that the St. Bernard be chosen as the point of crossing." [2]

In the meantime the organization of the Reserve Army at Geneva had been carried on with great vigour, yet the originally intended strength was not reached; by the

[1] C. N. To Napoleon. Dijon, 25th April.
[2] C. N. To Berthier. Paris, April, 4 p.m.

middle of April about 25,000 men were assembled, and consequently Berthier expressed the opinion in a letter to Napoleon, that he would cross the Alps with at most 30,000 infantry, adding: "As a general reckons, not as clerks do, a difference you will be able to appreciate more than any one else."[1] And therefore he requested that Moreau should receive urgent orders to send him Lecourbe with 15,000 men. Napoleon wrote almost daily to his general, entering most minutely upon all the details of organization, constantly stirring him up. For he had resolved, now that this Reserve Army was to play the principal part, to raise it to the highest strength possible, and he therefore issued a decree on the 5th May, that the Army of the Rhine was immediately to despatch 25,000 men to reinforce it, by the Gothard and the Simplon.

(26) On the 1st May, Berthier arrived at Geneva. On the 6th, at two a.m., Napoleon left Paris and reached Geneva during the night of the 8th—9th. The Reserve Army was now, by an order of the 10th May, divided as follows:—

Advance Guard: Lannes	... ...	8000 men.
Duhesme's Corps : Loison's Division	...	7000 „
Boudet's Division	...	8000 „
Victor's Corps: Monnier's Division	...	4000 „
Chambarlhac's Division		6000 „
Chabran's Division	...	5000 „
Cavalry Reserve: Murat ...	... ...	4000 „

Having here put the last touch with indefatigable zeal to the state of preparation of the army, Napoleon went on the 12th to Lausanne. The troops, which he had assembled for the invasion of Italy, were now disposed of as follows: Lannes was in advance at Martigny in the valley of the Rhone; the divisions of Boudet, Loison, Chambarlhac, and Monnier were behind him along the lake of Geneva from Villeneuve to Lausanne. The

[1] C. N. Dijon, 25th April.

division of Chabran lay in Savoy, and had orders to cross the Little St. Bernard. To the right of the army Thurreau, who had originally formed the extreme left wing of Massena's army, held the Mont Cenis pass; he was to march later towards Susa and then move to Ivrea. The left of the Reserve Army was formed by Moncey, who with 15,000 men (sent by Moreau) was marching towards the St. Gothard. Thus the whole force stood at the foot of the St. Bernard perfectly ready to cross, and Napoleon resolved to do so without delay. "I shall personally go to Italy. Events will succeed each other with great rapidity."[1]

The enemy stood at this time in the following positions: On the 21st April the investment proper of Massena in the fortress of Genoa had begun; the latter had here 12,000 men capable of bearing arms, and 16,000 sick and wounded. Melas had entrusted General Ott, who was at the head of 24,000 men, with the siege of this town. He himself turned with 28,000 men to the Riviera against Suchet, who had with 10,000 men formed Massena's left wing in the Alps, but who now, by the united advance of the Austrians upon Genoa, had been forced to retire from that town. Melas drove him along the coast and back over the French frontier, and reached the Var on the 14th May. The remainder of the Austrian army was thus placed: at Bellinzona 8000 men to watch the St. Gothard[2]; in the valley of the Dora Baltea 3000 men; in that of the Dora Riparia 5000 men; in the Stura valley 1000 men. Besides these there were 20,000 men in garrison throughout Upper Italy; 3000 in Tuscany and the Romagna; and 3000 in Istria. Melas had also ordered up 6000 men from the Romagna, and their van joined his forces at this moment.

On the 14th May, Napoleon ordered Lannes to advance towards St. Pierre, while Boudet marched to Bex, Loison to Aigle, and Chambarlhac to Villeneuve.

[1] C. N. To Brune. Geneva, 11th May.
[2] and Simplon.

Monnier's division forming the rearguard. On the 15th Lannes began to cross the pass and reached Etroubles with his first columns, forcing a weak Austrian outpost back from this village upon Aosta. On the 16th Lannes occupied Aosta. Behind him the main body of the army began to cross the highest point of the pass in the above order. Napoleon himself, according to his habit, remained behind in Lausanne for the present, so as not to give the enemy by his personal presence the certainty that the whole army was advancing. He urged upon Berthier to seize the fort of Bard as soon as possible, which, being situated in a narrow part of the Dora Baltea valley, was likely to offer a most serious obstacle to the success of the enterprise; apart from this, he advised him to push Lannes quickly forward to Ivrea, even though the rest of the army could not immediately follow; for it was, he said, of the utmost importance to obtain as soon as possible possession of this town, lying at the entrance to the plain.

At the same time as Lannes crossed the Great St. Bernard, Chabran had passed the Little St. Bernard, and on the 16th the heads of the columns joined at Aosta. On the 17th, according to Napoleon's plan, the French vanguard continued to descend the valley of the Dora Baltea, and on the 18th it drove the Austrians from their position at Chatillon. On the previous day Napoleon had arrived at Martigny. On the 19th Lannes reached the fortress of Bard, on which so much depended, and soon had the conviction forced on him that its garrison was fully determined to hold out, and also that it entirely blocked the valley. The moment was certainly critical. "Put it very plainly to General Lannes," wrote Berthier, who was at this time at Aosta, "that the fate of Italy, and possibly of the Republic, depends on the fortress of Bard."[1] But in view of the firm resolution of the Austrian commander and of the strength of the position

[1] To Dupont, 18th May.

of the fortress, it was not possible to capture it, and Lannes was obliged, in order to proceed on his way, to take a side-road to the left across Mount Albaredo, over which, however, no guns could be transported.

Napoleon himself crossed the pass on the 20th, and arrived in Etroubles. He was annoyed to find Bard not yet captured, and that consequently the vanguard, which had advanced beyond it, had to remain unsupported; he said to Berthier: "Be on your guard, Lannes will in three or four days have from 7000 to 8000 men upon him."[1] Otherwise, he saw in the resistance of Fort Bard a cause of delay, but no serious danger. He thought over other ways and means, and said to himself: "If the St. Bernard did not stop us, a mountain of the second rank will surely form no invincible obstacle in our march."[2] He therefore immediately gave orders to have the road over Mount Albaredo repaired: "It must indeed be very bad if it is worse than the St. Bernard, over which we transported our artillery; time and care overcome all sorts of obstacles."[3] The news which he had received from Suchet was that Melas was still on the Var on the 13th May; he reckoned, therefore, that he would not be able to attack his army in force before the 26th or 27th, and therefore was not alarmed by the state of affairs.

Lannes having successfully found his way round Bard and thrown the Austrian troops, destined for the defence of the valley, back upon Ivrea, attacked this town on the 22nd, but without success. But meanwhile some artillery began to arrive. Marmont, chief of the artillery of the army, had conceived the bold plan of getting some guns by night through the village of Bard, situated below the fortress. He had the village street covered with litter, and ordered the wheels and other movable parts of the guns to be wrapped in hay, and thus a large portion of

---

[1] C. N. Etroubles, 20th May, 9 p.m.
[2] C. N. To Berthier. Etroubles, 20th May, 9 p.m.
[3] Ibid.

the cannon were actually dragged past the fortress by the soldiers in the course of several nights. And although its defenders soon became aware of the enterprise and opened fire upon it, yet the fortress rose too perpendicularly from the valley for the fire to have much effect. With the assistance of these guns Lannes succeeded on the 23rd in taking the castle of Ivrea, and on the 24th he captured the town by assault, upon which Napoleon remarked: "It was time, for later on a regular siege would have been necessary."[1] In the meantime the other divisions of the army had likewise crossed the St. Bernard behind Lannes, and on the 22nd the passage was completed.

Now with respect to this crossing of the Alps, Napoleon has been reproached with not having made sufficiently careful preparations for it; it has been said that it was undertaken in too light-hearted a spirit, the whole affair might easily have failed, and that not only on account of Fort Bard; in fact, the happy success was entirely due to good luck. But this is not so. We have already seen that the quite unexpected resistance of this fortress did not in any way cause Napoleon to doubt the success of his plan; indeed, the event proved that though this fortress did not surrender, yet the passage of the Alps was entirely successful. And on the occasion of the ultimate fall of Bard, the Austrian account remarked: "Moreover, it had not been in any way expected that the enemy would cross the mountains of the St. Bernard with artillery, and use guns against a fortress which was only meant to resist musketry fire."[2]

That is just it; with Napoleon, on the other hand, nothing was ever left out of account, and more particularly nothing that might possibly be to his advantage; of course, he was far from thinking over every possible event in all its details beforehand, but he prepared his

---

[1] C. N. Rapport sur les prem. opér. de l'armée de rés. Chivasso, 28th May.
[2] Oesterr. Mil. Zeitschrift, 1822, IV. 252.

plans on a comprehensive scale, feeling sure that his skill and energy would, in the course of events, be able to take advantage of all the details or render them harmless. This neglect of details is indeed a quality inseparable from a great genius, for it is just because men of genius do not regard trivial things, but keep their eyes fixed upon the main object, the decisive point, that their success becomes so tremendous. It is said of Lee: "Lee never interfered as commander-in-chief in any of the details which lay outside his special province, but turned his whole power to the duty which was his;"[1] and of Gneisenau it is said: "Gneisenau passed lightly over details, confident of his presence of mind, his genius. It wearied him to weigh beforehand all eventualities, of which, indeed (as he used to remark), only one could happen, and that one never exactly as it was anticipated; he felt sure that he would know how to act if the right moment came; he credited all others with the same gift, and disregarded questions of time and space, the more so that he loved risk, and trusted to his own daring to overcome them."[2] A distinct example of the fact that he took tactical and topographical difficulties but little into consideration, once he had resolved upon a great strategical combination, is the case of Wartenburg; this was a sort of second edition of Bard, and yet here, as there, the great strategical plan was carried through in spite of all obstacles. "Genius is more a product of the heat of will than of the light of intellect,"[3] says Bülow, who has been so unjustly accused of sterile theorizing.

On the 24th May Boudet lay near Ivrea, Lannes had (27) captured that town, Loison was near Bard, Monnier at Chatillon, Chambarlhac at Aosta; Chabran had received orders to take the investment of Fort Bard in hand. Napoleon was at Aosta, and passed the following

[1] Scheibert: Der Bürgerkrieg in den Nordamerik-Staaten, 180.
[2] Müffling. Aus meinem Leben, 29.
[3] Feldzug von 1805, I. 203.

judgment upon the whole situation: "The enemy seems very surprised at our movement. He does not know what to do; as yet, he scarcely credits it. The following were the Austrian positions on the 18th May: 12,000 men at Nice, 6000 in Savona and in the littoral of Genoa, 25,000 men before Genoa, 8000 near Susa, Pignerol, &c., 3000 in the valley of Aosta, 8000 facing the Simplon and the St. Gothard."[1] It will thus be seen that he was most accurately informed of the Austrians' positions. Then he proceeded to state what had probably taken place meanwhile: "The enemy has remained in the above positions until the moment of our arrival at Ivrea. The 3000 men who were in this valley have been beaten and scattered. The whole corps, which lay towards Susa and Pignerol, has meantime taken up its position between Turin and Ivrea. Nice is probably evacuated by this time. I have information from Ivrea that Melas is said to have arrived in Turin, but this is not certain." In fact, the passage of the Alps had been entirely successful, the enemy had been surprised, he had no forces at hand to oppose the columns that issued from the mountains, and Napoleon was in a position to open the campaign in the plain in full security. On this point, he said: "I reckon upon having my whole army collected at Ivrea by the 26th or 27th; it will amount to about 33,000 men. I shall be master of the whole country between the Dora Baltea and the Sesia. By that day, Moncey will have crossed the St. Gothard with 15,000 men, Suchet and Massena will follow the enemy as soon as they are informed of our movement, and see that, in front of them, his force is diminishing."

Melas had at first, after his arrival on the Var, been led to believe that the Army of Reserve intended to march to Provence, in order to face him as he advanced along the Riviera. When, therefore, on the morning of the 18th May he received information from the general command-

[1] C. N. To Brune.

ing in Piedmont that Napoleon had crossed the Alps, he was entirely surprised by this movement, and lacked the forces necessary to oppose it immediately and effectively. He now left a corps of 17,000 men in position on the Var, for he did not like to resign all hopes of the speedy fall of Genoa, nor to evacuate the Riviera, and he himself hastened to Turin. Of his troops in the Riviera, he had sent about 9000 men back to Piedmont. On the 25th May he himself arrived in Turin, where he collected about 5000 men from the garrison and the troops who had retreated from the mountains. As to the siege of Genoa, he persisted in it, but he had also to face the enemy in the open; if we compare his action with that of Napoleon in 1796 before Mantua, and the ultimate results in each case, we shall again see that what Napoleon did then was the only right course.

Napoleon arrived in Ivrea in the evening of the 26th, full of confidence, elated by the rapid and successful issue of his passage of the Alps. "Within ten days," he said, "much will have happened."[1] But, as is characteristic of great generals, the success of a first enterprise only increased his aspirations, and though he had at first intended upon his entrance in the plain *viâ* Tortona to turn against Melas, and thus catch him between two fires, while relieving Massena, now that he was at Ivrea he formed a more ambitious plan. "It is possible," he said to himself, "that I may abandon this line of operations on the 29th or 30th."[2] Massena was still holding out in Genoa; why should not Napoleon take advantage of this fact and, marching to Milan, make himself master of Lombardy, and then crossing the Po, cut off completely all Melas' lines of retreat?

It is at such moments that the paths of an ordinary capable general of an army and those of a really great commander diverge. The former would have

[1] C. N. To the Consuls, 27th May.
[2] C. N. To Petiet and Dejean, 27th May.

marched from Ivrea to Turin, would have defeated Melas, relieved Genoa, and would then have entered on the conquest of Lombardy, only to meet the enemy again behind the Po or the Ticino. The latter cut off all the enemy's communications and offered him battle, which, if lost, must mean absolute ruin to him. The enemy succumbed and the one battle gave Napoleon possession of the whole of Upper Italy. A similar decision will be seen in 1809, when Archduke Charles was advancing victoriously between the corps of Davout and Napoleon, separated from each other through Berthier's fault. There also the commonplace general would have chosen the safer way, and turned aside to Ingolstadt, but the great commander took a bolder course; he operated against the enemy's communications, annihilated him, and won at one stroke the whole of Austria to the gates of its capital. And a third time, in October, 1813, we shall see Napoleon at Düben having to choose between turning aside behind the Saale, or advancing boldly across the Elbe, but, unlike himself, standing irresolute, until the advance of his opponent in his rear upon Leipzic dictated to him his course of action.

(28) On the 26th Lannes and Boudet attacked the Austrians, who opposed them once more at Romano, and, having thrown them back behind the Orco, reached Chivasso on the 27th. On the same day Murat with his cavalry and a part of Monnier's division took Vercelli; then, protected by these advanced corps, the rest of the army collected during these and the following days in and beyond Ivrea. Meanwhile also the divisions to the right and left of the army had pushed onward as ordered. Thurreau had begun his forward movement from Mont Cenis and Mont Genevre towards Susa on the 20th; he had driven back the Austrians posted at Susa, and then taken up a position at Bussoleno. Moncey crossed the St. Gothard on the 26th and 27th, and stood ready for an advance to Bellinzona on the 28th; he was in command of the

divisions Lapoype, Lorge, and Gilly; a detached column had crossed the Simplon and was on the march to Domo d'Ossola.

Napoleon now, in accordance with his project of marching to Milan, left Lannes behind at Chivasso, to protect this flank movement to the left from Turin, and ordered the army behind him to advance towards the Ticino. Murat, who was now in front, arrived on the 29th on the banks of the Sesia, where he drove back some weak Austrian detachments and reached Novara. He was immediately followed by Boudet and Loison, and later by Monnier and Chambarlhac; Moncey advanced on the same day as far as Bellinzona.

On the 30th all the French columns continued their advance towards the Ticino. On this river stood about 5000 of the Austrians, consisting partly of troops driven out of Piedmont, but for the greater part ordered up from Bellinzona; the division which had been watching the Simplon was also there. On the 31st Murat and Monnier reached the Ticino near Turbigo; they forced a passage, but were then prevented from any further advance by the enemy being still in possession of the great canal. However, during the night of the 1st June the Austrians retired to Milan; and the corps which had remained at Bellinzona to watch the Gothard route, fell back upon Como. Murat, Monnier and Boudet were occupied the same day in preparing for a passage of the Ticino at Turbigo and Buffalora, and crossed that river successfully during it. In the afternoon, at two o'clock, the vanguard reached Milan, whilst the Austrians retreated to Lodi. Napoleon, who had just been informed that Fort Bard had surrendered the day before, entered Milan in state three hours after the arrival of his vanguard. In the meantime, Lannes had also, on the 1st June, left his position near Chivasso and reached Vercelli on the same day, where he received orders to march to Pavia; he arrived there on the 3rd, whilst the other divisions assembled at Milan,

and Chabran followed from Bard. The pursuit of the
Austrians retreating towards Lodi had immediately been
entrusted to Loison, and he reached Lodi on the 4th;
but the Austrians had fallen back towards Crema during
the night.

Moncey had at first been ordered to pursue the Austrian
column retreating from Bellinzona *viâ* Como, but was
now commanded to move up as fast as possible to Milan.
After the capture of this capital, the next operation for
Napoleon was to cross the Po, so as to cut all the enemy's
communications. But if this was not to lead to his own
defeat, it had to be done with sufficient forces, therefore
it was necessary to await Moncey's arrival in Milan.

Napoleon had been informed as to the enemy's position
on the 4th by a spy who told him that their main body
was, in the last few days of May, still on the Genoese coast;
he consequently wrote: " I do not think the enemy has at
this moment on the Tanaro more than 10,000 infantry,
nor do I think he can possibly have 20,000 there before
the 9th or 10th."[1] As therefore no immediate serious
danger was to be apprehended from the enemy, he resolved, on the one hand, to push forward troops quickly
over the Po, in order to secure the points of crossing, and,
on the other hand, to force back the Austrian columns,
with whom he had been in touch as far as Milan, so far
that they would be unable to interfere any further. Murat
was consequently ordered forward to Piacenza, and the
corps of Victor started on its march to Pavia; whilst on
the other side Loison was commanded to pursue the retreating enemy beyond Crema and, if possible, to occupy
Orzinovi as well.

Melas had on his arrival in Turin expected that Napoleon would march first upon that town. But learning as
time went on of his march on Milan, he resolved on the
29th to take him in rear *viâ* Vercelli. Scarcely, however,
had he set the weak forces at his disposal in motion for

[1] C. N. To Lannes. Milan, 6th June.

this purpose, than he received on the 31st the news that the troops posted on the Ticino had been compelled to fall back before greatly superior forces, and that considerable bodies also were descending from the St. Gothard. He now first recognized his critical situation, and therewith the necessity of giving up Genoa and the Riviera. He therefore settled upon Alessandria as the point of concentration of his whole army, and sent orders to Ott, as well as to the column standing on the Var, to march to that place. This latter force had however meanwhile been compelled to fall back, before it received this order on the 1st June, for Suchet had been reinforced and had attacked and driven it back, and on its further retreat Suchet remained within striking distance, and inflicted such repeated losses on it that when it reached Ceva and Montenotte on the 7th, it only numbered some 8000 men.

Ott received also orders to march on the 1st June, but negotiations had already been entered upon, and the fall of Genoa was only a matter of a day or two. He therefore stopped a few days longer, and on the 4th Genoa surrendered. Massena had prolonged his resistance with admirable endurance and energy to the utmost, and then secured permission for the garrison to march out with the honours of war. His defence of Genoa is one of the most brilliant on record. On the 5th and 6th Ott's troops withdrew towards Alessandria.

Thus on the 5th June the situation was the following: Napoleon was at Milan, as yet unaware of the fall of Genoa; Moncey at only one day's march from that city; Murat and Boudet had arrived before the tête-de-pont of Piacenza, and had driven an insignificant force, a couple of hundred men, thence, at 10 p.m. Loison had reached Orzinovi; Lannes was at Pavia and Belgiojoso, towards which places Victor's corps the divisions of Chambarlhac and Gardanne (who had 4000 men of the Reserve Army, lately ordered up) and Monnier] was on the march. Chabran was still on the Orco, Thurreau in the valley of the Dora Riparia. On the enemy's side Melas was still at Turin, but was becoming more and more aware of the danger he was in, if the French army crossed the Po in full strength. The tête-de-pont of Piacenza was, as has been remarked above, only very feebly occupied, therefore no serious obstacles could be placed in the way of the enemy's crossing. At Turin lay 14,000 men; 8000 were on the march hither from the Riviera and approaching Ceva; Ott, with 12,000, was on the way from Genoa; and finally the column which had retreated before Loison, about 4000 men, had reached Cremona. Ott now received orders to march, not upon Alessandria, but with forced marches to Piacenza. The troops in Turin were to start on the 8th and take the road to Alessandria, to which place the troops on the march from Ceva were also to proceed.

On the 6th Loison pushed forward on the one side towards Brescia, on the other towards Pizzighettone, and at both places the enemy retired before him; after this, however, Loison set his whole force in motion in the direction of Cremona. Murat had not been able to cross at Piacenza, as this town was still occupied and the bridge partly destroyed. He had therefore turned a little down-stream, and began to cross early in the morning at Noceto. Advancing from this place, he seized the town. On the same day Lannes also had, according to Napoleon's instructions, begun to cross the Po, starting from Belgiojoso; and Monnier did the same a little lower down. One more engagement took place with the rearguard of the Austrians retreating *viâ* Stradella. Moncey on the same date reached Milan with his first column, where Napoleon himself still was.

The latter indeed knew of the successful crossing of the leading corps of Murat and Lannes, but as to what forces were opposed to them on the right bank he knew nothing, though he suspected that the resistance would be but feeble. On the 7th the army continued the passage of the Po, and concentrated at Stradella and Piacenza. As Napoleon was not yet informed of what had taken place at the latter town, he ordered Lannes to assist, if necessary, in its capture, but at the same time warned Berthier, who had gone to Pavia the day before, not to employ the whole of Lannes' force in that enterprise, for he might expect to be attacked at Stradella by some 20,000 men on the 9th at the latest. To Murat he sent an aide-de-camp in all haste to find out how things were with him. He intended himself to remain in Milan until he was quite clear as to the whole situation.

This he soon learned. Murat had captured a courier sent by Melas on the 5th from Turin to Vienna, and at 4 a.m. on the 8th Napoleon had a translation of his despatches in his hands, from which he learnt the surrender of Genoa and the movements and forces of the Austrians. He calculated from these, that they could not concentrate their whole strength at Alessandria before the 12th or 13th, and even then would not have more than 22,000 men there. Accordingly his instructions to Berthier, so cautious the day before, were now all in the opposite strain: " See to it, that the divisions advance vigorously and destroy all the troops they may encounter. The vanguard may push forward as far as Voghera."[1] " Should a corps present itself tomorrow before Stradella, as is possible, it must be attacked vigorously, so that we may make from 2000 to 3000 prisoners. It is certain it can only be a weak one." In a word, he resolved to defeat the enemy in detail.

In accordance with this command, Lannes started at 9 a.m. for Voghera, followed by Chambarlhac's division of Victor's corps; Gardanne being still engaged in crossing the Po. Meanwhile, Ott arrived at Casteggio about noon. Lannes immediately deployed for the attack, in conformity with Napoleon's reiterated order:

[1] C. N. To Berthier, Milan, 8th June.

"If any troops are seen between Voghera and Stradella, they are to be attacked without hesitation; they are certain to number less than 10,000 men."[1] Though at first successful, Lannes was soon attacked on his left flank and repulsed by reinforcements which reached the enemy, but he also was now reinforced by the arrival of Chambarlhac; the latter advanced in his turn against the Austrian right flank, and, Lannes receiving his frontal attack at the same time, forced the enemy to yield, and to fall back as far as the Scrivia.

(29)   Napoleon remained at Milan during the forenoon, awaiting Moncey, who arrived there during the day with his last troops. The latter was instructed to employ Lorge in clearing the country between the Oglio and the Chiese, to order Gilly to hold Milan occupied, to invest the citadel, and to send Lapoype forward along the Po, keeping pace with the army on the left bank. Then Napoleon went to Pavia, where he met Berthier. He found Murat and Boudet at Piacenza, Monnier, who had crossed the Po during the day, on the march to Stradella, Loison at Cremona. He resolved to keep the first two at Piacenza for this day and to move the latter up to the same place as a reserve; the day before he had already given orders to set Chabran in motion towards Vercelli. Then Napoleon rode forward as far as the scene of Lannes' engagement and inspected it in person, whereupon he moved his headquarters to Stradella. He acted on the same principle here as elsewhere; first he always remained behind the army at some great centre, where he calmly directed the march of his columns, preparing everything and hindering the enemy from judging of the real point of attack by his personal presence. But as soon as he had come in real touch with the enemy, he hastened from the rear in the shortest time possible, and, joining the foremost portion of his army, surveyed the situation personally.

[1] C. N. To Berthier, Milan, 8th June.

Of the Austrians, Ott, who had lost 4000 men in the engagement at Montebello, lay at Castelnuovo; Melas was still one or two days' march behind Alessandria. The situation was such as to excite our astonishment in no small degree. We cannot but recognize that Napoleon sinned here against one of those great principles which may rarely be violated with impunity. At this time, when everything pointed to a decisive battle within a few days, he did not concentrate all his forces for it, but employed no inconsiderable portions of them in enterprises of secondary importance. He had at his immediate disposal the divisions of Lannes, Victor, Monnier, Boudet, Murat, Loison[2]—in all, 34,000 men; Moncey, Chabran, Thurreau, with 23,000 men in all, were too far away to be of any immediate use. In view of these figures we cannot but agree with Jomini, when he says: "Still by some extraordinary chance the campaign of Marengo, which ended so brilliantly, was the one in which he departed most from his principles, at least in the measures he adopted."[1] The great mistakes which his opponent had already committed in the course of the campaign, did not admit of his concentrating his whole force against the 34,000 men of Napoleon, and proving to the latter by a defeat the risky, nay, we must use the word, the bungling nature of his proceedings.

But what was it that caused Napoleon to be thus untrue to himself, and neglect his great principle of concentrating for battle? It seems almost as if it had been the same that caused Frederick to commit a similar mistake at Kolin, namely, a self-confidence, rendered excessive by constant victories and a contempt for the enemy. But the former, who after all gained the victory, as well as the latter, who paid for his too great daring with defeat, recognized the strategical mistake and never repeated it. Still, the different result of these two battles had its effect upon the two generals. Who can say

[1] Hist. crit. et mil. des guerres de la Rév. VIII. 192.
[2] Wartenburg frequently uses the expression "the divisions of" meaning "the divisions comprising the command of". Here he means the corps of Lannes, Victor, and Murat, and the divisions of Monnier, Boudet, and Loison.

whether Frederick, had the venture of Kolin succeeded, might not have been led to undertake as stupendous enterprises as Napoleon was; or whether this latter, had Marengo been a defeat, would not have been taught moderation? As a general, Frederick, after Kolin, narrowed his aims; to him that battle may have appeared a blot on his fame, but I believe that defeat had at least as much to do with the enduring prosperity of the state he ruled as his most brilliant victories. Napoleon reached the highest summit of military glory, but we may possibly perceive in the victory of Marengo the source of those defeats, which later laid the edifice of Napoleon's empire of the world in the dust.

On the 10th June Ott retreated behind the Scrivia, and Melas' first columns arrived in Alessandria. Napoleon's troops remained on the whole stationary, but Murat and Boudet were brought a little nearer in; Loison, however, remained at Cremona and Piacenza, and his 6000 men were not destined to take part in the battle of Marengo. On the 11th Desaix, having returned from Egypt by Napoleon's orders, arrived in the headquarters at Stradella, and Napoleon immediately gave him the command of the divisions of Monnier and Boudet. On this day the French completed their concentration between Casteggio and Voghera, and on the morning of the 12th Napoleon started on his continued advance; in the evening of this day his troops stood in the following positions: Lannes at Castelnuovo, Desaix at Pontecurone, Murat in advance towards Tortona, Victor pushing forward in the same direction, forming the left wing. By the 12th Melas also had collected his army near Alessandria; moreover, Ott retreated at nightfall behind the Bormida, leaving only a rear-guard at Marengo.

On the morning of the 13th Napoleon crossed the Scrivia, Victor being in advance on the high road to Alessandria. However, contrary to his expectations, he did not meet with the Austrian army in the open plain between this river and the Bormida, where its best arm, the cavalry, would have found a good field for its evolutions, as Kellermann was to prove next day. Napoleon had for some days constantly contemplated the possibility that Melas might intend to avoid a battle, by turning aside, either towards Genoa or the left bank of the Po; and now this possibility bade fair to become a certainty; he therefore at once sent Desaix with the division of Boudet to the high road to Novi to block the Austrians' retreat to Genoa, whilst, in the other event, Lapoype and Chabran, the latter posted between Chivasso and Vercelli, were to stop Melas on the left bank of the Po. The detaching of Desaix was again a dangerous division of forces, and the army indeed was astonished at this action; the remark was made that Napoleon, contrary to his usual custom, " was busy catching the enemy, by occupying all his lines of retreat, before having defeated him. It would have been wiser, first to secure the means of defeating him, before making him prisoner."[1]

The advance guard, under Victor, came about five (30) o'clock in the afternoon on the Austrian rear-guard, left behind at Marengo, and drove it, after a short resistance, from its position back to the tête-de-pont on the Bormida, a circumstance which was naturally calculated to confirm Napoleon in his suspicion of the enemy's retreat. He therefore allowed his army, without massing it to its front, to remain for the night at the points just reached; Victor thus lay at Marengo, Lannes and Murat at San Giuliano, Desaix at Rivalta, Monnier at Torre di Garofoli, at which latter place Napoleon also passed the night; a false report moreover assured him that the Austrians had no bridge over the Bormida. In the meantime, however, Melas had resolved to attack the French army and to re-open his communications by a battle.

The Austrians began, therefore, to cross the Bormida in the early morning of the 14th June; their van-guard,

[1] Marmont, Mém. II. 126.

attacking Victor's position, drove Gardanne from Pietrabuona and threw him back upon Marengo. Napoleon had, as we have seen, not expected this attack; he now sent in all haste orders to Desaix to rejoin the army at San Giuliano. The ground being cleared by the success of its van-guard, the Austrian army now deployed its lines on the eastern bank of the Bormida. As regards the French, Victor was commanded to hold Marengo to the last, for as the army was not in the necessary state of concentration for a battle, the most important point was to gain time. Lannes was to come up to the right of Victor, and Murat to place two of his cavalry brigades behind the wings of the line; his third was posted at Sale, to oppose any attempted turning movement along the Tanaro.

(31) The first attacks of the Austrians upon Marengo failed, and Lannes gained time to take up his appointed position in the line; on his left Gardanne defended Marengo, whilst Chambarlhac occupied the space from this place to the Bormida near the farm of Stortigliona. Meanwhile, General Ott had arrived in Castel Ceriolo with a strong column, without having met with any resistance; seeing no enemy there, he turned to the right and advanced against Lannes' right flank. At this time, ten o'clock, Monnier alone was at Napoleon's disposal at Torre di Garofoli. Desaix sent word that he would arrive with Boudet's division about four o'clock in the afternoon. All Napoleon's efforts had therefore to be directed to holding out until that hour.

(32) He now sent Monnier forward with orders to occupy Castel Ceriolo with two of his demi-brigades, but Ott opposed to these his second line. In the front Lannes and Victor could no longer resist the continued Austrian attack, Marengo was captured from them, and their whole force retreated along the high road. By this retreat the defenders of Castel Ceriolo saw themselves isolated; they therefore also abandoned their position and retreated on Torre di Garofoli. It was now noon.

Napoleon then hurled the last fresh troops still at his disposal, the 800 men of his Consular guard, upon Ott, but while these were engaged in front by infantry, they were attacked in the flank and rear by some Austrian cavalry and entirely dispersed. It was now about one o'clock, and this last disaster had made the French retreat inevitable, and on the left wing, where Victor was, it soon degenerated into utter rout. One more combined effort of the Austrian army and their victory would have been secure. But Melas was not equal to the situation; a man of seventy, he was exhausted by the efforts of the forenoon, and when he saw the French in flight he thought it sufficient to order the pursuit, whilst he himself rode back to Alessandria. His chief of the staff now formed the bulk of the army in (33) one great column, and advanced along the road to San Giuliano, Ott marching to the left of it *viâ* Villanova towards the castle of La Ghilina. The head of the troops arrived about five o'clock in the afternoon before San Giuliano, whilst the French continued their flight past this town towards Torre di Garofoli.

But at this juncture Desaix came up with Boudet's division, and all the troops that still had any leaders joined him, whilst Napoleon sent his aides-de-camp over the battle-field, calling on all the fugitives to rally, and telling them that the army was again showing front and would advance afresh. Marmont assembled on Desaix's right wing a battery of eighteen guns to support his attack, and Kellermann's brigade (the same cavalry brigade which had covered Victor's left wing during the battle), moving round behind Desaix, appeared on the right flank of Marmont's artillery, and then advanced together with Desaix along the high road.

Desaix now flung his whole division impetuously upon the great Austrian column, and whilst this latter was thus checked, Kellermann fell with the first line of his cavalry upon its left flank, while his second line went to meet the Austrian cavalry advancing in the plain on one side of the

o

road to protect this flank. The latter evaded the shock, and Kellermann then threw this second line also upon the Austrian infantry column. The effect of these combined attacks of Desaix and Kellermann was decisive; the front half of the column was entirely scattered, cut down or taken prisoners, and the remainder, thrown into confusion by its own fugitives, succumbed also to the French, who were now advancing again on all sides. This decided the battle, the Austrians fled beyond the Bormida, but their rear-guard held the bridge-head until Ott came up again from Castel Ceriolo. The French van-guard encamped for the night near Pietrabuona, the main body at Marengo.

The next morning an officer bearing a flag of truce from Melas appeared, and on the same day an agreement was come to, in accordance with which the Austrian army evacuated the whole of Upper Italy with all the fortified places as far as the Mincio. On the 15th May Napoleon commenced crossing the Great St. Bernard, by the 15th June the campaign was at an end, the strategical idea which formed its foundation having been completely carried out.

Here we see the justification of the speech which Napoleon made to Jomini at the beginning of the campaign of 1806: "The secret of war lies in the secret of the lines of communications."[1] He who can determine the roads which will bring him most quickly and in full force upon the enemy's lines of communications without endangering his own, has found out the secret of success in strategy. And it is quite possible to acquire this power by study; therein lies the chief practical gain to be derived from reading military history.

Of course, study alone does not make a strategist, for that clear recognition of what is right in warfare, which may thus be gained, does not imply the capacity for carrying out what has been decided on,

[1] Traité, etc.. III. 18.

though it is one of the first conditions for doing so. Willisen says very justly: "There is always a great difference between knowing how a thing ought to be done, and being able to do it, still, you must begin by having that knowledge, and not with complete ignorance."
And Jomini amplifies the same thought: "All those brilliant conceptions, which threatened the very existence of the armies of Wurmser, Melas, Mack, and Brunswick, were in themselves clever manœuvres; they would alone have entailed the defeat of the enemy, but they would only have *threatened* the existence of those armies, they would not have *annihilated* them but for their splendid execution that energy and rapidity, which amazed the world." [2] In another place also he emphasizes the fact that the best plan only becomes valuable by the act of its execution, for he says: " Strategy does not consist in making half-hearted dashes at the enemy's communications, it consists in really mastering those communications, and then proceeding to give battle." [3]

This was done at Marengo, and therefore the great critic of those times says: [4] "These events were the natural outcome of the cleverly conceived plan of campaign, namely, to attack the enemy's lines of communications, without exposing one's own. Had Bonaparte been beaten at Marengo, we do not believe that, as many have maintained, *he would, shut in as he was within narrow limits, have of necessity been annihilated.*" [5] It cannot be denied that his line of retreat on the road to Stradella and then across the Po was perfectly open, and the same circumstance, which had made him appear too weak on the field of Marengo, viz., the wide dispersion of his force of troops, would then have allowed him to resume the fight with fresh troops. Indeed, he himself speaks

[1] Theorie des grossen Krieges I. 23.
[2] Traité, etc. III. 215.
[3] Ibid., IV. 34
[4] Jomini, Hist. crit. et mil., etc. XIII. 301.
[5] These words are found in Dumas, Précis, etc., III. 303.

thus of his situation : " I was in an exceptional position, and I risked a little on the chance of gaining much. Had I been beaten, I should have retreated to my fortified camp at Stradella, crossed the Po on my five bridges, covered by my batteries, without the enemy's army being able to stop me; I should have united my first corps with the divisions of Moncey, Lecchi and Thurreau; I should have allowed one of Melas' corps to cross the Po (and that was exactly what he wished it would do); and then I could have attacked him with superior numbers. Being victorious, I gained the same results. Melas' army, shut in between us and the river, was forced to lay down its arms and to surrender all the fortresses. Had I been beaten, which I believe would have been impossible, I should have resumed operations according to the ordinary rules, and called Switzerland to my aid."[1]

We have already drawn attention to the vast importance of Marengo to Napoleon, as well as to the contrast between his subsequent strategy and that of Frederick after Kolin; we must now consider the question under a different aspect. The final tactical aim of every war is the annihilation of the enemy, and therefore the offensive alone is, properly speaking, the way to attain it. We need therefore not be astonished to see that wherever the greatest results are achieved, the offensive is the predominating course. And here we may note a significant difference between the generals of Kolin and Marengo. Frederick's subsequent strategy was, in spite of apparent exceptions, necessarily defensive in its essence and based upon self-preservation; that of Napoleon became more and more pronouncedly offensive, aiming at the conquest of the world. Thus even in 1813 he did not conduct the war with a view to preserve himself, but to destroy his enemies; the fact that this was then no longer possible, Napoleon as a sovereign ought to have recognized, but since as a statesman he would not impose this self-

[1] Antommarchi, Mém. I. 184.

restraint upon himself, nay, fettered by his former actions, possibly could no longer do so, as a general he was right not to alter his manner of waging war, but to adhere to it, as he did; and we are right in admiring him for acting thus, though we may also confess that the final result could only be utter defeat.

CHAPTER IX.

ULM.

1805.

WITH the peace of Luneville the war on the continent had come to an end. Order had, during those first few years of the nineteenth century, been restored with a strong hand at home; indeed the country, exhausted by successive revolutions, was in need of it; the power and influence of the First Consul had grown more and more, to the exclusion of all others, until his work found at last its natural consummation, and the government of the country the stability it needed, in the establishment of the Empire on the 18th May, 1804. Napoleon could indeed afterwards say with justice: " I did not presume to claim the crown; I picked it up from the gutter, and the people put it on my head."[1]

The treaty of Amiens had only caused a short interval in the war with England. With the resumption of hostilities in May, 1803, Napoleon had, however, determined to deal that great rival of France a decisive blow; he intended to land his army in England and to subjugate the country altogether. This plan shows his genius at its full height. The idea, which underlay this landing, was perfectly correct, it was a "putting into practice of the highest rule of war, namely: Try to put your strong points as to time and space against the enemy's weak points."[2] Napoleon's strength lay in his

[1] Mém. de Ste. Hélène, I. 233.
[2] Willisen, Die Feldzüge der Jahre 1859 und 1866. Dedication.

army and in war on land, England's strength consisted in its fleet and in war at sea; to attack her in such a way that his strength might be brought to bear, was therefore assuredly good strategy. Napoleon has been condemned, because the execution of this plan is said to have been impossible. But if we remember all that has been declared impossible in the history of the world by contemporaries, and yet was achieved by the power of genius, who can say, that a landing of his army in England would have been an impossibility for Napoleon. Hannibal's great plan of crossing the Alps and attacking Rome in Italy and conquering it there, would perhaps be considered impossible now, if it had remained a plan only.

The fact that this landing was not effected and England not conquered, is generally considered by historians as the salvation of Europe, for one country at least escaped Napoleon's domination. I do not share this opinion. The states of the continent suffered at that time too severely and directly from Napoleon's tyranny for them to realize that England had no less exclusively, though in a more practical and more enduring manner, its own interests in view during that time, and by no means those of Europe. Had Napoleon entered England at the head of his army, his strength would on the one hand have been weakened thereby, and the continent would have preserved greater freedom of action, and on the other hand England, shaken to its very foundations at home, would not have been able to concentrate, as it did, almost the whole colonial possessions of the world in its own hands, and the continental powers would nowadays have a more equal share of them.

Napoleon directed all the powers of his mind to the execution of this plan of landing; he exerted all his indefatigable energy and keen and versatile understanding in the creation of the fleet of transports and the army necessary for it. The former, calculated by him at a total number of 2008 vessels, was to be capable of crossing the channel with 150,000 men and all the necessary equipment for

(34) such an army; the narrowest part, the neighbourhood of Boulogne, was chosen for the point of departure; the coast was covered with numerous batteries as a protection against any attempts of the English fleet, and enormous basins, moles, and fortifications were constructed. At the same time the army of invasion was organized. On the 14th June, 1803, orders were issued to form six corps, each of which was to be collected in a camp and drilled there. Five of these camps were placed along the coasts of the North Sea and the English Channel, at Ghent in the Netherlands, at St. Omer, Compiègne, and St. Malo. The collection and formation of these corps proceeded gradually in these camps. In July, Napoleon himself visited the north-eastern parts of France and Belgium, inspected the coast from the mouth of the Somme as far as Dunkirk, and studied the natural features which might affect the execution of his plan. The visit was repeated in November, and the troops in Soult's camp at St. Omer were then inspected. Soon after this, on the 12th December, a general order was issued, which divided the " Grand Army " into four corps, three at the camps of St. Omer, Bruges, and Montreuil, and the fourth in reserve.

Once more, in January, 1804, the troops were reviewed by Napoleon. The army was now distributed as follows: Bernadotte was in occupation of Hanover, Marmont lay at the camp of Utrecht, Davout at that of Bruges, Soult at that of St. Omer, and Ney at that of Montreuil. Behind these, as a second line, all the regiments of dragoons collected in divisions, lay in cantonments. There was in addition the camp at Brest under Augereau, the troops there being destined for a landing in Ireland. On the 16th August the new emperor assembled Soult's and Ney's troops at Boulogne, in order to inflame their enthusiasm for his person by a formal distribution of crosses of the Legion of Honour, for " the soul of every army is an honest attachment of all its parts to their leader." [1]

[1] C. N. N. to Gauteaume, St. Cloud, 23rd June, 1803.

These great preparations of Napoleon against England had, however, raised fears as well as hopes on the continent, and Austria more particularly, too much restricted in its legitimate influence on the fate of Europe in consequence of the peace of Luneville, was preparing to take advantage of the chances of the future. In October, 1804, this power established along the frontiers of Switzerland and Italy a so-called sanitary cordon, under the pretext of yellow fever being rife in Spain, and in January, 1805, matters came to such a pass, that Napoleon saw himself compelled for the moment to issue orders to his army to prepare to march. Moreover the Austrians had taken advantage of a concentration of French troops in Italy on the occasion of Napoleon's coronation as king of this country (26th May, 1805) to augment their own army in Carinthia and Venetia to 40,000 men.

Soon after this the Court of Vienna received from the Court of St. Petersburg proposals for combined action against France, and in July, 1805, Winzingerode arrived in Vienna to confer about their operations; on the 16th a convention was signed, in accordance with which Russia was to put two armies in the field; the first of which, 55,000 men, was to start from Brody on the 20th August, and, marching in six columns, was to reach Braunau on the Inn by the 20th October: the second, 40,000 men, was to start from Brest-Litovsk and proceed to Bohemia. Should the emperor or one of the archdukes command the Austrian army, the Russians were to be under his commands. Besides this, two corps, of 25,000 men each, were to be sent by sea, one to Naples, and the other to Pomerania, the latter in order to join hands with the Swedes and occupy Hanover.

The Austrian plan of campaign, drawn up by Archduke Charles, was based on the idea of taking the offensive with the bulk of the army in Upper Italy, and remaining on the defensive in Germany, until a decisive battle should have been won in Italy, or until the Russian army had arrived. In Italy 95,000 men were to be collected in the Tyrol, but to act with the Italian army, 33,000 men; in Germany 59,000.

Napoleon, who had been again at the camp of Boulogne since the 3rd August, now began more and more to see that he must for the present abandon crossing to England, and on the 23rd August he said to himself: " My mind is made up. My fleet set sail from Ferrol on the 14th August with thirty-four ships; it had no enemy in sight. If it obeys its orders and joins that of Brest, it will still be in time, I shall yet be master of England." [1] If this should not turn out so, " I shall attend to what is most urgent, strike my camp here, and order my third battalions to replace my field battalions; this will still give me a sufficiently strong force at Boulogne, and on the 23rd September I shall be in Germany with 200,000 men, and in the Kingdom of Naples with 25,000 men. I shall march to Vienna and shall not hold my hand till I am master of Naples and Venice, and have so increased the dominions of the Elector of Bavaria as to leave me nothing further to fear from Austria."

From this day he began to issue the preparatory orders for a concentration of the French army in Germany. Its distribution in the camps at this time was as follows: Bernadotte at Hanover, Marmont at Utrecht, Davout at Ambleteuse, Soult and the cavalry reserve under Murat at Boulogne, Mortier at Etaples, Ney at Wimereux, Augereau at Brest. Lombardy was held by Jourdan, whose place was however soon afterwards taken by Massena. Within two days the Emperor had taken his final resolution, and said: "I am resolved. My movements have begun, I shall be in Germany on the 17th September with 200,000 men." [2] The same day indeed he sent Murat and Bertrand to Germany, in order carefully to inspect the country in which the campaign was to be conducted; they were to reconnoitre minutely the fortresses, the roads, the tributaries of the

[1] C. N. To Talleyrand.   [2] Ibid.

Danube, as well as the banks of this stream itself, and gain all the information possible as to the passes leading into the Tyrol and into Bohemia, as well as those of the Black Forest.

On the 28th August Savary also was despatched thither, but by this time the Emperor's plan of campaign had assumed a more definite form, and the orders which he gave to this officer were more detailed. He was to reconnoitre the roads, which, starting from Philippsburg, Bruchsal, and Durlach, crossed the Neckar at Heilbronn, Cannstadt and Esslingen, and led thence to the Danube, Dillingen, Gundelfingen and Ulm, as well as the cross-roads between them. In these orders the Emperor's whole plan of campaign is revealed, and we should pay the greatest attention to them; for Napoleon, standing as he did at the head of the State, invested with absolute power and no longer fettered by any personal considerations, had now free play for his genius' and could put his ideas fully into practice.

To begin with, we note that he resolved to bring matters to an issue in Germany; we have already, when treating of the campaign of 1800, pointed to the fact that the decisive point lay there. He now placed the bulk of his army, 200,000 men, there, opposing only 50,000 men to the Austrian main army in Italy. Thus we have a more markedly admirable illustration than at any other time of his principle of appearing at the decisive point with overwhelming forces, neglecting all considerations of secondary importance. And just as in 1800, against Kray's left wing, these overwhelming forces were now set in motion against the right wing of the Austrian army in Germany, as indeed the reconnaissance of the roads by Savary led us to expect. This wing was the right one to attack, for it was the one first met with from the North-West and indeed from the North, whence two corps, those of Bernadotte and Marmont, were marching. Therefore, by attacking and turning this wing with superior strength, the Emperor would cut the Austrians entirely off from their communications with Vienna, and consequently annihilate them.

Here we must point out the difference which is shown between Napoleon's strategy and that in vogue nowadays. Napoleon, as appeared from his first plan in 1800, and as now may be more particularly noted here, effected the strategical concentration of his army in the first place on the enemy's flank, so that with a simple forward movement for battle he gained the latter's communications; hence the first encounter could not fail to prove an Ulm or a Jena. Nowadays this can no longer be done. Inasmuch as we must endeavour now to employ *all* the railway lines for our concentration, and inasmuch as the enemy also has to make use of all his railway lines leading towards the frontier, there will be in the main a frontal concentration on the part of both combatants, and it will no longer be possible to gain such an enormous advantage with respect to *space* in the first massing of forces, as Napoleon gained here by his strategical marches on the enemy's flank; it will only be possible to gain an advantage in point of time.

In Napoleon's day there was plenty of time during the march of the armies to the field (for then they had to march) to become acquainted with the enemy's formation and to direct one's own concentration to his flank, assuming of course a correct strategical perception of the situation. The modern rapidity of mobilization and of the strategical deployment by means of railways, have made the latter a task which must be arranged in all its details during peace; it is therefore impossible to alter it according to the position of the enemy's flank. Only after the armies have been massed and operations have begun, can a superiority of strategical calculation be displayed as to placing oneself on the flank or the rear of the enemy; hence the manœuvres with which Napoleon was in the habit of opening his campaigns, will only be possible after the first few encounters. We can no longer begin immediately with a Jena, but we can still, after a Wörth or a Spicheren, choose our lines of operation in such a manner that we may force the enemy to a Gravelotte.

Whilst the Emperor's confidential officers were thus, as ordered, examining the country to be traversed, he gave his chief of the staff, Berthier, the necessary instructions for the "counter-march of his whole army,"[1] and on the 31st August he exclaimed gleefully: "The Grand Army is in full march, it will have arrived entire on the Rhine by the 24th September."[2] *In extenso*, these marching orders ran as follows: "Bernadotte will collect his corps at Göttingen and arrive at Würzburg by the 23rd and 24th September. Marmont will march to Mainz, collect his troops there between the 20th and 25th September, and then join Bernadotte at Würzburg. Of the troops on the English Channel, the first divisions of the corps of Davout (left wing), Soult (centre), and Ney (right wing), will start on the 28th August; the next divisions will follow at an interval of two days' march, and the last in their turn at an interval of one day's march." The Emperor himself remained for the present at Boulogne, in order to divert the enemy's attention from this movement, but he appointed Murat his representative with the army, and ordered him to reach Strasburg by the 11th September. The Guards also, under Bessières, started for this latter place from Boulogne on the 31st August.

On the 29th August the Emperor arranged the following distribution of the "Grand Army of 1805":

In command: The Emperor.
Chief of the Staff: Berthier.

		Inf. Divs.	Cav. Divs.	
The Guards.	Bessières			6,000 men
I. Corps.	Bernadotte:	Drouet	Kellermann	18,000 men
		Rivaud		
II. Corps.	Marmont:	Boudet	Lacoste	
		Grouchy		
		Dumonceau		21,000 men

---

[1] C. N., 25th August.   [2] C. N. To Eugene, Camp of Boulogne.

		Inf. Divs.	*Light Cav. Divs.*	
III. Corps.	Davout:	Bisson Friant Gudin	Vialannes	27,000 men
IV. Corps.	Soult:	St. Hilaire Vandamme Legrand Suchet	Margaron	41,000 men
V. Corps.	Lannes:	Oudinot Gazan	Treilhard	18,000 men
VI. Corps	Ney:	Dupont Loison Malher	Tilly	24,000 men

Cavalry Reserve: Murat.

Cuirassier division:	Nansouty.	
" "	d'Hautpoul.	
Dragoon division:	Klein.	
" "	Walther.	
" "	Beaumont.	
" "	Bourcier.	
Dismounted dragoons:	Baraguey d'Hilliers	22,000 men

As a reserve there were still in the rear and in process of formation:

| VII. Corps. Augereau. | Inf. div.: | Desjardins | |
| | " " | M. Mathieu | 14,000 men |

In Germany he was joined by the following in addition:

Bavarian Corps:	Deroy	20,000 men
Württemburg contingent:	Seeger	5,000 men
Baden contingent:	Harrant	3,000 men

So that the grand total of the active army amounted to 219,000 men.

Of this army the Emperor proudly declared at that time: "Assuredly there is no finer army in Europe than mine is to-day;"[1] and even at the close of his life he called it "the best army that ever existed."[2] And indeed it was so constituted as to justify his praise. The men were, it is true, only to a small extent soldiers of long service, most of them belonged to the levy of the year before, but they had been uninterruptedly in camp for a year and a half, and had been drilled assiduously. One of their leaders at that time said: "The troops very rapidly reached a degree of perfection, which can hardly be imagined. I

---

[1] C. N. To Cambacérès. Camp of Boulogne, 13th August.
[2] Mém. de Ste. Hél. II. 319.

have never seen it attained in a like manner by any French troops."[1] Well drilled, well organized troops, whose powers of endurance are not yet weakened by their own personal experience of the sufferings, dangers, and hardships of war, are assuredly the best material.

But, above all, their commanders were excellent. Of the seven corps-leaders in the army destined for Germany only two, Augereau and Bernadotte had passed their fortieth year; three, Soult, Lannes and Ney, were contemporaries of the Emperor, then thirty-six years old; Davout was one year younger, and Marmont was not yet thirty-two. Of the commanders of divisions half were still in the thirties, and of the others d'Hautpoul alone had reached fifty. Thus all the men who commanded in the most important posts were still in their prime. All still had a future before them, and were therefore filled with an eager thirst for action, full of initiative and enterprise. And all moreover were well versed in war, most of them familiar with Napoleon's methods of strategy, and each accustomed to unconditional obedience.

Meanwhile, the Austrians also had set their forces in motion against the Bavarian frontier. The Archduke Ferdinand was entrusted with the chief command of this army, though the Emperor Francis reserved to himself the supreme direction of operations, and appointed for this purpose General Mack as his quartermaster-general. Napoleon had become acquainted with Mack in the year 1800, as a prisoner of war, and had at that time said of him: "Mack is one of the most mediocre men I ever met in my life. Full of conceit and vanity, he considers himself fit to do anything. He is nothing now, but I should like to see him some day opposed to one of our good generals, he would see fine things; he is very self-confident, and that is all; he is one of the most incapable men possible, and, in addition, he is unlucky."[2] It was this man, then, who was to be the Emperor's

[1] Marmont, Mém. II. 231.   [2] Bourrienne, Mem. III. 275.

special adviser, and the real conductor of the operations.

On the 2nd September, Mack arrived in Wels, and immediately gave orders for the army to advance into Bavaria. It was, as a matter of fact, not yet massed on the frontier, but as the French were still at a distance, Bavaria might, by prompt action, be forced to become an ally, or be disarmed before Napoleon's arrival. Here it could be said with justice: " Time presses and days are months." [1] But scarcely had the Austrians entered Bavaria, than they allowed themselves to be delayed by evasive negotiations on the part of the Elector, during which the Bavarian army, taking advantage of these, retreated behind the Danube, and only concentrated again at Amberg, and then at Bamberg. The Austrians marched, meanwhile, unconcernedly on along the south bank of the Danube, and on the 21st their front reached Memmingen. Mack inspected Ulm, and then reconnoitred the Iller, which river he had chosen as his line of defence. It is true the Archduke Ferdinand, who had arrived at Alt-Oetting on the 19th September, endeavoured to stop the forward march of the army, so as not to be forced to give battle in such an advanced and isolated position before the arrival of the Russians, but the Emperor Francis, who had reached Munich on the 20th, countermanded his orders, full of confidence in Mack, and the Austrians continued massing along the Iller. But on the 23rd September, Kienmaier was appointed to keep watch with one corps upon the Bavarians and Bernadotte, whose arrival at Mainz had become known; this corps was to take up a position along the line Neuburg—Ingolstadt.

In the meantime, Napoleon himself had, after having set his army in motion towards the Rhine, returned to St. Cloud, in order to conceal as long as possible the great offensive movement which he had set on foot.

[1] C. N. N. to Daru. Camp of Boulogne, 30th August.

With this same intention, he wrote to Fouché: "Prohibit all mention, in the newspapers, of the army on the banks of the Rhine; let it be as if it did not exist at all,"[1] and although the influence of the press at that time was far different from what it is nowadays, yet this precaution will surely be pronounced to have been very advisable, especially if we remember how greatly the French and Belgian newspapers hindered the chances of success of MacMahon's march in August, 1870. And whilst the Emperor thus took good care to hide his movements from the enemy, he himself received from Murat at Strasburg a preliminary notification, dated the 10th September, as to the result of the latter's reconnaissance. According to this, some 60,000 Austrians were then at Wels, 10,000 to 12,000 at Braunau, and about 15,000 near the lake of Constance; at Braunau a camp was being planned for 30,000 men, and enormous depôts established; finally, some 80,000 Russians were on the frontiers of Galicia.

On the 7th September, the Emperor had already issued orders for forming reserve camps. One of these was to be near Strasburg, under Kellermann, and another near Mainz, under Lefebvre. In addition, Mainz, Strasburg, Neu-Breisach, and Hüningen were to be placed in a state of defence. This method of ensuring the reinforcement of his army by the establishment of direct reserves, and of securing his base by fortifying the strong places near it, is one of those precautionary measures which this audacious but careful general always took.

Meanwhile, he continued to keep a watchful eye upon the Austrians. "It seems," he wrote on the 13th September, "the Austrians crossed the Inn on the 10th September."[2] But his own troops also were now approaching the Rhine, and accordingly the Emperor sent, on the 17th September, orders for the regulation of the passage of this river, and of the further lines of march

[1] C. N. St. Cloud, 12th September.   [2] C. N. To Eugène, St. Cloud.

of the individual corps. These orders form one of those documents which reveal Napoleon's strategical insight in the clearest light; the simplicity, clearness, and practical nature of all the instructions render them one of the most valuable lessons in studying, map in hand, how to arrange broadly the movements of an army.

And how did these orders come into existence, how did he work in order to obtain such a firm grip of the strategical situation? Let us inquire of one of those who saw him at work: "The Emperor was himself really his own chief of the staff; holding in his hand a pair of compasses, opened for a distance, by scale, of seven to eight leagues in a straight line (a distance which, reckoning the turnings of the roads, generally covers nine to ten leagues of march, at least), bent, nay, often lying over his map, on which the positions of his army corps and the supposed positions of the enemy were marked by pins of different colours, he arranged his own movements with a certainty of which we can scarcely form a just idea. Moving his compasses vigorously over his chart, he judged in a moment of the number of marches for each of his corps, which would be necessary so as to reach any point he wished it to reach on a fixed day, and then, sticking his pins into these fresh positions, and calculating the speed at which each column could move, he dictated those orders, which if they stood alone would entitle him to glory."[1]

It was only very rarely that the Emperor issued any orders dealing with his army as a whole. For he not only tried to avoid the possibility of the enemy getting wind of his intentions, in case they should capture an individual order, but he also shrank from making them known to his own army, as he was convinced that a secret known to many is sure to leak out somehow or other; whilst it was always a part of his plan to surprise the enemy as to space and time. In most cases, therefore, every corps leader re-

[1] Jomini, Précis, etc., 289.

ULM

ceived instructions only upon what he himself had to do, whilst, with respect to the general position of the army, he received additional information only concerning the corps next to his own. It is the careful study of these personal órders of the Emperor which is of the highest value for every officer; they contain the secrets of what the old school called "logistics," and what the modern school calls "staff duties." The Emperor referred in an incisive and definite manner to the movements as a whole, which he desired to see carried out; he did not indeed follow any fixed rule of sequence, but dictated, just as a thought occurred to him, and the originality and force of his diction, weakened by no formulæ, invested the orders he issued with a special emphasis, so that it was felt to be a simple impossibility not to execute an order couched in such terms. "Do not go to sleep before having sent me all these details."[1] "I congratulate you upon the successes you have gained. But do not give yourself any rest; pursue the enemy, with your sword at his ribs, and cut all his communications."[2] "Should the enemy not be in Memmingen, you will come down like lightning to our level."[3] "I recommend you to make your aides-de-camp and assistants ride their horses to death. Distribute them in relays upon the road to Weissenhorn, so that I may get your news as quickly as possible."[4] As to details, he only mentions them, if they have any special bearing upon the execution of the general plan, but in such cases he never fails to do so. It was Berthier's business to elaborate the orders, to regulate all particulars, to give to the whole the customary shape and to communicate them to the army.[5]

The above mentioned orders for the crossing of the

[1] C. N. To Bernadotte, Augsburg, 11th October, 1805, 3 p.m.
[2] C. N. To Murat, Abbey of Elchingen, 17th October, 1805, 2 p.m.
[3] C. N. To Soult, Augsburg, 12th October, 1805, 10.30 p.m.
[4] C. N To Soult, Augsburg, 12th October, 1805, 10.30 a.m.
[5] Berthier was chief of the staff in all Napoleon's campaigns from 1800 to 1814.—ED.

Rhine conveyed briefly the following instructions: In the first place the independent divisions of cavalry will cross. On the 25th September, Nansouty will reach Heidelberg, and Klein Bruchsal. The latter will advance to Bretten as soon as Soult's first division has crossed. Bourcier will cross at Kehl on the 25th, and then turn to the north, in order to cover Ney's passage, on the 26th he will proceed to Durlach. Beaumont and d'Hautpoul will cross at Kehl early in the morning of the 25th, the former will then march to Offenburg, the latter to Oberkirch. Baraguey d'Hilliers, with Walther under him, will cross at Neu Breisach on the 25th, and then proceed to Freiburg, clearing the country from this place towards Donaueschingen.

The army will follow in rear of the main body of the cavalry. Davout's first division will cross on the 26th at Mannheim, where he will establish his headquarters on this day; his other divisions will press on to Mannheim, his cavalry will advance as far as Sinsheim.

Soult's first division will cross at Germersheim on the 25th; it will then march to Bruchsal, where Soult will establish his headquarters on the 26th.

Ney's first division will cross at Selz on the 25th and proceed to Rastadt, where his headquarters will be established on the 26th.

Finally Lannes' first division will cross the Rhine at Kehl on the 25th.

The Rhine having been crossed, the army will execute the following movements:

Lannes will advance on the Kniebis road through Sand, Oberkirch, Freudenstadt, Rottenburg, Reutlingen, Urach to Ulm, where he will have to arrive on the 9th October. His march will begin on the 29th September.

Ney will also proceed *viâ* Durlach, Pforzheim, Stuttgart, Esslingen, Göppingen and Geisslingen to Ulm. His march will begin on the 27th September, and by the 7th October he must reach Ulm.

Soult will push forward on the road through Bruchsal, Bretten, Vaihingen, Ludwigsburg, Schorndorf, Gmünd to Aalen, which latter place he is to reach on the 9th October.

Davout will march on the 29th September and take the road *viâ* Mannheim, Heidelburg, Sinsheim, Heilbronn, Oehringen, Hall, Ellwangen, and is to reach Nördlingen on the 10th October.

Bernadotte and Marmont will start from Würzburg on the 30th September or 1st October, so as to reach Weissenburg by the 9th October.

On this latter day the Guards, the Reserve Cavalry and the Great Artillery Park will be at Gmünd.

In short, therefore, the main body of the army was, according to the above orders, to cross the Rhine along a line from Mannheim to Kehl, seventy miles in extent, on the 26th September, the independent divisions of cavalry having preceded it on the 25th by the same roads. The latter would arrive before the entrances to the defiles of the Black Forest and penetrate some way into them. Thus they would not only cover their own army during the passage of the Rhine, but also create in the enemy a mistaken impression as to the real direction of the Emperor's advance. For, as we see, the mass of the army was not to cross the Black Forest frontally, but turn to the left, so as to avoid its passes, and to stand by the 9th October on the line Weissenburg—Nördlingen—Aalen—Ulm.

This employment of the cavalry may be called masterly. It is indeed a characteristic, uniformly noticeable in the strategy of all the greatest generals, that they knew how to utilize their cavalry to the best advantage. For it is this arm, designed for a wide field and rapidity of movement, which requires superior officers of exceptionally large grasp and quick resolution, who, keeping only the great aims of a war in view, are able to set aside objects of secondary importance and to put up with heavy losses also, for cavalry employed over a large area must often get into situations from which it cannot withdraw without suffering them. Napoleon himself said: "The use of cavalry demands boldness and ability, above all it should not be handled with any miserly desire to keep it intact,"[1] and again, as we shall note in this very campaign: "I do not wish the horses to be spared, if they can catch men."[2] "Take no heed of the complaints of the cavalry, for if such great objects may be attained as the destruction of a whole hostile army, the state can afford to lose a few hundred horses from exhaustion."[3] This was Gneisenau's conviction, and as to what was effected by the cavalry of Lee's army, we need only mention the name of Stuart.

The above orders did not, however, include the final turning manœuvre, which was to place the army in full force upon the enemy's rear; they rather pointed to a direct advance *en masse*, for the Emperor did not yet know that the Austrians were going to push forward so far by themselves without waiting for the Russians; still the general idea of attacking the enemy's right wing in full strength appears clearly in them.

But twenty-four hours after the despatch of those orders, the Emperor learnt by telegraph that the Austrians had crossed the Lech, and on the 20th he received a letter from Murat, dated the 18th, informing him that the enemy was approaching Ulm. He therefore ordered a slight alteration in the lines of operation. Davout was now to march from Mannheim *viâ* Heidelberg, Neckarelz, Ilshofen, and Dinkelsbühl to Nördlingen. Soult was to cross the Rhine at Spires and proceed to Aalen through Sinsheim, Heilbronn, Oehringen and Hall; Ney was to cross at Pforz and take the high-road past Durlach, Pforzheim, Stuttgart and Gmünd to Giengen, and finally Lannes was to leave the Kniebis road at Rottenburg and

[1] Mém. de Ste. Hél. Notes sur l'introduction à l'hist. de la guerre &c., par Lloyd, III. 509.
[2] C. N. To Lannes, Znaym, 18th November, 11 p.m.
[3] Blücher to Yorck, Hohlstein, 31st August, 1813.

march to Göppingen *viâ* Tübingen, Grötzingen and Nürtingen. We see thus, that the corps were on the whole closer together, and that the general direction tended more to the left, that is, the idea of the turning movement is more apparent, and as the enemy was now at a less distance, the ability to quickly mass the whole army became the first consideration.

But still more definitely did the Emperor's plan become revealed in a short memorandum in his own hand, which he wrote down at that time for his own use; it is only to be regretted that it is not dated, but it must have been written shortly before the crossing of the Rhine, that is, between the 22nd and 24th September. It is as follows:

	28th Sept.	6th Oct.	9th Oct.	16th Oct.
Bernadotte	... Würzburg	Ansbach	Nürnberg	Regensburg
Marmont	... ″	″	″	″
Davout	... Mannheim	Mergentheim	Ansbach	Dietfurt
Ney	... Selz	Crailsheim	Weissenburg	Ingolstadt
Lannes	... Strasburg	Gmünd	Nördlingen	Neuburg
Soult	... Landau	Aalen	Donauwörth	

The above shows that Napoleon had for a time a more extensive turning-movement in his mind, undoubtedly under the supposition that the Austrians would not, on hearing of his forward march, remain stationary, but would fall back, and that he consequently must make a further sweep to turn their flank and cut them off. For the present, however, the orders given were not altered.

But when he saw that, contrary to his expectation, the Austrians remained stationary, he issued the final orders for turning them by a still shorter line, and on the 28th September Berthier despatched these to the army.

Davout was now to march through Heidelberg, Obrigheim, Möckmühl, Ingelfingen, Ilshofen, Dinkelsbühl, Oettingen and Monheim, and reach Neuburg on the 8th October.

Soult was to march *viâ* Heilbronn, Oehringen, Hall, Ellwangen and Nördlingen, and reach Donauwörth on the 8th.

Lannes was to take the road through Ludwigsburg, Schorndorf, Gmünd and Aalen, and arrive on the 8th in Neresheim.

Ney was to march along the road through Stuttgart, Esslingen and Weilheim, so as to reach Heidenheim on the 7th.

The cavalry, after having made a feint on the passes through the Black Forest, was to march through Stuttgart, Göppingen and Heidenheim, and be in Donauwörth on the 8th October.

Bernadotte received orders to march from Ansbach to Eichstädt, where he was to arrive on the 8th, and from which he was to operate towards Ingolstadt.

Marmont was to advance on Bernadotte's right *viâ* Rothenburg, Feuchtwangen and Wassertrüdingen, and to reach Treuchtlingen on the 7th, whence he was to take the direction towards Nassenfels.

And all these movements were executed with such precision and fidelity to the plan, that Napoleon could, three weeks after the passage of the Rhine, say: " I have attained my object; I have destroyed the Austrian army by sheer marching." [1]

The main body of the Grand Army crossed the Rhine on the 26th September. On the same day the Emperor having left Paris on the 24th, arrived in Strasburg. The corps took the road assigned to them, and no sooner had the Emperor set these movements going than he anticipated their full success. " Woe to the Austrians," he exclaimed, "if they allow me to gain a few marches upon them, I hope to have turned them and to find myself with my whole army between the Lech and the Iser," [2] and to Eugene he wrote: " The enemy seems entirely dumfounded by the direction, rapidity and vigour of our movements." [3]

---

[1] C. N. To Josephine, Elchingen, 19th October.
[2] C. N. To Augereau, Strasburg, 30th December.
[3] C. N. Strasburg, 30th September.

ULM

Whilst the French army was thus on the march to the Danube, Mack was still flattering himself that he was perfectly secure. In the middle of September he had, as mentioned above, inspected the line of the Iller and given orders to extend the fortifications in the neighbourhood of Ulm, with the intention of either awaiting there in a strong position the approach of the Russians, or of throwing himself upon one of the French columns as it advanced. But this idea was not justified either by the rapidity of his concentration or the numbers of the force he could collect. On the 3rd October the Austrian army stood in the following positions: General Jellacic, with 14,000 men, in the Vorarlberg; Generals Riesch, with 19,000 men, and Schwarzenberg, with 11,500 men, along the Iller and the Danube from Kempten as far as Günzburg. General Kienmaier's 6000 men were split up into small bodies in the north for purposes of observation round Neuberg, Ingolstadt, Eichstädt, Ellwangen and Amberg. From the rear and the Tyrol, reinforcements of some 18,000 men were on the march to join Mack.

The execution of Mack's plan of a concentration at Ulm was about to commence. On the 5th October Jellacic received orders to draw nearer to the Danube; in order to cover the district between this river and the lake of Constance, he was to arrive in Biberach on the 7th and 8th. The other corps had orders to march to Ulm, and on the 6th the main body of Schwarzenberg and Riesch stood near this town; on the right the front of the army extended to Günzburg, on the left to Illereichen. Kienmaier had collected his men at Neuburg. This concentration at Ulm did not escape the Emperor's attention, and on the evening of the 5th he said to himself: "The enemy is only becoming aware of our movement to-day, and is concentrating at Ulm."[1]

During the night of the 5th—6th the Emperor had slept

[1] C. N. Berthier to Soult, Gmünd, 10 p.m.

at Gmünd. On the morning of the 6th he moved his headquarters first to Aalen, but on the afternoon of the same day he reached Nördlingen. The more he advanced the more he saw his hopes realized. On the 2nd October he wrote: "The enemy is making marches and counter-marches, and seems to be in a state of embarrassment."[1] But he fully recognized that the enemy had not yet made up his mind to retreat. "It seems the enemy has already set some part of his forces in motion towards Donauwörth and Ingolstadt; but his movements are feeble and I do not think general. He still holds Stockach, Memmingen and the Tyrol."[2] However, he did not neglect warning his corps-leaders to support each other at once, if the enemy's army should take the offensive against either his right or left wing, and this support was certain to be effective and timely, considering the close order in which the Emperor's army advanced. For, as he himself said, with satisfaction: "Never has such a large mass of troops manœuvred in so small a space."[3]

He himself had during the advance moved his headquarters more and more towards the right wing of the army, for if the enemy took the offensive they must come in contact with this wing; but now that he recognized their inactivity and perceived that his own great flank-movement over the Danube would probably be effected without interruption, he went back to Nördlingen, to his centre. The various corps were in the following positions on the 6th October:

On the left wing Bernadotte (whom the Bavarians had joined at Würzburg on the 2nd) had reached Weissenburg and Marmont Wassertrüdingen; in the centre stood Davout at Oettingen, Soult at Nördlingen; the latter's advanced guard, under Vandamme, captured the bridge of Münster in the evening. Behind Soult stood

---

[1] C. N. To Joseph, Ettlingen.
[2] C. N. To Bernadotte, Ludwigsburg, 4th October.
[3] C. N. To Otto, Ludwigsburg, 5th October.

Lannes at Neresheim, and Bessières at Aalen. On the right wing Ney near Heidenheim protected the whole movement, as well as the communications of the army towards Ulm. Murat, with the divisions of Walther, Klein and Beaumont, was in a forward position near the Danube; Baraguey and Bourcier stood at Geisslingen to protect the right wing, and as rear-guards d'Hautpoul followed behind Bessières and Nansouty behind Soult.

Early on the 7th Murat first crossed the Danube at Donauwörth and then turned towards Rain; Soult followed, taking the direction of Augsburg. The other corps marching in their respective directions, reached: Bernadotte, Eichstädt; Marmont, Treuchtlingen; Lannes, Nördlingen; Davout, Monheim; d'Hautpoul now closed up to Nördlingen, Nansouty was ordered up quickly and arrived in front of Donauwörth. Ney, who had at first also had orders to march to Donauwörth, was now to remain stationary in the neighbourhood of Ulm, to cover the operation of crossing the river, and reached Giengen on the same day, Bourcier and Baraguey taking post at Heidenheim in support. But as soon as the army should have safely crossed the Danube, Ney was also, on his way to Ulm, to come nearer to the river, for the Emperor, ever anxious to have all his forces present for any possible battle, wished to be able to send Ney across the Danube, if necessary. (36)

Mack had resolved to collect his army at Günzburg, as soon as he heard, on the afternoon of the 7th, that the French had begun to cross the Danube. He immediately sent Riesch there, Schwarzenberg was to follow as soon as Jellacic, who had been ordered up, should have reached Ulm. Of the reinforcements, which had meanwhile arrived in Günzburg, one corps of 5000 men was sent to Wertingen, to hold in the first place such French forces as had already crossed.

Early on the 8th October Murat started from Rain and, turning westward, marched to Wertingen; in this movement Lannes and Nansouty, coming from Donauwörth, joined him. Soon after midday they reached Wertingen and there met the Austrian corps, which had just arrived; they advanced, moving round on both sides, against this place, which the Austrians defended, and the latter were entirely dispersed, cut down, or made prisoners. Murat pursued them and reached Zusmarshausen on the morning of the 9th. On the 8th Bernadotte began to cross the river at Ingolstadt, Soult drew near to Augsburg, Davout crossed at Neuburg and marched towards Aichach; behind him Marmont reached Neuburg, Bessières was in Donauwörth, where d'Hautpoul had already crossed, and Ney was on the march in two columns towards Ulm *viâ* Langenau and towards Günzburg *viâ* Gundelfingen; but an attempt to capture the bridge of Elchingen during the night of the 8th—9th failed. The Emperor arrived at Donauwörth and sent out orders upon order from here, to urge on his subordinate commanders to move forward as quickly as possible. "The least you can send me," he wrote to Soult, "is 3000 or 4000 prisoners;" and to Davout: " Do not lose an hour, and let me hear without delay that you are in possession of Aichach."

Kienmaier had avoided the enemy's combined forward movement by marching to Dachau, and on the 9th Davout reached Aichach, Bernadotte crossed the Danube at Ingolstadt and Marmont at Neuburg; Murat and Lannes reached Zusmarshausen; and Soult, advancing along both banks of the Lech, arrived in Augsburg and Friedberg about noon, closely followed by d'Hautpoul and Bessières.

Mack had, by the 9th, assembled the greater part of his army near Günzburg. The news now reached him of the disastrous fighting at Wertingen and the enemy's appearance at Augsburg and Zusmarshausen, but did not induce him to take any resolution; at last, in the evening, he determined to cross to the left bank of the Danube. In the meantime, Ney had arrived opposite Günzburg, in accordance with the Emperor's orders, and had taken possession of the bridge. Mack now abandoned his plan; and resolved to march back to Ulm, which resolve he carried out during the night, the 9th-10th, his army arriving there during the latter day. Kienmaier meanwhile continued his retrograde movement to the Inn, according to the orders he had received.

The Emperor, who had spent the night among Murat's troops at Zusmarshausen, remained there during the forenoon of the 10th October. He was now of opinion the enemy would not remain in Ulm, but endeavour to escape from the threatened investment, and the most probable direction of their retreat he considered to be towards Memmingen. "His Majesty does not think the enemy will be mad enough to cross to the left bank of the Danube, since all their magazines are at Memmingen, and they have every reason to remain in communication with the Tyrol."[1] He therefore ordered Ney to push forward quickly to Ulm, to take possession of that town, and then immediately start in pursuit of the Austrians. He himself intended to go to Munich, in order to oppose the Russians, whose advance across the Inn, for the purpose of relieving the Austrians, he now expected. In the first place, he fixed upon Davout, Bernadotte, and Marmont for this movement, holding Ney, Lannes, and the cavalry, all under the chief command of Murat, in readiness against Mack.

On the 10th Murat arrived in Burgau, Lannes was still at Zusmarshausen, Soult was collecting his corps at Augsburg, Marmont stood at Pöttmes, Davout was approaching Dachau, and Bernadotte was on the march to Munich. But in the evening, the Emperor, having arrived in Augsburg at nine o'clock, recognized from the news which reached him that the main body of the Austrians was still near Ulm, and that the Russians, on

(37)

[1] C. N. Berthier to Ney, 8th October.

their part, seemed to have no intention of taking the offensive, and he now resolved to have these latter watched by Bernadotte and Davout only, whilst he himself would advance with the remainder of the army towards Ulm, taking care at the same time to block the Austrian retreat to the Tyrol. Consequently, Soult was ordered to march to Landsberg, and Lannes to follow Murat to Burgau, Marmont was to move up to Augsburg, and Davout and Bernadotte, whom d'Hautpoul's cavalry division was to join, were to march on Dachau, and eventually Munich, with all possible speed. "I desire that you should clear all the country between the Iser and the Lech of the enemy."[1]

On the 10th Ney stood near Günzburg, Loison had been despatched to the right bank of the Danube, and Dupont and Bourcier, forming the right wing, were at Albeck. In accordance with the Emperor's commands Ney prepared for a general advance upon Ulm next day. Therefore Dupont started at 11 a.m. from Albeck, but met the bulk of the Austrian army drawn up near Ulm, and was repulsed by it with heavy losses to Albeck; Baraguey, who was to have come up to his support *viâ* Langenau, not having received his orders in time, and the rest of Ney's troops crossed to the right bank of the Danube in obedience to Murat's orders. Lannes approached Burgau, Soult reached Landsberg during the afternoon, the Emperor, with the Guards, remained in Augsburg, and Marmont arrived before this latter town; these corps could from here, according to the development of affairs on "this large theatre of war, which is changing every moment,"[2] be thrown into the scale either against Mack or against the Russians. Davout reached Dachau, and Bernadotte was in Freising. Kienmaier retreated hurriedly towards the Inn, and there received news that 8000 Russians had arrived in Braunau.

[1] C. N. To Bernadotte, Augsburg, 11th October, 3 p.m.
[2] Ibid.

Mack had fought an engagement on this day with Dupont, and learnt that Ney had crossed to the right bank of the Danube. He now hit upon the idea that Napoleon had turned against the Russians with the bulk of his army; he therefore projected an advance to Heidenheim, thus attacking Napoleon's lines of communication. However, before he could obtain the consent of the archduke Ferdinand, who was nominally commander-in-chief, the 12th October passed, and the execution of his plan could not begin until the 13th.

Now the Emperor was convinced that his opponent could no longer escape him. "The decisive moment has come,"[1] he said, but he wished his success to be a complete and crushing one, therefore he would not deliver his decisive blow until he had assembled his whole forces against Mack. "It is my intention," he said, in the morning of the 12th, "should the enemy continue in his present positions, and be ready to accept battle, to fight, not to-morrow, but the day after, so that Marshal Soult and his 30,000 men may take part in it; he will march to the enemy's right flank, and attack when he has turned it, a manœuvre which will assure us a decisive result."[2] Thus carefully did the Emperor always prepare for battle, so as to have beforehand every advantage on his side. For which reason he always kept the direction of the main outlines of his plan in his own hands to avoid untoward incidents from the independent action of his subordinates. "Everything," says Bülow, "with this extraordinary general is directed to the annihilation of the enemy."[3]

On the 12th, Bernadotte entered Munich as early as six o'clock a.m. Davout and d'Hautpoul stood fast at Dachau to watch the Russians. Soult reached Mindelheim, and Marmont's vanguard, closely followed by his whole corps, arrived at Tannhausen. Murat, with Lannes

---

[1] C. N. To Soult, Augsburg, 12th October, 10.30 a.m.
[2] C. N. To Murat, Augsburg, 9 o'clock.
[3] Der Feldzug von 1805, I. 213.

and his cavalry, was on the Rothbach on the line Wissenhorn—Pfaffenhofen—Fahlheim; on their right was Ney, of whose corps Dupont's and Bourcier's divisions were, however, still on the left bank of the Danube; these fell back that day to the east behind the Brenz, where they took up a position. Bessières was at Zusmarshausen. Thus the semicircle, which was to enclose Mack, was already closing in, two more marches, and it would be completed. "On the 14th, the day of the battle, the enemy will be annihilated, for he is hemmed in on all sides." [1]

Anticipating a certain victory, the emperor announced to his army that "Never will so much have been decided in so short a time"; [2] proudly he referred more than once to the resemblance between Mack's present situation and that of Melas at Marengo, and alluded to the lightning stroke which was to strike down the enemy. It is of advantage to show such confidence of victory to one's army, and thus to awaken the same in the men, but this will only be effected if the general is really confident in himself, for an army is exceedingly alive to the frame of mind of its leader. Certainly, modesty as to results would be out of place in warfare. Ever restless, the Emperor's thoughts already travelled beyond this success which he now held to be assured, "on the completion of this affair, his Majesty will return, so as to cross the Inn immediately." [3]

In the evening of the 12th October, at 10.30 p.m., the Emperor left Augsburg. At the moment of entering his carriage, he received a despatch from Murat, that the enemy was still at Ulm; Soult also now received orders to march to Ulm, though he had been up till then on the march towards Memmingen, with the intention of blocking Mack's escape to the Tyrol. Then the Emperor drove

---

[1] C. N. Berthier to Davout, Augsburg, 12h October, 8.30 p.m.
[2] Fifth bulletin, Augsburg, 12th October.
[3] C. N. Berthier to Davout, Augsburg, 12th October, 8.30 p.m.

through the night and the pouring rain, which had been continuous since the 8th, thirty miles to Pfaffenhofen.

On the 13th, Mack commenced his projected advance to Heidenheim; he marched part of his troops in that direction, part towards Gundelfingen, while sending Jellacic back into the Vorarlberg. The vanguard of the former column reached Heidenheim, but the other column met with a French detachment near the bridge of Elchingen, which it repulsed, occupying this village; the enemy, however, destroyed the bridge, and the Austrians could not advance any further. Mack now fell into the most egregious errors; he even went so far as to assume that Napoleon was endeavouring to force a return to France, as a rebellion had broken out in Paris and the English had landed in France! In consequence of this opinion, he retained half of his army, which was still at Ulm, in that town and did not send it after the other half, which had advanced towards Heidenheim and Elchingen. Napoleon said afterwards about him: " His arrangements have constantly been wrong, nor has he ever guessed my plans correctly."[1]

Whilst the Emperor had hitherto inclined to the (38) opinion that the enemy would try to escape to the Tyrol, by what was still the most open road, he now heard at Pfaffenhofen, on the morning of the 13th, of Dupont's defeat at Albeck, and immediately went to Ney's headquarters at Kussendorf, for he perceived that the enemy was endeavouring to break out towards the north, and sent Ney to Dupont's assistance across the bridge of Elchingen to the left bank of the Danube. On the 14th, therefore, Ney advanced towards Elchingen and Dupont towards Albeck; the former defeated the Austrians, who tried to defend Elchingen, took the town by assault, and drove the enemy back towards Ulm. Lannes approached Ulm and took up a position on the heights of Pfuhl;

[1] C.N. To Talleyrand, Abbey of Elchingen, 17th October.

whilst Marmont reached the Iller at Lower and Upper Kirchberg. During the night of the 13th, Soult appeared before Memmingen and summoned its garrison, a little over 4000 men, to surrender, which it did on the evening of the 14th. But the Emperor's attention was now fully directed to the northern bank of the Danube; he established his headquarters in the evening of the 14th at the abbey of Elchingen, and sent orders to Lannes, Bessières, and the greater part of the cavalry, to move up to that place before break of day; for on this bank of the Danube the main attack was to be delivered, whilst on the other, Marmont, in position at Pfuhl, was to endeavour, in conjunction with Beaumont and Baraguey, merely to hold the enemy in check.

Towards noon on the 15th, Ney also moved forward to Ulm, and occupied the Michelsberg, which commanded that town, but he could make no impression on the fortifications, though there were only 27,000 men there now. On the same day Soult reached Biberach. Ney sent a flag of truce into the town at six o'clock, summoning Mack to surrender, but for the present without success. After one hour's bombardment on the 16th the Emperor himself opened negotiations again, and in the afternoon of the 17th these were concluded. "My plan," he could now say with satisfaction, "was carried out exactly as I conceived it. I deceived the enemy completely, and of this army of 100,000 men more than half are prisoners, killed, wounded, or stragglers."[1] Mack had given his word to surrender if by midnight on the 25th no relief should have arrived. But he was induced to withdraw this reservation, and on the 20th, at 3 p.m., the Austrian army shut up in Ulm laid down its arms.

The column, which, as we have seen, had marched towards Heidenheim on the 13th, had safely reached Herbrechtingen on the 14th. But although no longer directly involved in the events at Ulm, it did not escape

[1] To Talleyrand, Abbey of Elchingen, 17th October.

the same fate. It had attempted at first to operate on the 15th against Napoleon's rear, and had marched towards Albeck, but there received orders from the Archduke Ferdinand, who had luckily escaped the investment with some cavalry, to march back to Aalen. It however attracted the notice of the Emperor on the morning of the 16th, and he at once despatched Dupont, Oudinot, and Murat's cavalry to pursue and cut it off. It was half annihilated, and the remnant laid down their arms at Trochtelfingen on the 18th.

Thus the Austrian army, which had invaded Bavaria, was entirely destroyed three weeks after Napoleon crossed the Rhine, and the first campaign of the war of 1805 was at an end.

It is only very rarely that a campaign can be conducted so exactly in accordance with the originally conceived plan, just like well-ordered manœuvres in peace time, and in such a manner, that we see clearly before us the birth of the resolution and its development and execution step by step. This campaign, therefore, is all the more instructive and an admirable testimony to the clearness, logic and force of Napoleon's strategy. His plan was framed, as every good plan of campaign ought to be, in such a manner, that in the main its execution was independent of chance occurrences. Whatever happened, Napoleon's great turning-movement with his whole massed forces was beyond the influence of circumstances.

Napoleon's strategy has been called "one-sided"; people have said: "He was really in his element only where the course of events allowed an unrestricted offensive, that is, strictly speaking, only at the head of superiors numbers."[1] But Bülow very justly points out, that he did not open this campaign with larger forces than Frederick did his, and 1796, as well as 1814, the beginning and end of his career, prove irrefutably that he was also able to vanquish an enemy much superior in numbers

[1] Bernhardi, Fredrich de Grosse als Feldherr, II. 645.

by means of his superior strategy. But even if he had always acted on the offensive and always been at the head of superior numbers, this would, far from telling against him, be the best proof of the greatness of his genius. The Archduke Charles said: "People wanted to lessen Bonaparte's glory by the remark, that he owed most of his successes to his superior forces. Could there be indeed any greater praise of a statesman, than that he never began any war or campaign, without being sure of such superiority? Even where his active forces were roughly equal to or perhaps weaker than the enemy's, as for example in the campaigns of 1796 and 1814, he knew how to ensure his superiority at decisive points and at the decisive moment."[1] Indeed 1805 is a proof of this, for the total strength of the Austrians and Russians was in no way inferior in numbers to Napoleon's forces, and yet the latter appeared at the decisive moment at the decisive point with an overwhelming superiority of numbers.

[1] Oesterr. Mil. Zeitschrift, 1865, I. 121.

CHAPTER X.

AUSTERLITZ.

SCARCELY was the first portion of the campaign at an end and the surrender of Mack's army an accomplished fact, than the Emperor started on his advance to the Inn with a view to improving his success. On the 21st October he left his headquarters in Elchingen at noon and went to Augsburg. His first care here was to establish a new base for his further advance, and he fixed upon the line of the Lech for this. Augsburg was chosen as his central magazine and depôt, and consequently, according to Napoleon's invariable custom, fortified and rendered safe against any hostile attack.

During the decisive days of the war, consisting mostly of marches, the Emperor replied to the complaints as to the commissariat: "In all his letters, General Marmont is always referring to the commissariat. I repeat that in the war of invasion and of rapid movements which the Emperor is waging there can be no depôts, and the commanding generals have themselves to see to it that they procure the necessary supplies from the countries which they traverse."[1] But scarcely was the pressure of circumstances over, scarcely was the "immediate base," as Jomini calls it, which had been chosen for the new chapter of the campaign, reached, than the commander-in-chief again allowed the question of his commissariat to be freely discussed, and expressed himself thus: "We have marched without depôts, circumstances have compelled us to do so. The season

[1] C. N. Berthier to Marmont, Augsburg, 11th October, a.m.

has been extraordinarily favourable for this, but though we were always victorious and could feed on the fruits of the earth, yet we have suffered much. At a season where there were no potatoes in the fields, or if the army had been beaten, the want of depôts would have been a most serious misfortune;"[1] he therefore gave immediate orders for the collection of stores.

In the meantime his corps had started so as to concentrate in the first place on the Iser. Marmont, who was collecting his troops at Weissenhorn on the 20th, received orders to march upon Munich, and Davout was to leave Dachau for Freising; Lannes, accompanied by Nansouty, started from Nördlingen for Landshut, Soult marched on the 21st from Memmingen towards Landsberg. Bernadotte, who was already at Munich, now collected his corps in that town. Ney remained for the present near Ulm. Augereau also was now ordered up from France and was to march to Kempten.

Little had meanwhile been done by the enemy. The Russian troops were assembling at Braunau, where the whole of their infantry had already arrived. The Austrians under Kienmaier were entrenching themselves at Mühldorf, in order to dispute the passage of the Inn at that point. As during the decisive events before Ulm, the French corps of Davout and Bernadotte, who faced them here, could naturally only play a defensive part, and since Kutusov, who had now assumed the chief-command over the united forces, Austrians, 22,000 men, Russians, 30,000 men, showed no desire to advance, there was nothing of any importance done here, until he received, in the evening of the 23rd, from Mack himself, who was passing through on his way to Vienna, official confirmation of the rumours current concerning events at Ulm. Kutusov now resolved to fall back to the Enns. On the 25th and 26th the whole force retreated behind the Inn; all the bridges were burnt, but the right bank was still held.

[1] C. N. To Petiet, Augsburg, 24th October.

On this last day the Emperor, who had arrived in Munich at 6 p.m. on the 24th, was with Lannes' corps at Landshut, Davout was in the neighbourhood of Dorfen, Bernadotte in front of Wasserburg; Marmont had reached Munich, where the Guards also were; Soult had already passed through this town and was on the road to Mühldorf; Augereau had just crossed the Rhine, and Ney was starting from Ulm for Landsberg. Of the cavalry, Walther, Beaumont and d'Hautpoul were at Hohenlinden under Murat; Nansouty under Lannes at Landshut, whither Klein also was on the march from Ingolstadt. In the rear, Bourcier and Baraguey were still standing at Augsburg and Ingolstadt; and the infantry divisions of Dumonceau and Dupont also had remained behind in these towns to cover the left flank of the general forward movement; they were to go to Passau during the further advance; thus Dupont ceased to form part of Ney's corps.

But on the 27th, whilst the Austrians were on the point of evacuating the line of the Inn, orders arrived from the Imperial Council of War in Vienna commanding this river to be defended; consequently they stood fast, the Russians assembling at Wels on the same day.

Of the French, Lannes advanced beyond Vilsbiburg, Murat marched viâ Ampfing to Mühldorf, where Davout joined him; they proceeded to restore the bridge there, Bernadotte doing the same at Wasserburg and Rosenheim. Marmont followed behind Bernadotte, and Soult behind Murat. A little resistance was met with at Mühldorf, it is true, but it was already clear that no real defence of the line of the Inn was contemplated. In the course of the night and on the morning of the 28th the bridge was completely restored, and at noon Murat began to cross; after which he turned towards Burghausen, which place he reached in the evening; at the same time giving orders to begin the restoration of the bridges at Neu-Oetting and Marktl. Davout crossed immediately after him by the bridge of Mühldorf. At the same time Bernadotte also commenced the passage of the river, and, in the second line, Lannes approached Braunau, Soult advanced to near Mühldorf, and Marmont to near Wasserburg. The headquarters were this day moved to Haag, where the Emperor arrived at 11 p.m.

Before daybreak on the 29th he proceeded to Mühldorf, and arrived there in time to see the last troops of Davout crossing; news had moreover come in that the enemy was in full retreat. As to his further forward movement towards the line of the Traun, where he anticipated finding the Russians and Austrians, his plan was to advance to his front towards the Traun to Wels and Lambach, with Murat in the van, followed by Lannes, Soult and Davout; whilst Marmont received orders to turn the enemy's left wing *viâ* Strasswalchen and Vöcklaburg in the direction of Steyer. Bernadotte was ordered to Salzburg, and Ney to Innsbruck, to cover the right flank of the combined advance against any forces that might be detached from the Austrian army in Italy, by occupying Salzburg and the Tyrol, and clearing them of all Austrian troops who might have taken refuge there; Augereau from Kempten was to help him. Should the Emperor meet with very considerable resistance in front, and only in that case, he would throw Bernadotte also upon the enemy's left flank.

On this day, the 29th, Lannes appeared before Braunau, occupied this fortress and the important bridge over the Inn without opposition. On the same evening, at five o'clock, the Emperor arrived at this town "charmed," as he himself said, "at the capture of Braunau, a fortress which I found full of stores, gunpowder and ammunition of all kinds. The enemy here have no longer any commander; they are seized with a panic."[1] He immediately constituted this town his principal depôt instead of Augsburg, thus pushing his "immediate base" forward from the Lech to the Inn. Murat had advanced beyond

[1] C. N. To Talleyrand, Braunau, 30th October.

Braunau as far as the neighbourhood of Altheim. Davout crossed at Burghausen to the right bank of the Selzach, Marmont reached Tittmoning, Soult passed the Inn at Mühldorf, and Bernadotte entered Salzburg. Whilst the Emperor remained for a few days at Braunau, these corps continued their forward movement uninterruptedly, so that on the 31st October Murat was in advance at Lambach on the Traun, Lannes on the left wing near Schärding in the direction of Linz, on his right Soult at Obernberg in the direction of Wels; then Davout further away at Haag in the direction of Lambach, and finally Marmont at Strasswalchen, in the direction of Vöcklaburg.

We see therefore that the Emperor utilized these days to "separate in order to live," but was ever desirous of "uniting in order to fight." He now impressed upon the commander of his vanguard, that it was necessary "to give time to every one to make his movements, therefore you must not advance too quickly;"[1] and furthermore, "you must be cautious in your advance. The Russians have not suffered yet and they know how to attack."[2] Thus he, who was so overbearing in his political successes, knew eminently how to combine in purely military matters caution and boldness. In this instance the Emperor had become aware of the need of caution by the fact, that on the preceding day, the 30th, Murat had again come in contact with the enemy; he had met the Austrian rear-guard at Ried, and had thrown it into the defile there.

The Austrians had in the meantime withdrawn their troops, which had been in position along the Inn and the Selzach, in small scattered detachments, their rear-guard holding the bridge of Lambach, whilst their main body stood behind Wimsbach; one division having been dispatched to Gmünden. The Russians were at Wels. On the 31st October Murat pushed with the leading corps of

[1] C. N. To Murat, Braunau, 31st October, 11 a.m.
[2] Ibid.

Davout's division forward towards Lambach, and drove the Austrians about noon beyond the Traun; the latter, however, destroyed the bridge and maintained themselves on the right bank, supported by a few Russian battalions which had come up, until evening. But the allied army immediately continued its retreat, and by the 2nd November the Russians stood behind the Enns at Strenberg with their rear-guard at Enns, the Austrians being at Steyer with their rear-guard on the Krems. Repeated orders arrived from Vienna to defend the Enns.

On the 1st November the Emperor himself arrived in Ried; the wretched wet weather which had continued since the taking of Ulm now changed to a dry cold. Once again he utilized the halt on the Traun to order his army to close up, and thus on the 2nd Lannes concentrated his corps at Linz, Soult at Wels, Davout at Lambach with the vanguard in front of Kremsmünster; Murat was on the far side of Wels; he was to support Lannes in his capture of the passage of the Traun at Ebelsberg; but he was again warned to await the concentration of the army, in the event of the enemy offering any serious opposition at Ebelsberg. As the Emperor had become convinced that the enemy would make one more stand before Vienna, Marmont, at Vöcklaburg, and Bernadotte, still at Salzburg, received orders to move up to Lambach and join the army. The headquarters were established at Haag.

The further advance was carried on by Murat, followed at about one day's march by Lannes and then by Soult, *viâ* Enns to Amstetten; Davout, meanwhile, followed at equal distances by Marmont and Bernadotte, marched by Kremsmünster to Steyer. This crowding of the whole army on two roads, necessitated by the absence of any others fit for use, was of course very unfavourable to massing the troops when required, and caused the Emperor considerable annoyance. " There is no road. Marshal Soult must come along the high-road. You must therefore close up, so that the tail may come to the assistance of the head."[1] "Close up, as much as you can, towards Marshal Lannes, for the nature of the soil allows us only to form one column; therefore, close up as much as possible, so that you may support each other from the front to the rear."[2]

On the 3rd Kutusov evacuated the left bank of the Enns and continued his retreat. Murat's cavalry quickly pursuing, came up with his rear-guard on the 5th near Amstetten, but was unable, although supported by Oudinot's division, to defeat the Russian rear-guard, posted there to cover the retreat. On the 7th Kutusov arrived at St. Pölten, and resolved to allow a day's rest to his army, considerably exhausted by the retreat. But with the evacuation of the line of the Enns, a large portion of the Austrians, 12,000 men, had left him in order to threaten the further advance of the French on their flank, by retracing their steps from Steyer up the Enns.

Between the 4th and 9th the Emperor remained at Linz, ready to halt the army and concentrate it, in case the enemy should offer any resistance before Vienna. "It is expected that the enemy will make a stand and entrench himself behind the heights of St. Pölten, ten hours from Vienna,"[3] he wrote on the 5th. He now began to take into consideration the left bank of the Danube, to note in time any crossing of the Russians to this bank, to watch the passes from Bohemia, and also to facilitate the advance. First he gave orders to form a flotilla on the Danube, "so that the Danube may cease to exist for me and I may be able to cross at a moment's notice;"[4] secondly, the divisions of Gazan and Klein were, on the 5th, ordered to cross to the left bank at Linz, and lastly, on the 6th, a new corps was formed under Mortier destined to operate on the left bank of the

---
[1] C. N. To Murat, Linz, 6th November.
[2] C. N. To Soult, Linz, 7th November, 11 p.m.
[3] 18th Bulletin.
[4] C. N. To Murat, Linz, 7th November, 11 p.m.

Danube, he being always kept somewhat in rear of Lannes' position on the right bank. To his corps were attached the divisions of Gazan, Dupont and Dumonceau —the last two being on the march up from Passau—as well as the cavalry division of Klein, the command of which he took over on the morning of the 7th. Gazan and Klein reached Grein that day, the other two Linz.

On the 7th Lannes arrived on the Ips in the neighbourhood of Neumarkt; Soult was at Amstetten, Bernadotte at Steyer. This latter town Davout had reached on the 4th and Marmont on the 5th; they had immediately continued their march to Waidhofen, but had then received counter-orders. Davout was now to march *viâ* Gaming to Lilienfeld, not only to turn the enemy on the left, in case they should make a stand near St. Pölten, but also in order to relieve the straight road to St. Pölten to some extent, for on this road the whole of the rest of the army was pushing forward. Marmont, who had got a little beyond Steyer, received orders to make forced marches from Steyer to Leoben, to rout whatever forces he might meet with, and cover the army on its right flank. Thus on the 7th Davout was at Gaming, Marmont at Weyer, and Murat's cavalry were scouting on the same day up to Mölk. During the 8th and 9th all kept advancing in the same directions as hitherto, so that the head of the main column—Murat's—appeared in front of St. Pölten. The Emperor himself left Linz on the 9th, hurried past all the columns of his army, and established his headquarters in the convent of Mölk.

Meanwhile the Austrian column, which, as we have seen, had separated from the main body since crossing the Enns at Steyer, had been forced back up that river by Marmont, and was now endeavouring to regain touch with the Russians at St. Pölten by a march *viâ* Mariazell and Annaberg, but found itself, through Davout's advance to Lilienfeld on the one hand and Marmont's march to Leoben on the other, between these two corps, and could only escape in a dispersed condition and with most heavy losses *viâ* Bruck to Graz.

Kutusov had no intention of fighting a frontal battle at St. Pölten in defence of Vienna against the superior forces of the French; he was for avoiding the threatening attack, and therefore moved his army during the night before the 9th to Mautern on the Danube, where he crossed to the northern bank, occupying a position near Krems and burning the bridge behind him. The Austrian cavalry remained at St. Pölten for the purpose of concealing this movement and then fell back to Vienna.

The Emperor had, it. is true, anticipated Kutusov's crossing to the left bank of the Danube, but did not alter his plans after this had taken place. "Push your outposts forward as far as the Vienna Forest, provided the enemy does not offer too much resistance. Keep ready and massed. Warn Soult to keep close up. Bernadotte will be in Amstetten to-morrow," he wrote to Murat in the evening of the 8th. Arrived in Mölk, he heard of the passage of the Russians, and in his confidence of victory he considered this movement to be merely a retreat to Moravia to join hands with the second Russian army. He therefore did not in any way interfere during the 8th with the advance of his own army, and consequently Murat-reached Sieghartskirchen, followed by Lannes, and stood beyond St. Pölten; Soult occupied a position on the Traisen, with one division in Mautern; Bernadotte arrived at Amstetten. Mortier had dispersed some weak Austrian outposts during the morning from Lower-Loiben, and taken up a position with Gazan in the defile of Dürrenstein; Dupont and Dumonceau being still a day's march behind at Mahrbach.

But in the course of this day Napoleon gained a more correct appreciation of the state of affairs; he now perceived that Kutusov had the option of defeating Mortier, who was at present isolated, or marching down the stream, seizing the bridge over the Danube in Vienna, and opposing the crossing of the French army there in a favourable position, and he therefore began to issue orders on the morning of the 11th to arrest the too rapid advance of the army to Vienna, and to place some forces at his own disposal in the neighbourhood of St. Pölten. Murat, to whom he addressed some very unjust reproaches on account of his too hasty advance to Vienna, was not to proceed beyond Purkersdorf, but to occupy Tulln and reconnoitre in the direction of Korneuburg. Soult, who had, at Murat's orders, commenced his further advance to Vienna, received counter-orders in the afternoon from the Emperor, who proceeded in person to St. Pölten, in order to be nearer to the scene of action; it was, however, only possible to stop one of his divisions at Mautern. Davout was not to go beyond Mödling, indeed he only completed one day's march beyond Lilienfeld; Marmont had reached Leoben on the preceding day. But the Emperor's measures did not come in time to avert from Mortier the danger he realized too late.

Kutusov, rendered anxious as to the safety of his own movement to the rear by Mortier's close approach, determined to get rid of him by attacking him. For this purpose he sent a division to Egelsee before daybreak, which was to advance thence to Weissenkirchen, and thus turning Mortier, entirely block his road back from the defile of Dürrenstein; another division was to attack him in the meantime in front from the direction of Stein. Mortier, however, not only resisted this latter attack, which began in the morning, but advancing in his turn, forced the Russians back again beyond Loiben, which they had already captured. For their turning column, starting only at noon from Egelsee, did not, as had been planned, attack the French in the rear. But when about four o'clock in the afternoon this turning column at last appeared in his rear at Dürrenstein and began to attack, Mortier had no alternative but to attempt to break through; in this only he himself and a few *débris* of the troops, who had been engaged, succeeded.; Gazan's division was annihilated. Mortier met Dupont during the evening near Spitz; he had in the morning, recognizing the danger of his situation, sent orders to him to hasten his march, but Dupont had not come up in time to take any effective part in the engagement.

This was the first occasion on which the Emperor's foresight was at fault, and on which he did not, with his customary clearness and rapidity, grasp all the possibilities of a given situation, and one of his corps had to pay for it with a most serious defeat. We cannot but refer in this connection to another corps of Napoleon, namely that of Vandamme at Kulm, which also, being isolated, found itself exposed to being surrounded by a superior enemy and was annihilated, separated as it was from the army by the Erz-gebirge, even as Mortier was here by the Danube. There, as here, the Emperor, careless and confident of success, left the pursuit of the beaten enemy to the zeal of his army; there, as here, he had set a single corps, separated from the army by a great natural obstacle, in motion against the enemy's line of retreat. But whilst the army of 1805 under its young leaders, eager for action, hastened too quickly past him in its pursuit of the enemy, that of 1813 under its veteran leaders, weary of war, delayed too much in its march. Thus Mortier in 1805 and Vandamme in 1813 were exposed unsupported to the attack of the whole hostile army and both were annihilated. In each case the great player had for a moment taken his eyes off a part of the chess-board, and in each case the penalty was the loss of an important piece.

But the fatality of 1805, due as it was to a superabundant confidence of victory in the general, and a thirst for action in his subordinate commanders, was soon retrieved by unwearying activity, whilst the same occurrence in 1813, caused as it was by a want of energy, had much more fatal consequences. If we then see here on the one hand, that a want of strategical foresight carries its penalty, and that, therefore, such foresight is a necessary qualification of a general, we see also, on the other hand, that it is not the highest requirement, for resolution and energy can retrieve its mistakes, whilst any want in these latter qualities cannot be made up for by greater strategical ability, "war must be carried on with vigour, resolution, and a firm will."[1]

We must in any case allow that a great military genius will contrive to gain victories even with the most imperfect tools, and that *it* therefore is the best guarantee of victory, for "in war men are nothing, *one* man is everything."[2] Yet such a genius is rare and, moreover, gets blunted by old age or is lost by death. Hence sound military institutions are better guarantees of lasting success. Where these exist, there the troops will always be officered, if not by exceptional men, still by capable, resolute, energetic leaders, and in the above examples we have just seen that this is, if not the whole, yet the most important primary condition of victory.

A year later it was to be demonstrated in a terrible manner what may become of an army, which, while its leader is devoid of genius, fails to cultivate sound military traditions. In these days particularly, when armies are so large, much depends on a general diffusion of excellence among the minor leaders; indeed, the annals of Napoleon's wars give a fresh proof of this assertion in 1813. At that time, when 400,000 men were in the field on either side, and these had to be divided into several smaller armies, the Emperor's plan failed in its execution through the faults of his marshals, whose energy and resolution were not equal to their tasks; Oudinot, Macdonald, and Ney were beaten, whilst Davout remained idle. On the other hand, Blücher and Gneisenau

[1] C. N. To Bertrand, Liegnitz, 6th June, 1813.
[2] C. N. Note on the Spanish affairs, St. Cloud, 30th August, 1808.

showed conspicuous ability, while Bülow rendered even Bernadotte's want of activity harmless by his own energy.

Moreover, sound military institutions will bring forth such leaders, and will not fail, as long as the whole nation is sound, and military service is an honour and not a burden; where this is no longer the case, the nation will fall and give place to a stronger and therefore better one, for in the relations between states might makes right, and "military authors teach the use of might for the maintenance of right."[1]

The Emperor was informed during the night of the disastrous result of the engagement of Dürrenstein, though at first without details; but he immediately perceived the advantage he could derive from it, if the Russians delayed at Krems in consequence; "At this moment our great business is to cross the Danube and to drive the Russians from Krems by getting into their rear." Therefore the speedy capture of the great bridge over the Danube at Vienna, before it could be destroyed, became of the utmost importance to him, "This alone can force the Emperor to take refuge in Vienna."[2] Murat was consequently to advance immediately, seize if possible the bridge over the Danube, and cross without delay; for which purpose Lannes and Davout were told off to his assistance. Bernadotte, on the other hand, received orders to remain stationary at Mölk; Soult also was not to advance any further; for in this direction also the Emperor wished to be in readiness to cross the Danube, in case the attempt on the Vienna bridge should fail, and with the object either of attacking Kutusov on two sides, or of lending a hand to Mortier, whom the Emperor believed to be still on the left bank of the Danube. However, the latter crossed again to the southern bank of this stream the same day, leaving Klein's cavalry division to reconnoitre towards the Bohemian frontier.

[1] Bülow, Campaign of 1805, II. 18.
[2] C. N. To Murat, St. Pölten, 12th November, 6 a.m.

In the meantime, an officer, sent by the Emperor Francis to open negotiations for a truce, arrived at Napoleon's headquarters, and while he was delivering his message, Murat's advance was postponed, but the negotiations were soon broken off without any result. Napoleon never doubted but that Kutusov would retire either to Bohemia or Moravia, "Everything leads me to believe that the Russians will start this very night;"[1] the third possibility, namely, their remaining stationary at Krems, he himself called "so senseless that it has only been mentioned as a remote possibility."[2] He therefore resolved upon a speedy advance, in order, if possible, to prevent Kutusov's junction with the second Russian army. He consequently sent his aide-de-camp, General Bertrand, to Murat, with instructions as to the capture of Vienna, and at 11 p.m. he gave him orders to occupy the bridge at day-break the following morning, and then immediately to push forward with his cavalry on the road to Brünn and Weikersdorf, that is to Moravia and Bohemia; the two nearest divisions of Soult were to follow without delay on the former road, and Lannes in the latter direction; whilst Soult's two other divisions, which were still in the rear, were to take up a position in reserve on the Vienna road.

In the early morning of the 13th Murat entered Vienna according to his orders at the head of his cavalry, closely followed by the divisions of Oudinot. Murat, Lannes and Bertrand now proceeded in person to the great bridge over the Danube, for the blowing up of which all preparations had been made, and succeeded by their bold front and assurances that a truce had been concluded, in so completely fooling the general, Prince Auersperg, who was in charge of the demolition of the bridge, that he allowed the French troops to approach without offering any resistance; they seized the bridge, demolished all the

[1] C. N. To Bernadotte, St. Pölten, 13th November.
[2] Ibid.

arrangements for blowing it up, and Auersperg retired. Thus lightly this important means of crossing was won. The Emperor was immediately informed of it. General Bertrand, who carried the news to him, met him at Purkersdorf, whither he had gone as soon as the information of the Russians' withdrawal from Krems reached him. Before this, Bernadotte had already received orders to cross at Krems, to occupy the position there, and then follow the Russians closely, as soon as they started. Mortier, of whose crossing to the right bank of the Danube the Emperor was still unaware, was to act as his reserve. In the evening, at eleven o'clock, the Emperor himself went to the bridge over the Danube, inspected it and crossed, in order to overtake his troops, who had hurried on in front. Catching them up, he established his outposts during the first few hours after midnight, and passed some severe strictures on the neglect which he discovered in this respect, for "one must always assume that the enemy has made movements during the night, in order to attack at daybreak."[1]

Thus the Emperor had, without in any way manœuvring, pushed along the straightest road from Ulm to the capital, "because a superior force should proceed straight to the goal. . . . He acted according to the law of least expenditure,"[2] and his enemy had done nothing but retreat still more hurriedly straight on Vienna. It was not till the Allies reached Krems, in retiring behind the Danube, that they deviated somewhat from their direct course, and this flank position immediately produced its effect. Napoleon had to consider the question of an attack on his left flank, and was forced to arrest his march, for "it is not the Emperor's intention to leave the Russians on his flank."[3] He immediately hastened forward to Vienna. We may note that the corps

[1] C. N. Order of the day of the 14th November.
[2] Bülow, Campaign of 1805, II. 3.
[3] C. N. Berthier to Soult, St. Pölten, 11th November, 4 p.m.

Lannes and Soult, which had left the line of the Inn on the 1st November, and arrived at Vienna on the 13th November, had marched in thirteen days 152 miles, and that not on a modern smooth high-road, but along country roads and without reckoning the détours. Davout, who reached the enemy's capital on the 14th, had marched *viâ* Gaming and Lilienfeld, 150 miles, as the crow flies, in sixteen days, and partly by most difficult mountain roads. Thus Napoleon did not, after all, vanquish his enemies so much by the battles of Ulm and Jena, however disastrous these were, as by his incredible marches.[1]

In the evening of the 13th Murat had reached Stockerau, and his cavalry had pushed forward on the road to Brünn. Lannes and Suchet's division of Soult's corps had crossed the bridge over the Danube on this day, and were half a day's march behind him. The Austrian garrison of Vienna, 13,000 strong, had, after the surrender of the bridge, retreated as far as Wolkersdorf, on the road to Brünn. On the same day Kutusov started from Krems, and reached Ebersbrunn. On the 14th Murat continued his march in the direction of Znaym, in order to cut Kutusov off, and arrived at Weikersdorf. Lannes immediately followed, but Soult fell further behind, as he could not leave Vienna before Davout's arrival there. The latter, however, entered this town in the afternoon, and the Emperor established his headquarters in the castle of Schönbrunn, assembling his Guards around him.

At the moment of crossing the Danube he once more surveyed the entire theatre of war; he saw his communications covered by Ney and Augereau, whilst Marmont, at Leoben, had hitherto secured the right flank of his advance against the army of the Archduke Charles in Italy. But now, by crossing the Danube, the Emperor exposed his direct rear to this latter army, and his right flank could now be turned from the side of Hungary. Once more, therefore, he was compelled to tell off a corps for

[1] Willisen, Theorie des grossen Krieges, I. 100.

the protection of his line of operations, and consequently Davout received orders to hold the road to Pressburg on the right bank of the Danube with Friant's division, while Caffarelli's [1] was to cover the road to Brünn, and Gudin at Neustadt to keep touch with Marmont. The latter was cautioned to remain strictly on the defensive. "You will have played your part satisfactorily if you prevent the enemy from seizing the Sömmering, and descending into the valley of the Danube." [2] Thus we see once more how lengthening the line of operations weakens the strength of the army, and for this reason the Emperor sent orders to Ney on this same day to leave the Bavarians to hold the Tyrol, and to march to Salzburg, where further orders would await him.

As the task of securing Vienna and the bridge over the Danube lay now in Davout's hands, the Emperor ordered Soult to advance that evening in the direction of Stockerau. Kutusov had reached Meissau on the same day, but Bernadotte had not yet succeeded in completing his bridge and crossing the Danube, a delay which caused the Emperor to reprimand him severely on the following day.

On the 15th Murat also kept pushing forward, urged on most earnestly by Napoleon, who felt sure of intercepting the Russian army, or at least inflicting heavy losses upon it. Since Soult's last division, that of St. Hilaire, could not reach Vienna before the afternoon of this day, he ordered Caffarelli to advance along the Stockerau road, to reinforce Murat in case of necessity. For a moment this was the decisive point, for here a battle might have to be fought, and therefore the Emperor did not hesitate to send all the forces he could in any way spare to this point: "All my troops are despatched against the Russians. I have not many,

[1] Until now under Bisson; the latter had been wounded at Lambach.
[2] C. N. To Marmont, Schönbrunn, 15th November, 4 p.m.

because I am forced to hold Vienna, and, as I intend to turn them in order to attack them effectually, I require more men than if I wanted simply to beat them."[1] It was ever his especial care to order up all his strength for battle, and he always emphasized the fact that nothing could excuse a breach of this rule. "People ascribe to me a little more talent than to others, and yet I never think I have enough troops to fight a battle with an enemy, whom I am accustomed to beat. I call up all the troops I can collect."[2]

In the meantime Kutusov had in the evening of the 14th set his army again in motion, and reached Schrattenthal on the morning of the 15th after an exhausting night march. Here he was forced to give some rest to his troops. He had sent Bagration with 6000 men to Hollabrunn to cover his further movements; the latter was to take up a position there, and block the road so as to give Kutusov time, by marching round behind him, to reach the great Znaym road at Jetzelsdorf before Murat. Now when Murat met Bagration in position at Schöngrabern, behind Hollabrunn, in the afternoon, he had besides his cavalry only Lannes with one division with him, since Gazan's had been detached, and he believed he had the whole Russian army before him. In order to gain time and to allow the rest of his forces to come up, he again tried the device which had delivered the Danube bridge into his hands; he amused the enemy with talk of a truce. But on this ground the wily Russian proved himself undoubtedly the master of the excitable Gascon. As nothing could be more welcome to Kutusov in his situation than to arrest Murat's progress in any way whatever, he not only immediately entered into a parley, but pretended to be fully aware that something of the sort was really pending between the combatants, and that he was entrusted with the further negotiations.

[1] C. N. To Marmont, Schönbrunn, 15th November, 4 p.m.
[2] C. N. To Savary, Mém. IV. 231.

He consequently sent an aide-de-camp of the Russian Emperor to Murat, for there was never a want of such officers at the Russian headquarters, and this envoy concluded an armistice with the French commander; Murat was not to advance any further, and Kutusov was immediately to begin his withdrawal from Germany as soon as the armistice was confirmed by Napoleon. Whilst, however, Murat forwarded this document to the Emperor, Bagration prepared for the defence of his position, and Kutusov immediately concentrated his troops upon Jetzelsdorf, and made preparations to continue his retreat next morning early *viâ* Znaym.

The messenger announcing the armistice, which had been concluded, only reached Schönbrunn about eight o'clock in the morning of the 16th. On receipt of this news the Emperor flew into a tremendous rage; he immediately perceived clearly that Kutusov was already on the road, and that a rear-guard only lay in front of Murat; with the most violent expressions of anger he therefore sent immediate orders to him to attack without delay. A few hours later he himself was on his way to him, after having set his Guards in motion towards Hollabrunn, and having ordered Davout to call up Gudin to Vienna, so as to be able to employ Caffarelli entirely against the Russians.

When Murat received the order to attack in the afternoon, Soult also joined him with three divisions, and Murat now advanced against Bagration with greatly superior forces, Oudinot attacked in front with Vandamme in reserve behind him, whilst Suchet turned the enemy's right and Legrand his left wing. Bagration offered a determined resistance until eleven o'clock at night, when he formed one column of all the men he could collect after his heavy losses, and broke through the French divisions that were trying to surround him. The Emperor arrived in Hollabrunn during the evening, and Kutusov reached Lechwitz in the course of the night.

On the 17th the French army, now urged on by the

Emperor in person, pushed forward in haste to Znaym; Murat reached this town, where the Emperor also arrived at 3 p.m., whilst Lannes, Soult, the division of Caffarelli and the Guards came up, partly during this day and partly during the night, after some very rapid forced marches. Bernadotte, who had at last crossed the Danube on the 15th, was still a day's march behind. Mortier, once more on the northern bank of the Danube, was at Krems. Of the cavalry divisions, at first left behind at Augsburg and Ingolstadt, Bourcier was on the march to Vienna, whilst Baraguey was scouting beyond Waldmünchen, as far as Pilsen. Beaumont had remained in Vienna with Davout and was keeping the road to Brünn clear. Klein continued to watch the south-eastern frontier of Bohemia. This distribution of the cavalry, as well as its whole handling up to this time, showed clearly that the Emperor, when forming a large "Cavalry Reserve," by no means intended to drag it along with him as a closed-up mass, in order to use it on the day of battle only, but that he expected from it the most far-reaching reconnaissances, whilst the rest of the cavalry, which had remained under Murat's immediate orders with the army, had uninterruptedly formed his vanguard since his departure from the Inn.

The Russians retreating further and further, reached on the 17th respectively: Bagration, Frainspitz and Kutusov, Pohrlitz; here the Austrian corps, which had evacuated Vienna, effected a junction with them, so that their strength now amounted to 45,000 men. Thus the Emperor's plan to cut off Kutusov had certainly failed, and his reproach to Murat: "You have made me lose the fruits of the whole campaign,"[1] proved true. Still he intended to push forward without delay to Brünn, "which is necessary to us, in order to secure our positions, for we cannot remain on outpost duty in a town like Vienna."[2]

[1] C. N. Schönbrunn, 16th November, 8 a.m.
[2] C. N. To Lannes, Znaym 18th November, 9 p.m.

Nevertheless he was compelled to grant his entirely exhausted troops a day's rest. He took advantage of this circumstance to inform them that, "he was induced to do so by the thought, that it would be better to gain a less complete victory, rather than expose such brave men to illness;"[1] and the world in general, that: "the Russians have retreated to Brünn, and our vanguard have pursued them halfway; but the Emperor, learning that the Emperor of Austria was there, wished to furnish a proof of his consideration for that monarch and arrested his march during the 18th."[2] Bernadotte received orders to march to Budwitz; Mortier was to leave Dumonceau behind at Krems, and occupy Vienna with the other two divisions, for Davout was now to take possession of Pressburg. The allied Russo-Austrian army went into camp near Schlappanitz on this day.

On the 19th November the French advance was resumed. Murat reached Brünn in the afternoon, Lannes Pohrlitz, to which the imperial headquarters also were transferred; Soult marched on the right of the Pohrlitz road to Niemtschitz· Bernadotte was at Znaym. Kutusov reached Wischau, and there effected a junction with the first portion, 14,000 men, of the second Russian army marching hither under Buxhöwden; falling back to Prossnitz on the next day, he met the second part of it, some 10,000 men. On this same date, the 20th November, at 10 a.m., Napoleon arrived in Brünn. Here he intended for the present to make a halt, for he was in need of a little breathing time, both in order to examine for himself the situation as a whole, and also to allow his army to gain strength and to get into good order, before the decisive battle, which he now considered inevitable, since Kutusov and Buxhöwden had joined forces, and the Emperor Alexander had, according to Napoleon's in-

[1] C. N. To Lannes, Znaym, 18th November, 9 p.m.
26th Bulletin, Znaym, 18th November.

formation, arrived in the camp and joined the Emperor Francis.

(41) During the next few days we find the French army posted as follows:—In Moravia the Emperor himself, his headquarters at Brünn, with the Guards 5300 men, and Lannes with Oudinot's and Suchet's divisions, 12,000 men; to the right of him, at Austerlitz: Soult, 26,000 men (divisions of St. Hilaire, Vandamme and Legrand); to the left Bernadotte, 19,000 men, with his two French divisions at Znaym and Budwitz, and with the Bavarian division of Wrede at Iglau. In front of this line Murat's cavalry, 4500 men (Nansouty, d'Hautpoul, Walther), were at Wischau, while behind were Caffarelli with 6000 men, at Pohrlitz, and Friant, 6000 men, at Nikolsburg. Baraguey, 4500 men, and Klein, 1100, were still on the way to Bohemia; the latter, however, was now sent to Pressburg, in order to replace the 2000 men of Bourcier, who was ordered to the front. Near Pressburg stood Davout with the division of Gudin, 8000 men, on the Danube; and Mortier, 6000 men (Dupont and Gazan's weak division), together with the cavalry division of Beaumont, 2000 men, occupied Vienna. Dumonceau, 4500 men, posted at Neustadt, formed the connecting link with Marmont, 9000 men, whose divisions, under Boudet and Grouchy, held the Mur valley at Leoben and Graz. The Army of Italy, under Massena, had advanced as far as Krain, and reached Laibach on the 29th November. From here an enterprising officer, pushing through the mountains of Carinthia and Styria with a patrol of dragoons, succeeded in opening communications with Marmont at Bruck. The Archduke Charles, compelled by events in Germany, had fallen back before Massena from the banks of the Adige; he was now in the lowlands on the Drave near Marburg; at which latter place the Archduke John also, having been driven from the Tyrol by Ney, arrived on the 26th; their collective forces numbered 80,000 men. Ney had cleared the

Tyrol of the enemy, and was now, having left the Bavarian division of Deroy, 9000 men, in it as a garrison, marching with the divisions Loison and Malher, 13,000 men, through the Puster valley, following upon the heels of the Archduke John; he started from Botzen in pursuit on the 21st November. The main army of the allies, which the Emperor Alexander had now also joined, occupied on the 22nd a camp near Ollschann, in front of Olmütz; it amounted to 89,000 men, having received some further reinforcements.

If we examine the situation, we shall find that the Emperor could have at Brünn or Austerlitz in twenty-four hours 53,800 men, within three days 74,800 men, and within four days, by calling up Wrede from Iglau and Baraguey's cavalry, 85,300 men. The enemy was forty-three miles to his front at Ollschann, and could only attack him on the morning of the fourth day, though he could then muster 89,000 men; still Napoleon could in that case begin a safe retreat with 74,800 men, after having, as doubtless he would, ordered up Davout, Mortier, and Klein, in case of the enemy's advance, so as to show front again after forty-eight hours with 102,400 men, thus ensuring victory. The allies, on the other hand, could not in any case effect a junction in time; if Kutusov wished to wait for the Archduke Charles' arrival, the latter could reach him safely only by a march through Hungary, as he had to reckon with Massena, Ney, and Marmont; moreover, such a march would not escape the attention of Davout at Pressburg, and the Emperor could throw himself upon Kutusov long before a junction could be effected. Montenotte, Castiglione and Arcola furnish proofs of this. Even if Kutusov and the Archduke had advanced simultaneously and concentrically upon Vienna, Napoleon would have stood on interior lines, and under any circumstances he could have assembled his whole forces, 172,000 men, long before the 169,000 men of his divided opponents could have arrived there; irrespective altogether of the fact that, during this divided advance, the Emperor could have stood on the defensive with a small force against one of his opponents, while attacking the other with his main body, thus repeating the lessons he had given Würmser and Quosdanovitch in 1796.

Thus we see that the Emperor, although covering in extended order a front of nearly 240 miles, yet stood in a more concentrated position than the enemy with his two masses, for the very reason that the latter had formed two isolated masses upon exterior lines of operation. If we compare this situation with that of the Prussian and Austrian armies in the middle of June, 1866, the former, with its two great bodies, separated by the Iser mountains on the Neisse and near Görlitz, if we reflect how easily a resolute commander might have assembled superior forces against either of them, and remember that there was no reason for considering Benedek incapable of the execution of such a plan, because little was known about the Austrian movements, we shall, it is true, have to pronounce the conduct of 1866 correct on the part of the Prussians, for political circumstances compelled them to act as they did, but we shall still hesitate to accept the Prussian system of concentric advance in separate bodies as one to be universally adopted. Napoleon indeed avoided such movements on principle.

The calm posture of defence which the Emperor assumed for the moment at Brünn, was intended partly to lead the enemy on to attack him, for nothing could be more favourable to Napoleon than to fight a battle soon, both before the Archduke Charles approached through Hungary, and also before the Cabinet of Berlin, which had also mobilized its army, could make up its mind to act. But since his line of communications was already very extended, it must have been a matter of congratulation to the Emperor that the allies came to him, rather than that he should be compelled to advance against their position at Ollschann. For the same reasons also, which made it desirable for

Napoleon to fight soon and to let the enemy attack him, the allies ought to have avoided this; but in their camp a forward policy prevailed, and thus it was determined on the 24th November to turn the enemy's right wing, and to force him by this pressure upon his communications to retreat to the Danube; should he, however, not fall back as expected, they would immediately proceed to attack his right wing.

For this purpose the army was set in motion on the 27th at 8 a.m., and reached the neighbourhood of Prossnitz. On the 28th the forward movement was continued; Murat's cavalry immediately evacuated Wischau before the enemy's advance-guard; Bagration and Kutusov on the same day were near this town and in front of it. Towards evening the Emperor was informed by his cavalry of the enemy's approach and expected their attack on the next day; he therefore issued the following orders at eight o'clock: "Caffarelli, Bourcier and Klein (the latter being still on the march to Pressburg) are to reach Brünn by 7 a.m. on the 29th; Davout, Bernadotte and Mortier are to hurry up by forced marches." An hour later he mounted his horse and rode to Soult's position at the posthouse of Posorzitz. He watched from the heights of (42) Austerlitz the movements of the enemy; but as only some small advance columns were to be seen, and as nothing indicated any immediate attack; he decided to remain stationary for the present. But late the same evening his aide-de-camp Savary, whom he had sent to Olmütz with an unimportant letter to the Emperor Alexander, but who was principally intended to gain information as to the state of affairs in the enemy's camp, returned and confirmed the news that the entire hostile army was on the march 'to attack him.

Consequently the Emperor drew back Soult at dawn on the 29th into the line Sokolnitz—Schlappanitz, evacuating Austerlitz. Caffarelli was in reserve near Latain, Suchet to the north of the Olmütz road behind

the hill of Bosenitz, called by the French soldiers the
"Santon," in memory of a similar hill in Egypt; behind
Suchet were the Guards and Oudinot at Kritschen. The
cavalry occupied Welatitz, Bosenitz, Girschkowitz and
the plateau of Pratzen. The Emperor, having immediately sent Savary back again to the enemy's camp,
established his bivouac on a hill affording an extensive
view to the south of the road to Brünn, in front of
Bellowitz. Dumonceau received orders to occupy Vienna,
and Marmont in his turn was to move closer up to that
capital. During the 29th Kutusov did nothing beyond
moving his army to the left under cover of his advance-
guard, for the purpose of turning the enemy's right wing
more easily. From all this the Emperor perceived that
the battle was after all not quite so imminent as he had
expected at first, and predicted it now for the 1st of
December. About noon Savary returned and informed
him that one of the Emperor Alexander's aides was
waiting for him near the outposts; for, more cautious
than the Russians, Napoleon did not allow such messen-
gers to penetrate without any ado to his presence in the
middle of the army. He now rode as far as the outposts,
and received the aide-de-camp's communication; but the
negotiations had no result.

On the 30th Kutusov ordered his outposts forward to
the line Schumitz—Walspitz—Satschan Pond; the army
again advanced by its left, and was now on both sides of
the river Littawa, with its front to the west, its last column
at Butschowitz, and its leading one at Hodjegitz. This
fresh respite led the Emperor to hope that he might still
be able to accept battle on the heights of Pratzen. Up
to now he had intended to fall back behind the Schwarz-
awa in case of a determined attack on the 29th or 30th,
for his expected reinforcements, Bernadotte and Davout,
could not come up before the 1st of December. But now
he saw that the issue would not be decided before the 2nd
of December, and he therefore prepared, on the 30th

November, the whole of the ground to the right of the Littawa, saying to himself: "If I occupy the plateau of Pratzen with my right wing on the Littawa, I shall frustrate the enemy's intention of turning this wing. But if I advance as far as that, the encounter might easily take place on the 1st, whilst the gain of one day renders the arrival of my reinforcements in time more certain. Besides, I can, it is true, repulse the enemy in the excellent safe position of Pratzen ("I can fight an ordinary battle,"[1] as he said); but if I do not occupy that position I shall probably induce him to attempt to turn my right wing, which will then not be so well in touch with the rest of the army; and while the enemy is engaged in this too extended movement, I shall advance in close order and inflict a complete defeat upon him."

And here we find again in the province of tactics the same truth which we noted in the province of strategy in 1800 on the occasion of Napoleon's march to Milan, namely, the difference of the procedure between a capable general of the ordinary type and a general of genius. The former would undoubtedly have taken up the safe position afforded by the plateau of Pratzen, and would, by forcing the enemy to a frontal attack, have won "an ordinary battle," to use the Emperor's words. The latter, however, took up a position which, if taken up in a "war game," would assuredly be found fault with; indeed all the principles of simple common-sense tactics are opposed to it, and only a full consciousness of superiority in tactics could excuse any general for taking it up. But Napoleon anticipated with the eye of genius what mistakes the enemy would commit, and how quickly he himself would be able to develop his forces, closely concentrated as they were between Schlappanitz and the road to Brünn, towards the plateau of Pratzen, and what delays the crossing at Sokolnitz and Tellnitz would occasion in the turning manœuvre of his enemy; he

[1] Hist. des campagnes de l'Emp. N. en 1805-6 and 1807-9, I. 141.

did not desire any "ordinary battle," but a decisive victory.

Therefore he posted his army on the 1st December in the following manner:—Suchet from the "Santon" to near Girschkowitz, with one regiment as a firm point of support for the left wing entrenched on the Santon, and Caffarelli behind Suchet; Bernadotte, who arrived during the afternoon, took up a position behind Caffarelli on both sides of the Brünn road. Wrede was left behind at Iglau to keep off the Archduke Ferdinand, who had collected about 18,000 men near Prague. Oudinot stood to the right of the Brünn road, in front of the imperial bivouac, and the Guards behind the latter. Murat, with his cavalry, was behind the lines of Caffarelli and Oudinot. Of Soult's corps, Vandamme's and St. Hilaire's divisions stood to the west of the Bosenitz hill, facing Puntowitz; Legrand was behind Kobelnitz, holding Sokolnitz and Tellnitz. During the night Davout also reached Raigern with Friant and Bourcier.

On this day the enemy again advanced wheeling to the left; their army was, as it had been on the whole march from Olmütz, divided into five columns, which now took up the following positions:—The 1st, Docturov, 8500 men, along the line: Klein Hostjeradek—Augezd; the 2nd, Langeron, 11,600 men, on its right, on the heights of Pratzen; the 3rd, Prschibitschewski, 13,800 men, between Krzenowitz and Pratzen; the 4th, Kollovrat, 25,400 men, behind the latter in front of Krzenowitz; and the 5th, the cavalry under Lichtenstein, 4600 men, between the second and third columns at the foot of the plateau of Pratzen. As a reserve the Guards, under the Grand Duke Constantine, 8500 men, stood at Krzenowitz, where the headquarters were. The vanguard, 13,000 men, under Bagration, stood in front of Raussnitz on the Twaroschna. They had the intention of doing exactly what Napoleon had anticipated, namely, to take possession, by a movement to the left, of the passes at

Sokolnitz and Tellnitz, and then to outflank the French altogether.

The Emperor had contented himself with ordering his troops to take up their respective positions, and carefully observing the enemy's movements; "with unspeakable joy" he saw them enter the trap he had laid for them and begin their turning manœuvre. Later in the afternoon, whilst he was eating his dinner, he called his corps leaders around him and discussed with them the situation and his own intentions for the morrow's battle, assigning to each his part in it. Soult was to have Vandamme and St. Hilaire ready at 7 a.m. on the other side of the Bosenitz brook, to begin "the day's manœuvre, namely an advance in echelons, right shoulders forward;" in the meantime Legrand was to hold the crossings at Sokolnitz and Tellnitz. Murat, with Beaumont, was to form the centre to the right of Soult; Caffarelli was likewise to have crossed the Bosenitz brook by seven o'clock, and was to march into position to the right of Suchet, the latter making room for him by taking a deeper formation; the two divisions under the command of Lannes were to remain under cover of the heights. Bernadotte was to advance behind Lannes and form his second line; on his right Oudinot, and behind both, the Guards. Davout was to start as early as 5 a.m. from Raigern and come up on Soult's right; in this way he would come direct on the flank of whatever troops might force the passes of Sokolnitz and Tellnitz.

Having given these orders, the Emperor strolled in the falling darkness through the bivouacs of his troops, inspiring them by his words and presence. Already confident of victory, he announced to them what the enemy would do: "Whilst they march to my right wing, they will expose their flank to me." Meanwhile musketry fire had become audible on his right wing in the neighbourhood of Sokolnitz; this rendered the Emperor somewhat uneasy, for, as a matter of fact, if the

S

enemy by a resolute advance had seized the passes of Sokolnitz and Tellnitz that evening, the Emperor's right wing would have been really endangered, and his whole position as well. This, indeed, was one of those risks to which the plans of genius are always open; but to take such risks and to judge how far the enemy was capable of profiting by his situation, was exactly what Napoleon called the divine side of the art of war. However, the Emperor retired to rest, after having sent his aide-de-camp, Savary, to the threatened point, to see what was going on there. Upon his report, that the Russians were concentrating there, but did not seem to have any intention of proceeding to an attack during the night, the Emperor rode thither with Soult, about 1 a.m., in order to inspect, as far as the darkness permitted, the enemy's dispositions, after which he slept for a few hours.

(43) At five in the morning Napoleon began to occupy his positions; he himself took post on the hill where he had bivouacked, surrounded by his corps leaders. As yet a thick fog covered the ground before them, which, however, began gradually to lift; by seven o'clock the outlook over the more elevated parts was tolerably clear, but in the valley the fog was still thick. At this moment the allies began their march. Docturov moved towards Tellnitz, with Langeron on his right, Prschibitschewski advanced towards the castle of Sokolnitz, and Kollowrat towards the low-lying ground between Sokolnitz and Kobelnitz. As soon as these columns should have crossed the Goldbach and approached the wood of Turas, Bagration also, covered on his left flank by the 5th column, the cavalry, and supported by the reserve, the Guards, was to advance along the Brünn road, for the decisive onslaught against the position of the enemy, who was suspected to be behind Schlappanitz and Bellowitz, and consequently to be completely turned. Thus, to begin with, the whole left wing of the allies was set in motion towards the Goldbach.

From the heights the Emperor noticed about 7.30 that

the plateau of Pratzen was becoming more and more denuded of troops, and turned to Soult, and asked: "How long will it take you to reach the heights of Pratzen with your divisions?" "Less than twenty minutes," was the marshal's reply. "In that case," said the Emperor, "we will wait another quarter of an hour." In a short time the sustained infantry fire on the right wing announced that the fighting near the passage over the Goldbach had begun; indeed, shortly after eight o'clock Docturov's column broke out from Augezd, and an hour later it had succeeded in seizing the crossing at Tellnitz. Now, whilst this column established itself in the village just won, Langeron appeared in front of Sokolnitz, and captured this place also. Prschibitschewski followed him, but could no longer find room enough to develop his lines. Whilst, therefore, the heads of the two first columns began to cross the Goldbach at these points, Davout appeared about nine o'clock before Tellnitz, having marched from Raigern, and immediately threw himself upon the enemy's columns, in support of Legrand. Thus at nine o'clock nearly half the allied army was engaged here.

In the meantime, however, Soult, in the centre, had commenced his forward movement, and the divisions of Vandamme and St. Hilaire were ascending the plateau of Pratzen. At this moment the head of Kollowrat's column, with which was Kutusov, reached Pratzen. The commander-in-chief, surprised by Napoleon's attack, now for the first time recognized the danger in which his army would be if the French should succeed in taking possession of the plateau of Pratzen. He therefore quickly threw two battalions into this village, and turned to the right with his column, but the forces at his disposal were inferior to those of the enemy. Still, for the time being, Kutusov offered a determined resistance.

Meanwhile, on the ground to the south of the Brünn

road, the fight had also begun. When Soult moved forward, Bernadotte crossed over the Bosenitz brook at Girschkowitz, whilst on his left Murat advanced upon Blasowitz. These were opposed by the Grand Duke Constantine, who was also on the march to the latter village, and who now encountered Rivaud's division on Bernadotte's left wing. On the Grand Duke's right, the cavalry under Lichtenstein now came up, and immediately attacked Murat, and one of those cavalry fights began which end indecisively, and in which each side claims the victory. In the meantime the combat between Rivaud and the Grand-Duke had also begun. Rivaud captured Blasowitz under the eyes of the Emperor, who had ridden forward to the heights above this village, and in spite of very determined efforts, the Russian Guards could not recapture it. The Emperor hurled the cavalry of his Guards against them, and at the same time Caffarelli attacked them in the right flank, so that they were soon after eleven o'clock forced definitely to fall back upon Krzenowitz.

Only a very short time after the Grand Duke Constantine, Bagration had come on the field, between nine and ten o'clock, and now, advancing towards Bosenitz, he met Lannes, who was also moving forward full in front. Whilst (44) the allies' entire right wing was thus under fire, the day was decided, about noon, at Pratzen. Kutusov, who had made a last desperate effort to gain possession of the heights, was completely repulsed by Soult, and his troops retreated in confusion down the slope to Krzenowitz and Great Hostjeradek. Drouet also assisted from the left, by the Emperor's orders, driving back the reserves, which were hastening up to Kutusov's support. By these movements the line of the allied army was broken through, all the forces fighting on the Goldbach were cut off from their line of retreat, and shut in in the angle formed by the Littawa and Goldbach at the pond of Satschan.

Shortly before this decisive turn of affairs the Grand

Duke Constantine also had, as we have seen, begun his retreat and now Lannes, with Suchet and Caffarelli, advanced to the attack of Bagration, who had meanwhile pushed forward as far as Bosenitz and taken possession of this village; on the left the cuirassier division of d'Hautpoul came into action and the right wing of the allies was also overthrown; Bagration fell back to Raussnitz, whence, between five and six o'clock, he turned towards Austerlitz.

The Emperor, having been present at the repulse of the Russian Guards at Blasowitz, and being convinced that his decisive movement against the enemy's centre had nothing further to apprehend on this side, now betook himself to Soult. The latter was at that moment near the Chapel of St. Anthony. He had, after the final occupation of the plateau of Pratzen, moving more and more towards the right, pushed forward with St. Hilaire upon Sokolnitz and with Vandamme upon Augezd, thus completing the isolation of the enemy's left wing. Drouet followed across the heights of Pratzen. Vandamme captured Augezd about two o'clock, whilst Davout, who had since nine o'clock, on the heights on the other bank of the Goldbach, prevented the enemy's advance from the low ground, now also pushed forward to the attack upon Sokolnitz and Tellnitz. With this the battle was decided. At two o'clock in the afternoon, the columns of Docturov, Langeron, and Prschibitschewski were completely surrounded and only some shattered remnants escaped, partly over the ice of the pond of Satschan, and partly along the embankment between this pond and that of Menitz.

The Emperor, who had witnessed from the chapel of St. Anthony the destruction of the enemy's whole left wing, rode with the beginning of dusk over the entire battle-field, as was always his custom after larger engagements, taking stock of the masses of dead and wounded with a kind of curiosity, which struck his suite as very strange; after midnight he established his headquarters in the posthouse of Posorzitz. Here an officer, despatched by the Emperor of Austria, arrived at four o'clock in the morning with proposals for an armistice and a personal interview between the two emperors. Neither in the French camp nor in that of the allies could the whole bearing of the victory and defeat respectively be clearly grasped at the time, but this message proved to Napoleon that his opponent acknowledged a complete beating. All the more he determined to use the 3rd December to prosecute his victory, and to increase the confusion and disintegration of the enemy's forces to such a degree, that no resumption of resistance should be possible; he therefore rejected the armistice, but consented to an interview with the Emperor Francis on the 4th. The officer was sent back with this decision, and Napoleon immediately, it being then 8 a.m., gave orders to all his corps to pursue the enemy vigorously. "The Emperor will personally follow close on the enemy's heels. It is his opinion, that in warfare nothing is done, as long as anything remains to be done; no victory is complete, as long as there is an enemy in the field. . . . In the position in which we are, there is only one order to be issued, viz. to inflict as great losses upon the enemy as possible and to improve our victory in every way."[1] This, in a few words, from the lips of the best of judges, is the whole theory of pursuit.

But the direction which the enemy had taken in their retreat was as yet unknown to the Emperor, and therefore (41) Murat was sent in haste along the Olmütz road as far as Prossnitz, and Lannes and Soult followed him; Bernadotte and Davout alone pursuing in a south-easterly direction. The division of Gudin, which had not succeeded in reaching the battle-field of Austerlitz in time, and was at Nikolsburg on the 2nd December, was now sent by Davout towards Göding. In the course of the day the Emperor gathered from his reports, that no enemy was

[1] C. N. To Soult, Austerlitz, 3rd December, 10 p.m.

to be found on the Olmütz road, but that they had seemingly retreated *viâ* Urschitz, that is, towards Hungary. Accordingly Soult and Lannes were instructed to push forward in this direction, *viâ* Hradish or Göding. As a matter of fact the allies had collected their troops in the evening of the 2nd, as well as was possible at the time, near Hodjegitz; they had then fallen back to Tscheitsch during the night, and arrived at this place during the forenoon of the 3rd. On the 4th they crossed the March at Göding and reached Holitsch. In the afternoon of this day the Emperor Francis visited Napoleon in his tent, which had been erected near the mill of Saroschitz, and this interview resulted in an agreement which put an end to the hostilities.

Thus Austerlitz brought the war of 1805 to a close; Napoleon had for the first time conducted a great pitched battle; for even Marengo had, after all, only consisted of two minor engagements, judging by modern standards, and therefore Jomini says: "The great pitched battles of our days date from 1805."[1] And he is right. In this first Napoleonic battle we may at once note all those characteristic points which distinguish modern battles from those of Frederick the Great. Under the latter the entire army was set in motion as one body, and had, during the whole course of the battle, to remain ready to manœuvre at the will of the leader; if its solidity were broken in one place, it was beaten. But in a modern battle the centre may be broken through, and yet the wings, turning the enemy, may gain the victory. One wing may be destroyed, and yet the other may crush the enemy; nay, in a well-conducted battle some such success will always be allowed to be gained by the opponent in one part of the battle-field, to enable the victor, in his turn, to appear at the decisive point with superior strength. Thus Napoleon sacrificed at Austerlitz his right wing, Legrand and Davout, (43)

[1] Oesterr. mil. zeitschrift, 1830, I. 113.

to the enemy's superior numbers, in order to appear at Pratzen in his full strength, though, on the whole, a little weaker than the enemy. In the same way he at Rivoli sacrificed his wings, in order to decide the issue in the centre. But, on the other hand, while no longer fearing any partial failure, the leader cannot direct all the varying phases of a battle. In modern battles the commander-in-chief has only two lines of action available—the direction in which to introduce fresh troops, and the moment at which he may do so. Once in action, the troops march straight forward, they may, indeed, leave the field again, but cannot be withdrawn at will. Thus Napoleon could here introduce Drouet on Soult's left wing, but he could not have withdrawn him again and employed him on Bernadotte's right wing. Drouet had to move on in the direction once given, *viâ* Pratzen.

The more the battles of modern times confirm this experience, the more it must be the endeavour of the commander-in-chief on a battle-field to secure to himself the mastery of these two points by which alone he can exert any influence upon the course of a battle once begun. In a word, he must keep his reserves in hand, so as to be able to bring them up where and when his plan demands it. If he has no fresh troops to send forward at the decisive moment or to the decisive point, he can no longer turn a doubtful battle into a victory; in that case the more or less able conduct of his subordinate officers, or the more or less favourable situation created by previous good strategy, will bring about the decision. Let us remember that the past-master of our art has said: "Battles are only won by reinforcing a line at the critical moment."[1] But in order to be able to do this, one must avoid playing one's last card too soon, one must act as Napoleon did, who, "when the first corps had become engaged, allowed them calmly to fight on, without troubling himself about their good or bad positions, and

[1] C. N. To Murat, Düben, 13th October, 1813.

only took good care not to yield too lightly to any requests for support on the part of their leaders."¹ Only when he saw "the decisive moment, which lies between the winning and losing of a battle"² appear, did he employ his carefully husbanded reserve. And how well he knew how to husband it, which is the first principle of the conduct of a battle, Austerlitz above all battles showed; even in the evening Oudinot and the Guards were untouched, they had not fired a shot, for Soult, Bernadotte and Lannes had been sufficient. Thus this Napoleonic battle, really his first, became at once a pattern for the conduct of battles in general, and illustrated Napoleon's words: "The task which the leader of an army has to fulfil is more difficult in modern armies than it was in those of antiquity. On the other hand, however, its influence upon the issue of the battle is greater."³

In the domain of strategy Austerlitz gives rise to the question : What would the Emperor have done, if he had been beaten ? His line of operations was already, even if we consider the Lech only as his base, of ominous length, and had taken a dangerous direction with his entry into Moravia. Would he not have been lost if he had met with a reverse in such a position ? Of course it has been said: "Did Alexander, Hannibal, or Cæsar trouble about their lines of retreat, when the moment appeared to dispute the empire of the world?"⁴ This remark is indeed justified in the sense that no anxiety about any lines of retreat should cause any secondary movements to be undertaken at the moment of a decisive battle, for victory will make all that good again. Still, the whole strategical position must, after all, have occupied the general's mind in the event of any tactical disaster. And of Napoleon above all others we are told: "Before

(41)

---

¹ Gouvion St. Cyr, Mém.
² Bulletin of the Grand Army, Lützen, 2nd May, 1813.
³ Notes sur l'art de la guerre. III. 397.
⁴ Fain, Manuscrit de, 1813.

he fought a battle, Bonaparte never troubled much about what he would do in the event of success, but very much about what he would have to do in the event of failure."[1] In the case before us he had resolved *not* to do what the enemy would expect him to do, namely, to return to Vienna, but to alter his line of operations and proceed through Bohemia to Passau or Regensburg; this Bülow's keen military judgment had indeed divined. For in 1806 the latter said: "Here I will venture to surmise: I believe he would have retired upon Znaym, or perhaps rather thrown himself into Bohemia, and crushed the Archduke Ferdinand there. He would then have been in the neighbourhood of Würzburg."[2] Indeed, Napoleon had always some such sudden inspiration in reserve as a surprise during his brilliant campaigns, and he himself said: "A change of the line of communications may be considered the most skilful manœuvre that strategy teaches."[3]

[1] Bourrienne, Mém. III. 215. [2] Campaign of 1805, II. 54.
[3] Précis des guerres de F., II.—IV. 233.

CHAPTER XI.

1806-1807.

JENA.

WE may look upon the Emperor's return after the peace of Pressburg as the beginning of a new chapter in his personal development and therefore in his history. His power in Europe had been great, but Austerlitz secured his undisputed supremacy. It was now that he began to create around him vassal princes; it was now that he began to heap upon his generals those magnificent rewards and princely titles, which served only to increase their desire for more, as was indeed the master's intention, who always took men's weaknesses into account and beheld the great qualities of his subordinate officers without apprehension, only when they were held in check by some weakness, which assured to himself his dominion over them. "He considered himself very much superior to the rest of the world, and yet dreaded all superiority in others. Who among those that were brought into close contact with him has not heard him say, that he preferred mediocrities?"[1]

More and more sharply did he define the distance between his imperial dignity and the rest of the world, and surrounded his person with a severe and rigid ceremonial; though personally simple in his tastes, he yet loved to see around him the greatest pomp as evidence of his power and of the dependence of others. "Napoleon's tastes were

[1] Mém. Mme. de Rémusat, III. 46.

simple and modest, but he loved glitter and pomp in his surroundings."[1] And he was marvellously skilled in letting everyone feel his own superiority. Already, as is also reported of Attila, no one dared to address him; not even Murat his brother-in-law, who was soon himself to be a king. No man ever was more skilful in employing " the two levers which move men, viz. fear and self-interest."[2]

With every new success his belief in his future became more firm, but the more he relied upon his star, the more he became prone to neglect the means by which success is reached. He had left far behind him the time when he said: "It is only by caution, wisdom, and much skill, that one reaches great ends and conquers all obstacles; there is no other road to success. One step only separates triumph from ruin. . . . It is characteristic of our nation to be too elated in time of prosperity. If we take for the basis of all our operations true policy, which is nothing else than the weighing of all combinations and possibilities, we shall for a long time be the Great Nation and the arbiter of Europe. I will go further and say, we hold the balance of Europe, we will let it rise or fall as we please. Indeed, if it be the will of Fate, I see no impossibility of our attaining those great results, which are the creations of an excited imagination, and which only an abnormally cool, logical, and reasoning man can attain."[3]

Now his confidence in his star was unwavering; when Fesch assailed his policy and would not give way to the Emperor's views, the latter led him out on to a balcony and said: "Look up, do you see anything there?" and when Fesch answered in the negative, he added: "Well, then you ought to be silent; as for me I see my star there and it guides me. Do not any longer compare your weak and imperfect faculties with my superior intelligence;"[4] and he even went so far as to say: "It is truly a proof of

---

[1] Bausset, Mém. I. 12.   [2] Bourrienne, Mém. III. 217.
[3] C. N. To the Minister of Foreign Affairs, Passeriano, 7th October, 1797.   [4] Marmont, Mém. III. 340.

the weakness of the human mind, that people think themselves able to resist me."[1]

Thus the notion grew more and more, that nothing was impossible to him. Up to now he had always seen things as they were, however much he endeavoured to represent them to others as he wished them to appear. But this constant effort to deceive his contemporaries and posterity with respect to himself and his work, had left their mark upon his own mind, and gradually he, who had acknowledged only facts and realities, whose successes even in military matters had been due to the fact that he always reckoned from correct data and saw things in their true proportions, even he reached the point at which people said: "that they thought he used now against himself that power of deceiving others, a power which he knew so well how to wield."[2] Marmont said of Napoleon after Tilsit, that he only believed in truth, when it agreed with his passions, his self-interest, or his humours.

As he continually persuaded himself more and more of the infallibility of his own views, and as his ever-increasing success seemed to justify this conviction, he soon would not listen to any divergent opinions, and all contradiction ceased. On the other hand, his soul, thirsting after glory, showed itself keenly alive to the applause of his contemporaries; flattery approached him with ease, since even in its most extravagant expressions it seemed scarcely to come near the truth as he saw it; "he could not resist believing everything that flatterers told him. A certain credulity may easily exist in a man's mind side by side with mistrust."[3]

With respect to military matters, this development of his character showed itself to begin with only in the fact that his plans, growing with his means, became more and more magnificent and comprehensive, and that his mode

[1] de Pradt, Ambassade, 54.
[2] Ségur, Hist. de N. et de la grande armée en 1812, I. 252.
[3] Mme. de Rémusat, Mém. II. 309.

of waging war became more and more the standard and pattern for others. It became ever more evident that the conception of the whole plan, the correct employment of masses renders victory so certain that mistakes in detail are of little moment, and, of course, the more armies increase, the less will the commander-in-chief be able to watch and control details, yet the more frequent also will be the occasions for mistakes in the execution. But in the control and conduct of the plan as a whole the Emperor's military genius had naturally grown in the same measure, as he rose in the world, and all seemed small compared with him. "What do I care for a million men?" he said in 1813 to Metternich, and de Pradt observed that it was one of the most striking traits of his character, that he was able to concentrate in an instant all his faculties upon any object which occupied his thoughts at the moment, "upon an individual as well as upon a whole hostile army."

But the more he concentrated his glance upon the whole, the more the details were neglected. Hitherto success had always come at his call; nobody ventured any longer to contradict him, and thus it came about that "the ready obedience he had ever met with finally made him believe that his own task consisted merely in commanding, and that his word must without fail be carried out."[1] "It is true he thus judged of many a movement only as a whole, and, without heeding the difficulties with which he was unacquainted, he gave orders for enterprises, which, on account of their minutely punctual execution by his generals, entailed great sacrifices of human life."[2] Of course, it is not the leader's business to look after secondary matters and details, for his mind has to be ever directed only to the great whole, the main points, as indeed the Emperor's always was; but in that case the education of the subordinate officers must ensure

[1] de Pradt, Ambassade, etc., XIV.
[2] O. von O., Napoleon's Feldzug in Sachsen im Jahre 1813, 193.

a correct execution of the details, and in this respect Napoleon's army was deficient.

Since the Emperor, as we have remarked above, loved an active, diligent, and blindly devoted mediocrity in those immediately about him, he had, it is true, at the head of his corps a series of brave and capable tacticians, but few thinking leaders, who could have conducted enterprises demanding more or less independent strategy. The campaign of 1806 will furnish an illustration of this truth, for Bernadotte showed himself incapable at Naumburg of grasping the strategical situation correctly. Adhering blindly to the orders once received, he marched towards Dornburg, thus exposing Davout unsupported to the onslaughts of the Prussian main army, while holding his own corps aloof during the whole of the 14th October. And as moreover the Emperor exacted more and more an unconditional subservience, and would listen to no contradiction, there was soon no possibility whatever of any objections reaching him with respect to orders, which were impossible to execute or fatal if executed. "People contented themselves with listening to him and obeying him without drawing his attention to anything, which a man as busy as he always was might have been forgiven for overlooking."[1] "His orders had to be executed, whatever the means at command. This habit of undertaking everything with insufficient means, this determination not to recognize any impossibilities, this boundless assurance of success, which in the beginning were the cause of our triumphs, in the end became fatal to us."[2]

Add to this, that the Emperor's personal energy began to diminish. The campaign against Prussia, indeed, he entered upon "with a kind of repugnance. The luxury and comfort around him began to affect him. The hardships of camp life alarmed his imagination."[3] He began at this time to become stout, and to be "occupied with

[1] Savary, Mém. V. 273.   [2] Fézensac, Souvenirs militaires, 118.
[3] Mme. de Rémusat, Mém. III. 59.

his comforts to such a degree that he looked upon them as essentials; he became careless, shunning all hardships, blunted, and indifferent in every respect."[1]

Of course, all these weaknesses were not fully developed in 1806, indeed, they only became thoroughly evident much later, in 1812 and 1813, but already they had begun to spring up and become noticeable.

(45) After the conclusion of the peace of Pressburg, the French army had by no means immediately returned home. Taking advantage of political difficulties, and especially of the pending affair of the mouths of the Cattaro, the Emperor kept it stationed in Southern Germany, and partly even on Austrian soil, thus burthening other countries with its maintenance, while it was a constant menace to Austria and Prussia. "My position is excellent, nay splendid, but the extent of my interests is such that I have to be most careful to keep my forces collected, and derive every possible advantage from them."[2] He therefore busied himself most assiduously in the completion of all his corps, and was constantly calculating what strength they had reached. "The muster-rolls of armies are for me the most agreeable literary works in my library, and I read them with the greatest satisfaction in my leisure hours."[3] We therefore see even in August, 1806, Bernadotte in Ansbach and Nuremberg, Soult on the Inn, Davout in the neighbourhood of Nördlingen, Lefebvre on the Lower Main, Ney on the Iller and the Upper Danube, and Augereau around Frankfort. Berthier in Munich had the chief command. At this period the Emperor computed his whole force in Germany at about 192,000 men.

(46) This is not the place to dwell on the political events which drove Prussia to war, nor to examine into the remoter causes of the disaster; the Prussian Government of that time showed indecision and weakness in its

[1] Marmont, Mém. VI. 275. [2] C. N. To Joseph, St. Cloud, 12th July.
[3] C. N. To Joseph, Paris, 9th February.

foreign affairs, and yet wished to derive benefit from the fluctuating condition of Europe. At home they attempted what Napoleon said Milan did: "in this country the impossible is attempted, namely to pay few taxes and have few troops and yet be a great nation; all this is nonsense." [7]

During the first few days of September the Emperor began to seriously contemplate war. As in 1805, his first measure was to despatch officers, who were to examine carefully the roads from Bamberg to Berlin, as well as the rivers Saale, Elster, Pleisse, Mulde and Elbe. For his base he chose; to begin with, the line of the Rhine, Strasburg, Mannheim, and Mainz, and intended to direct his line of operation from it on Würzburg, then a fortified town. For his further advance he searched eagerly for a point of support, situated conveniently in the neighbourhood of the Upper Main; nay, he even despatched officers to look out for additional fortified places on his line of march from Bamberg to Berlin, which he might make use of during the progress of operations after the choice of his immediate base; just as he had done with Augsburg and Braunau in 1805; indeed he hinted expressly at these latter eventualities.

Then he issued orders for the massing of his corps. On the 2rd and 3rd October Augereau was to reach Frankfort; Lefebvre, Königshofen; Davout and Bernadotte, Bamberg; Ney, Ansbach; and Soult, who was at first to have remained on the Inn to keep Austria in check, Amberg; the Guards were set in motion from Paris to Mainz; at the latter place a reserve-corps was formed under Kellermann. On the 28th September Berthier moved his headquarters to Würzburg, and in the morning of the same day the Emperor arrived in Mainz. During his stay in this town he moved the centre of gravity of his army more and more towards the right wing; Bernadotte received instructions to advance

[7] C. N. To Eugéne, St. Cloud, 14th April.

to Kronach; Ney was to march to Nuremberg; Murat was to collect the divisions of the cavalry reserve between Schweinfurt and Kronach; Lefebvre was given the direction of the highroad from Würzburg to Coburg; Soult received orders to march upon Bayreuth, with instructions to continue his march later on to Hof; one Bavarian auxiliary corps under Wrede was to move up to Nuremberg, and the Emperor concluded by saying: "It is my intention to be at Saalfeld before the enemy can appear there in any considerable force."[1]

Besides Würzburg, Forchheim also was fortified as a *point d'appui*, and on the 30th September the Emperor's plan was fully matured: "I intend to mass all my forces upon my extreme right, leaving the space between the Rhine and Bamberg entirely denuded of troops, so as to have about 200,000 men massed on one and the same line. Should the enemy send forward raiding parties between Mainz and Bamberg, it will not render me at all uneasy, because my lines of communication will have been changed to Forchheim, a small fortified place, and subsequently to Würzburg."[2] We see thus, how the Emperor massed his troops; he was going to collect his whole army between Bamberg and Bayreuth, and this mass he intended to bring to bear at the decisive point. For, advancing thence *viâ* Saalfeld and Hof round the left Prussian wing, he would fall upon the communications of the Prussian army which had the Elbe for its base, in the same way as he had in the preceding year cut Mack's communications by moving round the Austrian right wing.

But in order to appear there in full force, he had to sacrifice something in another direction, and that was, in this case, keeping in touch with Mainz, the most important point in his own base. He was obliged to do this, for the moment he concentrated towards his right wing, this line of communication lay to his left, and

---

[1] C. N. To Berthier, Mayence, 30th September.
[2] C. N. To Louis, Mayence.

with certainty that he would, in case the Prussians stood fast in the Thuringian Forest, choose their left wing as the object of his operations ; "the left wing of the allies would then become the goal of all our movements, the main object of which would be to gain the road from Bayreuth to Hof with superior forces, to crush this wing, then to pursue the remainder in detail, and always to hold the road on which the Russians might move up to their assistance."[1]

Here we may see the use of an intelligent study of the history of war. Jomini had not been content with watching how the Emperor had each time gained the victory, but he had deduced from his operations as a whole the general principles which equally underlay them all, and this qualified him now to predict the means by which the victor of 1805 would gain the victory in 1806, "for every war must follow certain lines, because it must be conducted in accordance with the principles and rules of the art and of common sense, and must have a definite object."[2]

Of the dispositions of the Prussians the Emperor had only a very imperfect knowledge. An advance-guard had appeared at Hof; some movements of troops were taking place in Westphalia, but on which wing his opponent was massing his main strength he did not know, and indeed did not care much. For he was determined to advance in the direction which most threatened the enemy's communications, and therefore the latter would either have to fall back quickly or to accept a battle, and as he intended to advance with concentrated forces "in a battalion square of 200,000 men," he would in any case be equal to his opponent in strength. "My first marches will menace the heart of the Prussian monarchy, and my forces will be massed in such an imposing and rapid manner, that probably all the Prussian army in

[1] Corresp. entre le Gén. Jomini et le Gén. Sarrazin, 44.
[2] Dix-huit notes, &c., III. 497.

Westphalia will fall back upon Magdeburg, and that the whole of it will set off by forced marches to defend the capital."[1]

At 9 p.m. on the 1st October the Emperor left Mainz, and arrived in Würzburg in the evening of the following day. He had no clear idea as yet of the state of affairs in the enemy's army; "the Prussian army is performing marches and countermarches; it seems as if their main point of concentration in front was to be Erfurt. The Emperor's armies are in position."[2] His corps received orders to occupy the following positions: Bernadotte was to take post at Lichtenfels, with detachments at Kronach and Coburg; Davout at Bamberg; Ney at Nuremberg; Lefebvre in front of Schweinfurt, with his advance guard at Königshofen; Augereau and the Guards at Würzburg; Murat's cavalry between Würzburg and Kronach; Soult at Amberg. After the Emperor had seen most carefully to the transport service during the 3rd and 4th October, and at the same time had allowed his corps time to move into the above-mentioned positions, he issued orders for a definite forward movement, and commenced operations.

His army was divided as follows:

The Emperor.
Chief of the Staff: Berthier.

		Inf. Divs.	Light Cavalry	
The Guards.	Infantry: Lefebvre			4,000 men
	Cavalry: Bessières			5,000 men
I. Corps.	Bernadotte:	Rivaud	Tilly	
		Drouet		
		Dupont[3]		25,000 men
III. Corps.	Davout:	Morand	Vialannes	
		Friant		
		Gudin		33,000 men
IV. Corps.	Soult:	St. Hilaire	Margaron	
		Leval		
		Legrand		35,000 men

[1] C. N. To Louis, Mayence, 30th September.
[2] C. N. Berthier to the King of Bavaria, Würzburg, 2nd October
[3] Detached from Ney's corps.

V. Corps. Lannes:[1]	Gazan	Treilhard	
	Suchet		23,000 men
VI. Corps. Ney:	Marchand	Colbert	
	Malher		21,000 men
VII. Corps. Augereau:	Desjardins	Durosnel	
	Heudelet		16,000 men

Cavalry Reserve: Murat.

Heavy Divisions.	*Dragoon Divisions.*	*Light Cavalry Brigades.*
Nansouty	Klein	Lasalle
d'Hautpoul	Beaumont	Milhaud
	Grouchy	
	Sahuc		20,000 men

Departmental troops . . . . . . 8,000 men
Bavarian Auxiliary Corps under Wrede . . . 8,000 men

Grand Total 198,000 men
Add the VIII. Corps, Mortier's, at Mainz . . 15,000 men

The army was directed to advance by three roads; the left wing, Lannes, was to reach Coburg early on the 8th October with Augereau, one day's march behind him, on the Bamberg road. In the centre Bernadotte was to march *via* Kronach on Lobenstein, and be on the 8th within a day's march of this latter place, whilst behind him Davout was to be before Kronach on the same day. Davout was to be followed by the Guards. On the right wing Soult had orders to be on the 8th at Münchberg, ready to continue his advance to Hof; one day's march behind him Ney was to move forward, with Wrede in rear; the latter was to reach Bayreuth on the 9th. The headquarters would be at Lichtenfels on the 8th. In their further advance the right wing would proceed *via* Hof, the centre *via* Lobenstein, and the left wing *via* Gräfenthal and Saalfeld.

Even if already dangerous features begun to develop in the Emperor's way of thinking, yet we recognize one thing in this strategical deployment, which is, that the great principles which guided his strategy were ever more closely followed and more marked and definite. The masses became more and more "in the

---
[1] *Vice* Lefebvre.

Emperor's hands like a battalion in the hands of a good commander, ready for anything."[1] Thus he advanced here along a front which extended, from Münchberg to Coburg, no more than thirty-eight miles, as the crow flies, whilst as to its depth, the army only covered two days' march, and was thus in close order, which would enable him to have within forty-eight hours his whole strength concentrated upon any given point. "You will understand, that with this enormous superiority of numbers, concentrated upon such a small space, I have no intention to leave anything to chance, but to attack the enemy, wherever he wants to make a stand, with double the strength he can dispose of."[2]

Here we may with advantage take a look at the Emperor's staff, and see the nature and working of the machine which moved such masses.

The entire personnel of the Emperor's headquarter staff stood under the direction of the Grand Marshal Duroc, who, as well as the Grand Master of the Horse, Caulaincourt, was present, wherever the Emperor rode or drove, in close attendance on him; the latter, moreover, always had the map of the district, in which he was at the time being, with him, ready for Napoleon's immediate use. The imperial carriage was so arranged that Napoleon, travelling as he often did all night, could lie down in it; next to him sat generally Berthier or Murat, and close to the carriage door rode Caulaincourt. Behind the carriage thronged the suite, each eager to be as near as possible, for it was well known with what impatience the Emperor always wished to see his desires, when made known, at once carried out. This suite consisted of the aides-de-camp and orderly officers, whose business it was to carry the Emperor's orders; in 1807 he had of the former seven and of the latter fourteen; besides these were four pages for

---

[1] Observations of a French officer on the official account of the battle of Austerlitz by Kutusov. *Moniteur* 21st April, 1806.
[2] C. N. To Soult, Würzburg, 5th October, 11 a.m.

the necessary personal service, as well as his Mamaluke attendant, Rustum, to wait on him. Two mounted chasseurs carried the most necessary maps and papers in leather portfolios, and a detachment of Chasseurs of the Guard acted as escort, of whom, if the Emperor for any reason left his carriage or dismounted, four immediately dismounted, fixed bayonets, and formed the four corners of a square round him; this square moved imperceptibly as the Emperor did, always leaving him a free view. Finally there followed equerries and grooms with led horses and all kinds of requisites for the escort; the Emperor himself always took eight or nine riding-horses with him on a campaign. It was only in 1813, when the inconvenience of such a large retinue, always close behind the Emperor, often made itself felt, that an order was issued, which settled once for all that only the following should personally attend the Emperor: Berthier, Caulaincourt (Duroc was dead), the field-marshal on duty, the commander of the escort, two aides, two orderly officers, two officers acquainted with the language of the country, one page, one groom, and Rustum. For the rapid performance of long distances, all the riding-horses were divided into relays of nine each, of which two were destined for the Emperor and seven for his most immediate suite. These relays were then distributed in advance along the road to be traversed in such a manner, that the Emperor found fresh horses every eight or ten miles. In like manner the carriage horses were divided into relays of three teams each, and held ready in the same way. Thus the Emperor travelled, for example, during a sharp frost from Valladolid to Burgos, eighty-six miles, in five hours and a half on horseback.

The staff proper was under Berthier; he had during this war 13 aides-de-camp, and, in addition, under 3 heads of departments, with 5 secretaries, 31 staff-officers and 30 belonging to the Survey Department. Songis, the artillery commander, had in 1807 a staff of

18; Chasseloup, the commanding engineer, one of 19 officers, and lastly, Daru, then quarter-master-general, had 43 officials at his disposal. However, these officers were not always all present at headquarters. On the contrary, all branches were so fully represented so that the chief might be able to order many away; more especially did the Emperor constantly despatch his orderly officers to his various corps, not only with orders, but also for the purpose of collecting news, so that he might not be compelled to wait until any corps sent the desired report; but might obtain information of anything which at the moment seemed most important to him.

When the Emperor arrived at the place selected for his headquarters, the first care was to arrange a study for him to work in; indeed he generally found one ready for him, as soon as he dismounted. In the middle of the room there would be a table, on which the best and largest available map of the scene of operations was spread out and marked by the director of the Survey Department, Colonel Bacler d'Albe, with the positions of the troops indicated by coloured pins. In the four corners of the room stood tables for his four private secretaries; these were the real transmitters of his orders, which he dictated to them, walking up and down in the room and speaking with incredible rapidity. These became the basis of Berthier's orders to the army, and of his instructions to the ministers of the various branches of the Government. Adjoining was the Emperor's bed-room, at the door of which Rustum always slept, and near it the apartment of the officers on duty. The rest of the escort had to shift for themselves. Only for Berthier a bed-room and office had always to be procured in the same house. If the headquarters bivouacked, five tents were erected, the Emperor's work-room, his living-room, one tent for Berthier and two for the suite.

Napoleon, who in times of peace generally went to sleep about eleven o'clock, rarely later than midnight, and rose between seven and eight o'clock, thus sleeping rather long, altered his habits during a campaign. Shortly after his dinner, which never lasted more than a quarter of an hour, as he was very frugal and ate little and very quickly, he usually lay down, about six or seven o'clock in the evening, and rose again about one o'clock to issue his orders for the coming day. This method had great practical advantages. If the general gives his orders for the next day during the evening before he retires to rest, his troops receive them in the middle of the night, and the rest of which they stand in need is interrupted. In Napoleon's method of sending out his orders, these reached the troops, it is true, only in the morning shortly before the time for marching, but this is, in by far the greater number of cases, quite soon enough, because it is after all the exception that preparations can be made during the night for the coming day's task. But another thing is still more important. In issuing his orders as early as eight or nine o'clock in the evening, the general will in most cases not be well posted in the details of the state of affairs. The corps will scarcely have finished their day's tasks, and probably from the more distant ones no reports will have been received as to how far they have marched during the day, and what the enemy has done during the latter part of it, in short all those details upon which the plan for the next day must be based. In consequence the evening's orders will frequently have to be altered on account of reports that come in during the night, and thus the troops, which have received one order during the night, may not receive their final orders till the morning. Napoleon, who issued his orders after midnight, was, on the other hand, then in possession of all the reports, and therefore of a sure basis on which to frame his instructions.

We saw how the French army began its advance in obedience to the orders of the 5th October. On the side of the enemy the state of affairs on this day was as follows.

In a council of war, held at Naumburg on the 24th and 25th September, it had been resolved to take the offensive and advance through the Thuringian Forest towards Schweinfurt. This advance had begun, and on the 5th of October Hohenlohe lay in the triangle Jena-Erfurt-Rudolstadt, with his outposts pushed forward towards Gräfenthal and Schleusingen and Eisfeld; Brunswick stood on the line Langensalza-Erfurt, with his van towards Gotha; Rüchel was near Eisenach, but one part of his corps, marching up from Westphalia under Blücher, had only reached Cassel. The reserve corps still stood at Magdeburg. If we measure on the map, to the north of the Thuringian Forest, the distances from Jena and Rudolstadt to Cassel, and to the south of it those from Münchberg to Coberg and Bamberg, if we in addition consider that on the former space there stood 106,000 men disunited, and on the latter 190,000 men concentrated, we shall have an arithmetical proof of the superiority of Napoleon's strategy.

At Erfurt long debates were again held during the 4th 5th, and 6th, but they remained ineffectual; the headquarters were indeed, as Napoleon said, "always holding councils, never agreed,"[1] for he knew very well how matters stood with his opponent. In the end, however, it was resolved to remain stationary on the northern slope of the Thuringian Forest, with the main army at Erfurt, Rüchel at Eisenach, Hohenlohe at Blankenhain; to send forward, into the mountain-passes, only some outposts and to await for the present the further developments of the enemy's plans.

Now the Emperor was well aware of the fact that some sort of concentration of the enemy's army was taking place; he considered that it threatened his left wing, and wrote therefore on the 5th: " From all the reports, which reach me to-day, it seems, that, if the enemy is moving at all, he is doing so towards my left flank, as his main forces

[1] Second Bulletin of the Grand Army, Auma, 12th October.

appear to be near Erfurt." [1]   At 10 p.m. on the same day he left Würzburg and went to Bamberg. His army now advanced during the next few days, as ordered, and on the 8th Lannes stood at Coburg, Augereau a day's march behind him, Murat at Saalburg, Bernadotte at Lobenstein, Davout at Nordhalben, the Guards at Kronach, Soult near Münchberg, Ney a good day's march behind him near Bayreuth. Only Murat had encountered the enemy, some weak outposts, at Saalburg, which, however, soon evacuated this town.

The Emperor had quitted Bamberg at 3 a.m., and arrived in Kronach at nine o'clock; as was always the case in such moments, he was very anxious to receive news about the enemy. "Before the expected reports arrived from his generals, especially when a probable engagement was impending, he was always tortured by restlessness;" [2] indeed he wrote to Soult, who was sure, as a matter of fact, to be the first to hit the most vulnerable point of the enemy's lines: "Do send me more frequent reports; in a war of combination, like this, we can only arrive at satisfactory results by frequent communications among ourselves; let this be your first care. This moment is the most important of the campaign; the enemy does not suspect what we intend to do, woe to him, if he hesitate or lose a single day." [3]

On the 9th the French columns continued their advance. In the centre Bernadotte met the enemy near Schleiz, a division of Hohenlohe's corps, some 7000 men, which had originally been posted at Hof, but had fallen back to Schleiz on the advance of the French right wing column. It was now attacked there and driven from its position. It retreated to Middle-Pöllnitz during the night. Behind Bernadotte, Davout arrived at Lobenstein.

---

[1] C. N. To Soult, Würzburg, 11 a.m.
[2] O. von O., Napoleon's Feldzug in Sachsen im Jahre 1813
[3] C. N. Kronach, 8th October, 3.30 p.m.

On the left wing Lannes reached Gräfenthal; Augereau was at Neustadt, whilst on the right wing Soult had arrived at Hof, and behind him Ney at Münchberg.

The Emperor had reached Nordhalben during the early morning hours; he left his office here for the present, and mounted his horse to personally head the centre column. He was present at the engagement of Schleiz, and then moved his headquarters to Ebersdorf, a part of his Guards also reaching this place. He was still ignorant whether to expect the main body of the enemy on his right or his left wing, though the latter seemed more likely to him. In the morning he sent a message to Lannes, that Saalfeld was probably strongly occupied, in which case he was not to attack before he was joined by Augereau; should, however, the enemy's main body be there, he was to remain on the defensive at Gräfenthal, for the emperor would attack the left flank of the enemy *viâ* Saalburg; this he would do, even if the enemy advanced; in this event Lannes was to fall back; should, however, the enemy retire, he was to occupy Saalfeld as quickly as possible. "What is most important at this juncture, is to send news three times daily to the Emperor about yourself and the enemy."[1]

As a matter of fact, no definite plan had as yet been adopted by the Prussians. Rüchel stood at Eisenach and Gotha; the main army at Erfurt; the advanced guard at Meiningen; their further operations were independent of each other; Hohenlohe was at Middle-Pöllnitz and in the neighbourhood of Saalfeld lay a considerable advance-guard. On the 10th Lannes advanced towards Saalfeld and met Hohenlohe's vanguard at ten o'clock, which had taken post there for the defence of the defile. Holding the enemy frontally by vigorous attacks, he turned their left flank, and finally, the enemy having been misled into holding Saalfeld too long and too obstinately, Lannes

[1] C. N. Berthier to Lannes, Nordhalben, 9th October.

brought his superior numbers fully to bear upon this Prussian advance-guard, which was completely dispersed.

The engagement of the day before at Schleiz, as well as the troops, which had come into action at Saalfeld, confirmed the Emperor in his opinion that his right wing had probably no considerable forces in front of it. He therefore sent orders to Ney to move up to Tanna, whilst Murat was to reconnoitre carefully in the direction of Auma and Saalfeld, in order to ascertain whether the enemy's main body was in front of Lannes or of the central column. Napoleon himself thought: "It seems as if the Prussians are minded to attack, and that their left wing intended to advance *viâ* Jena, Saalfeld and Coburg, and that Prince Hohenlohe's headquarters are at Jena and those of Prince Louis at Saalfeld; the other column seems to have advanced *viâ* Meiningen on Fulda."[1] Since he therefore believed the main force of the enemy to be facing himself and Lannes, he considered that the first thing was to be in sure communication with the latter. "As soon as our junction is effected I shall push forward as far as Neustadt and Triptis, and then I shall be delighted with whatever the enemy does; whether he attacks me or allows me to attack him; in any case I shall not miss him; should he retreat *viâ* Magdeburg, you (Soult) will be in Dresden before him. I greatly desire a battle,"[2] and as he was sure of interposing between the Elbe and the enemy, owing to the movements of his own right wing, he added: "After this battle I shall be in Dresden or Berlin before him." A despatch from Soult rendered it certain, that the Prussian army intended to concentrate near Gera, but the Emperor was of opinion that "it is doubtful, whether it can concentrate there, before my own arrival."[3]

Of the various corps, Soult reached Plauen on the 10th, but then received orders to change the direction of his march more to the left *viâ* Weida towards Gera; Ney,

---

[1] C. N. To Soult, Ebersdorf, 10th October, 8 a.m.
[2] The same.   [3] The same.

turning off to the left, according to his orders, reached Gefell; Bernadotte was near Auma; Davout, who had been ordered to hasten his march, reached Schleiz; and Augereau Gräfenthal. The Emperor now established his headquarters at Schleiz; late in the evening he received news of the capture of Saalfeld, though he had already judged from the distant artillery fire that Lannes was in possession of that place, and he now sent orders to him to march towards Neustadt the next morning. Thus all the columns of the army had been so directed as to converge upon Gera, " in Gera matters will be cleared up."[1]

In view of the general advance of the French, Hohenlohe had fallen back upon Kahla, moreover the main army now began, in consequence of the French advance upon Schleiz, to be alarmed for its communications with the Elbe, and therefore retreated towards Blankenhain. In the evening, however, it was decided, after the arrival of the news of the engagement near Saalfeld, to collect the whole army at Weimar. Rüchel had on the 10th closed up more towards Erfurt. We see, therefore, that although the Emperor was unacquainted with the enemy's positions in detail, yet his general view of the situation was correct, for the Prussian army retreating towards its communications, sought to concentrate towards the east, and Napoleon's advance on Gera would therefore hit the right point.

(49) On the 11th October the Emperor at first accompanied the central column. Of this Murat, with the light cavalry, and Bernadotte reached Gera, the latter being followed by the remainder of the cavalry reserve. Nothing was seen there of the enemy, and Murat therefore immediately ordered the cavalry forward to reconnoitre further in the direction of Zeitz and Jena. Davout reached Middle-Pöllnitz, Ney Schleiz, Soult was in the neighbourhood of Langen-Wetzendorf. Lannes on the left wing arrived in

[1] C. N. To Soult, Schleiz, 10th October, 6 p.m.

Neustadt, and Augereau in Saalfeld. The facts that Gera was unoccupied and that no considerable force of the enemy was visible in the district to the west of the Elster, had already aroused the Emperor's suspicion that the hostile army was still further to the west than he had originally believed. He rode back to Auma in the night, whither he had moved his headquarters, and became there convinced by the reports which reached him that the enemy's army still stood at Erfurt, or at any rate had not yet crossed the Saale. In consequence of this conviction he now resolved to turn to the left towards the Saale with his entire army, and to block all the enemy's lines of retreat towards the Elbe.

Orders to this effect were despatched to the army in the morning of the 12th; Murat was to advance to Zeitz, and if the enemy was still found to be really at Erfurt, to Naumburg; Bernadotte was to follow him; Soult was to march to Gera, Ney to Auma, Davout to Naumburg, Lannes to Jena, and Augereau to Kahla. On the side of the Prussians, Hohenlohe had retreated to Jena on the 11th, whilst the main army took up a position near Weimar, to which place Rüchel also moved forward.

On the 12th, therefore, the French corps advanced towards the points respectively fixed on. The Emperor returned to Gera in the morning, Bernadotte reached Zeitz, with Murat in advance of him; Soult arrived at Gera, Ney at Auma, Augereau at Kahla; Davout reached Naumburg on the same evening with his advance-guard, his main body being in the neighbourhood of Schkölen. Lannes arrived in front of Jena, and drove the enemy's outposts into that town. Here Hohenlohe's advance-guard now stood, whilst he himself had pitched his camp further in the rear, fronting the south-west, with his right wing at Kapellendorf and his left on the Schnecke.

In the course of the night the Emperor gathered from (49)

the reports from his different corps, that the enemy was still on the other side of the Saale, and he therefore still believed him near Erfurt. He now drew up in his own handwriting a memorandum of the general aspect of the situation, and fixed on the points at which he would direct his corps to cross the Saale during a general advance. In the first place he reviewed the preceding movements of his Guards, who had to a great extent remained rather far in the rear during the march, in order to ascertain at what date they could reach him. He then did the same with respect to the cavalry divisions of d'Hautpoul and Klein; in this latter case, however, his process of reasoning can now no longer be clearly traced. Finally he measured on the map the distances between the localities in question, and fixed the limits of the marches of all his corps.

The following is the text of this memorandum [1]:—

Guards: 10th Oct., in the evening, Bamberg; 11th, Lichtenfels; 12th, beyond Kronach; 13th, Lobenstein.

d'Hautpoul: 11th, two hours beyond Kronach; 14th, Auma; 15th Jena.

Klein: on the 11th, two hours beyond Kronach; 13th in Jena: 14th in Jena; 15th in Auma.

Klein: 12th in Lobenstein.

Jena to Weimar, four hours' march.

Naumburg to Weimar, seven hours.

Kahla to Weimar, five hours.

Neustadt to Jena, five hours.

Gera to Jena, seven hours.

From Zeitz to Jena, seven hours.

Reserve Cavalry, 14th in Jena.

Guards, 15th in Jena.

Park, 15th in Auma.

Davout, 14th in Apolda.

Lannes, 15th in Weimar.

Augereau, 14th in Mellingen.

Bernadotte, 14th in Dornburg.

Soult, 14th in Jena.

Ney, 14th in Kahla.

[1] C. N. Vol. 23, page 330. A footnote suggests it was written on the 10th October. ED.

We see, therefore, that he ordered his corps to close up in their advance, so as to proceed to the attack upon Erfurt with his whole army in close order; this, indeed, agrees with what he wrote to Murat: "If the enemy is at Erfurt, it is my plan to take my army to Weimar and to attack him on the 16th."[1] It is, moreover, invariably characteristic of Napoleon's strategy, that he, in his advance to a battle, always fixed the point of junction of his columns short of the anticipated battle-field, and never on the battle-field itself.

In agreement with the above memorandum, according to which the Saale was to be crossed on the 14th, he sent to tell his various corps that the army might rest on the 13th, only Ney was to proceed to Roda. However, as yet no news had come in from Lannes, and as he was the one who would be first to come in contact with the enemy, the Emperor sent one of his aides-de-camp to him at 7 a.m. in the morning of the 13th to ascertain how matters stood with him. A short time later, however, his report of his arrival in front of Jena, and of the troops observed there, came in, and the Emperor exclaimed: "At last the veil is rent, and the enemy is beginning his retreat towards Magdeburg."[2] He now ordered Murat to march as quickly as possible to Dornburg with the light cavalry and Bernadotte; he himself proceeded to Jena, to which place he also sent the rest of the cavalry-reserve. On the road, at Köstritz, he received news that Lannes had gained the left bank of the Saale, and immediately sent orders to Soult to come up as far as this place; then he continued his rapid march to Jena. A short distance from this town he heard that Lannes had about 50,000 men in front of him and expected to be attacked that very day. Without delay Davout and Bernadotte received instructions to move on to Jena, as soon as they heard firing

---

[1] C. N. Gera, 13th October, 7 a.m.
[2] C. N. To Murat, Gera, 13th October, 9 a.m.

there, otherwise they would receive further instructions during the night from the Emperor for the 14th. Arriving in Jena, Napoleon found Lannes in possession of this town and of the steep heights of the Landgrafenberg lying behind it on the left bank of the Saale. For in the early morning Hohenlohe's vanguard had moved from Jena to the rear, to the high ground on the left bank of the Saale, as far as the line Lützeroda-Closwitz, Lannes immediately following him and occupying the heights.

The Emperor himself immediately went to the top of the Landgrafenberg, where he arrived at four o'clock in the afternoon; he dismounted and approached the hostile lines within range, having now a view of Hohenlohe's position near Kapellendorf, and Lützeroda in front of him. It was one of the qualities which stamped him a born general, to take in at a glance the whole state of affairs and to form a correct judgment on it. "One look through his telescope and he had with incredible rapidity gained an insight into the position of a whole army. Thus, from some height, he would judge of a whole corps of 50,000 or 60,000 men according to space and position."[1] In this case he immediately estimated the army opposite to him, at 40,000 or 50,000 men, but thought it was the enemy's main body which was ready for battle; he also saw at once that the battle would take place here on the 14th, which he had believed would occur near Erfurt and on the 16th.

His first care now was to bring up that same day Lannes's entire corps on the heights, in order thus to keep the approaches to the fords of the Saale open for his army and to keep the enemy from them. With the fiery zeal peculiar to him, he was personally present everywhere, urging on his men and assigning to each corps its position. It was of such paramount importance to him, to remain in possession of the heights on the

---

[1] O. von O., Napoleon's Feldzug in Sachsen im Jahre 1813, 192.

left bank of the Saale, that he assumed the enemy would likewise be aware of their importance, and attempt in the evening of the same day to dislodge Lannes again from them. He therefore sent orders to Lefebvre and Soult to come up with all speed: "Let an aide-de-camp ride his horse to death if necessary." To Ney and Augereau also he sent orders to be at Jena by the 14th.

However, no attack was made. Hohenlohe remained quietly in his camp. The main army had indeed at last resolved during the evening of the preceding day to withdraw, and Hohenlohe was to cover this retreat, which exposed its flank to the enemy. But some further delays interfered with the execution of this plan and in the evening the main army stood at Auerstädt.

Rüchel had collected his troops around Weimar. On the side of the French, Davout and Bernadotte were in the evening of this day at Naumburg, the former held the pass of Kösen, Murat stood between Naumburg and Kamburg, whilst Lannes occupied, as mentioned above, the Landgrafenberg. Augereau arrived in Jena in the course of the night, resting on the Mühlbach, which flows into the Saale there from the left; the greater part of the Guards also reached Jena in the evening. Soult was on the march hither from Gera, Ney from Roda; the former brought up his cavalry and St. Hilaire's division during the same night, but Ney only reached the field with his advance-guard just before the beginning of the battle.

The expected evening attack was, however, not delivered, and at last the Emperor returned very late in the night to his bivouack on the Landgrafenberg. From here he issued after midnight his orders for the attack the next day. Augereau was to march into position on the plateau to the left of Lannes; Soult was to ascend the heights with daybreak by the valley of the Rau and form the right wing; Ney was to move into position on his left as soon as Lannes should have captured Closwitz, whereby room would be gained for deploying on the Landgrafenberg; the Guards were to be in reserve at the beginning of the ascent of this height. All the corps were told that, to begin with, it would only be a question of gaining the plateau; all further measures for the attack would have to be postponed, and would depend on the movements and strength of the enemy. Lannes was to provide the space necessary for the deployment of the army by opening the battle with an attack upon Cospeda and Closwitz.

At four o'clock in the morning the Emperor proceeded to this latter corps, addressed the men, informed them that the enemy's army was entirely cut off, and recalled to them the similar position of Mack on the same day a year before; at six o'clock the corps formed up and advanced in the thick fog of the cold October morning towards the enemy's position at Closwitz-Lützeroda. After a protracted artillery fire the fog began gradually to clear about eight o'clock, and the corps, which till now had been unable to distinguish the objects of attack, advanced against the much weaker vanguard of Hohenlohe, the right wing leading, drove it from Closwitz and forced it back with heavy losses, about nine o'clock, towards the Dornburg. Lannes immediately followed up the enemy's vanguard and dispersed it entirely; about ten o'clock he took up position on the line Closwitz-Lützeroda.

Thus sufficient room was won on the heights, and " the Emperor would now have preferred to delay two hours before coming to hand-to-hand fighting, in order to wait, in the position just occupied, for the troops, which were still to come up, and more particularly his cavalry;"[1] but he had to experience the truth of the observation, which we before ventured to dwell on in the case of Austerlitz, namely, that only the moment and direction of the opening movements of an attack lie in the general's hands, but that any stopping and resuming of the fighting at will is, as a rule, impossible.

[1] Fifth Bulletin, Jena, 15th October.

During the last efforts of Lannes, Soult also had (52) ascended the plateau, and stood at ten o'clock on the further side of Zwätzen. Here a hostile detachment advanced from Rödingen to attack him. This latter had been despatched by Hohenlohe on the evening before to Dornburg, to occupy the passage over the Saale there, and had now, in consequence of the artillery-fire, collected again at Rödingen. It did not succeed however in regaining its contact with the army, for Soult soon repulsed its attack and forced it back by Nerkwitz behind the brook there. It subsequently retired towards Apolda.

At the same time however, Hohenlohe had set himself in motion, and his army had advanced into the line Vierzehnheiligen-Isserstädt. Meanwhile some additional French troops had arrived on the plateau. Ney pushed forward with his vanguard south of Lannes's two divisions, towards Vierzehnheiligen, and occupied this village before the Prussians; the Guards marched into position as a reserve behind Lannes; Augereau deployed his lines on the Flohberg between Cospeda and the Schnecke. Now Hohenlohe advanced with his lines fully deployed against the French first line, composed of Ney at Vierzehnheiligen, Augereau on his left towards Isserstädt and Lannes to the right of Vierzehnheiligen. As to the Guards, the Emperor kept them where they were near the Dornburg, since he had for the present no other reserve.

Before the advancing line of Hohenlohe the French skirmishers retreated, and Isserstädt, only feebly occupied, was evacuated, but in front of Vierzehnheiligen the attack was checked, the batteries directed their fire against this village, and the Prussian infantry exchanged volleys in line with the enemy without advancing. Thus matters stood until about midday, the French defending themselves and (53) maintaining Vierzehnheiligen, and the Prussians hesitating to advance to a decisive attack. But at this time there arrived on the left bank of the Saale the divisions of Leval and Legrand of Soult's corps, and Marchand's division of Ney's, and the emperor, being at length in possession of fresh reserves, ordered the part of his army, already in action, to advance to a general attack upon the enemy's line. Soult turned towards their left wing; the Guards advanced towards Vierzehnheiligen, and Augereau moved towards Isserstädt and the Schnecke, where Hohenlohe's right wing, the Saxons, stood. The combined attack of such masses was too much for the Prussian line, already shaken by its two hours' exposure to the French artillery-fire; it fell back, and the retreat was soon changed into a complete rout by the French pressing after them. It was now two o'clock.

At this moment Rüchel arrived on the battle-field, but his weak corps could no longer turn the issue of the day; advancing *viâ* Kapellendorf towards Great-Römstadt, he compelled the foremost French division to fall back at first, but was soon attacked by superior forces and completely routed after a short struggle. The resistance also which the Saxons on the Prussian right on the Schnecke continued to offer, was now overcome. Whilst Augereau attacked them in front, the Emperor sent Marchand *viâ* Isserstädt against their flank, and thus they were cut off and a portion of them made prisoners. At four o'clock all was over; the Emperor was on all points completely master of the battle-field, and urged his columns forward to the pursuit in the direction of Weimar, towards which town the beaten enemy had retreated. The cavalry-reserve, which had just come up, and Ney's corps, now completely assembled, penetrated as far as Weimar, and, drove the enemy, who had wished to halt there, out of it. Lannes reached Umpferstädt and Soult Schwabdorf. The Emperor returned to Jena in the evening, still convinced that he had beaten the main army.

The latter had this day, however, been face to face with Davout. We have seen, that it had started on the 13th from Weimar to Freiburg and had reached

Auerstädt; the Prussians thought the pass of Kösen was only feebly occupied, and they would easily clear it and occupy it themselves during their further march. However, as we said, not only had Davout already reached Naumburg with his whole corps, but Bernadotte was in support of him near this town on the evening of the 13th. At three o'clock in the morning on the 14th, the former marshal received an order from the Emperor, dated "Bivouack near Jena, 13th October, 10 p.m.," in which he, thinking that he himself had the whole enemy's army in front of him, and that Davout would not meet with any considerable resistance, instructed the latter to march to Apolda and thus to attack the enemy's army, which the emperor himself would engage on the 14th, in the rear. In addition, the order contained the following: "If the Prince of Ponte-Corvo is with you, you can march together. But the Emperor hopes he is in the position which he had instructions to occupy near Dornburg." Bernadotte did not consider this to be any justification for his departing from the order issued to him from Gera on the morning of the 13th, to march to Dornburg, and immediately started upon his march to that place. Thus Davout was destined to meet the whole Prussian main army by himself, in carrying out the orders he had received for an advance.

At six o'clock he started for Hassenhausen in the midst of a thick fog, and at the same time the enemy also began his movement. But at Hassenhausen the Prussian cavalry, which was in advance, met the enemy's vanguard, which hastened to take up a position there. The Duke of Brunswick was obliged to deploy his infantry against it. Davout in his turn ordered his infantry, as it came up, to prolong the line to the right, in order to lengthen this wing threatened by a turning movement of the Prussian cavalry. Soon after eight o'clock a general cavalry attack began under the leadership of General Blücher, and actually threatened to envelop the right flank of the French infantry. But the cavalry was repulsed by the calmly delivered fire of the latter, and thrown into such confusion that they spurred back in full flight *viâ* Spielberg.

(52) At this moment Friant also began to come into position on the flank of Gudin's division, which had up till now stood alone near Hassenhausen; thus the line was lengthened as far as Spielberg, whilst the Prussian line, also lengthening out towards the right in its turn, began at nine o'clock an attack in force on Gudin's left wing, which stood near Hassenhausen. The Prussian line, as it advanced, drove all that it encountered in the open, back into the village, but Hassenhausen itself resisted all their attacks in line, as Vierzehnheiligen had done fifteen miles away.

The Prussian infantry became engaged in a stationary exchange of musketry, and suffered the severest losses, until at last, between eleven and twelve o'clock, the last division of Davout, Morand's, had crossed the Saale, and was led forward by the marshal himself, at the double,
(53) against the Prussians surrounding Gudin. The Prussian line, already seriously shaken by heavy losses, could not resist the attack of this fresh body; it was thrown back and retreated *viâ* Poppel and Tauchwitz upon its reserve, standing near Gernstädt. Now, however, the king ordered the general retreat of the army to Weimar, and
(54) therefore the movement was continued through Auerstädt under the incessant pressure of the pursuing French, who desisted from the pursuit only about five o'clock.

Bernadotte had reached Dornburg very late, and there the difficulties of the ground offered such obstacles to his crossing the Saale that his vanguard only reached Apolda as night fell.

Once more the Emperor had thus illustrated in the most magnificent manner his great principle of seizing the enemy's communications by a concentrated advance of his entire army in one direction. His successes against Melas and Mack had already led some military men to recognize that these manœuvres were not adopted merely on account of local circumstances, but that there lay in them a principle based upon the nature of things, and therefore universally true, and it was Bülow who first expressed it distinctly: "The lines of supply are the muscles, and to sever them paralyses the military body. Now, since these lie on the flank and in the rear, it follows that the flanks and the rear must be the objects of the enemy's operations."[1] But even he did not arrive at a full knowledge of what constitutes the effectiveness of these operations; he was still of opinion that the mere advance against the enemy's communications would have the effect of causing him to retreat, and that actual fighting could and must be avoided during such operations. It was reserved for Jomini to lay it down definitely, that the strategical turning movements only had their full effect if, after having reached the enemy's lines of communication, battle was offered. "It is not sufficient for the successful conduct of war to lead one's masses to the most important points; one must also know how to bring them into play. If one has arrived at those points and remains inactive, the principle has been forgotten; the enemy can make countermanœuvres, and in order to deprive him of this expedient, one must immediately, after having reached his communications or one of his flanks, make for him and give battle."[2]

It is of course only battle which lends effect to the turning movement. Up to the battle, it will easily be seen on looking at the map, that whoever turns the enemy exposes himself more or less to be turned also. A successful engagement alone averts this danger, and therefore we note how Napoleon always hastens, and especially in the case before us, with almost breathless eagerness, to give battle; indeed he was aware that this was one of his distinctive features as compared with his

[1] Geist des neueren Kriegssystems, 101.
[2] Traité des grandes opérations militaires, IV. 281.

enemies, for he said: "While they are debating the French army marches."[1]

On the other hand, moreover, we must note that Napoleon always guarded most carefully in all his turning-movements against the danger of being cut off in turn, by the choice of the direction of his lines of operation. And yet we cannot but acknowledge, that there was a possibility of his communications being temporarily cut in 1805. It is true such isolation would not have had any very serious consequences for him, inasmuch as his great superiority in numbers would have permitted him at any moment to bring matters to an issue by a battle, which would have cleared his rear again. Still we can note in 1806 an increase of precaution in his choice of base, although he again possessed great superiority of forces.

We know, that in case of an unfavourable turn of events, he intended to make the Danube the base of his main army, while retaining his base on the Rhine. Here Jomini already drew attention to the safety which such a command of two of the boundaries of the arena of war affords. He says: "And even if the Prussians had dreamed of cutting off this line of retreat (Saalfeld-Schleiz-Hof) by throwing themselves between Gera and Bayreuth, they would thereby only have opened out to him his most natural line, the fine road from Leipzic to Frankfort, besides the ten roads which lead from Saxony *viâ* Cassel to Coblenz, Cologne and Wesel."[2]

This indeed was the real reason for the instructions given on the 30th September to Louis, and why the army of Holland was posted at Wesel and Mortier at Mainz. Thus on the eve of Jena the Emperor's strategical position, considering his choice of a twofold retreat, seems to have been as carefully secured as is possible in the uncertainty of human affairs.

It is true he did not know, as is mostly the case in war,

[1] Third Bulletin, Gera, 13th October.
[2] Précis de l'art de la guerre, 133.

where the enemy was at the moment, indeed we have seen that he was mistaken and believed him to be further off than he really was. It was therefore quite possible, that in his continued advance over the Saale one of his corps should have unexpectedly met with the main force of the enemy and suffered defeat; but in that case Napoleon would have gained the necessary knowledge of where the enemy's army lay; he could then immediately have led his corps against him, and the close order of his whole advance warranted him in thinking he could have concentrated them all in time. More than the defeat of one French corps the Prussian army could not hope for nor Napoleon fear.

It will be seen from this that Jena was quite an unexpected encounter, at least as regards the Emperor; it was only on the eve of this battle, that he became aware of the fact that the enemy's army lay there and that the very next day must witness the meeting. Then he immediately did, what is needed in such a situation, i.e. he sent orders to all his corps to march up as speedily as possible. Undoubtedly there might now have happened what we mentioned above as possible: Lannes's isolated corps might, on the 13th, have suffered a reverse, but with that the whole campaign would neither have been won by the Prussian army nor lost for Napoleon. The Emperor had advanced in such close order, that he could be sure of having by noon on the 14th a force assembled, which would at least be equal to the Prussian army.

During the battle Napoleon again showed his desire, to keep its conduct in his own hands, by not employing all his troops before the supreme moment had come. Thus he left Ney's advance-guard and Lannes for two hours to their own resources, in spite of the very threatening look of Hohenlohe's attack; and when during these anxious moments he heard from the ranks of his Guards the cry of " Forward!" he said: " What does this mean?

It can only be a young, beardless man, who wishes to anticipate what I am going to do. Let him wait, until he has commanded in twenty battles, before he ventures to give me advice;"[1] and, watching the battle calmly, he waited until, by the arrival of fresh troops, the reserve was set free and he could use it for that general, decisive attack, which no one knew better than he how to deliver.

[1] Hist. des campagnes de l'emp. Nap. en 1805, 1806 et 1807-1809, II. 77.

CHAPTER XII.

EYLAU.

The consequences, which were sure to follow the battle of Jena, were immediately fully recognized by the Emperor. Indeed it was characteristic of him to rate a victory once gained too high, rather than too low; it was to this conviction that he owed the determination to aim at the greatest results which a victory could bring him, and the history of war proves that he attained them. On the very next day after the battle he already announced: "Considering that the result of yesterday's battle is the conquest of all the country this side of the Vistula, belonging to the King of Prussia, etc."[1] He must indeed have been far-sighted to use such words, while still on the banks of the Saale, but they were justified, for he felt that his untiring activity would not allow the beaten army to rest short of that point, and that he, who had gained the victory in a great pitched battle, had nothing further to fear, beyond not reaping its fruits.

On the morning of the 15th October he gave his corps orders for the pursuit: Bernadotte was to advance towards Neustadt and bar the road to Querfurt; Davout was to take up a position at Naumburg; Soult to march to Buttelstädt, Murat to Erfurt, and Ney to follow the latter. Lannes and Augereau were to remain near Weimar. The Prussian main army had proceeded northward past Weimar to Erfurt, and had then, on receipt of the news of Jena, changed its course towards Sömmerda, where it

[1] Decree, Jena, 15th October.

arrived on the morning of the 15th, much diminished in numbers through the night march. For not only had individual soldiers in great numbers left the ranks, but owing to the changes in the direction of the march, various bodies of troops had proceeded to Frankenhausen and Erfurt. For Hohenlohe also, Sömmerda was appointed as the place of concentration, but his troops had become fully disorganized; the retreat was to be continued to Magdeburg, where a junction was to be effected with the Reserve-Corps.

Soon after two o'clock in the afternoon, Murat arrived in front of Erfurt; immediately negotiations were begun, and in the course of the same night the town and citadel, and all the troops who had taken refuge there, surrendered; "this is a valuable acquisition, which will serve as our *point d'appui* during our future operations;"[1] was the Emperor's remark when he heard of it. Soult in his pursuit came up with the enemy's main column on the 16th near Greussen, attacked its rear-guard and inflicted some losses on it, whilst the main column continued its march to Nordhausen, reaching this town on the 17th. Here some 10,000 men of Hohenlohe's column also had assembled.

Napoleon immediately ordered Murat, Soult and Ney to go in pursuit of these troops to Nordhausen, whilst he himself, with the rest of the army, took the direct road to the Elbe, in order to block the road there to the retreating Prussians, and to force them northward and away from their capital and the direction to the Oder. Consequently Bernadotte was to march to Querfurt and Lannes *via* Naumburg to Merseburg; the latter was to be followed on the same road by the Guards and Augereau. Davout received the direction towards Leipzic. Mortier was now to move up to Fulda. The Emperor himself went on the 16th to Weimar.

Bernadotte, having reached Querfurt on the 16th,

[1] Ninth Bulletin, Weimar, 17th October.

heard that the Prussian Reserve-Corps had advanced from Magdeburg to Halle. He therefore started on the 17th, at 2 a.m., found it near Halle in position, attacked it, captured the bridges over the Saale, as well as the town, and then defeated the enemy completely. The latter, pursued by the French and half annihilated, fell back upon Dessau. On the 20th October the armies stood in the following positions: Murat had arrived in front of Magdeburg, Soult was close behind him at Great-Wauzleben, Ney had reached Halberstadt. The right wing of the army was disposed as follows: Bernadotte at Calbe, Lannes crossing the Elbe at Dessau, with Augereau close behind him; Davout was crossing the same river at Wittenberg and occupied that town, which was now to form the main depôt and point of support for the future operations, and was accordingly immediately fortified against any hostile attack. The headquarters and the Guards were at Halle.

As to the Prussians, the original main column, now under the command of Hohenlohe, had on this day reached Magdeburg, where the greatest disorder and confusion reigned. A second column, under Blücher, which had, on leaving Nordhausen, during the march through the Harz, taken a divergent direction, had afterwards been compelled, by the advance of the French, to give up its march to Magdeburg and had made for the mouth of the Havel; on the 20th it was five miles from Brunswick. Here Blücher effected a junction with a third column under the Duke of Weimar. This had originally been the vanguard of the main army, and had, on the 9th October, been ordered forward as far as the Werra, but had afterwards been recalled in time. The Duke had, after receipt of the news of Jena, reached the neighbourhood of Goslar on the 20th, by a considerable detour *viâ* Erfurt, Mühlhausen and Heiligenstadt, avoiding the Harz. Blücher and Weimar now resolved to continue their march in company, and on the 24th

x

the former, on the 26th the latter, crossed the Elbe at Sandau.

Soult, who was investing Magdeburg in conjunction with Ney, had been informed of the march of these troops, on the preceding day, and started immediately, on the 25th, to cut them off, but only came up on the 26th with the Prussian rear-guard at Altenzaun, where it had been placed to cover the passage of the Elbe, nor could he force it to yield.

In the meantime Hohenlohe had started from Magdeburg on the 21st, and reached the neighbourhood of Wusterhausen and Neustadt on the 24th, to the north of the Rhin-bruch. On the same day the Emperor arrived at Potsdam with Murat, Lannes and the Guards, Davout was near Tempelhof, at the gates of Berlin, only Bernadotte, who had been delayed in crossing the Elbe, was behind at Ziesar. This time the Emperor's anger against him broke out, and he reproached him in harsh terms, not only with the present delay, but also with remaining inactive between the two parts of the army engaged in fighting on the 14th. If we wish to have one more example of the marching, which was expected as a general rule from Napoleon's army, we have only to measure the distance which Davout traversed from Schleiz, where he arrived on the 10th October, to Berlin, which he entered on the 25th. We shall find that it amounted to 166 miles, as the crow flies, and was done in fourteen days, including the fighting of a battle.

At Potsdam, the Emperor received news of the march of Hohenlohe's corps towards the north-east, and gave orders to Murat in the night of the 24th, to despatch the light brigade of Lasalle to Oranienburg, from which place it was, by sending out strong patrols in all directions, to ascertain the actual direction of Hohenlohe's march. Murat and Lannes arrived on the 25th before Spandau, which place immediately surrendered, the same Spandau of which the Emperor, when it was in his own hands, said: "Spandau is a fortress, which the enemy will never be able to take."[1] On the same day Napoleon received a report from Bernadotte, informing him that Hohenlohe was marching in the direction of Stettin, and as he at the same time heard of the fall of Spandau, Murat and Lannes were immediately set in motion towards Oranienburg. Bernadotte, who arrived in Brandenburg on that day, was likewise to follow on the tracks of the enemy, and Soult received carte-blanche to assist in this operation according to his own judgment.

On the 26th Lasalle's cavalry came up with and defeated a division of the enemy near Zehdenick, which was to have covered Hohenlohe's right flank during his march *viâ* Prenzlau to Stettin, a march which had not been sufficiently rapid. For on the 28th Murat arrived at Prenzlau at the same time as Hohenlohe's column. The latter, it is true, managed to march through the town and to take up a position on the road to Pasewalk, but in this situation, which in any case was precarious, his chief-of-the-staff, Colonel Massenbach, whom he had sent to the enemy, and who had altogether lost his head, brought news that the enemy were advancing along the right bank of the Ucker on the Pasewalk road, 100,000 strong, and that they themselves would soon be completely outflanked. In reality, only Murat's cavalry was there, and no other troops were on the left bank of the Ucker; Massenbach had mistaken a small brook, which he had crossed, for the Ucker. Hohenlohe saw no further way of escape and laid down his arms. Two days later the fortress of Stettin was surrendered to Lasalle's light cavalry, which appeared unsupported before it.

Blücher's column had followed Hohenlohe, and received early in the morning of the 29th at Boitzenburg the news of the affair of Prenzlau. Blücher at once resolved to retreat towards the lower Elbe, and having been joined

[1] C. N. To Daru, Charlottenburg, 26th October.

by the division Weimar, now under the command of General Winning, he reached Waren on the 31st with these troops. Bernadotte had heard at the same time of both Hohenlohe's surrender and Blücher's march towards Strelitz; suspecting Stralsund to be the latter's goal, and intending to cut him off, he marched against him and reached Stargard on the 31st. On this day Soult was near Zechlin, where he heard of the situation of affairs. He now sent his cavalry alone in direct pursuit of Blücher, whilst resolving to move his infantry between him and the Elbe. On the 1st November Bernadotte came in touch with Blücher's rear-guard, and pursued it fighting as far as Old-Schwerin. Murat also was approaching from Stettin *viâ* Demmin.

Thus Blücher, closely pursued by Bernadotte and Soult, hurried towards the Elbe, intending to cross it at Boitzenburg. He soon deemed even this impossible, and on the 4th November he moved by Gadebush towards Lübeck, where he arrived at noon on the 5th; but the very next day this town was taken by storm by the French, and Blücher was obliged, considerably weakened, to fall back upon Ratkau. He wished to seek shelter in the works of Travemünde, but on the next day had to lay down his arms, in face of the considerably superior numbers of the French troops, who had followed him closely and threatened to attack at once. This made an end of all the Prussian troops still between the Elbe and Oder, as various other smaller and isolated bodies had also surrendered.

After the capture of Lübeck, the French soldiers made the most unheard-of use of their victory; the town was plundered and its inhabitants were subjected to the most licentious excesses and cruelties. Their prayers for mercy were answered by the French leaders with shrugs of the shoulders and indifference; they said they could do nothing, the town had been taken by assault, and in such a case " it was the custom of war." In this respect also it was a fatal thing for the army that their commander-in-chief had begun to care less and less about means, as long as he attained his ends.

Still, we cannot deny that the general only acted logically in this, and therefore was in the right. Whether his final aim was just or possible, is another question; but having once set up this aim, the means adopted were assuredly correct. His whole soul was set upon gaining the empire of the world, as Cæsar had done; this condemns his foresight as a statesman, but as a general he could only reach his highest aims by demanding enormous efforts, and could exact these only by fanning all the passions of his soldiers and permitting them to satisfy them; he could only conquer the world by abandoning its constituent parts to his instruments as their booty. "From the moment that Napoleon grasped supreme power, the morals of the army degenerated rapidly; the union of hearts disappeared with poverty, and the liking for material well-being and for the comforts of life found its way into our camps . . . The Emperor considered it advantageous to his policy to favour this degeneration. He considered it useful for his purposes as conducive to the total dependence of the army on himself."[1] This was the opinion of an officer of his army at the time, an officer very partial to Napoleon.

Men were bound to become thereby more and more a matter of indifference to him, not only in the sense that the fate of the vanquished became of less and less importance for him, but also in the sense, that he looked upon his own army only as an instrument to the inner moral qualities of which he was altogether indifferent. As long as they peformed the required tasks of marching and fought bravely upon the battle-fields, the soldiers might plunder, and the leaders steal, for ought he cared. What did he care, even if the effective strength of his army diminished more quickly than would have been the case

[1] Berthezène, Souvenirs milit. I. 328.

with more severe discipline? This was very soon remedied by reinforcements, and by drawing more freely upon the rising generation. Thus he levied in the December of 1806 80,000 men who were not liable for military service until September, 1807. If he had had any intention of educating his army or his nation, he would have needed peace, but he desired war, and by war the dominion of the world.

Thus we must repeat that, judging from the standpoint of the aim he wished to reach, he acted logically and was right, for:

> " Every individual mind is right
> That is at one within itself; there is
> No fault, but inconsistency."

Indeed, every leader who purposes to do great things must possess this callousness as to his means, this firmness of mind, which looks with indifference upon the evils inseparable from extraordinary efforts. "No ridiculous leniency; we shall always have time enough to be generous."[1] "We wage war in all its severity,"[2] this was the Emperor's principle, and assuredly if only his final ends had been desirable for France, politically speaking, all those sacrifices which the callousness of his method of waging war exacted would have been worth making.

Thus the Emperor's army soon took to plundering the conquered country wholesale, and to considering the vanquished as having no rights worth mentioning. "The soldiers used to dine with their hosts, and it may be imagined what pretensions they put forward, if we consider the temperament of the French, their greed and voracity, which did not exclude daintiness, their liking for wine, and the contempt which they have always shown for foreigners;"[3] and here they were quartered in peace time on an allied country; in the enemy's country they

---

[1] C. N. To Lannes, Schönbrunn, 14th November, 1805.
[2] C. N. To Joseph, Osterode, 1st March, 1807.
[3] Fézensac, Souvenirs milit. 84, 110.

behaved with still less ceremony: "Nor was looting ever carried on to a greater extent than during these marches; the want of discipline fell little short of insubordination."[1] The officers could not put a stop to it, for they themselves generally set a bad example. "The officers, too far separated from the common soldiers, could not suppress their excesses; especially as most of them set an example of insolence and rapacity. If they wished to take a drive they demanded horses and a carriage without ever paying for them. They received visits, gave dinners to their friends, and all at the expense of the country."[2]

The Emperor himself encouraged the leaders in their want of consideration. He was pleased if their excesses put them constantly in the wrong with respect to himself, it increased his power over them, and thus he condoned things, for which even the most able leader in any other army would have been cashiered. As early as 1805 we read: "The conquered countries saw themselves exposed to the rapacity of the conqueror, and many Austrian magnates and princes paid with the complete plunder of their castles for the obligation, forced upon them, of entertaining a general for a single night, aye, even for a few hours. . . . They could not prevent this or that marshal taking what he liked with him at his departure from the castle. I heard, after the return from this campaign, the wife of Marshal ——— relate laughingly that her husband, knowing her taste for music, had sent her an enormous collection, which he had found at the castle of, I forget what German prince; and in the same ingenuous manner she related to us that he had forwarded to her such a number of boxes full of Viennese candelabra and glass ware, which he had laid violent hands on in all sorts of quarters, that she did not know what to do with them all."[3]

[1] Fézensac, Souvenirs milit. 84, 110.
[2] Ibid, 85.
[3] Mme. de Rémusat, Mém. II. 210.

Of Massena the Emperor said: "He is a good soldier, but entirely a slave to his love of money; this is the only motive of his actions, and this alone will make him move, even under my own eyes. At first it was small sums, now milliards would not content him."[1] When he had entrusted Marmont in 1806 with the administration of Dalmatia, he was compelled to write soon afterwards: "Tell Marmont in confidence that all accounts are examined here with the greatest severity, that any irregularity might ruin him, and his friends too, that he will have all he can wish for when the members of the Grand Army get their share, and that he has to keep up a reputation for honesty."[2] And even Berthezène, ever anxious to publish the glory of the French army, relates quite calmly of Bernadotte: "On this retreat he lost a baggage-waggon, which contained the booty from Lübeck and the fruits of his campaign. However disagreeable this occurrence was to him, yet he pretended that he only regretted it because it prevented him giving his men gratuities;"[3] and Berthezène had no other remark to offer upon this except: "This witticism excited much hilarity."

To this rapacity insolence towards the vanquished was soon added. "In Wolborsh, de Pradt met the secretary of the bishop, Canon von Kujawien, wearing the riband and cross of his chapter, who showed me his cheek, considerably injured by the violent blows which General Vandamme had dealt him the day before, on account of his refusal to supply Tokay wine, demanded in an insolent tone by the general, and which the canon only refused because, as he said, the King of Westphalia, who had spent the preceding day in the castle, had loaded his carts with all their store of that

---

[1] C. N. To Joseph, St Cloud, 3rd June, 1806.
[2] C. N. To Eugène, St. Cloud, 9th August.
[3] Souvenirs militaires, I. 120.

wine;"[1] of Vandamme he moreover related that "thousands of traits of violence and rapacity were related of Vandamme; his name is still execrated in Poland;" and of Davout, that he "had filled Poland with terror. I have heard some terrible stories told about him, which created much prejudice against the French."

Now we do not wish to deny that all this was a matter of indifference as to the personal capacity of each as a general, for Massena above all, who in this respect laid himself open to the severest reproaches, was undoubtedly the most capable of Napoleon's generals, and whenever there was any question of employing him the Emperor's opinion was: "Massena has great military gifts, before which we must bow down; we must forget his faults, for everyone has them."[2] Very often indeed rapacity and violence go hand in hand with enterprise and boldness; still, in the whole army this generally spreading eagerness to acquire soon changed into an eagerness to enjoy the things acquired, and this latter, at any rate, is ruinous to a general. "The truth of the matter was that, generally speaking, the higher officers were tired of it all. I had loaded them with too many dignities, too many honours, too much riches. They had drunk of the cup of enjoyment, and now all they demanded was rest; this they were ready to purchase at any price; at any price, do you hear, marshals of the empire? at any price whatever. The sacred fire was extinct."[3] In this respect we certainly cannot deny that the insatiable Napoleon, as compared with his over satiated companions in arms, was the more ideal soldier.

The Emperor had from Charlottenburg, and afterwards from Berlin, followed and directed with great attention the movements of his corps, to cut off Hohenlohe, Blücher, and Weimar. "If military events do no longer offer the

---

[1] Ambassade, etc. 73, 80, 142.
[2] C. N. To Eugène, Burghausen, 30th April, 1809.
[3] Gohier, Mém. II. 239.

interest of uncertainty in their development, they still offer the interest of combinations, marches and manœuvres,"[1] said he, contemplating the situation of affairs with the eye of a connoisseur. For the rest he occupied himself with putting administrative affairs in order, as far as he always did in conquered countries, in such a way, namely, that they might be suited for collecting the requisitions and war contributions he imposed. "It is my wish that Berlin should furnish me in abundance with all my army requires, and that nothing should be spared, so that my soldiers may enjoy abundance in every respect."[2]

In the meantime Ney continued his siege of Magdeburg, and on the 8th November this fortress also surrendered. Augereau and the Guards had remained in Berlin, Davout had been sent forward from there to Frankfort, where he arrived on the 31st October. On the following day Küstrin was surrendered to the division of Gudin, sent thither by Davout; thus one after another the fortresses fell, which, according to Willisen's expression, might have been the "breakwaters" of the invasion, and indeed without any defence or even the attempt at any. In the presence of the young and reckless French leaders, the old, weak and irresolute Prussian commandants showed themselves simply incapable of resistance; when the framework of the military system, which had alone lent them some sort of stability, had been once broken, they had no longer the strength to stand. The Emperor was more careful in dismissing his officers as soon as they became old; "the third battalions are full of officers, who have a right to be pensioned off, and who on account of physical incapacity can no longer serve; the body of officers must be rejuvenated."[3] And here we must note, that the

[1] Twentieth Bulletin, Charlottenburg, 27th October.
[2] C. N. To Daru, Berlin, 28th October.
[3] C. N. To Lacuée, Mayence, 29th September, 1806.

rapacious Massena and the uncouth Davout were far more attractive personalities to the soldier, than men like Kleist and Ingersleben.

Thus Prussia lay entirely prostrate at the victor's feet, and was obliged to accept any conditions which he was pleased to impose. For a moment it seemed as if some sort of agreement would be come to between Napoleon and Prussia, and Frederic William had already, on his side, signed the Emperor's hard conditions, when the latter, who in the meantime had received news of the fall of Prenzlau, Lübeck, Stettin and Küstrin, broke off all negotiations. He already looked beyond Prussia, saw the Russians approaching, and thus a vista of new successes opening, which must break even the last resistance in Europe.

And again we must say that, judged from the standpoint of a conquering general, he was right. It was better not to allow the Russians any time for further preparations, but to continue the war with his strong victorious army, which could now take the Oder as its base, by immediately following up the tremendous results just achieved, so that the opening of the new campaign would at the same time include the last realization of the advantages gained during the one just completed. A purely military situation is always spoilt by moderation ; a general may, if necessary, be commanded to stop in the midst of a successful career, but it is never advisable to do so. A statesman, indeed, might have based a permanent political system upon the victory of Jena, and would have commanded his general to stop. Bismarck, who signed peace at Nikolsburg and arrested the leaders of his victorious army at the gates of Vienna, would have concluded a lasting peace at Berlin, but the man, we are treating of, was only a general.

In the first place the Emperor had no certain news as (56) to how far the Russians had already advanced and in what strength. He therefore ordered Davout to march in the direction of Posen, in order to find out how matters really stood; he was however to avoid any serious engagement. Somewhat in his rear, to the left and the right of Davout, followed Augereau and the newly formed IX. corps of Bavarians and Württembergers, under Jerôme. Then news came that the Russians were, on the 9th October, still at Kamenez Podolsk, and on the 5th November the emperor calculated, that in this case, they could not reach Warsaw before the 20th November. He therefore sent orders to Davout to continue his march to Posen, and on the 7th the Emperor resolved to assemble his whole army near there, "for at that place I intend to fight a battle with the Russians, if they desire to advance."[1]

But on this same day definite reports came in, that the Russians, under Bennigsen, 56,000 men, forming four columns, were between Jurburg and Grodno, on the 23rd October, and that they would be able to cross the eastern frontier of Prussia, and reach Thorn with their first troops on the 7th or 8th, and with their last on the 18th or 20th November. In this case the Emperor did not wish to march beyond Posen, and was in hopes of being able to concentrate there Augereau, Lannes, Davout, Jerôme, the Guards and some cavalry before the 18th. "If, on the contrary, the Russians have delayed their movements, things would be different, and I should determine upon some other plan."[2]

On the 9th Davout had arrived in Posen, and as there was no sign of any Russian advance visible as yet, he received orders to continue his march immediately towards Warsaw, whilst Augereau was to march to Thorn, and Jerôme to Kalisch. Lannes had been ordered to move up to Thorn *viâ* Bromberg. The corps of the second line, Ney, Soult, Bernadotte and Murat, which were now likewise free to advance, approached Berlin, and were then to follow across the Oder. It is true, the fore-

[1] C. N. To Berthier, Berlin.
[2] C. N. To Davout, Berlin, 7th November, 3 p.m.

most corps had to spread out, since their principal aim was at this moment to gain information as to the enemy, and they could safely do so, for the enemy was still at a distance. Yet the thought of a possible junction at the right time never left the Emperor; it was too much the Alpha and Omega of his strategy. " In all this there is only one really important thing, and that is, that my three corps and my cavalry should be able to effect a junction in a short time, whenever the movements of the Russians render it necessary."[1] He now estimated his forces in the first line at 80,400 men, and placed them under the chief-command of Murat, who had personally hastened on in advance to Posen.

At 2 a.m. on the 25th November the Emperor also left Berlin, and arrived in Posen at 10 p.m. on the 27th. He found his corps in the following positions. The vanguard of Murat's cavalry met some hostile cavalry at Blonje on the 27th, and drove it back to Warsaw. Davout followed a day's march behind; Lannes was at Lowitsch, Augereau at Gostynin, the Guards and Ney were at Posen; Soult had advanced beyond Frankfort, Bernadotte was still near Berlin. Finally, Jerôme was at Kalisch, but now received orders to proceed into Silesia, in order to occupy the fortresses in this province, and thus still further to secure and extend the base of the Oder. In Mecklenburg and Hither-Pomerania Mortier was left behind. On the 28th Warsaw was evacuated by the Russians, who only retained the suburb Praga on the right bank of the Vistula. On the same day Murat entered the town with the cavalry, followed on the 30th by Davout.

The Russians now had two armies in the field, of (57a) which the first, 55,000 men under Bennigsen, had been posted near Pultusk since the middle of November, the second, 36,000 men under Buxhöwden, being still on the march and as yet far behind. At Thorn there stood a

[1] C. N. To Davout, Berlin, 13th November, 4 p.m.

Prussian corps of 15,000 men under Lestocq. But, in view of Napoleon's offensive and of his own relative weakness, Bennigsen had good reason to fear that the Emperor might turn his left wing and bring about a second Jena. He therefore evacuated Praga on the 1st December, and withdrew his whole army to the Narev. Lestocq was now put under his orders and retreated to Strasburg.

Napoleon wanted to go in immediate pursuit. "Should the enemy commit the stupid mistake of evacuating Praha, you must occupy that suburb. . . . I should be very pleased if you crossed the Vistula there. You will at once endeavour to cross the Bug as well."[1] Accordingly Murat and Davout crossed the Vistula during the early days of December, and advanced towards the lower Bug, whilst Lannes arrived in Warsaw and Ney occupied Thorn.

Still uncertain as to the actual position of the Russians, the Emperor, at Posen, kept urging Murat to throw bridges over the Bug and the Narev, and then to establish a strong *tête-de-pont* at the confluence of the Narev and the Vistula, at the spot where in our days the Russians have built Novogeorgievsk; after that he was to occupy positions at Pultusk with his cavalry and at Scherozk with Davout. But Bennigsen soon advanced again. He had in the first place fallen back upon Ostrolenka, but now, when Buxhöwden came up, he advanced again to Pultusk and despatched Lestocq to Thorn.

Meanwhile, the Emperor was still in doubt as to the enemy's intentions, whether he meant to avoid any serious attack or make a stand; on the 13th he resolved to bring matters to a head by sending his corps across the Vistula, thus compelling the enemy to declare his intentions. He formed a second corps from the cavalry-reserve under Bessières, which was to advance from Thorn to Rypin, and establish communication between Ney and

[1] C. N. To Murat, Posen, 1st December, 10 a.m.

Soult, and, moreover, reconnoitre the whole country to the north of the Vistula; Murat was to do the same on his side; the infantry corps were then to follow across the Vistula, Davout at Novy-Dwor, Augereau at Sakrotschin, Soult at Vlozlavk; Ney was to advance to Strasburg, Bernadotte and the Guards replacing him at Thorn.

Thus advancing, on a front of eighty miles, against the line of the Wkra, he thought he must gain certainty as to the enemy's plans; if the latter should remain stationary at Pultusk, he would turn [1] him with his advanced left wing, Ney, Soult and Bernadotte, and force him to the Austrian frontier, " but our greatest difficulty will be the question of supplies."[2] These words show how the circumstances on the Polish theatre of war, as contrasted with those of Italy and Germany, were already beginning to make themselves felt. In those countries the Emperor had never considered the commissariat his main difficulty; but they show also that the general recognized this difference and took it into consideration. " Circumstances have forced me to return to the system of depôts."[3] In the second half of the month of December, therefore, Ney proceeded to Strasburg, Bernadotte advanced to Thorn; Augereau prepared for crossing the Vistula at Sakrotschin, and Soult at Wyschogrod; Davout was to throw a bridge across the Narev at Okunin. In the evening of the 15th the Emperor left Posen and arrived in Warsaw at midnight of the 18th—19th December. Bennigsen was at Pultusk, with his troops forward as far as the Wkra; Buxhöwden had reached Ostrolenka; Lestocq had, as already mentioned,

---

[1] We must remember that at that time the Austrian frontier ran along the Piliza and then along the Vistula; about five miles above Warsaw it turned aside from this river and ran to the confluence of the Bug and Narev

[2] C. N. General directions for the campaign beyond the Vistula. Posen, 13th December.

[3] C. N. To Daru, Willenberg, 2nd February, 1807.

been despatched forward to Thorn, had met Ney there, and had fallen back upon Lautenburg.

This advance of the Russians upon Pultusk had not remained unnoticed by the Emperor, and he now ordered all his corps to march in that direction, so as to attack the enemy. On the 22nd Augereau advanced towards Plonsk, Soult crossed the Vistula at Dobrshykov; Bessières and Bernadotte were in the neighbourhood of Byeshun, Ney at Strasburg, Lannes in Warsaw; Davout was collecting his troops by the bridge which he had thrown over the Narev at Okunin, and crossed towards evening. Here the Emperor also arrived on the 23rd at 9 a.m. and reconnoitred in person the river Wkra. Behind the latter stood a division of the enemy in the line Tscharnovo-Pomyechovo, between the Narev and the Wkra.

(57b) The Emperor examined this position most carefully, he ascended by a ladder to the roof of a house on the little island at the confluence of the Wkra and the Narev, after which he dictated his orders for the attack. The bridges for the crossing were to be thrown across the entrance of the Wkra, from the little island; Morand was then to cross first and attack the enemy's left wing at Tscharnovo, one part of Gudin's division was to follow him and turn towards Pomyechowo, whilst the larger portion of this division would remain as a reserve at the *tête-de-pont* of the Narev. Towards evening the French began to cross the Wkra in the manner ordered, and during a night attack they forced the Russians from their position; the latter retreated to Nassielsk. Lannes had been moved up closer to the Narev bridge.

For the 24th the Emperor, having now the enemy before him, but not being able as yet to ascertain his strength, ordered Lannes to cross the Narev and the Guards to move up to the bridge from Warsaw. Augereau was to advance to Novemyesto, and Soult to follow him to Plonsk. Davout was to pursue the enemy towards Nassielsk.

The Russian armies were at this time, nominally at

least, under the chief command of Kamenski, an old man of seventy-six, mentally and physically weak. The latter ordered, upon the news of the French crossing the Wkra, a portion of the troops at Novemyesto to join the division at Nassielsk. When, on the 24th, about noon, Davout's vanguard arrived before this place, the Russians resisted until evening and then retreated towards Strshegozin. The Emperor established his headquarters in Nassielsk, and ordered Lannes, who had crossed the Wkra on this day, to join him as early as possible the next morning. During the engagement which ensued at Nassielsk, Kamenski had withdrawn the troops stationed along the river at Novemyesto and Koloshomb to Pultusk; but here Augereau encountered them and forced the passage of the stream.

On the 25th early Davout continued his march in pursuit of the Russians towards Strshegozin. The Emperor, who had gone to Schlostovo, in order to be equidistant from his two wings, Davout and Augereau, and to be able to hasten to whichever most needed him, now saw that he had broken the enemy's line on the Wkra, and that the latter had not concentrated his forces; but he was still ignorant of all details as to where the various hostile corps lay. In this situation he resolved not to allow Lannes, as he had at first ordered, to follow Davout by Nassielsk, but to send him to Pultusk, in order to bar the enemy's line of retreat at that important passage over the Narev.

When, a few days later, this phase of the campaign was finished, and the Russians had retreated, without, however, having suffered any actual defeat, or still less lost a great battle, we shall see how in Napoleon's letters and bulletins one sentence is continually recurring, namely that, had the days not been so short, and above all, had the roads not been so impassable, not a man of the Russian army would have escaped. This is as much as to confess that, after all, the general had not been successful in all he attempted

Y

and the world had expected. But we shall not be able to accept without hesitation the reasons he mentions; for, were not the days just as short, and the road just as impassable for the Russians, and did not the general know that he was manœuvring in the month of December and in Poland, and could he not have calculated and taken into consideration these circumstances as well as others? And such indeed was the case. These same impassable roads, which afterwards had to excuse the absence of success, had to serve in the beginning as a pretext to demand from his subordinate leader the infliction of double loss upon the enemy. " Since the roads are bad, their artillery and baggage ought to fall into your hands." [1]

I hold that the decisive moment, which was the reason why this campaign of Pultusk, in striking contrast with those of Aboukir, Ulm and Jena, ended without any great decisive blow, though such a blow was designed, was the despatch of Lannes to Pultusk. Here the Emperor forsook his great principle, which he elsewhere always followed. In the campaign of Jena also the Emperor did not know where he had to look for the enemy's main body; but he kept his columns close together and was, therefore, ready for any encounter, wherever it might take place. Here, however, he attempted to surround the enemy on all sides, even before he could be sure where the tactical issue would be decided. But for this purpose he had to separate his corps and could not therefore effect a junction as he usually did with the wings of his army, which were advancing on two separate lines of operation from Thorn and Warsaw, before the enemy was met with, that is, to the west of Wkra. But he separated them still more, after having crossed that river and come in touch with the enemy. For he sent, as we have seen, Lannes to Pultusk, and in addition, as we shall see presently, Soult through Zechanov to Makov.

[1] C. N. Berthier to Murat, Lopatschin, 26th December.

As happens so easily in such extensive concentric turning-movements, the enemy's main body is not found where it is expected. One corps meets no enemy at all, another does not arrive in time at the appointed spot, and a third sees itself suddenly opposed by superior forces. Thus it happened here, the enemy broke through the too widely-spread net at one point and, had the leader and armies been equally matched, the campaign might easily have been lost. In these operations to the north of the Vistula, we no longer recognize the general of 1796, of Ulm, and of Jena.

The Emperor felt convinced that the main mass of the Russians had retreated to Golymin; he therefore ordered, on the 25th, Davout to follow them on this road. The latter reached Strshegozin, and Murat Schlubova. Lannes advanced as far as Sbroschki, Augereau to Schonsk, and Soult as far as Schochotschin; Bessières and Bernadotte were still in the neighbourhood of Bieshun. Ney, who had continued pressing Lestocq back, reached Soldau and Mlava on this day, in close touch with his enemy. As to the Russians, Bennigsen's troops effected a junction with a portion of those of Buxhöwden at Pultusk on the 25th, whilst the remainder of Buxhöwden's divisions were at Makov and Golymin.

In the morning of the 26th Lannes started to continue his march to Pultusk. Arriving in front of this place about ten o'clock, he saw the enemy in position there and resolved to attack him. With heavy losses on both sides the fighting continued into the afternoon, when, about two o'clock, Gudin's division, which had been sent in the morning from Strshegozin to Pultusk, and now hastened up on hearing the sound of the guns, arrived at Moschin, and immediately came into action against the Russian right wing. Bennigsen withdrew the latter, it is true, at first, but his superiority in numbers had permitted him to keep on this very wing some untouched reserves, in spite of the fighting having lasted over four hours with great violence.

He threw these reserves against Gudin, penetrated between him and Lannes, and drove him, with heavy losses, by the evening, back to Moschin. In the meantime Lannes attempted a second attack towards evening, but was repulsed, after a short success, and retreated as night fell.

On the same day Davout advanced to Golymin. The Emperor had moved his headquarters on the preceding day to Lopatschin, and now sent Augereau also towards Golymin, for at this place he still expected to meet with the Russian main body. Murat was still to stand fast at Schlubova, but he soon received orders to support Davout's advance. Soult was to push forward to Zechanov, in order to gain from there the enemy's line of retreat towards Ostrolenka, and Bernadotte, going still further round, was to march to Koschevò on the Omulev. All this confirms the view, just expressed, as to the Emperor's plan of operations on this occasion.

At Golymin the Russians only kept up a rear-guard engagement against Murat, Davout and Augereau, whose troops arrived gradually; after which they retired, unpursued, to Makov. Soult reached Zechanov only with the greatest difficulty on this day. On the left wing Lestocq had fallen back before Ney as far as Neidenburg; Ney remained stationary during the 26th. The Emperor had gone to Paluki for the night; when he saw the Russians retreating, and received the news of Pultusk, he resolved to look upon the campaign as over, and indeed it would have been impossible, considering the condition of the roads, the lateness of the season and the exhausted state of the army, to undertake any effective pursuit of the enemy.

The study of the annals of war furnishes us with two reasons for the discontinuation of the pursuit. The first made itself felt more particularly in the days of Frederick, namely an insufficient recognition of the value and importance of effective pursuit, due to the impossibility, as it was considered at that time, of departing from the principle of having short lines of operations, so as not to move far from the base of supplies; even Frederick was unable to shake off this idea. The second reason is that the general himself succumbs to his own exhaustion and the effects of the over-fatigue of his troops. That the first reason had very little influence upon Napoleon, his whole mode of carrying on war has taught us; but may not the second for once have had some effect even upon his determined character?

It is true we must look with some suspicion upon the assertion, that his troops were really too exhausted to carry on the pursuit. It has been made again and again in the history of war, and yet we find again and again that where a man of extraordinary energy was in command it was still possible to accomplish the unexpected. " In the pursuit of a flying enemy, who every hour suffers loss in prisoners or stragglers, it is of no importance whatever to march in close brigades or even in close battalions and squadrons. What remains behind, remains behind and must follow later on; as soon as the battalions become weaker, one can dispense even with officers, and leave them behind for that purpose." [1]

But here there seems for once, and as an exception, to have been a case of impossibility. The tremendous exertions which he demanded in 1796, and after Ulm and Jena, from his soldiers, show too clearly that the Emperor's mind was inaccessible to all ideas of sparing them. But here he found such quagmires of roads, that he had not been able to bring his artillery into action even in the fight at Golymin. The days were short; the weather was extremely unfavourable, cold and wet. Moreover the country, drained as it was already by the Russians, offered scarcely anything in the way of supplies. Thus he was forced to confess, that even if it had still been possible to send troops in pursuit of the Russians,

[1] Blücher to York, Holstein, 31st August, 1813.

his army would thereby have been split up and fatally weakened, besides being compelled to advance further and further into Russia. On the other hand, the pursuit could not, and this was the most important point, in any way increase the sum total of his success. The mere fact of having to retreat was bound to entail great losses on the Russians, just because nature was so unpropitious. The kind of pursuit, which alone would have been possible in the morasses of Poland, could hardly add to these. The momentum of the blow dealt at Jena had here lost its effect, and his army was absolutely forced to collect new strength for new exertions. Besides, in the ranks of the French army, that grumbling which Cæsar's legions indulged in at the prospect of every fresh campaign, began to be audible. "You cannot be quite right in your head," they cried to the Emperor as he rode by, "to lead us about on such roads without any food."[1] But he felt what lay behind this half-playful criticism on the part of his men, and therefore he allowed them to go into winter quarters.

During the last few days of December he issued the preliminary orders, and followed them up from Warsaw, on the 7th January, by definite regulations as to the quarters.

(38a) Bernadotte was sent to the Drevenz to cover the Lower Vistula; he was to station himself at Osterode and extend his lines as far as the neighbourhood of Elbing, with his magazines at Marienwerder; Ney was to cover Thorn and the siege of Graudenz, and to take up his position at Soldau-Mlava-Chorshele, with his stores at Thorn. Soult was near Zechanov, Prassnych and Makov, depôt at Plock; behind him on the Vistula Augereau, in the neighbourhood of Novemyesto, depôt at Wyschogrod. Davout stood in the angle between the Bug and the Narev, extending in front as far as Ostrolenka, and on the left beyond the Narev as far as Pultusk and Golymin,

[1] Savary, Mém. III. 23.

with Pultusk as his depôt. Schyerozk and the ground between the Bug and the Vistula were assigned to Lannes, who occupied Praga also and had his depôt in Warsaw. At the latter town the Guards were stationed, and the Emperor himself returned there on the 1st January, 1807. Should the enemy resume the offensive the various corps were to concentrate at the following places: Bernadotte at Osterode, Ney at Mlava, Soult at Golymin, Augereau at Plonsk, Davout at Pultusk, and Lannes at Schyerozk.

In this extended formation, the army was thoroughly to enjoy the rest of which it stood in such need, so as to be all the sooner ready for operations when the cadres were completed as far as possible. The Emperor now devoted himself to the urgent business of regulating the supply of the army, calling up reinforcements, taking steps for the administration of Poland, and especially with organizing the auxiliaries put in the field by that country. At the moment of the resumption of operations we may calculate Bernadotte at 18,000, Ney at 16,000, Soult at 28,000, Augereau at 16,000, Davout at 20,000, Lannes at 18,000, the Guards at 15,000, and Murat at 14,000 men. The Emperor, anxious, in accordance with his usual custom, to receive news as soon as possible of the first movements of the enemy, ordered one of his higher staff officers, with two gallopers and two aides-de-camp, to remain permanently with the advanced cavalry, who were doing outpost duty. In addition to this, to ensure the concentration of his corps in time, he gave orders for the erection and fortifying of bridge-heads at the bridges at Schyerozk, Modlin, Pultusk and Praga. He also cautioned his corps expressly not to incite the enemy by any offensive movement to an attack, but only to observe them. For since the army was to rest, it was to do so thoroughly.

Bennigsen had in the first place retreated, after the battle of Pultusk, over the Narev in the direction of Bielostok, whilst Buxhöwden had fallen back on the north of the Narev towards Grodno. Afterwards, however, the two armies effected a junction in the neighbourhood of Schtschutschin, and Bennigsen was entrusted with the chief command. Lestocq had withdrawn to Angerburg.

This position of the Prussians, which left the direct road to Königsberg open, suggested to Ney the idea of attempting to surprise this town, and make for himself an opportunity of special distinction. He consequently started in the beginning of January from Neidenburg and advanced *viâ* Wartenberg, Gutstadt and Bartenstein, but here, on the Alle, Lestocq, who had just arrived, opposed him with 13,000 men. After some skirmishing between the 11th and the 16th, however, Ney became convinced that he would have to give the enterprise up, and, rightly apprehensive as to the Emperor's reception of his acting without orders, he sent an officer to him from Bartenstein on the 15th to explain matters.

In the meantime, however, Bennigsen had set his army, 63,000 men, in motion toward Prussia; his plan was to surprise Ney and annihilate him, and then to repulse Bernadotte also behind the Vistula; after which he would, based upon Danzig, pass the winter in East Prussia. On the 17th and 18th his army arrived in the neighbourhood of Rhein.

Meanwhile the Emperor had received information of Ney's advance, and was extremely angry at this departure from his instructions. "The Emperor, Marshal, has, in forming his plans, no need either of advice, or of any one acting on his own responsibility; no one knows his thoughts, it is our duty to obey."[1] In addition to a sharp letter, in which he ordered him to return to the quarters assigned to him, the Emperor sent Jomini to him, to convey his displeasure by word of mouth. Ney now retreated slowly in accordance with his orders, and arrived on the 23rd in the neighbourhood of Neidenburg.

(58b) On this day Bennigsen was at Bischofstein, Lestocq being again under his command; he then continued his

[1] C. N. Berthier to Ney, Warsaw, 8th January.

advance through Heilsberg, and on the 25th January his vanguard met the enemy at Mohrungen. This was Bernadotte, who, upon the news of Ney's retreat after the Russians' advance, had collected his forces on the sea line, Osterode, Prussisch-Holland, and who now repulsed the Russian vanguard at Mohrungen. During the next few days, however, Bernadotte, being well aware that he had superior numbers in front of him, fell back upon Löbau. Bennigsen did not go in pursuit, but allowed his army, around Mohrungen, to go into winter quarters cantoned over a line of some length.

The Emperor had in the first place, in connection with Ney's unauthorized movement, once more sharply enjoined his subordinate leaders to allow the troops a thorough rest, nor did he consider the movements, which were observed on the part of the enemy, to indicate any general offensive at present. "His Majesty believes the extraordinary position of the enemy to be due to the rash manœuvre made by Marshal Ney."[1] On the 23rd he issued orders for the formation of a Xth corps, 22,000 men, under Lefebvre, which was to besiege Danzig. But two days later he began to feel alarmed. "Various reports, Marshal, lead me to believe, that the different movements which the enemy is making, are preparatory to an advance."[2] The corps therefore received orders to prepare to march, and Lefebvre was ordered to leave Dantzig alone for the present and to cover Thorn.

The value which the Emperor henceforth attaches to Thorn is remarkable. We have already pointed out, after Jena, with what anxious care he looked after his communications. Now also he considered that he would be unable, during an advance into Eastern Prussia (which might possibly become necessary) to keep up his direct line of communication with Warsaw. For it was exposed to a flank attack from Russia; and the

[1] C. N. Berthier to Soult, Warsaw, 24th January.
[2] C. N. Berthier to Lefebvre, Warsaw.

further his line of operations extended, the more would this danger increase. The Emperor determined therefore, while there was yet time to choose the shorter and safer line to Thorn, and for this purpose he determined to hold this latter fortress at any cost. The positions of his lines of operation were here exactly the same as in 1805 before Vienna. At first the direct, natural line, Berlin-Warsaw, as in 1805 Augsburg-Vienna, so that his communications were directly in rear of the army and covered by it. Then while pursuing the enemy, the line turned at right angles to the north, and was dangerously exposed to the east of Warsaw-Bartenstein, as in 1805 that of Vienna-Brünn had been. Hence, in both cases, the determination to abandon this line in case of disaster and to adopt a new one, which was not exposed and led directly to the base.

On the 27th January the Emperor determined definitely to resume operations; he therefore ordered his army to take the field, and the corps to concentrate. "The enemy seems to intend to make a stand at Elbing, in order to defend his communications with Danzig. This being so, I shall leave my winter quarters and make a counter-march."[1] Murat and Soult were to assemble at Willenberg, Ney at Neidenburg, Augereau at Mlava, Davout at Pultusk, Lannes at Brok. The Emperor reckoned that this concentration would be completed within three or four days. Bernadotte was to fall back upon Thorn, if he could not hold Osterode, so as to cover the former place.

On the following day Davout and Augereau received instructions to concentrate further to the front; the former was to take post at Myschinez, the latter at Neidenburg, whilst Ney was to proceed to Gilgenburg. Murat was to advance a little, to Ortelsburg, so as to make room, but he was to be very careful "that no movement is observed. You must fly before the Cossacks, and avoid

[1] C. N. To Clarke, Warsaw, 27th January.

everything that might render the enemy suspicious."[1] The enemy was to be delayed another three days, and then "the Emperor will be on the 1st February before daybreak with his vanguard beyond Willenberg, and take the offensive against the enemy with all his forces. . . . It is the Emperor's intention to pierce the enemy's centre, and to drive back right and left all his forces which have not retreated in time."[2]

After having in addition during the 28th and 29th regulated the commissariat and settled a number of questions of administration, the Emperor left Warsaw on the 30th at 6 a.m. At Pultusk he met Marshal Lannes, who had fallen sick and was unable to continue in command of his corps; he gave orders for his removal to Warsaw, and then continued his drive to Prassnych, where he arrived during the night. Here he sent for Savary and entrusted him with the command of Lannes' corps, which was intended to secure at Brok the offensive operations of the army on the right flank against a hostile corps, 18,000 men, which lay at Briansk under General Essen. The Emperor impressed upon Savary that this was his only task, and that he was not to allow himself to be tempted to attack, in the hope of any tactical success, if he was not altogether sure of his position. His principal aim would be to cover the Narev line from Schyerozk as far as the Omulev.

If we examine the situation with which the Emperor was confronted at Prassnych, we shall again recognize and admire the great master in the art of moving and concentrating masses. On the fourth day after giving orders for the advance, he stood with 100,000 men assembled and ready for action on the line Myschinez-Willenberg-Gilgenburg-Mlava-Prassnych, whilst 18,000 men protected his right flank, and 40,000 on his left flank were in position, either to support his advance or, if necessary, to

[1] C. N. To Murat, Warsaw, 28th January.
[2] C. N. Berthier to Bernadotte, Warsaw, 28th January.

hold the line of the Vistula from Bromberg to Thorn, and in particular this latter important place. And what could Bennigsen do to resist the onslaught with superior numbers on his flank, or to protect his threatened line of operations? If he accepted battle and went to meet the Emperor with his own 76,000 men, which besides were not yet fully assembled, his defeat was as good as certain; and if he retreated in hot haste, he gave up the campaign just begun as lost. The Emperor might thus be said to be the undoubted victor from the very outset.

He had decided upon the 1st February as the day to begin the advance, and on the 31st January the final orders for it were issued from Willenberg. One of these orders, addressed to Bernadotte, and explaining in detail the whole situation of the army to that marshal, who was still in a manner separated from the rest, fell into the enemy's hands, and was handed to Bennigsen on the 1st February. Bernadotte thus failed to receive the orders, contained in this letter, to move up to Gilgenburg and to take part in the general advance. On the other hand, Bennigsen obtained information as to the danger threatening him, and immediately ordered the concentration of his army in the position of Jonkendorf.

(59a) On the same day, the 1st February, the Emperor began his advance. Murat and Soult drove some Russian outposts from Passenheim. Davout remained near Myschinez, Ney moved to Hohenstein, Augereau was at Neidenburg. The next day Murat and Soult reached Allenstein, the Russian vanguard falling back before them to Gettkendorf; Ney came up within half a day's march of Allenstein, Augereau to Demben Ofen, Davout to Ortelsburg. Bennigsen had assembled the main body of the Russian corps at Jonkendorf. On the second the Emperor had gone to Passenheim; he thought the enemy was on the retreat to Gutstadt. "It is easy to see that our manœuvre does not suit him, and he would like to prevent it, which leads me to think that he has come to a dead-lock. It is rumoured everywhere that he is retreating on all sides, so as to try and avoid the impending blow."[1] The Emperor considered that the enemy would run enormous risks if he stayed where he was; "it is impossible to assume he will allow his left flank to be turned;"[2] though of course "it is possible that the enemy will fight to-day with the 30,000 or 40,000 men he has, so as to gain time."[3]

On the morning of the 3rd he received from Murat, who, together with Soult, had advanced in that direction, a report of the enemy's massing at Jonkendorf. He immediately hurried thither, reconnoitred the position, and then issued his orders for the attack. Murat and Ney, of whom the latter had arrived in Allenstein, were to attack frontally; Soult received orders to capture the bridge over the Alle at Bergfried and to advance on the enemy's rear. Davout also was ordered to march for the same purpose to Spiegelberg. While waiting for Soult's turning movement, the Emperor contented himself with a cannonade in the front, but Soult did not succeed in occupying the point of crossing at Bergfried until nightfall. Augereau reached Allenstein on that day, and Davout lay to the south of Wartenberg. The Emperor, who had bivouacked at Gettkendorf, thought Bennigsen would accept battle the next day, and made every preparation for it.

But when he advanced the next morning, he soon became aware that Bennigsen had only left a rear-guard there, and had withdrawn during the night; he therefore immediately ordered a rapid pursuit in order to ascertain the direction of his retreat. Murat reached Deppen, Ney Schlitt, Soult Heiligenthal, Davout's advance-guard Rosengarten, and Augereau Pupkeim. The Emperor's headquarters were removed to Schlitt.

[1] C. N. To Talleyrand, Passenheim, 3rd February.
[2] C. N. To Murat, Passenheim, 3rd February, 6 a.m.
[3] C. N. To Davout, Passenheim, 3rd February, 6 a.m.

Bennigsen had retreated to Arensdorf, and had ordered Lestocq thither also. The latter had at the commencement of the Emperor's advance been at Freistadt, and arrived now, on the 4th February, at Mohrungen. Napoleon saw through these movements: "The Emperor is of opinion, Prince, that the enemy's aim is to reach Landsberg before us, it is therefore likely that he made his escape between Liebstadt and Gutstadt. . . . The Emperor hopes you will get news of the enemy near the village of Arensdorf, a large place situated at the intersection of the roads from Gutstadt to Landsberg. His Majesty would not be astonished if the enemy were to concentrate there to-day."[1]

On the 5th Lestocq, now aware of the threatening proximity of the enemy, withdrew, *via* Pfarrersfelden, in order to reach the crossing of the Passarge at Spanden. The Emperor sent in the first place Murat and Ney in pursuit of the enemy towards Arensdorf, whilst Soult and Davout threatened his left flank from the direction of Gutstadt; Augereau followed as a reserve towards Arensdorf. These movements had just begun when the Emperor received news of Lestocq's march towards the Passarge. He now ordered Ney, with whose corps he was then, to change his direction at once towards Liebstadt and to intercept this column. Should the latter, however, for greater safety have kept far to the west, he was not to follow him a long way, "because the Emperor wishes to have his whole army together to give battle to the Russians, in case he succeeds in outflanking them."[2]

Ney came across at Waltersdorf a detachment sent thither by Lestocq for the protection of his march, and drove it back completely upon Mohrungen; then he himself reached Liebstadt, whilst Lestocq, continuing his march behind the above mentioned detachment, succeeded in crossing the Passarge at Spanden and reaching Wusen.

[1] C. N. Berthier to Murat, Schlitt, 5th February.
[2] C. N. Berthier to Ney. In bivouac, 5th February.

Murat and Soult arrived at Freimarkt, as well as one of Davout's divisions (Friant's); the remainder of the latter's corps was around Gutstadt and Augereau at Lauterwalde. The Emperor established his headquarters in Arensdorf. As to Bernadotte, touch with him had been lost, as indeed this is usually the case in such movements; but the Emperor presumed he was somewhere near Osterode, and hoped he was also pushing forward to Liebstadt. Bennigsen had retreated to Drevenz on the road from Mehlsack to Heilsberg; but during the night he continued his march, and in the morning of the 6th was at Landsberg.

Napoleon was, with good reason, extremely satisfied with the situation. "Our affairs are going on splendidly. One corps of 20,000 men is cut off. The Russian army is flying without knowing whither, and in the greatest disorder."[1] This was not altogether the case, but such confidence is of advantage to a general. Indeed, generally speaking, we may remark that the Emperor at this time was taking good care of his full physical comforts. The sensual part of his nature, which the young general of 1796 suppressed, as he had to be carefully on his guard before his older subordinates, had in the meantime come more into evidence. Even in Egypt it was known that the young wife of Lieutenant Fourés was his mistress. Afterwards the First Consul put less and less restraint upon his passions, and at this time, since his arrival in Warsaw, the Emperor was in the enjoyment of the love of a noble Polish lady, who indeed kept up her connection with him later and visited him even at Elba.[2]

Josephine complained bitterly of these amours of her husband; she went so far as to accuse him of seducing his own sisters; "did he not indeed consider himself of such exalted position in the world, that he could satisfy all his whims?"[3] And it was to no purpose that Napoleon

[1] C. N. To Talleyrand, Arensdorf, 6th February.
[2] Mme. Walewska.—ED.
[3] Mme. de Rémusat, Mém. I. 204, 114.

answered angrily : " You must submit to all my whims, and look upon it as quite natural, that I should permit myself such amusements. I have a right to reply to all your complaints with an invariable ' Je le veux.' I am different from others and do not accept anyone's conditions."[1] The short letters which he wrote in great number to Josephine during this campaign, show how little she was able to suppress her complaints.

As all excitement of the senses is followed in the first place by an increase of physical and mental well-being, the Emperor felt indeed in excellent health during this campaign. " My health has never been better, so that I have become more gallant than I was formerly."[2] " In the midst of these great hardships every one has been more or less ill. As to myself, I never felt stronger, and I have become stouter."[3] Physical health is of the greatest importance to a general. For although the energy of a strong mind can often conquer physical suffering, yet one can never be sure that it may not occur just at the moment when the situation may demand from the general the endurance of great hardships. Charras points to the fact, that in the decisive days of 1815 the Emperor's illness greatly interfered with his work, and the latter himself, when speaking about Massena having lost his reputation in Portugal, added that this was to be ascribed to the state of his health, " which did not allow him to ride, or to look to things himself. A general who has to see things through other people's eyes, will never be in a condition to command an army in the way it ought to be commanded."[4] But more important still is the influence of the physical condition upon the mind. Bodily comfort will ever induce us to look at things in a more favourable light, whilst suffering will have

[1] Mme. de Rémusat, Mém. I 204, 114.
[2] C. N. To Joseph, Warsaw, 29th January.
[3] C. N. To Joseph, Osterode, 1st March.
[4] O'Méara, Nap. en exil, II. 377.

the opposite effect, and even though a strong spirit will overcome this, yet it will in the act of conquering lose a part of its energy. The Emperor possessed a healthy and strong constitution, and, with the exception of the above mentioned indulgences, he lived very frugally. Even a skin disease of an eruptive nature, which he had contracted at Toulon, and which returned from time to time, only seems to have served to provide some kind of outlet to the humours of his blood.

On the 6th February, at 2 a.m., orders were issued for the continuation of the pursuit; Murat and Soult were to advance by Freimarkt, Davout by Heilsberg, Augereau was to follow them, and Ney to push forward to Wormditt, in order to complete Lestocq's separation from the Russians. Bernadotte was also to assist in this, but did not reach Osterode till this date, having only on the 4th received news of the army. Bennigsen had, in the morning of the 6th, already taken the preparatory measures for the continuation of his retreat to Prussisch-Eylau, and placed a rear-guard beyond Hof to cover the same; Heilsberg also was still held. At both places, however, the Russians were compelled to fall back before the advancing French columns.

In the morning the Emperor had gone to Freimarkt, where he awaited Augereau's corps; he then advanced at the head of the latter; his centre encamped for the night in the neighbourhood of Hof; Davout was at Heilsberg, his vanguard near Schwelmen; Ney at Wormditt. Bennigsen continued his retreat, during the night, and reached Prussisch-Eylau in the morning of the 7th. Lestocq had arrived at Engelswalde on the 6th. The Emperor had at first expected Bennigsen would make a stand at Landsberg, but as soon as he became aware of his continued retreat, he ordered Ney to march in the direction of Kreuzburg, and Davout along the road from Bartenstein to Prussisch-Eylau.

Early on the 7th Murat encountered the Russian rear-guard, left behind at Landsberg, and compelled it to fall back though still fighting; about 2 p.m. Murat appeared before Prussisch-Eylau. The Russian rear-guard made a stand this side of the town, but was gradually forced into the town, and defended itself there obstinately. Soult, it is true, entered it, but was soon thrown out again by the reinforcements, which Bennigsen, who had placed his army in position in the line Serpallen-Schloditten, had sent up. But at 6.30 p.m. the Russians voluntarily evacuated it at Bennigsen's orders, and the French occupied the town. Thus the Emperor had, in and near this town, on the evening of the 7th, Murat, Soult, Augereau and the Guards; Ney stood at Orschen, Davout on the road from Bartenstein to Prussisch-Eylau, a little beyond the first named place. The Emperor himself was in bivouac behind Prussisch-Eylau, on the heights near the brickfields. Lestocq reached Rositten in the night, where he received orders from Bennigsen to move up the next day to Althof, in readiness for battle.

(60) With the early morning of the 8th February Bennigsen commenced the battle by a cannonade. The Emperor seeing him thus determined to fight, sent a messenger in haste to Ney to come up to Althof. He himself ascended the hill near the church at the south-east end of Eylau, and ordered, to begin with, numerous batteries to be placed in position, to reply to the enemy's artillery. In the meantime the Guards marched into line behind the hill, Augereau to the right of them, Soult to the left and in front beyond Eylau as far as the windmill, with the cavalry on the two wings. One of Soult's divisions, St. Hilaire's, was, however, on Augereau's right wing. This wing was to strike the decisive blow, according to the Emperor's intention, as soon as Davout's arrival should have threatened the enemy's line of retreat. Accordingly the French left wing, against which the Russians advanced about nine o'clock, was withdrawn to Eylau, without

having offered any serious resistance, but on the right wing St. Hilaire and Augereau received orders to attack the Russian left wing, taking Eylau as their pivot and wheeling to the left as they advanced.

In the midst of a violent snow-storm, however, the direction was lost, St. Hilaire and Augereau became more and more separated, and the former, marching in the direction of Serpallen, was attacked in his isolated position by some Russian cavalry and driven back. Augereau chanced upon the enemy's centre, was attacked by superior numbers, repulsed after a desperate resistance, and, half annihilated, pursued by the Russian cavalry straight to the point where the Emperor himself stood, causing great uneasiness to be felt in his vicinity. Berthier ordered the horses to be led up; Bessières, still more excited, brought up the Chasseurs of the Guard, exclaiming: "Save the Emperor!" But the latter remained quite unmoved, and rejected all these measures with some show of annoyance, for his practised eye had judged correctly that the enemy's cavalry would not have enough breath or cohesion left to charge up the Cemetery Hill, and he therefore calmly posted a battalion of his Guards in front of him, and said only several times, looking at the approaching Russians: "What boldness! What boldness!" And indeed the latter, tired out by the long pursuit, were startled by the appearance of the infantry of the Guards and fell back.

Thereupon, however, the Emperor ordered Murat to advance to the counter-attack with the collected cavalry of the right wing, to stop up the gap between St. Hilaire and Augereau, and to arrest the retrograde movement of the right wing. This end was in the main accomplished, the Russian and French cavalry forces being alternately successful. Exhaustion and most heavy losses, however, forced both sides to resume the artillery duel. But at this moment, about noon, Davout's corps put in an appearance on the battle-field, and advanced against (61)

Serpallen; the Russians evacuated this village and fell back upon Little Sausgarten. Now St. Hilaire also resumed his forward movement, inclining towards Davout on his right. These two forced the left wing of the Russian line further and further back. Kutschitten in its rear was occupied, and heavy fighting was in progress around the key of the position, the farm of Anklappen, when, about four o'clock, Lestocq appeared on the scene.

(62) The latter had started in the morning, in order to march to Althof as ordered. In this march, Ney, who was advancing in the same direction, met his vanguard at Wackern. But whilst this latter made front against Ney, Lestocq himself made a detour to the north *via* Graventin, and although forced to detach a few troops to protect his right flank against Ney's attack, he was on the whole successful in reaching Bennigsen's battle-field without being stopped. He moved on Kutschitten, drove the enemy from this village and forced him, in conjunction with the left wing, which again advanced back upon Little Sausgarten. Darkness now came on, however, and put an end to the combat here, when Ney, who had not received his orders to come up until 2 p.m., arrived at Schloditten. But Bennigsen sent late in the evening to dislodge him from that place, as he saw his communications with Königsberg endangered by Ney's stay there, and then began his retreat at midnight.

The Emperor had returned to his bivouac for the night, but his troops rested wherever the darkness found them. He was at first rather anxious about his position, his expressions immediately after the battle were much less confident than usual, and to his intimate companion Duroc he expressed himself thus: "Yesterday a very severe battle took place at Eylau. We remained masters of the battle-field, but although the losses on both sides were very heavy, yet my distance from my base renders mine more serious to me. . . . It is possible that I may return to the left bank of the Vistula, so as to go into quiet winter quarters, protected from these Cossacks and this swarm of light troops."[1] Accordingly, his next measures were extremely cautious ones, aiming at his own safety only. Lefebvre was ordered up to Osterode as a general reserve, and the line of communications of the army was shifted from Warsaw to Thorn, and thence along the left bank of the Vistula.

But when it was observed with the break of day that the Russians had withdrawn, and that only swarms of Cossacks were to be seen in front of the French line, the Emperor immediately determined to act as if he was the undoubted victor, although of course the tremendously thinned ranks of his completely exhausted troops rendered any energetic pursuit out of the question. He therefore remained stationary during the 9th, but his descriptions of the victory of Eylau in his various despatches on the evening of this day, already bore a very different colouring.

On the 10th Murat received orders to march along the road to Königsberg behind the enemy, whilst the corps around Eylau were ordered to separate somewhat more, so as to recuperate more at their ease; at the same time Ney was to push on along the Königsberg road behind Murat. On the 11th Murat advanced across the Frisching to Wittenberg, and continued during the next few days in touch with Bennigsen, who had now taken up a position in front of Königsberg. This induced the Emperor to send successively Davout, Ney, and Bernadotte, who had now also joined the army, towards the Frisching as supports the cavalry. Nevertheless it was not his intention to resume operations, but to allow some rest to his troops in quarters on the Passarge, and on the 16th February he issued orders for the beginning of the retrograde movement.

What is most remarkable in this campaign on the part of the Emperor, is the way in which he immediately reassumed the initiative, after Bennigsen had for a moment

[1] C. N. Eylau, 9th February.

deprived him of it by his advance. The advantage which the possession of the initiative gives a general in his movements is rightly considered very great; here we can note that it is only preserved by persistence in the execution of a resolve once taken, and we feel the truth of Napoleon's dictum: "In the beginning of a campaign one ought carefully to weigh, whether to advance or not, but once the offensive is assumed, it must be persisted in as long as possible."[1] Bennigsen's resolution, quite correct in itself, slackened at Mohrungen; he had conceived a great plan, a plan which in the hands of a Napoleon opposed to a Beaulieu would have had great results. But the Emperor opposed his own resolution to it, and never hesitated, but carried it through with increasing obstinacy; indeed, it may be said that Bennigsen fell back even more before the strength of Napoleon's intelligence than before his superiority in numbers. "The most important qualities for the leader of an army will ever be, great character or moral courage, which allows mighty resolves to be formed, and then coolness or physical courage, which triumphs over all dangers. Actual military science only comes in the third place, but it will be a very strong auxiliary; one must indeed be blind not to recognize this."[2]

[1] Précis des guerres de Fr. II. XXXII. 263.
[2] Jomini, Précis, etc., 69.

CHAPTER XIII.

FRIEDLAND.

AFTER having proceeded to carry out his resolution of (63a) retiring to the Passarge, the Emperor distributed his corps in the following manner: Bernadotte at Prussisch-Holland, his vanguard at Braunsberg, his transport at Saalfeld; Soult at Mohrungen, vanguard at Wormditt, transport at Liebemühl; Davout at Hohenstein, transport at Gilgenburg. In front of these corps, as a kind of outpost, stood Ney along the Alle on the line Gutstadt-Allenstein; the cavalry reserve was distributed along the whole line. "There will be no serious action undertaken, and the moment the enemy appears in mass, every marshal can by himself concentrate his corps upon his reserves, in order to be ready to march thence at the first warning to any chosen point."[1] The corps of Augereau, which had suffered most severely of all, and with the leader of which the Emperor was somewhat dissatisfied for having left the battle-field when wounded, was broken up on the 21st February and distributed among the other corps.

The Emperor went to Osterode on the 22nd, where he established his headquarters for a considerable period. He now gave orders that all the administrative branches of the Headquarter Staff were to be transferred from Warsaw to Thorn, and thus he abandoned Warsaw altogether as a base, and adopted the line through Thorn

[1] C. N. Orders, issued the 20th February, 1807, with respect to the position of the army.

to Posen, the most prudent course to pursue. His Guards likewise were encamped around Osterode, which place, should occasion arise, would be the general point of concentration of the army.

The Emperor's first thoughts after his retreat to the Passarge were of a defensive nature; should the enemy advance, he was "determined to make a stand on the plateau of Osterode, where I can concentrate in a day and a half more than 95,000 men."[1] It was, indeed, only a principle laid down by himself as essential, which he thus obeyed in concentrating to his rear. "The point of concentration of an army in case of a surprise must always be fixed in its rear, so that all the corps may be able to reach it before the enemy."[2] Still less enterprising was the state of mind of the men near him, indeed, they desired a retreat to the Vistula, and Berthier himself is said to have put before the Emperor proposals to that effect. Of course, Napoleon was obliged, for the sake of France and Europe, to avoid such a step, as long as there was any possibility of doing so. His first and most urgent care was again, as must always be the case in any defensive position occupied for any length of time, the commissariat. "Our position will be excellent here, as soon as our provisions are absolutely safe."[3] "My position would be excellent, if I only had provisions; the want of which renders it but moderately good."[4]

On the Narev the Vth corps was to continue safeguarding the Emperor's extreme right flank, which had already been, as we know, the task of this corps during the month of February under Savary. It is true, at that time General Essen, who lay facing it, had, in the middle of the month, endeavoured to threaten the Emperor's flank. This movement, however, had been observed by Savary; he went

[1] C. N. To Soult, Osterode, 26th February, 11.30 p.m.
[2] Précis des guerres du Maréchal de Turenne, XXXII. 149.
[3] C. N. To Soult, Osterode, 26th February, 5 p.m.
[4] C. N. To Talleyrand, Osterode, 27th February.

out to meet the Russians, and defeated them on the 16th February at Ostrolenka. But Savary, who was one of the Emperor's favourite mouthpieces, was now recalled to personal attendance, and the command of the Vth corps, which had been reinforced by a Bavarian division under Wrede, was handed over to Massena on the 24th February. It was to remain on the defensive as before.

The Emperor's chief concern was now the siege of Danzig; on the 17th Lefebvre received orders to proceed to the investment of this place. In this connection we can no longer avoid one question, the reply to which, of whatever nature it be, must in any case be of importance in estimating the qualities of a general, namely, what was this general's attitude with respect to the art of fortification, what did he expect from it, what use did he make of it? And the more the nature of Napoleon's method of waging war was offensive in principle, the more will what he thought of the value of fortifications, and what use he made of them, be of decisive weight, according to the axiom, just in itself, but easily misunderstood, that, "All fortification borrows its importance only from its close connection with strategical movements."[1]

Napoleon had a high opinion of the value of the art of fortification; he called it "a difficult science, in which the least mistakes may have a great influence upon the success of a campaign and the fate of a nation;"[2] he said: "There are some military men who ask, what is the use of fortresses, entrenched camps, and all the science of engineering? I, in my turn, should like to ask these men, how it is possible to manœuvre with inferior or equal forces without the assistance of positions, fortifications, and all such accessories of our art?"[3] One feature is more especially to be noted in his opinion on all questions

[1] Willisen, "Ueber grosse Landesvertheidigung," II. 343.
[2] C. N. To the Directory, Alexandria, 28th July, 1799.
[3] Précis des guerres du Maréchal de Turenne, XXXII. 155.

of fortification, and that is the one which constituted his great strength even in the field, namely, a uniformly correct appreciation of the true nature of things and a disregard for all minor considerations. He drew a sharp distinction between what the art of fortification could perform in each individual case and what it could not, and never expected from one of its branches, or from it as a whole, what it could not in fact perform.

As to the art of field-fortification, he himself wrote a treatise of some length,[1] in which he accurately determined its scope, distinguishing definitely between its various tasks. He refers to works which may be thrown up in five, fifteen, thirty minutes with the ordinary pioneer tools every soldier should carry with him, and which, generally speaking, are merely shelter-trenches; and he refers to works which may, it is true, afford some kind of resistance after an hour's labour, but which must be planned in such a manner, that the labour of twenty hours more, developing the original plan, may increase their strength to such an extent, that under their protection an effective resistance may be offered to an army twice as numerous as the defenders, and in this respect he adds his opinion that: "The natural positions, which one usually finds, cannot protect an army in face of a superior army, without the assistance of art."[2]

On the other hand, as a class altogether different from field-fortifications, he mentions temporary works, which are to be resorted to along the line of communications for the protection of important places. In this case a heavier form of fortifications is to be employed, and regular engineers, not the troops themselves, should throw them up. Their completion may occupy some days, and it is specially mentioned that wood and light masonry should be employed. The engineers are reproached with the fact that they use the latter too little,

---

[1] Essai sur la fortification de campagne, XXXI. 562.
[2] Précis des guerres du Maréchal de Turenne, XXXII. 155.

and are advised to become familiar with this idea. As to the employment of wood, we read: "Wooden-revetments were used with the best effect during the 1807 campaign in Poland, at Praga, and at Modlin, and during that of 1809 at Passau."[1] We have seen how during all his campaigns he immediately ordered the places which he chose for his depôts, to be put in a state of defence against a *coup-de-main;* how the important bridges over the rivers, which he took as his bases, were provided with strong bridge-heads, and how, for this very reason, he could lengthen out his lines of operations with impunity. The opinion is still too much in vogue, though often vaguely expressed, that the employment of fortification is necessarily incompatible with the offensive.

The Emperor had a great idea that much could be effected by improvised works: "With wood, tools, and arms, a fortress can be created where there was not one before."[2] But in spite of this favourable opinion of the capability for defence of temporary fortifications, he yet never forgot that they require defenders far more numerous and reliable than are needed for permanent ones. "It is my opinion, that an earthwork occasionally has some advantages over a work in masonry, because cannon balls occasionally bury themselves in it; but masonry has the advantage of allowing of economy with respect to the garrison required."[3] "Magdeburg," he said in 1813, "is a large, beautiful and strongly fortified place, which can be left to itself, as often and as long as may be necessary, without any fear that it will be captured by a sudden attack, however vigorous, as might have happened to Dresden during the three days that the allies remained before it, if they had been commanded by a man of any ability."[4]

[1] Essai sur la fortification de campagne, XXXI. 562.
[2] C. N. To Berthier, St. Cloud, 19th September, 1806. Note on the defence of the Inn and the occupation of Brandau.
[3] C. N. Notes on the defence of Italy, Valladolid, 14th January, 1808.
[4] Gouvion, St. Cyr, Mém.

Now in what light did Napoleon view permanent fortifications, what part did fortresses play in his opinion? In a most valuable letter to Dejean,[1] which in itself is a complete treatise on the theory of fortresses, he explains his views on this point: "We must here," he said, "set down clearly our thoughts as to the use of fortified places," and he then laid down three distinct instances: (i.) a fort blocking a mountain pass, (ii.) a fortress, and (iii.) a complete system of frontier defence. These remarks were occasioned by the question of the fortification of Peschiera, and he examines under which of those three heads this place would come. It is not a fort blocking a pass, nor is it a bridge-head, for the Mincio is not sufficiently important for this; as a fortress it was inferior to Mantua, and one such was sufficient for every frontier; finally, it could not be looked upon as a link in the system of frontier defence, for no system existed apart from the fortresses of Mantua and Peschiera, and so the enemy would simply avoid these places, or mask them.

Consequently he asks the questions, "Is then this place Peschiera of no use? Must we therefore have no Peschiera?"[2] And, with his inborn appreciation of facts as they are, he replies at once: "If it were possible to move Peschiera to S. Giorgio, or to any other point commanded by Mantua, that is, if a place of the value of Peschiera could be found in any other position, so that its communication with Mantua could not be cut, I should not hesitate a moment. But Peschiera stands where it stands."[3] Thus he emphasizes the fact, that the importance of possessing a place may in itself be of sufficient weight to compel the establishment of a fortress there, even if it could affect the campaign in no other way than by keeping out the enemy.

Moreover, in another document, when Osoppo was in

[1] C. N. St. Cloud, 27th June, 1806.   [2] Ibid.   [3] Ibid.

question,[1] he laid down two conditions as indispensable in a fortress, first that it should be capable of defence by a minimum of men, and secondly that a whole division should be able to find shelter in it; but he denies any real connection between fortresses and field armies. "Therefore I do not desire an entrenched camp, because, even if we assume that it could fulfil the second condition, it would not fulfil the first."[2] Indeed it was part of his experience as a general, that it must be one of the necessary qualifications of permanent fortresses that they should lend themselves to a defence by few or inferior troops. Even as a young officer he had said: "Only old troops are able to face successfully the chances of a siege;"[3] and at the end of his career the experienced general knew that it was the essential task of fortresses to set armies free for the decisive campaign, and not swallow them up as garrisons, and he said: "The garrisons of fortresses must be recruited from the population, and not from the armies in the field. This is the duty of the Local Militia regiments, and the most honourable privilege of the National Guard."[4]

Thus, generally speaking, he expected nothing from his fortresses, beyond securing certain important towns for him; he looked for no effective assistance from them, nor for any immediate support of the field army in the latter's task, i.e. the gaining victories. When for example, in 1807, the question of a retreat to Thorn had to be included in the Emperor's considerations, he continued to advise Lefebvre and Bernadotte, the two corps within reach of that place, that they were only to cover Thorn, and not to seek or find any protection or reinforcement there. And yet "fortified places are as useful in defensive as in offensive warfare. Doubtlessly they cannot by themselves take the place of an army, but they are the

[1] C. N. To Eugene, Warsaw, 19th January, 1807.
[2] Ibid. [3] Souper de Beaucaire.
[4] Dixhuit, notes sur l'art de la guerre, etc., xxxi. 499.

only possible means of stopping a victorious enemy, to disturb, weaken and harass him;"[1] and he declares the real part a fortress should play is: "to allow a small body of men, protected by its fortifications, to defend themselves; to stop the enemy and preserve the magazines in their charge against the attacks of considerably superior numbers."[2]

But though the Emperor considered the defence of a town as the first and most important task of a fortress, he did not fail to recognize also, that, as a matter of fact, the influence of a fortress may extend beyond the range of the guns on its walls. This influence he describes when treating of the system of frontier fortification, i.e. national defence on a large scale. As an example, in dealing with the effectiveness of the line of the Rhine, he supposes that a Prussian army desires to make its way to Brussels, in order to effect a junction there with an English army. The first obstacle would in this case be the line of fortresses Wesel, Venloo, Maestricht and Stevensworth. "If on the other hand," he continues, "this army crossed the Rhine at Cologne, in order to be less within the reach of Wesel, it would have to invest Jülich;" he therefore ascribes to Wesel a certain sphere of influence, to use the modern technical term. This is still further confirmed by his continuing thus: "An enemy crossing the Rhine at Coblenz, would in the first place approach the sphere of Mainz, would meet with obstacles in all the narrow Moselle valleys; he could not penetrate to Jülich without passing Bonn, because there is no other road, and he would therefore again come within the reach of the 'system' of which we have already spoken (namely Wesel)." Thus he considered himself safe along the whole extent of the Rhine by the "systems" of Mainz and of Wesel and the territory they command. On the other hand he rejects the idea of a complete frontier blockade, such

[1] Dixhuit, notes, etc., xxxi. 499.
[2] Précis des guerres de Fréd. II. xxxii. 265.

as modern French engineering has established on the Eastern Frontier. "It is no use trying to seal hermetically a territory like that of France."

But indeed the condition of the fortification of France itself up to the year 1870 was not altogether in consonance with the principles which the Emperor held. Thus he emphasized the fact, that, considering the great number of French fortresses, France ought to employ her money only in bringing the most important ones up to the standard of modern requirements and leave the others alone. "Here the principle must be laid down, that every fortress is valuable. I should like to have one at Orleans as the central point, which would contain all the depôts of France. But it is not a question of writing romances, and what we have to consider is this: the Government has only 1,200,000 or 1,500,000 francs to spend on keeping up its fortresses; is it better to use this money to keep up carefully the fortresses of the first line, or to distribute it over a number of places, leaving the frontier in a bad condition?"[1] And how little did the condition of Strasburg in the August of 1870 correspond to Napoleon's principle, that "the defence of a fortress is not complete unless all military buildings are bomb-proof. . . . At the moment of investment it is too late to erect bomb-proofs."[2] "You know my views as to buildings and barracks that are not bomb-proof; they are always a pretext for the surrender of a place."[3]

It is true, the system of detached forts round a fortress of the first rank was not yet fully developed in Napoleon's time, yet he frequently wrote in terms which point to his approval of it, and speaks of the advantages it offers. Thus he said in a "Note on the defence of Corfu,"[4] if one had a fortified camp near the fortress, it might happen

[1] C. N. To Clarke, Paris, 13th February, 1810.
[2] C. N. Orders with respect to the fortresses of Italy, Compiègne, 19th April, 1810.
[3] C. N. To Clarke, Trianon, 7th August, 1810.
[4] C. N. St. Cloud, 21st June, 1810.

that 5000 or 6000 Frenchmen would beat the enemy and compel them as the result of that victory to embark again, but if one were shut up in a fortress, one could no longer take the offensive, and there would be no possibility of further success. He therefore advised that five or six earthworks should be constructed, and "care should be taken that the sides exposed to the enemy's attack should have a *siege profile*," that is, should be *secure against assault;* "the *tracing* should be so arranged that the works flank each other mutually." He was further of opinion that this would compel the enemy to open trenches against one or two of those earthworks, but then the garrison would proceed to construct counter-approaches and establish batteries in these, which "will prevent the besieged from being reduced to a passive part. Thus a commander and good officers could bring to bear all the resources of war. In a siege so conducted, the time necessary for mastering such works cannot be accurately calculated." If any great naval arsenal is in question, containing numerous and irreplaceable war material, he added as a reason for the construction of detached works: "To keep the bombardment at a distance by means of these works;"[1] and also he said with respect to their defence: "If, as soon as the enemy is discovered opening trenches against a fort, counter-approaches are begun from the two nearest forts, the resistance will become much enhanced, and the time during which the first fort would be able to resist will be indefinitely prolonged." But the question of the fortification of any great naval base had for him another side also. On the 27th July, 1810, he dictated in a meeting of the administrative council of the navy, a note[2] in which he demonstrated that a mere bombardment would not be sufficient for the enemy's purposes; it must rather be their intention to actually enter the area of the fortress, in order to thoroughly destroy its war materials, its basins, etc.; in

---

[1] C. N. Note on Cherbourg, Rambouillet, 8th July, 1810.
[2] C. N. St. Cloud.

this case only, they could inflict a really great loss, and, therefore, he concluded, that the place must be not only surrounded by outlying forts, but must also be provided with a closed enceinte. For the rest, he was convinced that land artillery is much superior to sea artillery: "at sea the artillery is of but little account, on land its superiority is immense; the difference is in the proportion of one to seven; i.e. ten mortars on land are as effective as seventy at sea." [1]

Bennigsen had set out on the 20th February and had followed the retreating French corps, and when these took up their positions, he posted himself in front of them in the neighbourhood of Prussisch Eylau, the outposts on both sides being in close contact. But Bennigsen was of opinion that the Emperor would fall back behind the Vistula, he would then immediately follow, whilst Lestocq, at present near Heilsberg, was to march towards Elbing. This view remained no secret to the Emperor. "There is no doubt but that the enemy wish us to retire behind the Vistula, but it is also probable that they do not wish as yet to run the risk of a battle." [2] Consequently Lestocq advanced by Wormditt and occupied Braunsberg on the 24th, which place the French evacuated. On the 26th, however, Bernadotte ordered, at the Emperor's command, this place to be taken again, and the Prussians were driven back behind the Passarge. Thus secure on his left wing, the Emperor now turned his attention to his right.

Here he saw the enemy very active owing to Bennigsen's recent arrival, but still remained convinced that no general advance was intended. "I am of opinion that the enemy is not ready, and that he is playing the fool." [3] Should he, however, seriously advance towards Mohrungen *via* Gutstadt, the Emperor intended to fall

[1] C. N. To Clarke, 21st October, 1809.
[2] C. N. Berthier to Ney, Osterode, 26th February.
[3] C. N. To Soult, Osterode, 27th February, 4.30 p.m.

upon his right flank, through Mehlsack. In the meantime, however, he enjoined Ney to hold Gutstadt, and thus to cover the Passarge line, or, if he had evacuated that place, to reoccupy it. Ney had in fact evacuated Gutstadt during the night of the 26th-27th February, in view of the threatening approach of Bennigsen, and had retreated to Allenstein. Accordingly the Emperor, determining to recover his outpost-line on the Alle in order to cover the right flank of the line of the Passarge, sent orders to Ney to recapture Gutstadt. But as there was a possibility of strong resistance, the following corps were placed so as to afford support, if needed: Bernadotte at Spanden, Soult at Liebstadt, Davout at Mohrungen.

This forward movement was moreover to serve the purpose of "capturing the enemy's cannon, frightening them, routing their infantry, and giving them a hint not to bring their artillery so close again, but to content themselves with observing us with their cavalry,"[1] or, as the Emperor very appositely expressed it in one sentence: "This enterprise may be considered in the same light as a sortie from a fortress;"[2] this moreover confirms the fact that he looked upon the position he held as a mere defensive one.

Ney therefore occupied Gutstadt on the 3rd March without any particular difficulty, and then the corps went back into their former positions. Now began that period of defence for the protection of the siege of Danzig, about which the Emperor said at St. Helena, "Nothing was more correctly planned . . . than the defensive position on the Passarge in 1807, to cover the siege of Danzig."[3]

This period, during which, it is true, a few movements and occasional concentrations, but no real change in the positions, took place, is best characterized by the Emperor's own words: "We have here a few marches and counter-

[1] C. N. Orders and movements for the 2nd and 3rd, Osterode, 1st March, 10 p.m.   [2] Ibid.
[3] Dixhuit, notes, etc., xxxi. 430.

marches, a little artillery-firing, but nothing of importance. I have given orders to drive the enemy from Gutstadt. As their outposts had taken up their position on the Passarge, I had them swept away to a distance of ten hours' march."[1] Still he thought, if only his commissariat were safer and the weather more favourable, he would be able to take the offensive, beat the enemy in detail and reach Königsberg, for "the enemy have committed many blunders."[2]

As it was, however, he was determined to keep on the defensive, though not quite passively. "A river or any line can only be defended by occupying some offensive points, for if one has done nothing but defend oneself, one has run risks without having gained any results whatever; but if one can combine with the defence a few offensive movements, the enemy will have run greater risks than the corps attacked."[3] Therefore he gave urgent orders for bridge-heads to be constructed along the Passarge, so that he might be in a position to push forward whenever and wherever the necessity should arise. This opinion of the Emperor as to the defence of a river remained unchanged; in 1808 he said: "No river, though it be as wide as the Vistula, or as rapid as the Danube near its mouth, is any obstacle, provided one has free access to the opposite bank and is always ready to resume the offensive;"[4] and even in 1813 he expresses himself in exactly the same manner as regards the Elbe: "No river has ever yet been looked upon as an obstacle which could stop an advance more than a few days, and its passage can only be defended by placing troops in large numbers in bridge-heads on the opposite bank, ready to assume the offensive as soon as the enemy begins crossing.

"Nothing is more dangerous than to try to defend a river seriously by occupying the near bank in force, for as soon

[1] C. N. To Talleyrand, Osterode, 6th March.
[2] C. N. To Bernadotte, Osterode, 6th March, midnight.
[3] Ibid.
[4] C. N. Note on the Spanish affairs, St. Cloud, 30th August.

as the enemy has forced a passage by a surprise—and he always does force it—he finds the army in a very much extended defensive position, and can prevent it concentrating."[1] If one be determined, as the Emperor resolved to do behind the Passarge, to limit oneself altogether to the defensive, "there is no other means than to place one's troops in such positions that one can concentrate them in mass and fall upon the enemy before he can complete his passage."[2] This concentration in mass had, in this instance, as we know already, been planned at Osterode, in case Bennigsen should resume the offensive with his whole army. Against any partial offensive, however, an active defence by forward movements from the têtes-de-pont was to suffice.

But the manner in which the engineer here protected his immediate base and possible line of defence, the Vistula, by bridge-heads, did not meet with the Emperor's approval. For these, being constructed too close to the river, did not seem to him to offer the necessary space for affording shelter to the troops during the protracted operation of crossing the river in case of a forced retreat. At St. Helena he said on this subject: "They (the engineers) ought to leave room between the works and the river, so that an army without having to enter them, a movement which might endanger its safety, can form into line and assemble between the works and the bridge. . . . The bridge-heads which the engineers constructed in front of Marienwerder were quite close to the Vistula, and would have been of but little use to the army if it had been forced to cross that river in its retreat."[3]

The Emperor's untiring activity soon succeeded in regulating the difficult questions of commissariat and putting the army in a secure position. The reinforcements also and the transport of the wounded to the rear were

---

[1] C. N. To Eugene, Trianon, 15th March.
[2] Ibid.
[3] Précis des guerres du Maréchal de Turenne.

seen to very carefully, and the Emperor again ordered a levy of 80,000 fresh recruits, who, by law, were not liable until 1808. His activity indeed was extraordinary during these weeks, he dictated as many as twenty letters in one day. On the 1st April he moved his headquarters to the castle of Finkenstein, " a very handsome chateau in the style of that of Bessières, where I have many open fireplaces, which is very pleasant for me, for, as I often get up in the night, I like to see a fire." The Guards also were moved to the neighbourhood of Finkenstein.

The only military action of any importance during this period was the siege of Danzig, which was prosecuted most vigorously This town had been invested since the 12th March, and only after its surrender were the operations in the field to be resumed. " I am waiting until the season is more favourable, until Danzig is taken and until all my provisional regiments have come up, in order to deal a knock-down blow." To secure his communications with the besieging corps, the Emperor also ordered bridges to be thrown across at Marienwerder and Marienburg, and bridge-heads to be constructed there.

Then he turned his attention to his extreme right wing, where Massena lay, and sent him instructions as to the manner in which he might best place his corps in position. This corps, he said, had three purposes to serve: first, to cover Warsaw; secondly, to form the right wing of the army; and thirdly, to assume an offensive attitude, in order to occupy the enemy. Now, which would be the best position to answer all three purposes? The enemy might advance against Warsaw either along the Bug or along the Narev. Accordingly Massena's best position for the first purpose would be at Schyerozk, for the higher up the Narev his position was the less he could cover Warsaw. The second purpose, on the other hand, would

[1] C. N. To Kellerman, Elbing. 8th May

demand a position on the Omulev, near Willenberg and near Ostrolenka, whilst the third would be best answered by a position at Ostrolenka. For this latter would either invite the enemy in this direction, in which case its natural strength would become a great factor, or from it an attack could be made upon the flank and rear of the enemy, should he advance along the Bug. Therefore Massena was advised to place one division in a fortified camp at Ostrolenka and the other at Willenberg.

In the meantime the siege of Danzig had been energetically prosecuted, though the Emperor saw himself compelled to spur on Lefebvre's energy by frequent and resolute exhortations. For this Marshal exhibited too much care and caution, and listened to every suggestion. The Emperor admonished him repeatedly to adhere to the plan once adopted, and advised him "to get rid of all these little critics by kicking them out."[1] At last on the 26th May this bravely defended place had to be surrendered. With this event the main condition was fulfilled, which the Emperor had fixed for leaving the defensive, and he settled upon the 10th June for the resumption of operations; but Bennigsen once more anticipated him.

(63b) The situation of the two armies was at this time as follows. In consequence of the orders of the 5th May, the French corps had left their cantonments and gone into huts; Bernadotte, with 27,000 men, lay on the Lower Passarge; Soult, with 31,000 men, around Liebstadt on the Middle Passarge; Davout, with 29,000 men, on the upper course of this little river. Ney, with 17,000 men, was still in his advanced position near Gutstadt on the Alle; the Guards, as already mentioned, 8000 strong, lay at Finkenstein; Murat's cavalry, 21,000 men, were divided up. Finally, on the right flank, stood Massena, with 26,000 men, on the Omulev and the Narev; the latter had, however, not fully carried out

[1] C. N. Finkenstein, 18th May, 11 a.m.

Napoleon's instructions, and was, therefore, neither in possession of Ostrolenka, nor in command of the Narev. In addition, there had been formed, on the 5th May, a reserve corps, 15,000 men, under Lannes, consisting of the divisions of Oudinot and Verdier, which now stood at Marienburg, and lastly Mortier, with 14,000 men, had been moved up to Danzig. The Xth Corps, Lefebvre's, however, which had besieged Danzig, was broken up and partly employed as a garrison of this place, and partly incorporated in the other corps. Finally, in the rear of the army, there was a corps of observation, newly formed on the 29th April, 32,000 men, under Brune, for the protection of the North Sea coast and the North German lowlands. Facing them stood Bennigsen at Heilsberg and Bartenstein with 74,000 men, Lestocq with 18,000 men at Heiligenbeil in front of the Lower Passarge, and Tolstoi with 15,000 men, at Ostrolenka and on the Narev.

In the execution of his offensive plan Bennigsen intended thus to march forward against Ney, on the 5th June, in five columns, attacking him on every side, whilst 10,000 men were to take up a position at Elditten so as to occupy Soult, and Lestocq was to hold Bernadotte. Accordingly Ney saw himself on the 5th from 6 a.m., continually forced back upon Gutstadt by increasing forces of the enemy, and reported this attack immediately to the Emperor. The latter was loth, it is true, to believe as yet in a general offensive movement on the part of the enemy, still he informed the other marshals of the news, as soon as it reached him, at 2 p.m., and ordered Murat to assemble his cavalry divisions, namely, Lasalle and Latour-Maubourg at Elbing, Espagne at Marienburg, Nansouty at Christburg, St. Sulpice at Bischofswerder, Grouchy at Strasburg, and Milhaud at Soldau.

Meanwhile Ney had assembled his corps at Gutstadt, and had, in view of the superior forces threatening him, begun his retreat to Ankendorf. Soult also had been attacked by the column sent against him, and Bernadotte by Lestocq. They had, however, held the bridges over the Passarge at Lomitten and Spanden. Further reports from Ney had, meanwhile, convinced the Emperor that the Russians were really in earnest with their offensive, and he therefore gave Lannes orders to start on the 6th as early as possible and to march to Christburg; Mortier, who had reached Dirschau, was to follow close upon his heels. At the same time the Emperor sent an aide-de-camp to Deppen, who was personally to examine the situation of affairs on this portion of the field of operations.

During the night the report of Ney's retreat came in, and in the morning of the 6th the Emperor sent to Ney to make a stand at Ankendorf, if possible; if not, he was to fall back towards the South of the Narien Lake. Soult he ordered to Mohrungen, and Bernadotte to Prussisch-Holland. The latter marshal, who had been wounded on the 5th, was on the 6th replaced in his command by Victor. Davout was to move up to the Passarge towards Alt-Ramten, and the cavalry divisions of Grouchy and Milhaud to Osterode; finally, the Guards were set in motion towards Saalfeld. As usual, the Emperor wished, if the enemy continued his offensive, to concentrate his army before beginning operations. He thus drew back his more advanced corps and advanced those in the rear, all in the general direction of Saalfeld; here was to be the central point of concentration of the army, and to this place he also betook himself. In this way he had, it is true, set the concentration of all his forces going by noon on the 6th June, but how and in what direction he would advance with them, he left for the present to depend on the further reports which would come in about the enemy, until the moment when he himself would be ready to move. He calculated that the whole of the 7th June would pass before this would be the case.

Ney continued his retreat on the 6th, before Bennigsen, who was still advancing, and crossed the Passarge unmolested at Deppen, taking up a position there. No further attacks had been made upon the other marshals. Thus the Emperor, on his arrival in Saalfeld, about 10 o'clock in the evening, found himself still in possession of the Passarge, while Bennigsen's offensive seemed to him to have come to a stop. He credited the latter for the moment with the project of turning the French right wing *viâ* Allenstein, thereby cutting the French off from their base on the Vistula at Thorn. The Emperor, however, laid stress upon the fact that this was a mistake, and that his base was the Lower Vistula, and that he had adopted the line of communication Marienwerder-Marienburg-Danzig; consequently his plan was still to use Davout, who was to move up as quickly as possible to Osterode, as a pivot, and thus to force the enemy away from Königsberg, turning his right wing. Therefore the Emperor had in the evening of the 6th June: Victor at Spanden, Braunsberg remaining in the occupation of the division of Dupont; Soult at Liebstadt; Ney at Deppen, Davout at Allenstein; Lannes and Mortier in the neighbourhood of Christburg; the cavalry concentrated on the different points mentioned. In front of him stood Bennigsen at Heiligenthal with his outposts on the Passarge; Lestocq at Mehlsack and Heiligenbeil, with his outposts likewise forward as far as the Passarge. (64a)

On the 7th this situation underwent a change. Bennigsen became convinced that his purpose of attacking one of the enemy's corps in an isolated position had failed, and that he now stood with inferior numbers before the Emperor's army, which would soon be fully assembled; he therefore resolved to fall back into a favourable defensive position, and to begin with, he retreated in the evening of that day to Queetz. The Emperor on his side, however, recognized that the enemy's offensive had come to an end against the bridge-heads on the Passarge, and he resolved in his turn to take the offensive as soon as he had all his corps at hand. The 7th was, therefore, utilized, to order Lannes and Mortier up to Mohrungen, at which place and at Deppen Murat's divisions were also concentrated, whilst Soult and Victor were at the same time instructed to advance across the Passarge, in order to find out the enemy's intentions. " I am still trying to guess what the enemy really intends to do; the whole affair looks to me very much like an ill-considered stroke. I am this day assembling my infantry and cavalry reserves near Mohrungen and shall try to discover the enemy, so as to force him to a pitched battle and make an end of it all."[1] He himself went towards evening to join Ney, and established his headquarters at Alt-Reichau.

Early on the 8th Soult advanced *viâ* Elditten towards Wolfsdorf and forced some hostile troops, without any particular difficulty, to evacuate this place, whilst Victor engaged Lestocq's attention by various feints; in front the Emperor allowed only reconnoitring parties to cross the Passarge at Deppen on this day. In the meantime the enemy's main army retreated to Glottau, and then during the night as far as Gutstadt. On the next morning the (64b) Emperor set off at 3 o'clock and advanced with his whole army towards Gutstadt; the enemy's rearguard, stationed at Queetz, was thrown back, and in the evening the main mass of his army stood in and behind Gutstadt, Davout at Ankendorf, Soult at Altkirch, Mortier being still a day's march behind on the other side of the Passarge. Bennigsen had continued his retreat and reached Heilsberg, where he occupied a position he had prepared and entrenched some time before, on the two sides of the Gutstadt road, with his right wing on the Alle and his left resting on a marshy brook, the Sims.

But the Emperor did not intend to follow him on the right bank of the Alle; but rather to turn the enemy's

[1] C. N. To Bernadotte, Saalfeld, 7th June, 11 a.m.

right wing entirely, so as to cut him off from his communication with Königsberg. He therefore ordered Soult and Lannes, with Murat in advance of them, to march along the left bank of the Alle and to move towards Heilsberg, in order to arrest the enemy there, whilst Davout and Mortier were to proceed with the turning movement. Ney and the Guards were kept in reserve. Victor was to continue occupying Lestocq's attention.

In executing these orders Murat encountered at 8 o'clock on the morning of the 10th at Launau, a weak Russian vanguard, stationed there, on the left bank of the Alle, and threw it back upon Bewernicken; thereupon Soult came up and captured the village of Lavden, in spite of the fact that the Russians brought up more and more troops from the right bank, whilst Murat continued his advance *via* Langwiese. Though Bennigsen now kept ordering up troops from the right bank of the Alle to the left, the French continued their advance and the Russians had to fall back upon Heilsberg. About 10 o'clock the Emperor arrived on the field of battle, and when he observed that the Russians were falling back upon Heilsberg, without having offered any particularly obstinate resistance, he immediately ordered Murat and Soult in vigorous pursuit, though he had no other forces at hand. For it was part of his plan to arrest and occupy his enemy here as much as ever possible.

However, close before Heilsberg he met at 6 p.m. with (65a) a determined resistance at the earthworks thrown up there, and the enemy soon mustered courage to make a counter attack and threw the French with heavy loss back behind the Spui brook. But soon after 9 o'clock Lannes arrived on the battle-field, and, the Emperor, annoyed at seeing the day end with failure, immediately ordered him to attack the Russians, but Lannes also was soon forced back again and with most severe loss. It was now past 11 o'clock, and night put an end to the fighting, very opportunely for the French, as one of the combatants,

Savary, confesses. Of the other corps, Davout had reached Altkirch, Ney and the Guards were within reach of Gutstadt, and Mortier was in the neighbourhood of Heiligenthal. The Emperor bivouacked for the night on the hills to the north-west of Bewernicken; the final failure of the day had put him in a bad humour; still he expected to see the enemy retreat the next morning, and hoped thus to pose as a victor after all.

But the morning of the 11th June showed this expectation to have been altogether false; the Russian army had remained in its position at Heilsberg, and the Emperor, enlightened by his severe losses of the preceding day as to their powers of resistance, now resolved first to order up the whole mass of his army and to initiate his turning movement before risking a fresh appeal to arms. Accordingly Ney and the Guards were ordered up to Launau and Mortier to Altkirch, whilst Davout was to march towards Grossendorf, and thus gain Bennigsen's right flank. This latter movement rendered the position at Heilsberg untenable, and the Russian General therefore withdrew his army with the fall of night to the right bank of the Alle and marched to Bartenstein, where he arrived during the afternoon of the 12th.

On the morning of the 12th the Emperor also, observing the position of Heilsberg to be evacuated, started, but not in pursuit of the Russian army; on the contrary, he took the direction of Prussisch-Eylau, so as to intercept Bennigsen from Königsberg; only some cavalry was sent in pursuit of the Russians. Consequently Davout marched to Prussisch-Eylau, Murat, Soult, and Lannes following him on the road to this place; Ney marched to Eichhorn and Mortier to Heilsberg; to this latter place the Imperial Headquarters also were moved. Victor also received orders to come up to Prussisch-Eylau; he had on the morning of the 10th been ordered to repulse Lestocq beyond Mehlsack. On this wing the adversaries tranquilly remained face to face until the evening of the 11th, but then Victor started, according to his orders, during the night, *viâ* Spanden, and marched upon Mehlsack. Lestocq, who had captured the first officer sent to Victor with this order, had thereby gained information of his intentions, and retreated before daybreak on the 12th to Zinten.

During the night from the 12th to the 13th, Bennigsen again started, reached Schippenbeil in the morning and took up a position behind this town; but being informed of the presence of the French at Domnau, he immediately continued his retreat to Friedland, where his army arrived in the course of the evening. Lestocq had fallen back upon Königsberg that day, and taken up a position in front of this town at Gollau during the afternoon. The Emperor, who had arrived at Prussisch-Eylau in the early morning of the 13th, was in doubt as to the direction of Bennigsen's march. He therefore sent, at 11 o'clock, orders to Murat to advance towards Königsberg, in order to clear up the situation, Soult and Davout having before this already been set in motion in the same direction, the former towards Königsberg, the latter towards Wittenberg, whilst Lannes advanced on the right flank to Lampasch and his cavalry reconnoitred in the direction of Domnau. Ney, Mortier and Victor were all to come up to Prussisch-Eylau, and then the Emperor intended to wait in the centre of all these movements, to see at what point he should finally throw the force massed at Eylau into the scale.

In the afternoon he received news of Bennigsen's march to Schippenbeil, and at once instructed Lannes to go to Domnau. Meanwhile Murat had met with Lestocq at Gollau, but could not engage him seriously with his cavalry. But from Lannes there came news during the evening, that the enemy appeared to be at Friedland, though the Emperor did not think it could be his main body there. He therefore ordered Lannes to advance to Friedland, and contented himself with sending only the

(65b)

cavalry division of Grouchy after the Russians. Murat, Soult and Davout were to continue their march towards Königsberg and to try to reach this town with all speed. Thus, in the evening of the 13th, Murat stood at Wittenberg, with Davout behind him on the Frisching; Soult at Kreuzburg, Ney at Schmoditten, and Mortier at Lampasch; the latter, however, started in the same night to follow Lannes; the Guards and Victor were at Prussisch-Eylau, and Lannes on the march *viâ* Domnau to Friedland.

(66a) About 3 a.m. on the 14th June the leading column of Lannes' corps, Oudinot's division, appeared in front of Friedland, and took up a position at Posthenen near the mill-dam. Bennigsen, who still persisted in his plan of continuing his march to Wehlau, determined, however, first to attack Lannes, whom he thought to encounter by himself, and thus to gain a partial success. He therefore began to move his army through Friedland, to the left bank of the Alle, and to place it in position there; this was done at 9 o'clock in such a manner that Heinrichsdorf lay in front of his right wing, whilst his left leant upon the forest of Sortlack.

Bennigsen now wished to advance, and to capture Heinrichsdorf with his right wing, for Lannes had occupied this village also by extending his line. At the same time, however, the head of Mortier's corps, the division of Dupas, arrived; the Russians were repulsed and retreated to their former position, where they remained stationary for a few hours, without undertaking anything of importance; only the artillery duel continued with varying intensity. During this time there
(66b) arrived there in succession the rest of Lannes' corps, Ney, the Guards, and Victor, who had been hurriedly despatched thither by the Emperor after the receipt of the repeated reports from Lannes as to the state of affairs. The Emperor himself, hastening on in front, reached the battle-field about noon, and, taking advantage

of Bennigsen's inactivity, made his preparations and reconnoitred the enemy minutely. At three o'clock he issued from his bivouac at Posthenen the orders for the attack, when all his corps had come up; these orders we quote here verbatim, as an example of the simple and clear wording of his commands, and as an example of how he addressed only the officers immediately under him, and left to these all the details of execution, merely indicating the movement as a whole in firm and bold outlines:—

"Marshal Ney will form the right wing from Posthenen as far as Sortlack and rest upon General Oudinot's previous position. Marshal Lannes will form the centre, taking up the line on the left of Marshal Ney at Heinrichsdorf, and extending to about opposite the village of Posthenen. Oudinot's Grenadiers, which at present form Marshal Lannes' right wing, will gradually move to the left, in order to attract the enemy's attention to them. Marshal Lannes will withdraw his divisions as much as possible, so as to have the chance of forming them into two lines. Marshal Mortier will form the left wing, and draw up his lines facing the Russian right wing, whilst keeping a hold on Heinrichsdorf and the Königsberg road. Marshal Mortier will not advance at all, as the movement is to be executed by our right wing, which will wheel round on the left as a pivot.

"General Espagne's cavalry and General Grouchy's dragoons, joining the cavalry of the left wing, will manœuvre in such a manner as to inflict the greatest possible loss upon the enemy, as soon as the vigorous attack of our right wing forces him to see the necessity of retreating.

"General Victor and the Imperial Guards, horse and foot, will form the reserve and be stationed at Grünhof, Bothkeim, and behind Posthenen.

"Lahoussaye's division of dragoons will receive its orders from General Victor; Latour-Maubourg's division of dragoons will look to Marshal Ney for its orders; General Nansouty's heavy cavalry division will place itself at Marshal Lannes' disposal and take part in the battle along with the cavalry of the reserve corps in the centre.

" I shall be with the reserve.

" The advance is to be made from the right and the initiative is to be left to Marshal Ney, who will wait for my orders before starting.

" At the moment when the right wing advances against the enemy, all the cannon along the whole line will redouble their fire in the given direction, so as to support the attack of that wing."

This order contained everything essential; every officer knew what was expected of him, and what his position was to be in the line of battle; a force was told off as a reserve; the place where the commander-in-chief was to be found fixed, and Napoleon reserved to himself the beginning of the attack. On the other hand, the Emperor avoided giving instructions or fixing positions by the map so exactly that the troops would afterwards, when on the spot, either endeavour to execute the orders too literally, and thereby encounter undreamed-of difficulties, or be compelled after all to depart from them, a proceeding which would have a bad effect in proportion to the minuteness of the details given. He who gives too minute orders, and weighs all chances in advance, only accustoms his subordinates to a want of self-reliance, without ensuring that his instructions will be any better carried out. We see thus, that it was the Emperor's general idea, only to engage the enemy's attention with his left wing, whilst making an attack upon Friedland with his right wing, supported by the fire of his combined artillery, capturing the bridges, thus blocking the Russian retreat and exposing them to utter destruction.

At 5 o'clock the Emperor gave the signal for the

attack. Bennigsen had already taken steps for a retreat behind the Alle, when his troops were by the enemy's attack compelled to show front again. In accordance with the orders, Ney began the movement by advancing vigorously along the Alle towards Friedland. He came (66c) indeed close to this town, but was here received by the Russian left wing, which had fallen back as far as this, with such an overwhelming fire, that his corps wavered and began to fall into confusion: the Russians took advantage of this, and Ney was completely routed.

But in the meantime the Emperor had already moved up Victor through Posthenen, and his foremost division, Dupont's, made its way through the midst of Ney's disorganized troops and threw the Russians back again on Friedland. Immediately after this General Senarmont brought the entire artillery of Victor's corps, thirty-six guns, which he had collected under his command, in one mass close up to the Russian line, and the fire of these enormously increased the confusion of the Russians, crowded together near Friedland. The latter retreated (66d) now as fast as they possibly could, through Friedland and across the Alle, whilst Ney, who had reorganized his troops somewhat, went in pursuit, and Dupont, crossing the mill-stream, entered the town along the Königsberg road. At 8 o'clock Friedland was in the hands of the French. In the centre and on the left wing, Lannes and Mortier had, according to the Emperor's plan, remained stationary to begin with, and had then contented themselves with repulsing an attack of the Russian right wing; this latter now also began, in consequence of the events described above, its retreat to Friedland, in order to escape over the lower Alle bridge. But Lannes went in pursuit; the bridge was burnt down prematurely, before the Russians had all crossed, and their right wing, thus cut off, was annihilated by the artillery-fire of the French. By this time night had completely come on, and in the course of it Bennigsen fell back upon Wehlau.

(67a) Whilst the Emperor fought a battle at Friedland, Murat, Soult and Davout had, on the 14th, advanced further towards Königsberg; they forced Lestocq into that place and invested it from the left bank of the Pregel.

(67b) With Friedland the war was at an end. During the next few days Bennigsen, having crossed the Pregel in the forenoon of the 15th at Wehlau, retreated to Tilsit, whither Lestocq also moved, having given up Königsberg. On the 18th the army crossed the Niemen. The Emperor had followed Bennigsen on the right bank of the Alle with some cavalry only; but with the mass of his army he proceeded along the left bank to Wehlau, where he crossed the Pregel on the 16th and 17th; on the 18th he lay beyond Great Schrannau and established his headquarters in Great Skaisgirren. He was determined "to march to Tilsit and fight a battle with the enemy, if he should have the audacity to make a show of awaiting us";[1] but should the enemy, without concluding peace, retreat into the interior of Russia, he would not follow, but, resuming the defensive, give his troops some rest, and await, on the Niemen, the renewed appearance of the enemy. The next day, the 19th, Murat entered Tilsit. On the same day, however, proposals for an armistice, on the part of Bennigsen, were accepted by the Emperor, and the hostilities came herewith to an end.

The battle of Friedland had, it is true, like Jena, come about through the Emperor's encountering the enemy where he did not expect him, yet it does not in any way bear the stamp of an accidental battle, but was, just like Austerlitz, prepared for and led up to according to a fixed plan. Two circumstances were of importance for the tactical decision of this battle: the direction of the various corps and the full utilization of the fighting strength of the troops. But the fighting strength in modern tactics is equivalent to the firing strength, for "battles are nowadays decided by fire and not by

[1] C. N. To Murat.

shock."[1] The direction of the troops is the business of the leader, and we saw at Austerlitz how much the Emperor was master of this art. But the value of the other factor rests upon the organization and education of the armies themselves, namely, upon the possession of a practical method of fighting and upon a thorough excellence of the individual soldiers in shooting. If the troops have not proper tactical methods, so as to render their excellence in shooting of effect, they may, like the English lately in Africa, fail even against savages;[2] and if, on the other hand, the individual soldier is not thoroughly drilled in shooting, the best weapon and the best tactical methods will fail to render their fire effective. The Emperor knew this very well. "It is not sufficient that the soldier should shoot, he must shoot well;"[3] and the right tactical form he had found to lie in those close swarms of sharpshooters which preceded his attacks, led up to them, nay, often decided them. The importance of artillery-fire also he recognized and dwelt on. "A good infantry is without doubt the backbone of the army. but if it had to fight long against superior artillery, it would be discouraged and disorganized;"[4] and as to the employment of artillery, his principle was: "The artillery, like the other arms, must be collected in mass, if one wishes to attain a decisive result."[5] Of the manner in which he applied this principle, Senarmont's action gives us an example here.

With respect to its strategy, the campaign of Friedland is one of the most interesting fought by the Emperor, and furnishes food for much reflection. The great critic of this epoch does not approve of the conduct of the campaign in question. Arrived at Gutstadt, two ways were (64b) open to the Emperor, *either* to advance along the right

[1] Mém. de Ste. Hél. Essai sur la fortification de la campagne, xxxi. 551.
[2] The author is alluding to Zululand.—ED.
[3] C. N. To Eugene. Posen, 5th December, 1806.
[4] Dixhuit, Notes, &c., xxxi. 395.
[5] C. N. To Eugene. Schönbrunn, 16th June, 1809, 5 p.m.

bank of the Alle, with his right wing forward, and to throw the enemy back upon Königsberg and towards the sea; strategy, according to Jomini, should have prompted this course; *or*, to advance on the left bank of the Alle, left wing forward, cut off the enemy from Königsberg, throw him back completely, but still in the direction of his own frontiers; this is what the Emperor did. Abstract criticisms and the study of the campaign on the map will always compel us to agree with Jomini. With the operation against the left wing of the enemy the war itself would have been decided, whether Bennigsen were driven into Königsberg or forced back towards the sea. What was it then that induced the Emperor to march with his left forward?

In contradiction to his whole procedure hitherto, it was his consideration of secondary circumstances, though these were very weighty in themselves. He had selected his line of communication with Danzig through a very fertile country, for he had just had some experience of the misery arising from want of food. It was difficult now to change his base once more to Thorn, and by a line passing through an exhausted country; the army already trended more towards the left than the right; the enemy was not at all unwilling, as it seemed, to go to Königsberg, and it is, as a rule, advisable to act contrary to the enemy's intentions. All these were good and practical reasons, which led the Emperor to act as he did.

Still we must say that what is characteristic of a general of genius as contrasted with the merely able general, is to put aside all such difficulties or to overcome them, where it is a question of fixing on the point which will decide the whole campaign irrevocably. For a Bennigsen, a Soult, the campaign of Friedland would have been a glorious one, on account of its vigorous and excellent strategy, but the Emperor had accustomed us to greater things; he had accustomed us to find from the first in his plan of operations the strategical thought, which must necessarily lead to the ultimate decision; it was by so acting that he has become our ideal. But here it was different, and the result proves the correctness of Jomini's criticism. In spite of a brilliant carrying out of his plan, in spite of a complete victory, the Emperor, having arrived on the Niemen, was forced to acknowledge that he was not yet the absolute master of his opponent's movements, nor of the situation, and that his opponent, by a mere retreat within his own frontiers, could, though beaten, force him to resume his defensive. Such had not been the case after Marengo, after Ulm, after Jena, nor could it have become so. What would have happened if Bennigsen had retreated into Russia, perhaps even, as might have happened, without having been beaten at all, if the Emperor Alexander had not concluded peace? It would have been impossible to follow him; this would only have led to a kind of preliminary rehearsal of 1812, indeed, to remain stationary on the defensive on the Niemen was the only thing left to the Emperor, and, as we have seen, this was what he resolved to do; but what a miserable ending to a campaign! Thus, it is true, the campaign of Friedland proved once more that resolution and energy are the principal factors in the conduct of war. But although the Emperor did gain the victory, and assuredly it was well deserved, we no longer find a conception which must inevitably bring the whole war to an issue, and that a successful one. (67b)

The Emperor's military genius had reached high-water mark, and its waves were beginning to fluctuate. It was still capable of great things, but although the ebb had not yet commenced, there were no longer any indications of a rising tide.

END OF VOL. I.

www.ingramcontent.com/pod-product-compliance
Lightning Source LLC
Chambersburg PA
CBHW030357230426
43664CB00007BB/627